CW00555579

EGYPTIAN MUMMIES AND MODERN SCIENCE

Egyptian mummies have always aroused popular and scientific interest; however, most modern studies, although significantly increased in number and range, have been published in specialist journals. Now, this unique book, written by a long-established team of scientists based at the University of Manchester (England), brings this exciting, cross-disciplinary area of research to a wider readership. Its main aim is to show how this team's multidisciplinary, investigative methods and the unique resource of the Egyptian Mummy Tissue Bank are being used for new major international investigations of disease evolution and ancient Egyptian pharmacy and pharmacology. It also assesses the current status of palaeopathology and ancient DNA research and the treatments available for conserving mummified remains. Descriptions of the historical development of Egyptian mummifications and medicine and detailed references to previous scientific investigations provide the context for firsthand accounts of cutting-edge research by prominent specialists in this field, demonstrating how these techniques can contribute to a new perspective on Egyptology.

Rosalie David is KNH Professor and Director of the KNH Centre for Biomedical Egyptology at the University of Manchester. She was awarded the Order of the British Empire (OBE) in the New Year Honours List of 2003 for her services to Egyptology, and she is the author and editor of twenty-seven books, most recently *Religion and Magic in Ancient Egypt*.

Egyptian Mummies and Modern Science

Edited by

ROSALIE DAVID

University of Manchester

CAMBRIDGE UNIVERSITY PRESS
Cambridge, New York, Melbourne, Madrid, Cape Town, Singapore, São Paulo, Delhi

Cambridge University Press
32 Avenue of the Americas, New York, NY 10013-2473, USA

www.cambridge.org
Information on this title: www.cambridge.org/9780521865791

© Cambridge Universtiy Press 2008

This publication is in copyright. Subject to statutory exception
and to the provisions of relevant collective licensing agreements,
no reproduction of any part may take place without
the written permission of Cambridge University Press.

First published 2008

Printed in the United States of America

A catalog record for this publication is available from the British Library.

Library of Congress Cataloging in Publication Data

David, A. Rosalie / Egyptian mummies and modern science
　　p.　cm.
Includes bibliographical references and index.
ISBN 978-0-521-86579-1 (hardback)
1. Mummies – Egypt.　2. Paleopathology – Egypt.　3. Medical archaeology – Egypt.
I. Title.
DT62.M7D35　2008
932 – dc22　　　　2007020004

ISBN　978-0-521-86579-1 hardback

Cambridge University Press has no responsibility for
the persistence or accuracy of URLs for external or
third-party Internet Web sites referred to in this publication
and does not guarantee that any content on such
Web sites is, or will remain, accurate or appropriate.

Contents

List of Plates

List of Figures

Contributors

The following contributors to this book are actively engaged in the research performed by the Manchester Egyptian Mummy Project, and in the teaching programmes of the KNH Centre for Biomedical Egyptology, University of Manchester (UK).

EDITOR

Professor Rosalie David, OBE
KNH Professor of Biomedical Egyptology and Director of the KNH Centre for Biomedical Egyptology, University of Manchester (UK). Director of the Manchester Mummy Research Project since 1973.

CONTRIBUTORS

Professor Judith E. Adams
Professor of Diagnostic Radiology, Clinical Radiology, Imaging Science and Biomedical Engineering, Faculty of Medicine, University of Manchester (UK). Member of the Manchester Mummy Project since 1998.

Chrissie W. Alsop
Manager of Clinical and Research Imaging Facilities, Clinical Radiology, Imaging Science and Biomedical Engineering, Faculty of Medicine, University of Manchester (UK). Member of the Manchester Mummy Project for more than twenty years.

Jacqueline M. Campbell
Research Associate, KNH Centre for Biomedical Egyptology, University of Manchester (UK). Specialising in the history of pharmacy in ancient Egypt,

particularly medicinal plants and their relevance to current medicine and nutrition.

Dr David J. Counsell

Consultant Anaesthetist, NHS Trust, Wrexham (UK). His research focuses on drug history in ancient Egypt.

Antony E. David

Formerly Manager of Support Services, Lancashire County Museums Service (UK). A forty-year career in conservation, specialising in artefacts and Egyptian mummified remains.

John Denton

Pathology Research Fellow, Division of Laboratory and Regenerative Medicine, University of Manchester (UK). He has nearly forty years of experience of the histological investigation of biological tissues in diagnostic and research environments.

Dr Andrew P. Giże

Senior Lecturer, School of Earth Atmospheric and Environmental Sciences, University of Manchester (UK). He runs the organic analytical facility (gas chromatography–mass spectrometry and microscopy), and uses microprobe techniques for research on Egyptology and Late Minoan projects.

Dr Maria Jeziorska

Lecturer in Molecular Pathology, Division of Laboratory and Regenerative Medicine, University of Manchester (UK). She is engaged in research and teaching on the use of immunohistochemical methods in contemporary and ancient human remains.

Dr Judith Miller

Orthodontist, Research Affiliate at the Wellcome Trust for the History of Medicine, London, and Honorary Fellow in the KNH Centre for Biomedical Egyptology, University of Manchester. Her specialist study is the history of dentistry in ancient Egypt.

Dr Patricia Rutherford

Research Associate (until 2006), KNH Centre for Biomedical Egyptology, University of Manchester (UK). Pioneered and developed the use of immunocytochemistry as a diagnostic tool for detecting the presence of schistosomiasis in mummified tissue.

Roger Speak
Experimental Officer, Department of Chemistry, University of Manchester (UK). In addition to mass spectrometry, he provides infrared microscopy (a unique facility) for archaeological projects.

Ken Wildsmith
With a background in engineering, and a career in sales for major companies manufacturing industrial endoscopes, optical measuring equipment and microscopes, he has pioneered and developed the application of endoscopic techniques for Egyptian mummies since he joined the Manchester Mummy Project in the 1980s.

Dr Caroline M. Wilkinson
Formerly Head of the Unit for Art in Medicine, University of Manchester (UK), and now Senior Lecturer, Wellcome Unit, University of Dundee (UK). Her pioneering work on techniques of scientific facial reconstruction for both forensic and archaeological purposes has received wide media coverage.

Acknowledgments

The diverse and complex nature of the research we undertake is only made possible by the generous support we have received over the past four decades from many individuals and organisations. Although it is not possible to thank them all here, we wish particularly to acknowledge those who have provided the opportunities and facilities for our most recent studies.

First, we are indebted to the support we receive from 'KNH' whose generosity enabled a unique centre (which carries her initials) to be set up in 2003 at the University of Manchester, and to the two Deans, Professor Alan North, FRS (Dean and Vice-President, Faculty of Life Sciences, 2004–present), and Professor Maynard Case (Dean, School of Biological Sciences, 2001–2004), who have both played crucial roles in the centre's establishment and development.

We wish to record our gratitude to The Leverhulme Trust (UK) for its support of the interdisciplinary, international projects we undertake. The Leverhulme Trust has provided significant funding towards our research in the form of two Research Grants. The first (1996–1999) facilitated the establishment of the International Ancient Egyptian Mummy Tissue Bank, and the current grant (2006–2009) was awarded for the Pharmacy in Ancient Egypt Project.

We should also like to express our gratitude to Dr Keith Hall, the founder and Managing Director of Hall Analytical Laboratories, Manchester (UK), one of the premier organic mass spectrometry facilities in the United Kingdom, which is involved in both analysis and development. Dr Hall has played a key role in providing additional, essential facilities for our work, and he and his colleagues have been actively involved in the research and interpretation associated with many of the archaeological projects undertaken at the KNH Centre.

At the University of Manchester, we are grateful to many departments for giving us access to their facilities. In particular, we should like to thank Dr Paul Taylor, Clinical Director of Radiology, Central Manchester and Manchester Royal Children's University Hospitals NHS Trust (CMMC) for permitting the use of the radiographic equipment and computed tomography scanner for imaging of the mummies; the radiographers (Simone Brooke and Nicola Moran) who performed the imaging; and the CMMC Research Endowment for funding the out-of-hours imaging that has been undertaken. We are indebted to Professor Mark W. J. Ferguson for his support in allowing Dr Patricia Rutherford the use of his laboratories for her research. We are grateful to all the depositors to the International Ancient Egyptian Mummy Tissue Bank, and would like to record here that the substantial loans of material made by Professor A. C. Aufderheide, Professor D. Van Gervan, the Manchester Museum and the Leicester Museum have provided significant resources for many of the current projects discussed in this book.

Indeed, many institutions have made their collections, facilities and expertise available to the Manchester team. In particular, we would like to record our gratitude to staff and colleagues at the following: the Agricultural Museum, Cairo, Egypt; the British Museum, London; the Chelsea Physic Garden, London; the Duckworth Collection, University of Cambridge; the Egyptian Museum, Cairo, Egypt; the Forensic Science Laboratory, Exton Hall, Chorley, Lancashire (UK); the Georges-Labit Museum, Toulouse, France; the Glyptotek Museum, Copenhagen; the Groningen Museum, the Netherlands; the Leicester Museum, Leicester, UK; Manchester Royal Infirmary, Manchester; the Medical Toxicology Laboratory at Guy's and St. Thomas' Hospital, London; the Metropolitan Museum of Fine Art, New York; the National Museums of Scotland; the National Research Centre, Cairo, Egypt; the Natural History Museum, London; the Manchester Museum, University of Manchester; PDR, Cardiff (UK); the Polish Centre for Archaeology, Cairo, Egypt; the Royal Botanic Gardens, Kew (UK); the South Sinai Environmental Agency, Egypt (United Nations Development Programme); Stapeley Water Gardens, Staffordshire (UK); VAC-SERA (the Egyptian Organisation for Vaccine and Biological Production, Cairo, Egypt); and the Vivi Tackholme Herbarium, University of Cairo, Egypt.

We should also like to express our gratitude to the following individuals for supporting and making various contributions to our work: Frank Barnett; Dr Jenefer Cockitt; Professor M. Doenhoff, University of Bangor, Wales (UK); Professor K. H. El-Batanony, National Scientific Advisor to the

Egyptian Government; Professor M. El-Demerdash, Director, South Sinai Environmental Agency; Dr W. El-Saddick, Director, Egyptian Museum, Cairo; Dr Azza el-Sarry; Dr B. Harer; Dr N. Hepper; Professor Faiza Hamouda; Professor N. M. Hassan; Professor Fawzia Helmi Hussien; Emeritus Professor M. Kassas; Professor E. Rabino Massa, University of Turin, Italy; Professor A. J. Mills; Professor Moushira Erfan; Caroline Needham; Richard Neave; Dr P. T. Nicholson; Chris Rynn; Denise Smyth; and Dr J. Taylor.

It has been a pleasure to work with the staff at Cambridge University Press, and we are particularly grateful to Publications Director Beatrice Rehl and Senior Editor Simon Whitmore, for their advice and support during the commissioning and production of this book.

To my husband, Antony E. David, I give my personal thanks, for his academic input and significant practical contribution towards preparing this manuscript for publication, and for providing constant support and encouragement for my work.

Finally, we should like to acknowledge the contribution made by our students, whose enthusiasm and interest in this field continually inspire us to pursue new goals and developments.

Rosalie David
Manchester, December 2006

Preface

Rosalie David

The main aims of this book are to show how biomedical and scientific techniques have led to a new understanding of some aspects of ancient Egyptian society, and to demonstrate how the focused, multidisciplinary research of one team, working continuously in this area for more than thirty years, has been able to contribute to this field.

There has been a remarkable and significant increase in the number and range of scientific studies undertaken on mummies over the past couple of decades, and people are now aware of the information that can be derived from such investigations, in terms of explaining the cultural context of human remains and in adding to knowledge of how disease has evolved and developed from ancient to modern times. Much of this work, however, is published in scientific journals or conference papers, and is not readily accessible to the reader who has a general interest in the field.

The Manchester Egyptian Mummy Research Project, established at the University of Manchester in 1973, has conducted pioneering research on the methodology of using scientific techniques to investigate ancient Egyptian mummified remains. It has run the longest continuous research programme in the field of biomedical Egyptology, and this has led to the establishment (in 2003) of a university specialisation and a dedicated facility – the KNH Centre for Biomedical Egyptology in the Faculty of Life Sciences at the University of Manchester (UK).

The earliest phase of this project was published in A. R. David (ed.), *The Manchester Museum Mummy Project* (1979). The team has made major advances since then, and mummy studies in general have progressed and taken advantage of the many new techniques that can contribute to this field. This book provides the first opportunity to present the complete picture of the Manchester team's more recent studies. The contributors have not adopted a uniform approach: some chapters provide detailed descriptions of techniques, others concentrate on the significance of results, and some assess the current role and status of the various fields of interest. Taken as a whole, we hope this book will demonstrate how scientific studies on mummies can provide new insight into the ancient Egyptians' attitudes to life and death.

The book is divided into five parts. The first, *An introduction to the scientific study of mummies*, considers the aims, methods and development of the Manchester Mummy Project within the wider context of scientific studies on Egyptian mummies; it also provides a brief introduction to the prehistory and history of ancient Egypt and a summary of why and how Egyptian mummies were produced.

The second part, *Diet, disease and death in ancient Egypt: diagnostic and investigative techniques*, describes the Manchester studies on human and animal remains, with particular reference to disease, and demonstrates how a wide range of scientific techniques can be developed and used as diagnostic tools in this research.

The third section, *The treatment of disease in ancient Egypt*, uses information derived from the Manchester studies to explore the ancient Egyptian medical system and the role of medical practitioners, and to assess the extent to which these analytical studies can confirm the ancient literary evidence. It also considers the ancient Egyptian use of narcotics and pain relief in religious, medical and social contexts, and presents the latest research on the scope and possible therapeutic efficacy of their pharmaceutical treatments.

The fourth part, *Resources for studying mummies*, describes the establishment and role of the International Ancient Egyptian Mummy Tissue Bank, and surveys the conservation methods available for the treatment of Egyptian mummified remains. The final section, *The future of biomedical and scientific studies in Egyptology*, provides a summary of the contributions that biomedical and scientific techniques can make to the study of ancient Egypt, and considers some of the directions that this field of research might take in the future.

Each chapter is written by an expert in the relevant field, scientists at the cutting edge of this research who, working together as members of the Manchester Mummy Project, have conducted this original work themselves. Although this is primarily a firsthand account of the group's own research and results, the investigations are described within the wider context of mummy studies, and an extensive list of references to other work in this field is included.

Much of the research undertaken at Manchester in recent years has involved the application of new techniques. To provide sufficient space in the book for explanation and discussion of these new techniques, we have decided to omit techniques (such as serology and finger-printing) described in our earlier publications that are no longer part of mainstream mummy research.

PART 1

An introduction to the scientific study of mummies

CHAPTER 1

The background of the Manchester Mummy Project

Rosalie David

Early investigations

From the Renaissance, Egyptian mummies have attracted the interest of antiquarian collectors, who brought them from Egypt to enhance the collections of museums, learned societies, and wealthy individuals in Britain, Europe, and later the United States of America. From the sixteenth century onwards, some of these mummies were 'unrolled' (unwrapped) at frivolous social events in front of invited audiences. Most of these unwrappings had little scientific value; however, some were performed by serious investigators whose detailed publications still provide valuable evidence.

These researchers include Thomas Pettigrew (1791–1865), a London surgeon who unwrapped a series of mummies in London (Pettigrew 1834); Augustus Bozzi Granville (1783–1872), another London doctor who reported evidence of ovarian disease in an Egyptian mummy (Granville 1825); and members of the Leeds Philosophical and Literary Society, who undertook an interdisciplinary study on a mummy in 1825 (Osburn 1828).

In the early twentieth century, various pioneering projects laid the basis for mummy research. Armand Ruffer, Professor of Bacteriology in Cairo, developed methods of rehydrating ancient tissues (Ruffer 1921), and invented the term *palaeopathology* for the study of disease in ancient populations.

Grafton Elliot Smith, Professor of Anatomy in Cairo, performed extensive examinations of the mummies of the rulers of the New Kingdom, discovered at Thebes in 1871 and 1898 (Smith 1912). With his co-workers W. R. Dawson and F. W. Jones, Smith also undertook an important study on some 6,000 ancient bodies retrieved during the Archaeological Survey of Nubia, a heritage rescue operation that was established when the first dam was built at Aswan in the early twentieth century (Smith and Wood Jones 1910). A third scientist, Alfred Lucas (1867–1945), also based in Cairo, performed analyses of many ancient materials and substances, and was the first to demonstrate that Herodotus' account of mummification was accurate.

Mummy research has progressed steadily throughout the twentieth century, although this development has not shown any continuous or regular pattern. Nevertheless, the route has been highlighted by many important studies which are too extensive to list here, but the following provide just some examples.

Continuing research on royal mummies has included a radiological survey (Harris and Wente 1980), an interdisciplinary study of the mummy of Ramesses II (Balout and Roubet 1985), and various investigations of the mummies of Tutankhamun and the body found in Tomb 55 in the Valley of the Kings. An extensive radiological survey of nonroyal human remains in other major collections (Dawson and Gray 1968) has formed the basis for many subsequent studies, and much information has been derived from the series of autopsies and scientific studies undertaken in the 1970s on several mummies in the Detroit Institute of Art, Pennsylvania University Museum, and the Royal Ontario Museum in Toronto (Cockburn and Cockburn 1980).

The role of the Manchester researchers can now be considered within the context of these earlier and contemporary projects.

Autopsy of the Two Brothers at Manchester

The pioneering work of Dr Margaret Murray at the University of Manchester characterised the new approach to examining mummified remains that emerged in the early twentieth century. As the first curator of Egyptology at the Manchester Museum, she undertook one of the earliest scientific investigations of Egyptian mummies, heading an interdisciplinary team of specialists in anatomy, chemical analysis, and textile studies.

In 1908, before an invited audience in the University's Chemistry Theatre, the team unwrapped and performed autopsies on the mummies of two brothers from a tomb (c. 1900 B.C.) at Der Rifeh. The results of subsequent medical, scientific, and archaeological investigations, which provided information about the tomb, bodies, and funerary possessions, were published in a book (Murray 1910).

The Manchester Mummy Project: initial phase (1973–1979)

Shortly after I was appointed in 1972 to curate the Egyptology collection at the Manchester Museum, I initiated a similar investigation. The Manchester Mummy Project, as it became known, was established to examine all the Egyptian mummified remains at the museum, although eventually it also encompassed collections held in other institutions. A rare set of circumstances – a university museum with a significant mummy collection, located near teaching departments and hospitals with sophisticated, specialised equipment, and supportive university authorities – ensured that the project had unprecedented access to extensive scientific resources.

An interdisciplinary team of specialists, drawn from the university and associated teaching hospitals, had the primary aim of establishing a methodology for examining mummies based on the availability of a range of techniques and specialist equipment that could be used under near-ideal conditions. Subsequently, other researchers have been able to utilise all or some of the approaches and principles set out in this 'Manchester Method,' to form the basis for their own contributions in this field (Dawson et al. 2002; Taylor 2004; Raven and Taconis 2005).

In examining this group of mummies, the team's second aim was to gain as much information as possible about disease, diet, living conditions, the process of mummification, and religious and funerary customs in ancient Egypt (David 1997).

Techniques used in the first phase of the project (1973–1979) included a radiological survey; rehydration and processing of mummified tissue to produce histological sections that could be examined by light and electron microscopy to demonstrate the framework and cellular detail of the tissue and any evidence of disease; electron microscopy to identify insect remains associated with the mummies; palaeo-odontology; the development and application of special fingerprinting techniques; and the scientific reconstruction of selected mummified heads. In addition, experiments were undertaken to investigate the actual process of mummification, and to assess the accuracy of ancient literary accounts.

In 1975, it was decided to unwrap and perform an autopsy on one of the mummies, Number 1770, in the Manchester collection, to demonstrate how these techniques could provide maximum information about the mummy. As the first scientific autopsy of a mummy in Britain since Murray's project some seventy years earlier, it attracted considerable media interest.

Additional methods of analysis included the macroscopic and microscopic examination of the textiles associated with this mummy; chromatography to isolate and characterise the substances applied to the bandages; and radiocarbon dating to establish and compare the approximate age of the bones and bandages.

This first phase was published in a scientific book (David 1979) and a more general account (David 1978). In 1979, an international symposium entitled *Science in Egyptology* attracted more than 100 delegates to the University of Manchester to discuss the application of medical and scientific techniques to Egyptological projects. Although earlier Egyptology conferences had sometimes included sessions on palaeopathology, and some scientific meetings had surveyed disease in ancient man, this was a new concept because it focused exclusively on the application of science to Egyptology. The joint proceedings of this successful meeting and another symposium held at Manchester in 1984 were published later (David 1986).

The BBC produced a television documentary in the *Chronicle* series that examined the team's research and recorded the autopsy of Mummy 1770. The Audio-Visual Department of the University of Manchester also made two films which demonstrated the Manchester techniques and key events in the unwrapping of 1770. These films, produced for general use in teaching departments, won awards from the British Association for the Advancement of Science. A public exhibition at the Manchester Museum (1979–1980) presented the team's results within the context of Egyptian funerary beliefs and customs; it attracted many visitors, and received the Sotheby's Award in the Museum of the Year Awards (1980).

The Manchester Mummy Project: second phase (1979–1995)

After 1979, the project moved in new directions (David and Tapp 1984). An important decision to promote virtually nondestructive methods of investigating mummies introduced the use of endoscopy as a means of obtaining tissue from inside a mummy for histological and other studies. Also, acting on a proposal made at the 1979 symposium, an International Mummy Database was established at Manchester to gather, store, and respond to requests for research data about disease found in Egyptian mummies in collections across the world.

This phase of the project was recorded in a second BBC *Chronicle* documentary, and another film, made by the Central Office for Information for distribution outside Britain, related how techniques developed for the project also contributed to contemporary forensic work and plastic surgery.

A major redisplay of the permanent Egyptian galleries at the Manchester Museum highlighted the research and results of the Mummy Project and was judged for the Museum of the Year Award, which Manchester won in 1987.

In the 1990s, Manchester's innovative, virtually nondestructive approach led to invitations to examine mummies in other collections. Pioneering research in identifying DNA in mummies (Pääbo 1985) now opened up new possibilities, and in 1992, at the invitation of Professor N. Kanawati of

Macquarie University, Sydney, Australia, the Manchester team undertook pathological and genetic studies on six mummies discovered in a tomb at El-Hagarsa in Egypt (Elles et al. 1993).

In 1989, P. C. Brears, then Director of the Leeds City Museum, proposed that the Manchester team should undertake a new scientific investigation of the 'Leeds Mummy,' which originally underwent autopsy in 1825 (Osburn 1828). The new study gave the Manchester team the unique opportunity to compare their own techniques and results with those of the earlier researchers (David and Tapp 1992).

The Manchester Mummy Project: third phase (1995–present)

A major development in this phase was the establishment, in 2003, of a university specialisation in biomedical Egyptology within a dedicated centre – the KNH Centre for Biomedical Egyptology in the Faculty of Life Sciences at the University of Manchester (UK) (see Chapter 17). This is now the base for the Manchester Mummy Team and its various projects.

The schistosomiasis in ancient and modern Egypt project

Until the mid-1990s, palaeopathological studies had concentrated on detailed investigations of individual mummies or defined groups of bodies, but in 1995, the Manchester researchers were invited to collaborate with scientists in Egypt on an epidemiological project. The scientists were pursuing a ten-year programme, the Schistosomiasis Research Project, designed to identify contemporary epidemiological patterns of a parasitic disease, schistosomiasis, and to find more effective methods of treating the condition.

The aim of this joint study was to construct epidemiological profiles of schistosomiasis in ancient and contemporary Egypt, and then compare the incidence patterns from the twenty-sixth century B.C. to the seventh century A.D. with the modern evidence, thus describing the evolution of the disease over a 5,000-year period. Resources for this study would include evidence of the disease that occurred in mummies, and contemporary infection data collected by the Schistosomiasis Research Project on some 100,000 people living in villages between the north and south of Egypt (Contis and David 1996; David 2000).

Other researchers have used various diagnostic techniques to detect schistosomiasis in mummies, including radiographic examination to identify secondary pathological indications of the disease, and histological investigation of mummified tissue to detect the presence of worms and eggs. The latter method was used by Ruffer, who first identified the disease in mummies in 1910. More recent studies show the effectiveness of immunological analysis of tissue or bone samples by using the enzyme-linked immunosorbent assay (ELISA). This can detect the presence of circulating anodic antigen (a glycoprotein regurgitated from the gut of the schistosome) in the mummy, which will confirm if the infection was active at the time of the person's death.

To attempt to trace the pattern of schistosomiasis over the millennia, it was necessary for the Manchester researchers to gather data from a large number of mummies, drawn from different locations and chronological periods (see Chapter 15). For this project, it was decided not to use radiography or histology, because the former would be expensive and dependent on access to specialised x-ray equipment, and the latter would be successful only if tissue could be obtained from specific areas of a mummy.

The Manchester researcher, Dr Patricia Rutherford, therefore decided to adopt an immunological approach: she pioneered the use of immunocytochemistry to detect this disease in mummies (see Chapter 8; Pain 2001), and then confirmed the results by means of ELISA and DNA (Chapter 9). Further success was achieved when, for the first time, the DNA of the causative parasite was identified in one of the samples.

The International Ancient Egyptian Mummy Tissue Bank

To ensure that a sufficient quantity of tissue samples was available for this project, the International Ancient Egyptian Mummy Tissue Bank was established at Manchester (see Chapter 15). The bank was initially funded by a research grant from The Leverhulme Trust to collect and store samples (mainly tissue, but also some hair and bone) from mummies held in collections across the world (apart from Egypt, where there are plans to establish a similar tissue bank). The bank thus provides a new resource of specially selected material for ongoing disease studies and other research.

Instrumental methods

In addition to existing techniques, the Manchester group now has access to a range of instrumental methods, involving organic and inorganic analyses, which are available to forensic scientists who wish to investigate ancient and conserved remains and residues (see Chapters 10 and 13).

For example, these mass spectrometric and other protocols are being applied in a unique study to determine if narcotics and pain-relieving agents were used in religious, medical, and social contexts in ancient Egypt. This study is also investigating the problem of false results produced by contamination, which may arise from mummification methods, environmental conditions, or diagenesis.

The pharmacy in ancient Egypt project

The most recent area of research in Manchester focuses on the use of pharmaceutical treatments in ancient Egypt. This study is supported by a research grant from The Leverhulme Trust, and combines historical and scientific methodology to investigate the therapeutic potential of these regimes (see Chapter 14).

In a pilot study of more than 1,000 prescriptions found in four Egyptian medical papyri, 379 drug substances have been analysed and formatted in the style of the British National Formulary, detailing their active ingredients and therapeutic efficacy. This initial work, comparing the compounding and administration of these prescriptions with contemporary pharmacy, has demonstrated that some 70 per cent of the identified substances used by ancient Egyptian physicians remained in use in the twentieth century A.D. Researchers working on this project include specialists in many fields who have unprecedented access to both the International Tissue Bank and collections of modern and ancient plants in Britain and Egypt. This provides a unique opportunity to use scientific analytical methods to assess the validity of the literary evidence.

These studies are investigating ancient and contemporary plant and inorganic remains from Egypt, identifying any traces of pharmaceutical residues in mummified tissue samples, and tracing the places of origin and the trade routes by which the raw materials may have entered Egypt.

It is hoped that the results of this research will not only revolutionise our understanding of the scope and significance of ancient Egyptian treatments, but will contribute new information to the history of medicine and pharmacy.

CHAPTER 2

Egyptian mummies: an overview

Rosalie David

Historical background

Mummification (the artificial preservation of the body after death) may have been practised in Egypt for more than 4,000 years, and perhaps developed as early as c. 4500 B.C., when Neolithic communities lived in scattered settlements in the Egyptian Delta and along the banks of the Nile. Gradually, these villages merged into larger groups, drawn together by the common need to develop irrigation systems, and eventually, the north and south were ruled as two separate kingdoms. Egyptologists describe this whole era (c. 5000 B.C.–3100 B.C.) as the Predynastic Period.

In c. 3100 B.C., a southern ruler conquered the northern kingdom, unified the two lands, and founded dynastic Egypt. Thousands of years later, an Egyptian priest, Manetho (323–245 B.C.), composed a chronicle of kings who ruled Egypt between c. 3100 B.C. and 332 B.C., and this king-list has survived in the writings of later historians. It divides the reigns of Egyptian kings into thirty dynasties and these, plus a thirty-first dynasty added by a later chronographer, form the basis for the modern chronology of ancient Egypt.

Contemporary historians arrange these dynasties into a series of major periods: the Archaic Period (c. 3100–c. 2686 B.C.), the Old Kingdom (c. 2686–c. 2181 B.C.), the First Intermediate Period (c. 2181–1991 B.C.), the Middle Kingdom (1991–1786 B.C.), the Second Intermediate Period (1786–1567 B.C.), the New Kingdom (1567–1085 B.C.), the Third Intermediate Period (1085–668 B.C.), and the Late Period (664–332 B.C.).

The conquest of Egypt by Alexander the Great of Macedon in 332 B.C. ushered in the Ptolemaic Period. On Alexander's death, Egypt passed to his general who became King Ptolemy I, and his descendants (the Ptolemies) ruled until the death of Cleopatra VII, the last of the dynasty. The next stage of Egypt's history, when the country was ruled as a province of the Roman Empire, is known as the Roman Period (30 B.C.–641 A.D.).

Source material

Apart from the mummified remains themselves, sources relating to mummification include inscriptions and funerary illustrations, but these generally concentrate on methods of anointing and wrapping. The earliest detailed descriptions of mummification were written by Classical authors who visited Egypt: Herodotus in the fifth century B.C. (*Histories*: vol.2, 86–88; see de Selincourt 1976), and Diodorus Siculus in the first century B.C. (*Universal History*: vol. 1, 7; see Geer 1954).

The environmental context

Egypt is a land of contrasts: most of the country is desert, but in antiquity the annual inundation of the Nile brought down water and silt, which created a triangle of fertile land in the north (the Delta), and a strip of cultivated land on either side of the river. Continuous irrigation and ceaseless vigilance were needed to maintain this scarce agricultural land, which supported the people, and their crops and animals.

From Neolithic times, towns and villages became established here, and because this cultivated area could not be sacrificed for the burial of the dead, the corpses – usually covered by a reed or skin mat – were placed in shallow graves in the nearby desert.

It may have been religious beliefs that first inspired the Egyptians to try to preserve the bodies of the dead in as enduring and lifelike a state as possible, but geographical and environmental factors also played a significant role in the development of mummification.

Natural and artificial mummification

A combination of the hot, dry climate and the location of the shallow graves in porous sand provided conditions that ensured that these bodies were preserved indefinitely. The body fluids of the newly buried corpse evaporated and were absorbed by the sand, a process that arrested decomposition and produced desiccated, practically sterile bodies that could last indefinitely in the right environmental conditions. Such corpses, complete with skin and hair, are excellent examples of 'natural mummification,' and indeed may have been the inspiration for later attempts at artificial preservation.

Although this method of burial continued in use for the poorer classes throughout the historical period (c. 3100–332 B.C.), intentional preservation of the corpse (mummification) was introduced first for the elite burials, and eventually for all who could afford this method.

The reasons for artificial mummification, and the date when it was first introduced in Egypt, cannot yet be confirmed. Until recently, Egyptologists associated this development with a new type of grave built for the kings and wealthier classes in the Archaic Period. Their bodies now rapidly decomposed because they were interred in an underground burial chamber lined with mudbrick or wood, rather than being in direct contact with the sand.

Even at this date, the Egyptians probably believed that preservation of the body was essential to enable the deceased owner's immortal spirit to return to the corpse and use it to derive spiritual sustenance from food offerings regularly placed at the tomb. Thus, Egyptologists have speculated that artificial preservation was possibly introduced now to provide an alternative method of preserving the lifelike form and features of the deceased.

New evidence indicates, however, that features that may be associated with early artificial mummification (i.e., enclosing parts of the corpse in tight-fitting linen wrappings and impregnating this material with resinous substances) were already present in the Badarian Period (c. 4500–4100 B.C.), at Badari and Mostagedda.

Elsewhere, in predynastic cemeteries (Naqada IIa-b) at Hieraconpolis (Davies and Friedman 1998: 206–208) and Adaima (c. 3500 B.C.), some stages of intentional mummification have also been observed (wrapping the body and applying resin to the bandages and to selective areas of the body). This is not, however, conclusive evidence of intentional preservation; it may simply represent aspects of the funerary ritual (Jones 2002: 7).

There is new confirmatory evidence from Abydos that some features associated with intentional mummification were already in use in the earliest dynasties. A photograph taken by Petrie during excavations of the royal tombs at Umm el-Qaab, Abydos, during 1899–1900 (Petrie 1901: vol. 2, 16, pl. ii) shows a wrapped forearm, complete with four bracelets, which was concealed in a hole in the wall of the tomb of King Djer (first Dynasty). This arm may have belonged to his queen. Recent studies have demonstrated that textiles associated with this arm appear to have been impregnated with a substance that may be resin (Jones 2002: 5–6).

Another early attempt at mummification was noted by Quibell in the second Dynasty necropolis at Saqqara (Quibell 1923: 11, 19, 28, 32. Pl.XXIX(3)). The body of a woman had been wrapped in many layers of bandaging, and between the bandages and bones, there was a large mass of very corroded linen, suggesting that crude natron or some other substance may have been applied to the surface of the body as a preservative.

Natron is a natural deposit that occurs at El-Kab and in a desert valley known today as the Wadi en-Natrun; it consists of sodium carbonate and bicarbonate, and sometimes includes small amounts of sodium chloride and sulphate. When artificial mummification was practised in later periods, natron was used as the main dehydrating agent (Nicholson and Shaw 2002: 383–4).

Even in the Old Kingdom, the evidence for artificial mummification is scant. A mummy discovered by Petrie at Medum (and later presented to the Royal College of Surgeons in London where it was destroyed during an air raid in 1941) probably dates to the fifth Dynasty, and demonstrates that the embalmers had moulded the outer bandages, saturated with resin, to attempt to recreate the body contours and facial features (Petrie 1892: 17–18). In 1913, Reisner's excavations at Giza revealed a similar mummy (Reisner 1913: vol. 11, 58, fig. 9).

Mummification in the Old Kingdom

Generally, the outer appearance of the body was emphasised in mummies of this period: the limbs were separately wrapped in tight-fitting linen bandages, and the facial features, breasts, and genitalia were moulded in a gummy substance with the details added in paint. Although Junker, also working at Giza, found examples in which the head or entire body (covered first with a fine linen cloth) was coated with a layer of stucco-plaster (Junker 1929–1959: vol. 6, 226; vol. 3, 224), and details of the bodily features and the head were carefully depicted.

The end result, however, was still unsatisfactory because underneath the elaborately wrapped and moulded form, the body continued to decompose. A successful method of artificial mummification still had to be found. A major advance was introduced in the early fourth Dynasty: the evisceration of the abdominal and thoracic cavities. This was probably a deliberate and conscious attempt to arrest decomposition, which now replaced earlier efforts to recreate a modelled likeness of the body.

The first definite evidence of evisceration is provided by the contents of Queen Hetepheres' tomb, discovered near the pyramid of her son, Khufu, at Giza (Reisner 1928: vol. 26, 80–81). Although the mummy itself was missing (possibly removed by tomb robbers from the original burial site), this reburial contained packets of viscera that had been treated with natron (Lucas 1962: 271). Thus, the two crucial procedures required for artificial mummification – evisceration and the use of natron to dehydrate the bodily tissues – were already in use by the early fourth Dynasty.

Around the same period, the practise of burying the body in the contracted position was discontinued, and the mummy was now placed in the extended position, on its left hand side. From the New Kingdom onwards, this changed again to the dorsal position.

Mummification in the First Intermediate Period and Middle Kingdom

More mummies are available for study from the First Intermediate Period and Middle Kingdom, but standards declined: whereas the outer appearance of the mummy is often elaborate, less attention was paid to preservation of the body itself. In 1903, archaeologists discovered an interesting group of mummies belonging to princesses of the eleventh Dynasty (Naville and Hall 1907–13: vol. 1, 44). These mummies showed no evidence of a flank incision for removing the viscera, but possibly another method – partial evisceration *per anum* – was used.

Winlock's expedition in the same area some years later led to the discovery of more royal bodies (Winlock 1921: 37–52); again, there is no evidence of evisceration, and the bodies were probably preserved by injection of resinous material into the alimentary canal *per anum*. Their generally poor state of preservation, however, was probably due to incomplete desiccation of the tissues, either because they were treated for only a short time with natron before they were wrapped up or because natron was not used at all.

Generally, during this period, evisceration through the flank incision was performed for nonroyal persons, but the dehydration process was minimal. The thin coat of resin customarily applied to the surface of the skin achieved only incomplete desiccation, and this caused the body to decompose. Even the two mummies discovered by Petrie in an intact tomb at Rifeh, that subsequently underwent autopsy and study in Manchester in 1908 (Murray 1910: 31), were poorly preserved, although they had both been eviscerated.

In the Second Intermediate Period, few examples of artificial mummification are available for study, but the body of Seqenenre, a ruler of the seventeenth Dynasty, is of particular interest. He died as the result of a severe head wound, probably falling on the battlefield, which would explain why his body was cursorily mummified (Smith 1912: 4–6).

New Kingdom mummies

The discovery of two caches of royal mummies at Thebes between 1881 and 1898 A.D. provided the anatomist Elliot Smith, and later palaeopathologists, with the means of studying the development of mummification in the New Kingdom (Smith and Dawson 1924). These royal mummies represent only one social group, but they provide information that is also relevant when studying nonroyal human remains of this period.

In the New Kingdom, various types of resin and oils were applied to the body to preserve the tissues and mask odours associated with putrefaction and the mummification process.

Brain removal (excerebration) was well established and widely practised at this period, although it may have been introduced as early as the fifth Dynasty (Strouhal 1986: 141–154). The most common method was to insert an iron hook into the cranial cavity through the nostril and ethmoid bone to reduce the brain to fragments that could then be scooped out with a spatula.

More unusually, the embalmer gained access to the brain through the foramen magnum or a trepanned orbit (eye socket). Excerebration was always incomplete, however, and residual brain tissue was left in the cranial cavity. Because the Egyptians believed that the heart, and not the brain, was the locus of the personality and intellect, any extracted brain tissue was subsequently discarded.

During the reign of Tuthmosis III (1504–1450 B.C.), the location of the flank incision for evisceration and the positioning of the arms (generally dictated by gender and historical period) were changed. The hands of female mummies were usually placed alongside their thighs, whereas the male's arms were fully extended, with their hands placed over the pubic area. From the reign of Tuthmosis II (c. 1512–1504 B.C.) until the twenty-first Dynasty, kings' arms were crossed over the chest.

Two outstanding examples of the embalmer's art date to the nineteenth Dynasty: the head of King Sethos I (1318–1304 B.C.) demonstrates the excellent results that could be achieved, although the body is less well preserved, whereas in the mummy of his son, Ramesses II (1304–1237 B.C.), innovative methods have retained the skin's natural light tones, in contrast to the blackening and discolouration associated with earlier mummies.

Mummification in the Third Intermediate Period

Mummification reached its peak in the Third Intermediate Period. During the twenty-first Dynasty, an official project was launched to rescue and restore royal mummies damaged by tomb robbers seeking treasure during the previous centuries. In the course of re-bandaging the mummies, the embalmers may have recognised that mummification did not preserve an accurate or lifelike image of the deceased, and this may have led them to experiment with new techniques.

These innovations were first discovered when nine royal and more than forty priests' mummies from the twenty-first Dynasty were examined (Smith 1912: 94–111). Later studies on other mummies of this period supported these findings; however, the new techniques were apparently first introduced in the eighteenth Dynasty for the mummy of the obese pharaoh, Amenhotep III (1417–1379 B.C.). Subcutaneous packing (stuffing inserted under the skin of the legs, arms, and neck) was used to simulate the king's ample form when he was alive.

During the Old Kingdom, the embalmers had added external padding to the body surface to reproduce the bodily contours. In the twenty-first Dynasty, subcutaneous packing was widely used to achieve the desired result. Small incisions made in the skin's surface allowed the embalmer to insert sawdust, butter, linen, and mud; these materials were also used to fill the thoracic and abdominal cavities and to pack out the neck and cheeks.

An interesting transitional example from this period is the mummy of Queen Nodjme, in which the older method of external packing had been used, but there is no evidence of subcutaneous packing, although the face was stuffed with sawdust, introduced through the mouth.

In the twenty-first Dynasty, the viscera, instead of being placed in Canopic jars, were wrapped in four parcels, each containing a wax figure of one of the protective Four Sons of Horus, and returned to the body cavities. Further realism was achieved by inserting artificial eyes in the orbits, using false hair extensions, and painting the faces (and sometimes the entire body) of men and women with red and yellow ochre, respectively.

Mummification in later times

These innovations were practised until the end of the Third Intermediate Period, but in the Late Period, standards gradually declined. Subcutaneous packing and painting of the skin became less common, and the viscera were no longer returned to the bodily cavities. Instead, the viscera parcels were placed between the legs or, once again, stored in Canopic jars. Generally, the external appearance of the mummy was more important than preservation of the body, although resin was used extensively in the body cavities and on the skin. As in earlier periods, however, it did not ensure complete dehydration of the tissues.

In the Ptolemaic Period, a dynasty of foreign rulers and the arrival of Greek and other settlers introduced many changes. Egyptian religious beliefs were gradually eroded, and although some of the immigrants adopted mummification and it was more widely practised, the procedure was now dominated by commercial rather than religious factors.

All of these changes led to a general decline in mummification standards. As the outer wrappings of the mummy became more elaborate, less attention was given to preserving the body. Sometimes the viscera were removed and treated, and then returned randomly to the bodily cavities. Often the mummy was not eviscerated or the cavities were filled with linen, mud, and broken pottery.

Resin, now the main embalming agent, was poured into the cavities and the skull, applied directly to the skin surface, and used to plug the nostrils. As a result, the skin of these mummies is characteristically dark, hard, and shiny. Many bodies were in an advanced state of decomposition when they arrived at the embalmers' workshop, and the molten resin often trapped and preserved the insects that were attacking the tissues.

Mummification continued to decline during the Roman Period. The mummy was now often buried without a coffin, and so the outer wrappings and decoration were elaborate, sometimes incorporating a painted panel portrait. Some of these portraits appear to represent a true likeness of the deceased. Most of these bodies were poorly preserved, and it is often difficult to confirm if the mummy has been eviscerated or excerebrated. Resin was applied to the skin surface to arrest total decay, and sometimes missing limbs were replaced by prostheses.

Even when Roman rule declined and Egypt embraced Christianity, mummification continued in parts of Egypt and Nubia, and was even practised by members of monastic communities. The bodies were no longer eviscerated, but natron and other substances were applied to the skin, and the body was wrapped in embroidered clothes and linen sheets. Mummification gradually disappeared after the introduction of Islam, following the Arab invasion of Egypt in A.D. 641.

The contribution of mummy studies

Mummies are a unique resource for studying the lives of the ancient Egyptians, because they provide unbiased evidence about disease, medical treatment, diet, genetics, mummification techniques, and religious customs.

Favourable environmental conditions and the custom of burying possessions with the dead have preserved a wealth of evidence for studying ancient Egypt, and until the late twentieth century, our interpretation of this civilisation was mainly based on the archaeological sites, monuments, artefacts, art, and inscriptions.

Art and literature in particular can present a deliberately distorted or propagandist picture that does not represent reality. For example, religious art associated with the elite tombs usually represents the owner, his family, and friends as youthful and free from illness to ensure that they would enjoy perfection and health in the life after death. Only the lower classes are occasionally portrayed with physical signs of ageing, deformity, or illness.

Scientific evidence from human remains, however, should provide a more accurate insight into the past, and multidisciplinary, analytical studies have an important contribution to make to Egyptology, although researchers should be always be aware that with some techniques it may be difficult to obtain accurate results. Also, if scientific evidence is to be accepted by Egyptologists, it is essential that investigators demonstrate that they have interpreted their data correctly.

PART 2

Diet, disease, and death in ancient Egypt: diagnostic and investigative techniques

CHAPTER 3

Imaging in Egyptian mummies

Judith E. Adams and Chrissie W. Alsop

Historical background

The application of radiography to the study of Egyptian mummies followed soon after the discovery of x-rays by Wilhelm Roentgen in December 1895 (Boni et al. 2004). Four months later, in March 1896, Walter Koenig obtained radiographs of a mummified child and a cat from the Senckenberg Museum in Frankfurt, Germany (Koenig 1896). In the same year, Thurston Holland obtained a radiograph of a mummified bird in Liverpool, United Kingdom (UK) (Holland 1937).

At this time, the radiographic equipment was mobile and used on site but was quite primitive, with limited tube rating (exposure limited, and so it may have been impossible for the x-ray beam to penetrate through very thick and dense material of the sarcophagus/cartonnage) and exposure times were long (3 minutes or more).

In 1898, William Flinders Petrie, Professor of Egyptology at University College London, and a major figure in the history of mummies and archaeological sciences, applied x-rays to the examination of mummified human remains from Deshasheh, south of Cairo (Petrie 1898). In 1904, the anatomist and anthropologist in Cairo, Sir Grafton Elliot Smith, assisted by Howard Carter, applied x-ray examination to the mummy of Tuthmosis IV, determining the age of the king at death (Smith 1912).

In 1931, Moodie surveyed the Egyptian and Peruvian mummies in the Chicago Field Museum in one of the earliest comprehensive radiographic studies of such collections (Moodie 1931). In 1960, Gray and collaborators documented the radiographic findings of some 193 ancient Egyptian mummies housed in various museums in the UK and Europe (Gray 1973), including the British Museum (Dawson and Gray 1968), the City of Liverpool

Museum (Gray and Slow 1968), and the Rijksmuseum in Leiden, Netherlands (Gray 1966).

Head computed tomography (CT) scanning was introduced in 1972 and
body CT in 1975 (Hounsfield 1973, 1976). The first applications of CT to
the study of Egyptian mummies were made in Canada by Harwood-Nash
and by Isherwood and colleagues in the UK who examined the Manchester
Museum mummy collection by using radiography and CT (Harwood-Nash
1979; Isherwood et al. 1979). Radiography and CT have now been applied
to study most of the major collections of Egyptian mummies throughout
the world (Chhem and Ruhli 2004).

Imaging methods

Radiographs

X-rays are produced when electrons are accelerated in a vacuum tube to an
anode, and from which a cone beam of x-rays is then emitted. The energy of
the x-ray beam can be altered according to the thickness and density of the
object being radiographed. Some x-rays will be absorbed (attenuated) in the
object, and some will pass through the object and reach the radiographic
film, changing the silver crystals to form the latent image; the radiograph is
then processed to develop the image on it. The attenuation of x-ray photons
is determined by the x-ray beam energy and the atomic number and electron
density of the structures though which the beam passes.

High atomic number materials (e.g. calcium in bones and metal) attenuate the x-ray beam and so few photons reach the film and the area is white
(radiodense) on a radiograph (see Figure 1). In areas of the object of low
x-ray attenuation (e.g. air) through which most of the photons pass to the film
the region will be black (radiolucent) (see Figure 1). Soft tissues of the body
are various levels of gray scale between these extremes of black and white
(Curry et al. 1990; Farr and Allisy-Roberts 1997; Dendy and Heaton 1999).

Because of the cone beam shape of the x-ray beam, the further an object is
from the film the greater the magnification of the object. To minimise such
magnification the object needs to be as close as possible to the film (contact
radiograph), and a long Film-Focus Distance (FFD – the distance between
the x-ray tube and the radiographic film) of 100 to 180 cm is required. To
minimise geometric lack of sharpness in the radiographic image, a focal spot
of 1 mm or less (0.6 mm) is required. Although contact radiographs can be
made of bone specimens, this is impossible for mummies in cartonnage
and wrappings. If accurate measurements are required to be made from

(a)

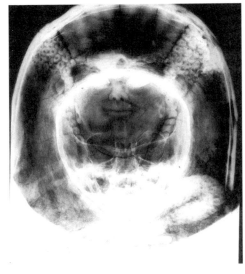

(b)

FIGURE 1. *Mummy of a child.* (a) The mummy is encased in linen wrappings and a gilded cartonnage cover. *Credit: The Manchester Museum, The University of Manchester.* (b) Anteroposterior (AP) radiograph of the same mummy (1a) showing disposition of skull within the cartonnage. Note that the bones of the skull vault are radiodense (white) and the area between the cartonnage and the skull is radiolucent (black), because this area is filled with air. *Credit: Judith Adams.* (c) AP radiograph of the same mummy showing remainder of the skeleton, which is articulated and in a good state of preservation. The gilding of the cartonnage can be visualised as radiodense areas, due to the high atomic number of the gold paint superimposed on the thorax of the mummified body. Note how there is the problem of superimposition of structures on the 2D radiograph of the 3D body structure. *Credit: Judith Adams.*

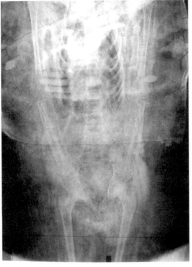

(c)

radiographs of mummies, then a radiodense object of known dimensions (coin, metal ruler) has to be placed at the same level from the tabletop as the structure to be measured, so that the degree of magnification can be calculated and an appropriate correction applied to measurements made.

Many of the early radiographic studies of Egyptian mummies were performed in the field with portable equipment that had limited tube current (limited beam energy). If the specimens to be examined cannot be removed from their place of origin then portable or specially manufactured radiographic equipment on site has to be used. Equipment in a modern radiology department will be technically superior to field equipment and will provide higher quality images and more ideal positioning of mummies than it is feasible to obtain in the field. Radiography of mummified remains will have to be performed during nonworking hours in a clinical radiology department.

Although, in the early days of radiology, the differentially attenuated x-ray beam changed the film directly, now to reduce radiation doses to patients, films are inserted into a cassette, in which there is a radiosensitive phosphor screen. This emits light in relation to the x-ray photons reaching it, and the light forms the image (shadowgram) on the film.

Radiographic tomography

If a patient moves during x-ray exposure, the moving structures are blurred and consequently not clearly seen, as they are not in the same position during the x-ray exposure. Tomography (from the Greek word 'tomos' meaning slice) uses such movement to blur out structures that overlay the item of interest. This blurring out is achieved by the x-ray tube and the radiographic film moving simultaneously in equal but opposite directions.

The fulcrum around which this movement takes place can be varied from its distance from the tabletop and provides the 'in focus' plane, with everything above and below this fulcrum plane being blurred out by the movement. The larger the angle of movement of the x-ray tube, the thinner is the section of the in focus plane. Tomography had to be widely used before the introduction of CT, but is now not so necessary in clinical practice. Current radiographic tomographic equipment uses linear movement of approximately 20° and provides a slice thickness of 10 mm.

Computed radiography (CR)

With technical developments and the introduction of Picture Archiving and Communications Systems (PACS) to the majority of modern radiology departments, the images are recorded electronically instead of on radiographic film, resulting in 'filmless' departments. In CR systems, the projection x-ray image through the object is acquired on a photo-stimulated storage phosphor; this image is then transformed by a CR reader into an electronic latent image, which is then converted electronically into a digital image. When radiographing mummies, ensure that you know how the images are stored electronically in the department and for how long; otherwise the original image data may not be available long term, in which case you should request that the data are transferred for you to DVD as soon after acquisition as possible.

Fluoroscopy

In this method, the x-ray photons transmitted reach a phosphor screen and are intensified by electronic or geometric means. The image can be recorded photographically by a 'spot' camera for static images or on a television monitor which allows real time imaging. This may be relevant in imaging mummies when endoscopy is being performed, and it is important to identify the anatomical position of the end of the endoscope (e.g. when a biopsy is being taken) (Notman et al. 1986).

Computed tomography (CT)

CT of the head was introduced in 1972, and transformed clinical imaging of the brain (Hounsfield 1973). CT enabled a transverse axial slice of the body to be obtained. The image is made up of a number of picture elements (pixels) in which the slice thickness determines the volume elements (voxels); the latter are given an attenuation value dependent upon how much the x-ray photons of the beam are absorbed by the material within the voxel. These attenuation characteristics are defined as Hounsfield Units (HUs), after Sir Godfrey Hounsfield, who was awarded the Nobel Prize in 1979 (Hounsfield 1980) for devising CT.

CT can be used for quantitation (QCT) and is applied to the measurement of bone density with the use of a bone equivalent phantom to transform HUs into bone mineral density units. Because QCT, and dual energy x-ray absorptiometry (DXA) – another method for making quantitative measures of the skeleton (Adams 2003; Mughal et al. 2005) – depend on the bone being measured being adjacent to normally hydrated soft tissues, quantitation methods cannot easily be applied to mummified tissue. In CT, for the attenuation value to be representative of the substance being measured, the entire voxel has to be filled uniformly with the substance. If the voxel is filled with tissues of different x-ray attenuations (e.g. bone and air, fabric and air), there will be partial volume averaging and the HU will be a mean value and not representative of the individual components.

The original head scanners used a pencil beam of x-rays and a single detector that rotated around the head to obtain the transmitted radiation readings from different angles around the head. With the introduction of body scanners in 1975, the pencil x-ray beam was replaced by a fan beam and the single detector was replaced with a curvilinear bank of detectors. This allowed faster scanning of the larger volume of tissue; each slice still took 20 seconds to acquire and was 10 mm in thickness.

Over the past decade, there have continued to be remarkable technical developments in CT, with the x-ray tube rotating continuously to acquire the images (spiral CT), and multiple rows of detectors (initially four, then sixteen, thirty-two, and currently sixty-four rows) (multidetector CT – MDCT) to record the transmitted radiation at different angles around the body. This enables very fast acquisition (20 seconds for the whole torso) of a large number of images (100 s), thinner sections (approximately 1 mm), three-dimensional (3D) volume imaging, and a spatial resolution in the longitudinal plane that is the same as that for the cross-sectional plane, which was not the case for individual slices of the rotate/translate scanners (Kalender 2000, 2006; Hoffman et al. 2002). CT is now widely used to image mummies and has also been used to guide biopsy sampling in palaeopathological research (Ruhli et al. 2002).

Magnetic resonance imaging (MRI)

The technique of MRI was introduced in the early 1980s and has had important implications for imaging human patients. The principle is that when the body is placed within a strong magnetic field (current clinical MRI scanners are usually 1.5 Tesla in field strength), the water protons in the body tissues align along the magnetic field. When exposed to certain radiofrequencies, the protons are perturbed through 90° or 180°. When they realign to the magnetic field they emit a radiosignal that is detected by a receiver coil. MRI has high tissue contrast and can image directly in any anatomical plane, and is widely used in medical diagnosis. It depends, however, on water being present in the tissue, so unless mummified tissue is rehydrated, MRI has no role in the imaging of desiccated mummies.

Ultrasound (US)

The technique of US imaging was introduced in the early 1970s, originally for the scanning of the foetus in utero, as it does not involve ionising

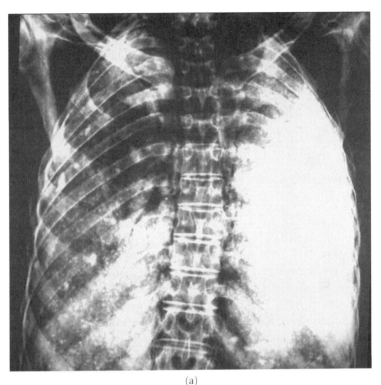

(a)

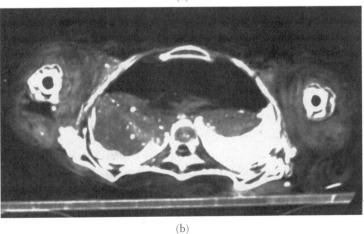

(b)

FIGURE 2. *Resin and mud in the thoracic region of a mummy.* (a) AP radiograph of the thoracic (chest) region of a mummy showing radiodense resin in both the left and right hemithoraces; the resin is very extensive and dense on the left. *Credit: Judith Adams.* (b) CT through the thorax of the same mummy showing cross-sectional anatomy without overlap, and the layering of resin and other materials (perhaps mud, which is less radiodense) posteriorly, confirming that the body was supine during the mummification process. *Credit: Judith Adams.*

radiation. It is now applied widely for scanning in all body sites. Ultrasound waves are emitted from a transducer; some are reflected off surfaces within the body and some are transmitted, particularly through fluid. The differential reflection of the US waves is received by the transducer and the image is formed. This technique also depends on water within tissue, and so has no application to desiccated mummified tissue.

Strengths and limitations

MRI and US, which require hydrated tissue, have no role in the examination of mummified items. The study of mummies requires techniques that use ionising radiation (x-rays) – radiography, conventional tomography, fluoroscopy, and CT scanning. Radiography is the most widely available technique, is the least expensive, and can be most easily applied in the field at the site of the mummified artefacts.

Radiographs have the highest spatial resolution (capability of resolving small structures so long as there is sufficient contrast difference between the two structures, e.g. bone trabeculae containing calcified bone and measuring between 0.05 and 0.20 mm and which are adjacent to marrow fat) of approximately 0.1 mm. CR, which is used increasingly in clinical radiology departments, has a slightly less good spatial resolution of 0.25 mm. CT has higher contrast resolution than radiographs, and so may demonstrate structures not identified on radiographs. However, the spatial resolution of CT is not as good as radiography with spatial resolution between 0.4 mm for single CT slices and 1 mm and 0.2 mm for MDCT.

A radiograph is a two-dimensional (2D) image of a 3D object and has the problem of overlap of anatomical structures, so that the object of interest might be obscured by superimposition of anatomical structures or artefacts (see Figure 2). Radiographic tomography enables this to be overcome to some extent, but the introduction of CT has largely made this imaging method obsolete. Because CT provides transverse axial sections through the body, it does not have the problem of overlapping structures found in radiographs (Figure 2). MDCT allows rapid 3D volume imaging that can depict either the soft tissue or bone facial or entire features of a mummy within its wrappings, depending on the threshold HU used to display the images (Figure 3). Such 3D images of the skull and facial bones might assist in the construction of models that have been made to illustrate how the mummified person might have looked in life (Neave 1979; Manley et al. 2002). CT involves a higher radiation dose than radiography, but whether this is of detriment to mummified tissue (e.g. possible damage to any remaining DNA) is uncertain at present.

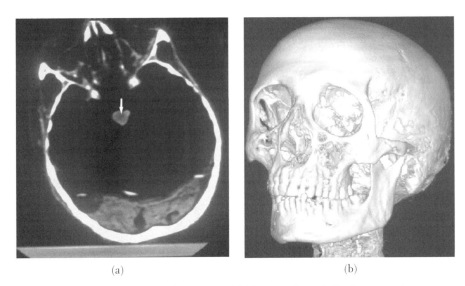

(a)   (b)

FIGURE 3. *CT scan of the head of a mummy.* (a) CT scan through the head showing layering of resin posteriorly in the skull vault. More anteriorly, there is a round structure (arrow) that was identifiable on all sections below and extended into the body through the foramen magnum, indicating that it is a rod used by the embalmers to stabilise the position of the body. *Credit: Judith Adams.* (b) From CT sections such as in 3a, a 3D volume image can either be reconstructed or acquired directly with MDCT, and with appropriate thresholding can depict either bone, as in this illustration, or soft tissue features of the mummy. *Credit: Judith Adams.*

Applications of imaging to the study of Egyptian mummies

The main attribute of imaging in the study of mummies is that it provides a noninvasive method of examination. The images can provide information about mummification practices used and important aspects of the person whose mummified remains are being studied.

State of the mummy and disposition of the body in the cartonnage

Radiography can provide an indication as to the disposition of the skeleton in relation to the outer cartonnage and wrappings, if these are not too radiodense (Figure 1). The images can also indicate whether the mummy is in a good or poor state of preservation (see Figures 1 and 4). If the mummification process was of poor quality or if the mummy has not been kept in ideal conditions (e.g. cartonnage placed erect in unfavourable conditions for temperature and/or humidity, which cause the ligaments/tendons across joints [e.g. sacroiliac joints] to break under sheer forces) the skeleton becomes disrupted (see Figure 4).

Wrapping and amulets

The material wrappings are better demonstrated on CT than radiographs, but the latter can indicate the site of metallic amulets within the wrappings and other decorations of high atomic number material (gold paint, glass, or ornamental stones). Such decorations and artefacts can indicate rewrapping of a mummy (see Figure 5).

Mummification process

As most of the organs were removed prior to wrapping, the cranium, thorax, and abdomen of the mummy will be largely filled with air, packages (see below), resin, the skeletal remains, and desiccated soft tissue. The latter will attenuate x-rays to a greater extent than they do in the living human. The radiographic contrast between this desiccated soft tissue and air will be greater than under normal clinical conditions, and it is important that the appearances are not misinterpreted as disease (e.g. ankylosing spondylitis).

Resin residue can be identified in the dependent part of the body (posterior of skull vault, spinal canal, abdomen, and thorax), confirming that the body was supine when the mummification process was undertaken. Sometimes, more dense mud may also be mixed with the resin (Figures 2 and 3).

Packages and artificial appendages

Organs such as the intestines, liver, heart, lungs, and spleen were removed before mummification and either placed in Canopic jars or placed in packages in the cavities of the body or between the limbs. These can be visualised on radiographs but are better seen on CT scans (Figure 6).

It was the aim of the embalmers to try and make the mummified body as close in appearance to that of the individual in life. This resulted in packing in the cheeks (infratemporal fossa), oropharynx, neck, and elsewhere in the soft tissues, which can be identified on radiographs, but again are better visualised on CT (see Figure 7).

The natural soft tissues of the eyes would shrink on desiccation and false eyes were placed within the relatively empty orbits (Gray 1971). Such false eyes may be identified on radiographs, dependent on the radiodensity of the

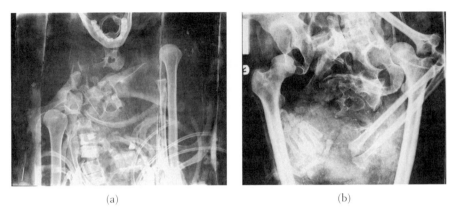

(a) (b)

FIGURE 4. *Poor preservation (jumbled bones) inside a mummy.* If the mummification process has been poor, or the conditions in which the mummy had been stored were unfavourable, then the integrity of the mummy is lost, the skeleton is no longer articulated and the bones are a jumble as is evident in the upper (a) and lower (b) portion of this mummy. *Credit: Judith Adams.*

material used, but are more clearly seen on CT scans (see Figure 8). The desiccated native orbital tissue structures can be identified on CT posterior to the artificial eyes. As the phallus also shrivelled on desiccation on some male mummies, an artificial phallus may be identified. To keep the body in

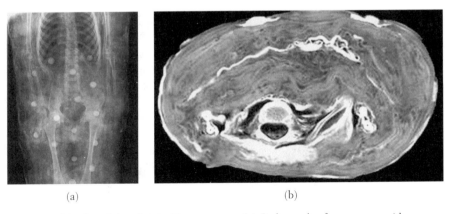

(a) (b)

FIGURE 5. *Metal studs/amulets inside a mummy.* (a) Radiograph of a mummy with evidence of metallic studs/amulets scattered throughout the wrappings. *Credit: Judith Adams.* (b) CT scan showing the thick wrappings around the pelvic region of the mummy. The metal studs can be seen on the surface of the wrapping anteriorly. There is a layer in the middle of the wrappings that is high in attenuation, suggesting gold paint and that the mummy may have been rewrapped at some time. *Credit: Judith Adams.*

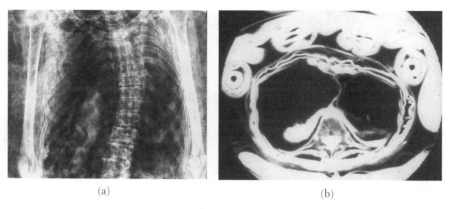

(a)   (b)

FIGURE 6. *Packages in right thorax of a mummy*. The organs were removed before mummification and placed in Canopic jars or in packages, which were placed into the body cavities. These packages can be identified in the right thorax on this AP radiograph (a), as the package is of soft tissue attenuation and surrounded by air. The package is better visualised to the right of the spine on the CT scan (b). There are also two packages/fabric rolls lying anteriorly between the chest and the wrappings. *Credit: Judith Adams.*

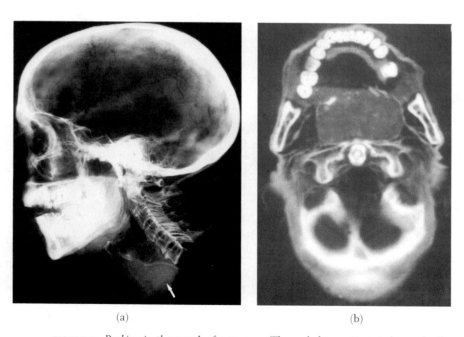

(a)   (b)

FIGURE 7. *Packing in the mouth of a mummy*. The embalmers attempted to make the mummified body appear as it had in life. To achieve this, packing was placed in the mouth (area of the mandible appears more dense) and neck (arrow), as seen on this lateral radiograph (a) of the skull and neck. The CT scan (b) shows the packing in the oropharynx. *Credit: Judith Adams.*

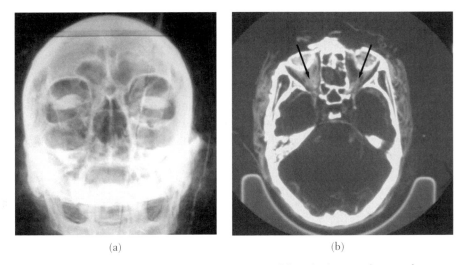

(a)   (b)

FIGURE 8. *False eyes in a mummy*. As the native tissues of the orbit became desiccated during the mummification process, the embalmers often placed false eyes into the orbital cavities. These were made of a variety of materials; if radiopaque, these can be visualised on radiographs as on this frontal skull projection (a), but would not be evident if made of fabric. The false eyes and their construction are better visualised on b) CT scans in which the desiccated native orbital structures (optic nerve and rectus muscles) (arrows) can be seen deep within the orbital cavity, posterior to the false eyes. *Credit: Judith Adams*.

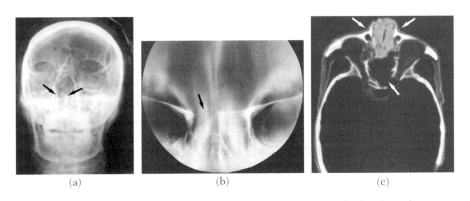

(a)   (b)   (c)

FIGURE 9. *Brain removal during mummification*. The brain was removed either through the foramen magnum or the anterior approach through the ethmoid and cribriform plate. There will be radiographic evidence of the anterior approach with absence of the ethmoid bones and air cells, (a) which would normally be seen through the nose on the frontal radiograph of the skull (with cranial angle of the x-ray tube) with no bone structures being present (arrows). *Credit: Judith Adams*. (b) coronal radiographic tomography showing absence of the right ethmoid bone and cribriform plate (arrow). *Credit: Judith Adams*. (c) CT scan showing destruction of the right and left ethmoid air cells (arrow). Note that anterior to this bone destruction there is material packing in the nasal cavities (arrowheads). *Credit: Judith Adams*.

the straight disposition it held in life, rods were inserted that may be visible on CT (Figure 3).

Some mummies have been found to have artificial limbs. These were usually added after mummification (restoration limbs), in persons who had lost a limb before death, to make the body whole in the afterlife. Some, however, were intended to be functional limbs during life (prosthesis) (Gray 1967; Finch 2005).

Organ removal

The intestinal organs were generally removed through an incision in the left side of the abdomen, the position of which may be indicated by a metal cover, or through the perineum, which can be demonstrated to be deficient on CT.

The brain was surgically removed before mummification via an anterior approach through the ethmoid air cells and cribriform plate (Leek 1969) on either side (Hoffman and Hudgins 2002). The consequent bone destruction can be demonstrated on both radiographs and CT scans (see Figure 9). Sometimes the surgical instruments would be forced so far into the brain that the dorsum sellae (posterior bone margin of the pituitary fossa) would be displaced (Isherwood et al. 1979).

The brain was also sometimes removed through the foramen magnum, at the junction between the skull and the spinal canal in the posterior aspect of the skull, but no radiological evidence of this will be seen on imaging. Mostly, the skulls of mummies are filled with air; sometimes there is resin layered posteriorly within the skull vault (Figure 3); only occasionally can the gyri of remnants of brain be identified on imaging (Lewin and Harwood-Nash 1977).

Imaging of forensic anthropology

Study of the skeletal remains by imaging can provide information about the age and sex of the mummified person and perhaps give insight into diet (through the dentition), lifestyle and disease during life, and the cause of death (Ruhli et al. 2004). There may be sparse information on the latter because, presumably, systemic infection may have commonly accounted for death in these times and there will be no skeletal signature of such acute events.

Sex

Often there will be information on the cartonnage/wrappings of the mummy as to the details of the individual contained within. Imaging (radiographs)

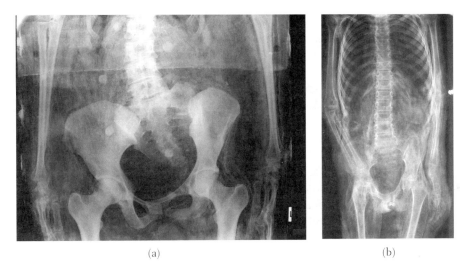

(a)   (b)

FIGURE 10. *Radiographic evidence indicating gender in a mummy.* The gender of the mummified body can be determined from certain skeletal features, one of which is the shape of the pelvis. The pelvis of a female is more oval (a), whereas in a male it is more pear shaped (b), where there is also evidence of the construction of a false phallus overlying the symphysis pubis. The pelvis may be distorted in shape if the wrappings are very tight. *Credit: Judith Adams.*

can sometimes be helpful in differentiating whether the body was that of a male or female. This is best assessed from the shape of the pelvis on a radiograph or making measurements of the pelvis on a CT scan. The female pelvis is oval, whereas the male pelvis is pear shaped (see Figure 10). Care has to be taken, however, when interpreting these signs that the pelvis has not been narrowed into a male shape by tight wrappings, particularly in a child.

Age at death

It is easy to differentiate the skeleton of a child from that of an adult because the growth plates, where enchondral ossification enables growth to take place up to the time of skeletal maturity, and the epiphyses will be evident (see Figure 11). Females reach skeletal maturity at between 16 and 18 years in modern times and males later, at between 18 and 20 years.

In modern times, an assessment of skeletal ageing is made from a radiograph of the nondominant hand, using either the method of Greulich and Pyle (gathered from American Caucasian children) or that of Tanner and Whitehouse, both of which assess the size and shape of the carpal bones and epiphyses (Greulich and Pyle 1971; Tanner and Whitehouse 1975). It can be problematic applying these parameters to mummified children because the hands are often superimposed on the pelvis on radiographs, making the bone detail difficult to define. Also, these reference databases may not be appropriate to the early Egyptian population.

The dentition can also contribute to the process of differentiating between a young child and an adult (primary, unerupted teeth visible) (Figure 11), and the teeth that have erupted and their development can define more accurately the age of the child (Demirjian et al. 1973; Liversidge et al. 2006; Dhanjal et al. 2006).

In an adult, it becomes more difficult to define the exact age at death. Degenerative changes in the spine and joints or skeletal diseases more common in the elderly (e.g. osteoporosis), if present, may suggest that the person was of more advanced age. Such changes are not as common in imaging of mummies as they are in a contemporary population, presumably because most people in ancient times did not reach the same advanced age as modern individuals.

State of body

Mummies may be in a good condition and wholly intact, which reflects a high-quality mummification process and maintenance in an ideal environment since mummification. Poor mummification may be associated with some putrefaction of tissue and postmortem fractures of bones and dislocation at joints. Alternatively, a poor environment and storage since mummification could result in disruption of the mummy.

Status of the individual

The quality of mummification, wrappings, ornamentation, and disposition of the arms may give an indication of the status of the person.

Disease

Because most of the organs have been removed and placed into packages, only the teeth and skeleton are left to provide an indication of disease. Harris growth arrest lines (thin horizontal sclerotic lines in the ends of long bones) indicate that some episode (illness or malnutrition) at that stage of skeletal development caused cessation of enchondral ossification; the provisional zone of cartilage calcified is not resorbed as is normal, and remains as an indicator of disease (Harris 1933; Schwager 1969; Ashby 2001) (Figure 12).

Premortem trauma may be seen in long bones as fractures that have evidence of healing (callus formation). Osteomyelitis may be evident by

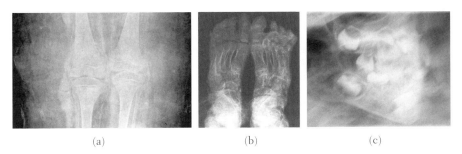

(a)   (b)   (c)

FIGURE 11. *Age determination in mummies.* The age of the mummified person at death can be determined by the dentition and skeleton. In children there will be evidence of epiphyses, as seen here in the AP radiograph of the knees (a) and in the bones of the feet (b), and unerupted teeth (c), depending on the age. *Credit: Judith Adams.*

periosteal reaction, cloacae, and sequestra. Septic arthritis may be evidenced by bone destruction or healing by bone ankylosis (Isherwood et al. 1979). In the more elderly, there may be features of osteoporosis (thinned cortices, reduced trabecular number, prominent vertical striation in the vertebrae of the spine as the horizontal trabeculae are lost preferentially, and fractures in sites of the skeleton rich in trabecular bone such as the spine) or degenerative joint disease (osteophytes, subchondral sclerosis, cyst formation, and joint space narrowing). Degenerative changes may, however, also indicate that the person had been involved in heavy manual labour as compared with a more sedentary lifestyle.

The tramline calcification in soft tissues indicates calcification in arteries, which could reflect arteriosclerosis or diabetes (Ruffer 1921; Sandison 1962). Calcification in the bladder wall is most likely to indicate bilharzia infection; other infestations may cause soft tissue calcification.

It is difficult to make detailed scientific assessments of the prevalence of disease in this early Egyptian population because each mummy is just a 'snap-shot' of that individual and the time and environment in which he or she lived. The mummified remains that have been studied are relatively rare and span an enormous period of time.

Lifestyle

Degenerative changes may indicate that the individual was involved in heavy manual work rather than a sedentary way of life. Harris growth arrest lines could indicate periods of malnutrition (Figure 12). Because food contained quite a lot of sand, the cusps of the teeth became eroded (attrition), giving a flat upper surface, which is best visualised on radiographs (Leek

1979). If this erosion was severe, the dental canal became open and infection could pass from the mouth through the tooth (caries) to the mandible where there may be radiographic evidence of dental abscess (Figure 12) (see Chapter 5).

Artefacts

The process of mummification can cause changes on images that may mimic disease processes. The cartilage in joints and intervertebral discs may appear more radiodense, through dessication, than is the case in living humans and may be adjacent to air in mummies, resulting in greater contrast difference. Joints may appear narrowed as a consequence; the absence of associated erosive (juxtaarticular erosions) or degenerative (osteophytes, subchondral cyst, and sclerosis) arthritic changes help to distinguish when the narrowed joint is the result of the mummification process rather than premorbid disease. Intervertebral discs may also be calcified (Figure 12). This was initially considered to be due to onchronosis (alkaptonuria), an inborn error of tyrosine metabolism, but has now been confirmed to be artefactual and due to the process of mummification, with the deposition of natron in the disc (Gray 1967; Wells and Maxwell 1962; Walgren et al. 1986; Baunstein et al. 1989; Phomphutkui et al. 2003).

The paravertebral ligaments may also appear more dense, through dessication, and more prominent because of increased contrast difference between ligaments and adjacent air in mummies. These features must not be misinterpreted as paravertebral ossification of ankylosing spondylitis; normal sacroiliac joint excludes this pathological diagnosis. Forestier's (senile) hyperostosis (diffuse idiopathic skeletal hyperostosis [DISH]) also causes paravertebral ossification, and has been misinterpreted as ankylosing spondylitis in the mummy of Ramesses II (Chhem et al.), although there are distinct radiographic appearances that distinguish these two conditions (Resnick and Niwayama 1976).

Animal mummies

The mummification of animals was closely linked to the desire to preserve bodily remains for eternity. The reasons for animals being mummified can be attributed to the following:

Categories

Certain animals were regarded as godlike, and so were worshipped as cult animals. Others were mummified as they had been beloved pets during life

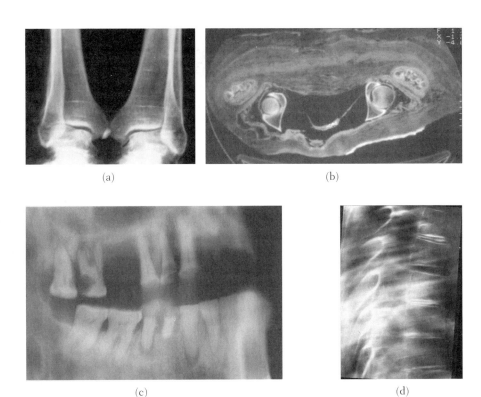

(a)   (b)

(c)   (d)

FIGURE 12. *Disease processes in mummies.* (a) AP radiograph of the ankles showing the dense horizontal Harris lines in the distal tibiae, which indicate some episode (e.g. illness, malnutrition) at that stage of skeletal development that caused enchondral ossification to cease for a period, leaving this line of the zone of provisional calcification. *Credit: Judith Adams.* (b) CT scan of the pelvis showing calcification in residual tissue in the anatomical region of the bladder. Through image-guided (fluoroscopy) endoscopic biopsy this bladder calcification was confirmed to be due to bilharzia. *Credit: Judith Adams.* (c) Food contained sand, which caused abrasion of the cusps of the teeth and predisposed to dental infection. The teeth have flat superior surfaces on this lateral radiograph of the mandible and maxilla, with evidence of caries and some apical bone resorption. *Credit: Judith Adams.* (d) Sagittal tomography of the thoracic spine showing the intervertebral discs to be increased in density. This may, in part, be related to the desiccated cartilage of the disc being adjacent to air (increased contrast difference compared with that in living humans). Calcification of the intervertebral disc also occurs, which is now known to be related to the process of mummification and not due to alkaptonuria, as initially surmised. *Credit: Judith Adams.*

and so would be preserved to accompany the person into eternity. Some animals were bred for slaughter in the temples so that they could become votive offering to the gods, whereas other animals would serve as food (victuals) in the afterlife for the tomb owner. It is thought that animals intended for food would not be wrapped but simply placed in a box or on a platter (Briers 1996).

Animal types

A wide variety of animals fulfilled the various categories for animal mummification (Armitage and Clutton-Brock 1981; Owen 2001). These included cats, dogs, predatory birds (kestrels, sparrow hawks), other birds (ibis), insectivores, Nile crocodiles, and fish. Radiography can noninvasively confirm an animal skeleton within the wrapped mummy and, from the skeletal characteristics, can confirm the type of animal mummy it contains (Figure 13). It has still to be determined whether CT will add further to knowledge of these animal mummies and the mummification process.

Fakes

In some mummies where the external wrappings indicate the shape and features of a specific animal, imaging reveals that no skeleton is present (see Figure 13). Presumably the embalmers ran out of the supply of certain animal types and so created these artificial animal mummies, or if the cost of high-quality mummification was not affordable, then less expensive fake copies of animals may have been provided to accompany the owner into eternity.

Conclusions

Imaging is an important tool that provides information about the contents of a mummy, human or animal, without damage to the mummy or its wrappings (Chhem and Ruhli 2004). The most widely applied imaging method is radiography, which has been feasible in the field for many decades, and so is the easiest to perform with the items in the place where they have been found. Radiographs have advantages (least expensive, most widely available, high spatial resolution), but also some limitations (superimposition of structures on 2D images; magnification of objects some distance from the film; limited contrast resolution; difficult sometimes to position the mummy ideally for the best projection to be obtained; if the wrapping

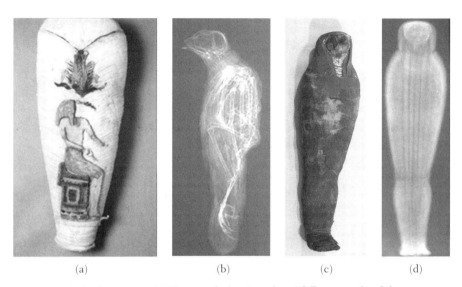

(a)   (b)   (c)   (d)

FIGURE 13. *Animal mummies.* (a) Photograph showing a beautifully wrapped and decorated animal mummy. *Credit: Judith Adams.* (b) The radiograph of an animal mummy confirms that the wrappings contain the skeleton of a bird. *Credit: Judith Adams.* (c) Photograph of a mummy purporting to contain a bird. *Credit: Judith Adams.* (d) Radiograph showing that there are no bones in the wrappings and that the mummy consists simply of material and reeds (vertical linear structures). *Credit: Judith Adams.*

is very dense, then the energy of the x-ray beam obtainable may not be adequate to penetrate to visualise the mummy structure adequately). The quality of images will generally be higher if the radiography is performed in a modern, well-equipped clinical radiology department with experienced radiographic staff performing the radiography.

CT has been increasingly applied to the examination of Egyptian remains since the mid-1970s. The advantages of CT over radiographs are that there is no overlap of anatomical structures on cross-sectional images, greater contrast resolution, and quantisation is feasible (contents of voxel can be based on its attenuation characteristics), but this cannot be exploited to the same extent as in the living human because of the mummification process and desiccation of tissues. There are some limitations (expense, limited availability in some parts of the world, not generally available in the field [although recently a mobile CT unit has been made available for imaging of the mummy of Tutankhamun in the Valley of the Kings], partial volume effect, and less good spatial resolution than radiographs). The quality (spatial resolution, 3D volume imaging) of CT images and the speed of acquisition have improved greatly over the past decade or more (MDCT), but huge numbers of images (approximately 1,200 for an entire human mummy) are required.

For all such imaging, high-quality equipment and skilled technical radiographic staff are important, as is having radiological, in addition to Egyptological expertise for the interpretation of imaging features and differentiating among premortem disease, postmortem changes, and artefact (technical and due to mummification process).

CHAPTER 4

Endoscopy and mummy research

Ken Wildsmith

Medical and industrial applications of endoscopy

Endoscopy is a medical technique whereby a narrow tube is introduced through one of the natural orifices of the body or through a small incision in the chest, abdominal wall, or knee joint. The aim is to allow the doctor to see structures that cannot normally be examined and allow parts of these structures to be removed by biopsy for subsequent examination under the microscope.

One of the most common areas to be examined by endoscopy is the stomach, in cases in which it is suspected that an ulcer is present. Indeed, there are many instances in which endoscopy can be used as an alternative to major surgery. For example, by viewing the ulcer through the endoscope, the medical investigator can often identify whether or not the ulcer is malignant, and if part of the ulcer is then removed for histological examination, a firm diagnosis can usually be made. If the ulcer is not malignant, it can be treated medically, thus avoiding the need for major surgical intervention. Similar examinations of the rectum and colon are made via the anus; another common surgical procedure involves passing the endoscope through the urethra and into the bladder during the investigation of symptoms arising in the urinary tract.

Currently, the endoscope is used extensively in 'keyhole surgery,' and removal of the appendix, gall bladder treatments, female sterilisation, and repairs to ligaments in the knee are regular procedures.

The technique of endoscopy is also used extensively in industry, where it facilitates the nondestructive examination of otherwise inaccessible areas in, for example, gas turbines, cavity walls, and water mains. Industrial endoscopes are often known by other names such as borescopes, introscopes, and endoprobes. As in medicine, endoscopy can save time and money because it facilitates examination without the need to dismantle an engine or other complicated machinery.

The history of endoscopy

The technique of endoscopy is very old and, indeed, it may have been practised in ancient Greece and Egypt. Evidence for its use in ancient Egypt is provided by an enamelled earthenware statuette that dates to the twelfth Dynasty (c. 1900 B.C.). In this piece, a woman kneels with her head between her knees, while a man, seated behind her with his hands placed on her buttocks, is apparently viewing her anus. This was originally regarded as an erotic statuette, but more recently it has been suggested that it may represent a physician performing anoscopy. Certainly, some Egyptian physicians were highly specialised and some may have been skilled in treating diseases of the anus. It is known that, at an early date, some officials carried the title 'Shepherd of the Anus,' but it remains uncertain whether these men were medical specialists, or whether they merely administered the royal enemas.

The earliest endoscopes were possibly made of either copper or silver with the internal surface polished to allow sunlight or candlelight to be reflected down the tube. In the next development, the surgeon wore a lamp on his head, which shone light down the tube with a slotted mirror to reflect the light passing down the tube in parallel rays. When the light bulb was invented in the late nineteenth century A.D., this was incorporated into the end of the tube, with a system of lenses to transmit the image back to an eyepiece. This only added to the discomfort already experienced by the patient as these early instruments measured up to 25 mm in diameter. Prisms and mirrors were also included in the distal end of the endoscope to enable the user to obtain different viewing angles inside the patient.

In 1953, there was a major breakthrough with the invention of 'fibreoptics,' based on a principle that John Tyndall first demonstrated to the Royal Society in London in 1870. The basic principle was that a stream of water flowing from an illuminated vessel conducted light along its length by the phenomena of total internal reflection.

When this principle was applied to a strand of glass coated with a glass of different refractive index, it resulted in the term *fibreoptics*. When a bundle of these fibres, bonded together in a resin, was incorporated into the endoscope, light could be transmitted along them from a remote light source of higher power without discomfort to the patient, as the fibres did not transmit the infrared part of the spectrum and the light was known as 'cold light.'

Subsequently, a bundle of these fibres was constructed with each fibre in the same geometric position at each end. This allowed an image to be transmitted via lenses at the distal end to an eyepiece at the proximal end. These bundles were encased in a plastic tube, creating the instrument known as the 'fibrescope.' These early instruments suffered from a slight lack of flexibility, but the technology soon began to facilitate the manufacture of increasingly smaller fibres, with the result that the instruments became more flexible. Typically, a high-specification instrument would have up to 50,000 fibres in the image bundle. This gives very good image resolution and a high degree of flexibility.

Further developments included the incorporation of a system of wires connected to the distal end of the fibrescope to allow angulation of the tip section and channels to allow suction and infusion through the instrument. Channels were also added to allow the use of small forceps to enable biopsy sampling.

Rapid advances in the electronics field have now added a new dimension to endoscopy. The invention of the charge-coupled device, which is the imaging system in digital cameras and mobile phones, has now been incorporated into the endoscope. This technology considerably improves the image quality through the flexible endoscope and they are now usually known as 'videoscopes.' As the image is now produced digitally, the instrument no longer has an eyepiece, but instead the output is fed directly to a television screen and to video recording, if required. Some instruments have a small LCD screen incorporated in the proximal end of the videoscope, together with a joystick control for the angulation of the distal end.

Endoscopy and Egyptian mummies

Approximately thirty years ago, the Manchester Egyptian Mummy team began to experiment with nondestructive investigative techniques (see Chapter 1). At first, attempts were made to take specimens from the abdominal cavities of the mummies by using narrow hollow needles, typically those used in medicine to obtain liver and renal biopsies. The needles were not, however, very successful for this application, as they rely to a certain extent on the slight movement of the organ to be sampled into a groove in the needle, and the dry and rigid tissue found in Egyptian mummies was difficult to removal in this way.

Next, a larger hollow needle with a diameter of 0.5 cm and a cutting edge at one end was tried, with the aim of obtaining solid cores of mummy tissue. This method was partly successful, but the dry, crumbling nature of the mummified tissue prevented the researchers from obtaining satisfactory samples, and so it was decided to investigate the potential of endoscopy (Tapp and Wildsmith 1986: 351), a technique used some years earlier by other researchers in this field (Manialawi et al. 1978).

At a lecture given by Rosalie David to the Institute of Chartered Surveyors, a member of the audience suggested that the Manchester Mummy team might develop the application of an industrial borescope of the type used by surveyors to examine the inside of cavity walls. Keymed (Medical & Industrial Instruments) Ltd., a firm that manufactures endoscopes for use in both the medical and industrial fields, was willing to assist the team in exploring the use of endoscopy in Egyptian mummies.

Professor David and her colleagues soon recognised the advantages offered by industrial endoscopy, and the team proceeded to purchase six scopes to facilitate their research. It was not only the team members who were enthusiastic about this project – as the company representative who demonstrated the equipment, I was enthralled by the whole subject. I was invited to join the team as the resident endoscopist, a role that occupies much of my spare time, with responsibility for endoscoping the mummies and obtaining all the photographs taken through the instruments.

To obtain successful endoscopy results in Egyptian mummies, it is necessary that the tissues to be viewed inside the body have an air-filled space on at least one aspect, into which the endoscope can be introduced. Therefore, the scopes cannot be used, as they are in medicine, to examine the gastrointestinal tract or the bladder, because the pathways inside the mummy have collapsed and cannot be expanded by the introduction of air. Endoscopes have, however, been introduced into mummies by less conventional routes, and the technique has provided valuable information regarding mummification and disease in ancient Egypt (Tapp and Wildsmith 1992: 152–153).

Some case studies

The mummy of Asru, Chantress of Amun

Egyptian embalmers frequently removed the lungs from mummies, leaving the thoracic cavity empty, and so this offered a good site to pursue the use of endoscopic techniques. The first mummy to be examined with an endoscope belonged to Asru, a Chantress in the Temple of Amun at Karnak, and the subject of previous investigations by the team. When a private donor had given the mummy to the Manchester collection in 1825, the bandages had already been removed and a bandaged package containing her viscera (removed from the body during mummification) lay between her legs. In the team's previous research, histological examination of tissue from this package had demonstrated that, when alive, this woman had suffered from a parasitic infestation, caused by a worm of the genus *Strongyloides.*

There was no evidence of an incision in the abdominal wall and the embalmers appeared to have removed the intestine and other internal organs through the pelvic floor. The anatomy of the anus and vagina could not be established with certainty but in the dried state, there appeared to be a common orifice through which the organs had been extracted. X-ray films of the chest showed radiopaque tissue, which, it was thought, probably represented collapsed lung or the heart in the central part of the chest, but the thoracic cavities appeared to be empty.

The skin and subcutaneous tissue on the chest wall were of a hard leathery consistency but two holes each less than 1 cm in diameter were bored through the chest wall from the back on either side and a variety of rigid industrial endoscopes were used to examine the thoracic cavity. An excellent view of the inside of the thorax was obtained and, as suspected from the x-rays, the lungs were collapsed down to the midline.

There was no evidence of resin within the chest. The thin membrane (pleura) lining the inside of the cavity and the underlying ribs could be seen quite clearly, and appeared to be free from disease. The backbone could be seen and showed no evidence of disease. Part of the diaphragm, the thin layer of muscle separating the chest and abdominal cavities, was evident and appeared to have been damaged at one point, presumably when the embalmers removed the contents of the abdomen.

Radiographs of the collapsed lung tissue showed peculiar striped markings, and the researchers attempted to find out what these were, while looking for evidence of lung disease. To take the investigation a step further, small retrieval forceps attached to the endoscope and manipulated from outside the chest were used to take samples of the presumed lung tissue. Direct visualisation of the tip of the endoscope on a radiographic screen was used to position the endoscope within the chest so that the biopsy could be taken more exactly from the desired site.

The histological examination of this tissue showed scarring of the pleura and the lung tissue. It also revealed that not only did Asru suffer from a *Strongyloides* infestation but also that a hydatid cyst, caused by another parasitic worm, *Echinococcus*, was present within the lung. Further examination included introduction of the endoscope through the common anal/vaginal orifice, but unfortunately, the absence of air within the cavity limited the view within the abdomen. The embalmers had cleared out this area, and as a result, the abdominal wall had collapsed backwards and obliterated the cavity. Biopsies were taken of muscle and blood vessels from the wall of the pelvic cavity, but histological examination of these specimens did not reveal any significant abnormalities.

Finally, attempts were made to examine the inside of the skull. In some mummies, successful access to the skull can be gained by passing the endoscope up the nose and through the defect made by the embalmers in the base of the skull. Unfortunately, in this instance, the soft tissue in the nose had collapsed and so it was not possible to use this route; however, the eye sockets were empty and the hole in the back of the socket through which the optic nerve enters the brain was open, enabling a narrow-bore rigid industrial instrument to be passed through this hole, which provided a satisfactory view of the inside of the skull. There appeared to be some brain tissue in the skull, but due to the small size of the access hole, it was impossible to retrieve tissue for a biopsy.

It was necessary to make a burr hole in the skull to allow any remaining brain tissue to be removed for histological examination. Several intact larval skins were seen lying free within the skull and these were photographed through the endoscope and then removed with fine retrieval forceps. They appeared to be very similar to those examined previously from the intestines of this mummy, which were identified as *Chrysomyia albiceps*.

The mummy of Khary, Priest of Amun

The mummy of Khary, a Priest of Amun in the Temple of Amun at Karnak, was the second mummy in the Manchester collection to be investigated using endoscopic techniques. This mummy retained most of its bandages, and therefore presented an even greater endoscopic challenge because all normal external landmarks of the body were concealed.

To proceed, small holes were made in the chest area, causing minimal damage to the bandages, and endoscopes of various types were then used to examine inside the chest. In this case, the views were quite different from those found inside the mummy of Asru. Here, the lungs were only partially collapsed and in some places, they were attached to the pleura over the rib cage. These adhesions are usually the result of inflammation in the lungs and pleura during life. When present, they prevent the lungs from collapsing completely as the air is gradually absorbed from them after death; in this instance, the view from one side of the chest cavity to the other was obscured, and in fact, the chest cavity was divided into three sections.

There was a significant amount of resin on the surface of the lungs, but it was possible to use the endoscope and the biopsy forceps to examine several areas and to take biopsies for histological examination. Later, microscopic examination of this tissue produced evidence of sand pneumoconiosis, a condition observed in Nekht-Ankh, another mummy in the Manchester collection.

Detached heads in the Manchester Museum collection

The Egyptian mummy collection in the Manchester Museum includes several detached heads. Many of these have now been investigated using endoscopic techniques, and interesting information has been obtained regarding embalming procedures and disease (Tapp and Wildsmith 1984: 73–77). Previous radiological studies demonstrated that, in many mummies, there are defects in the base of the skull. Presumably these were made by embalmers introducing instruments through the nose and into the skull to remove the brain. This procedure was usually performed a few days after death so that postmortem autolysis would cause some liquefaction of the brain, making it easier to extract by this route.

In some instances, the defect in the base of the skull provided a pathway for the endoscope. Because it was sometimes difficult to manoeuvre through this route, flexible endoscopes were particularly appropriate. When the endoscope was introduced through the nose, there was usually a good view of the pathway ahead and the defect in the base of the skull could be seen.

On emerging through this into the skull cavity, a general view of the anterior part of the cavity (anterior cranial fossa) could be seen, and as the instrument was moved around, the membranes lining the skull and dividing it into compartments (falx cerebri and tentorium cerebelli) could also be visualised.

Additionally, the central part of the cavity (middle cranial fossa) was visible. It was often possible to see the groove on these bones in which, during life, the middle meningeal artery was situated. This vessel is important because it is often damaged when the side of the skull is fractured, and this may lead to a very dangerous haemorrhage, which quickly threatens life if it is not stopped by a neurosurgeon.

The endoscope could then be manipulated so that it pointed backwards towards the posterior cranial fossa and the area of the base of the skull that encloses the posterior cranial fossa, so that the area of the base of the skull, which encloses the pituitary gland (sella turcica), could be seen. The bone behind the pituitary gland (dorsum sellae) protrudes from the base of the skull, and consequently was in danger of being damaged by the ancient Egyptian embalmers when they introduced their instruments. In the case of one mummified head (No. 5275) dating to the Ptolemaic Period

(c. 300 B.C.), the radiological evidence indicated that this may have occurred, resulting in displacement of the bone that was embedded in either resin or brain tissue at the back of the skull where it had been pushed by the embalmers some 2,000 years before.

In detached mummy heads, it is sometimes possible to introduce flexible endoscopes through the space within the bones of the neck, which normally contains the spinal cord (vertebral canal). Passing an endoscope upwards through this passage allows access to the cranial cavity through the foramen magnum where, during life, the brain merges with the spinal cord.

It should be pointed out that the endoscope has been of particular value in investigating the 'fluid' levels seen radiologically in several skulls. Through the endoscope, it is possible to observe that in some instances these 'fluid' levels have a smooth flat surface, and when a biopsy of the material forming these surfaces is taken, it is found to consist of resin. The position of these resin levels indicates that the body lay prone for some time after the resin was poured in, and indeed, there was time for it to set hard before the body was moved. In the case of one detached head (No. 1981/575), the resin level showed that the body was propped up at an angle from the horizontal position during the mummification procedure.

Endoscopic examination also provided further information about the fluid levels observed on the x-rays. For example, in some instances, where the surface of the fluid level was irregular and fissured, endoscopic biopsies showed that the fluid forming the fluid level was indeed decomposing brain. It was evident that the brain had been incompletely removed, and as it liquefied, it sank to the back of the skull, forming the fluid level. The body must have been left prone for a considerable time, as the brain must have dried out and rehardened in this position for the fluid level to have persisted after the body had been moved.

Finally, in one head (No. 22940) where none of the aforementioned routes into the skull was available, a burr hole was made using tools employed routinely in neurosurgical operations. These tools consist of a brace and bit very similar to those used in carpentry. The normal size of a drill hole made by a neurosurgeon is approximately 1 cm in diameter, and during an operation, the surgeon may make several of these around an area of the skull that is to be removed to operate on the brain below.

It was sufficient, in this detached mummy head, to make one burr hole through an area of the skull that was shown radiologically to be away from brain tissue. An endoscope introduced through the hole gave an excellent view of the interior of the skull and also allowed a brain biopsy to be taken. The histological examination of this biopsy specimen showed evidence of a hydatid cyst, and it is evident that this was another example of *Echinococcus* worm infestation.

Endoscopy continues to play a major role in providing a minimally invasive means of obtaining mummified tissue. Additionally, tissue samples obtained in this manner over many years now form the basis of the International Ancient Egyptian Mummy Tissue Bank (see Chapter 15), which provides material for current studies undertaken by the Manchester team and other researchers.

CHAPTER 5

Dental health and disease in ancient Egypt

Judith Miller

Introduction

This survey of ancient Egyptian palaeodontology draws not only on all available sources and previous studies (e.g. Harris et al. 1980; Bennike and Fredebo 1986; Harris et al. 1980; Smith 1986), but is also based on research conducted by the author on more than 500 ancient Egyptian skulls from the Duckworth Collection in Cambridge and the Natural History Museum, London. These collections contain more than 5,000 skulls from sites in Upper and Lower Egypt dating from the Predynastic to Ptolemaic Periods, a time span of almost 5,000 years. Many skulls display severe dental pathology, which varies over the millennia and can be explained by the influence of the diet.

In addition to considering the incidence of dental disease, this chapter examines the diet of the ancient Egyptians, the role of medical practitioners who had the title of dentist, and the prescriptions of dental relevance found in the medical papyri. Finally, there is an assessment of the evidence that researchers have proposed in support of the theory that dental treatment was practised in ancient Egypt.

Diet and dental disease in ancient Egypt

After death, when other structures of the body have disintegrated, teeth are often all that remain intact as they are more resistant to postmortem decomposition than bone, and appear to be unaffected by the chemicals used in mummification. The dentition provides information about the diet and health of a population at a specific period in antiquity.

The historical background

For this study, specimens from the Predynastic Period; the Old, Middle, and New Kingdoms; and the Graeco-Roman dynasties have been considered as separate groups. Where possible, more than one site from each period has been investigated, and the findings have been related to known differences in diet in the various geographical regions and time periods.

During the Palaeolithic Period, the Predynastic populations lived on the edge of the desert because the Nile Valley was under water and the vegetation abounded with wildlife. These people, whose weapons have been found, were hunters. More information is available from the Mesolithic Period: for example, near the village of Sebil in the Kom Ombo plain, there is evidence of three different periods of occupation known as the Sebilian culture (Saffiro 1969). The plain had originally been under water and, as this dried up, the population settled at successively lower levels to be near the water.

The second and third period excavations have yielded millstones and stone pestles. In the refuse heaps, archaeologists discovered the remains of molluscs, fish bones, and herbivore bones, which had been opened to extract the marrow. Butchered hippopotamus skeletons have also been found: the flesh of these would yield as much meat as forty or more sheep; the bones were used to fashion fishhooks and other implements (Midant-Reynes 1992).

At the site of El Omari, which may even predate the Predynastic community at El Badari (Midant-Reynes 1992), the remains of granaries and dwellings lined with matting, cakes made of wheat, fragments of wheat and barley, bread, sycamore figs and dates, and stalks of wild sugarcane (*Saccharum spontaneum* L) (the earliest examples recorded in Egypt) have been discovered. Among the animal remains found were pig, hippopotamus, crocodile, snail, ostrich, antelope, goat, and fish bones (Hayes 1964).

A major change in nutrition occurred around 4,000 B.C. when the inhabitants of the Nile Valley evolved from hunter-gatherers to settled agriculturists and pastoralists. The cultivation of grain as a main source of food and the concomitant reduction in hunting for animals resulted in an increased intake of carbohydrates and a decrease in proteins. Because of the settled lifestyle, the population rapidly increased, and at times, this would result in famine.

The ancient Egyptian diet

The influences of the variation in diet engendered by this transition, together with the periods of drought and flooding that have been recorded throughout the chronicled history of Egypt had a profound effect on the dentition. There were years of abundance when the inundation of the Nile was optimum, but these were interspersed with periods of famine when there was harvest failure. Other cultural modifications arose within the Dynastic Period as the result of invasions from neighbouring countries, the capture of prisoners, and expanding trade, which brought the addition of imported crops. A reduction in the average stature in communities who ate a mainly cereal diet has been noted, and even today, the height of the hunter-gatherers has not been regained (Brewer et al. 1994).

As the water level began to fall after the annual inundation, crops were sown in November, and harvested in April before the next inundation. Barley (*Hordeum vulgare*) and emmer, a species of wheat (*Triticum dicoccum*), were the cereals most frequently produced. There was an abundant supply of vegetables such as lentils, beans, cucumbers, leeks, garlic, radishes, and, in particular, onions. Fruits were also plentiful, and there is evidence of grapes, dates, figs, and pomegranates (Gardiner 1961).

Much of the information about the diet has come from the contents of tombs (Darby et al. 1977), including tomb models, stelae, wall reliefs, and paintings that depict a variety of consumables, and well-preserved food offerings, deposited for the afterlife, such as mummified meat and fowl, and bread. Analyses of the viscera contained in Canopic jars have identified food particles. Literary sources include texts on papyri listing the rations given to soldiers and workmen, and inscriptions on temple walls that detail the food offerings presented to the gods.

References also occur to oil produced from the fruit of the *b3q* tree, which is now thought to be ben-oil from the moringa tree (Gardiner 1961). Although there is no evidence of oil palms in predynastic Egypt, a fragment of the pericarp of an oil palm was found in a Mesolithic site in the Sudan, which may mean that food substances were moved between regions.

Fruit and vegetables, the main components of the diet, were enjoyed and eaten in abundance. In discussing the pyramid builders, Herodotus (Book II: para.125) (Selincourt 1972: 151–52) reported that an inscription on the Great Pyramid at Giza recorded the substantial payments spent on food for the labourers, which included radishes, onions, and leeks. In addition, they would have been supplied with bread, the staple of the ancient Egyptian diet. Nowadays the diet would be considered very healthy but the effect on the teeth was often devastating, mainly because of the wear. The causes of these problems can be explained by the geography of Egypt, the diet, and the social conditions that continued for some 4,000 years.

The dietary effect on dentition

The dentition is the only part of the skeleton that, in health, is exposed to the external environment. Diet has been shown to affect the dentition either indirectly or directly. Indirectly, dietary deficiencies causing hypoplasia and hypocalcification can be seen in the developing teeth. Although the cause is the same, no direct relationship has yet been found between Harris lines in the long bones and dental hypoplasia. Direct effects of diet on the dentition can cause caries, wear, and periodontal disease.

Although the dental condition that most afflicted the Egyptians has been labelled *attrition*, this is a misnomer because the problem was not caused by attrition alone. Attrition is defined as 'The physiological wearing of teeth as a result of mastication' (Shafer et al. 1958), or 'loss of tooth substance as a result of tooth to tooth contact' (Soames and Southam 1998).

It occurs on the occlusal and interproximal surfaces. The occlusal surface loses enamel and the cusps flatten. When the wear is sufficient to expose the dentine, the odontoblasts (the cells that form dentine lining the pulp chamber) are stimulated to form secondary dentine to protect the pulp from exposure and its subsequent death. The interproximal wear appears at the contact points of adjacent teeth because of their vertical movement within the periodontal membrane during mastication. The contact between adjacent teeth progresses from a contact point to a complete surface of contact.

Attrition, *per se*, is not pathological. It is found in groups of people who have a fibrous diet (Begg and Kesling 1977; Hinton 1982). Although the diet partly explains the severe wear in the dentition of the ancient Egyptians, it does not completely clarify the aetiology of the pathology that has often been found. In addition to the fibrous diet there are quartz phytoliths included in the cellulose structure, which have an abrasive effect.

There are several scoring systems used to assess attrition but the scheme illustrated by Molnar (1972) is the most detailed. Contamination of the bread led to the initial effect being aggravated by abrasion, a condition described as 'the pathologic wearing away of tooth substance by the friction of a foreign body independent of occlusion' (Soames and Southam 1998). Most of the papers referring to the extreme wear found in the dentitions of ancient Egyptians identify this wear as attrition (Grilletto 1969; Leek 1973, 1986); however, severe attrition alone is unlikely to have caused the devastation seen in these dentitions.

Begg (1954) describes the attrition observed in the Stone Age Australian Aboriginal, in whom the dentition was frequently worn down so that the roots had erupted into the occlusal plane, and he comments on the recession of the pulp chamber with no exposure of the pulp. The Egyptians often experienced the exposure of the pulp because the laying down of the secondary dentine was overtaken by the rapid wear of the dentine. This is an example of tooth wear with a major component of abrasion.

The distinction between attrition and abrasion cannot be clearly defined; there is an element of both in each condition. A better term is *wear*, and Soames and Southam (1998) give a more accurate description of the process: 'Tooth wear with a major component of attrition/abrasion.'

Samples of bread from several museum collections (from different sites and dating to between c. 3000 and c. 1085 B.C.) have been analysed and compared with other types of bread (Leek 1973). Almost all the ancient samples appeared to have whole grains on the surface and inorganic contaminants. When the fragments were softened, the whole grains were found to be husks, but this is because the endosperm had degenerated with the passage of time.

The samples were then examined by x-ray with 4× magnification to show the inorganic contaminants more clearly. After treating the specimens to isolate the particles, they were photographed and magnified at ×105 and compared with samples of sand from sites in Egypt. The particles were identified in the Department of Mineralogy at the Natural History Museum, London. Most were rounded grains of quartz, which were recognised as sand, but grains of feldspar, mica, and hornblende were also present. Only the samples of English bread had no inorganic contaminants.

Leek (1984) cited the statement by Pliny the Elder (23–79 A.D.) that the Carthaginians added sand and chalk to the grain to aid the crushing of the grain. The Egyptians may have applied the same technique but it is also possible that the accidentally incorporated particles may have had the desired effect in breaking down the corn. These particles came from soil itself and from the flint-tooth sickle harvesting tools seen in eighteenth Dynasty tomb paintings. Wind-blown sand may also have been incorporated during winnowing.

Additionally, another contribution was made by abrasions from the surfaces of querns and saddle-stones, used continuously in the grinding process. There are also illustrations of stone ovens with bread baked on the outside where the surface of the bread might have been further adulterated by sand and granules of stone.

Other dental conditions and diseases

THE INCIDENCE OF CARIES. Although less common than today, caries occurred in ancient Egypt, caused by residual dental plaque from a carbohydrate diet. The plaque is colonised by oral bacteria that create an acidic salivary pH. Decalcification of the enamel, followed by the breakdown of the matrix, results in cavity formation, allowing the ingress of bacteria to attack

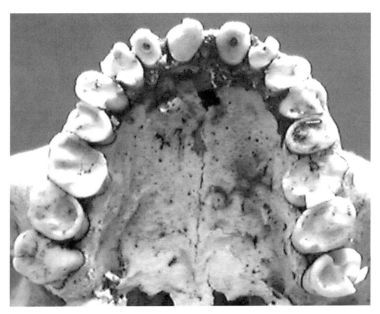

FIGURE 14. *Severe wear with pulp exposure of 2/12.* The main reason for this condition is the contamination of the bread, which was so important to the Egyptians' diet that they were known as 'eaters of bread' (*'artophagi'*). *Credit: Judith Miller.*

the pulp. The site of this attack varied at different time periods because of changes in the diet. In the Predynastic Period, there were many examples of root caries but later periods showed a distribution of interstitial caries, similar to the present day, which is caused by an increase of sucrose in the diet.

The cause of caries was thought to be a 'worm.' In the *Legend of the Tooth-worm*, a Babylonian magical text, toothache is attributed to a demon, represented by a worm, which must be destroyed to cure the pain. Maggots found in figs were analogous to the tooth-worm (Weinberger 1948). An even earlier example occurs in Papyrus Anastasii IV (1200 B.C.) in which an Egyptian official describes the physical afflictions of a scribal companion, and states that a *fnt*-worm (translated as a real or metaphorical intestinal worm) has invaded his tooth.

PERIAPICAL LESIONS. Both severe wear and caries could have led to the high incidence of bone lesions thought to have been caused by periapical abscesses. Some of the periapical lesions that the ancient Egyptian developed were caused by caries, which allowed the migration of bacteria through the dentinal tubules into the pulp chamber. They were, however, mainly the result of the relentless attrition/abrasion that wore away even the secondary dentine and resulted in exposure of the pulp. In the Predynastic Period, the site of the caries was predominantly in the cervical region of the tooth.

The incidence of caries decreased in the Dynastic Period from 33.33 per cent to 28.1 per cent of individuals examined and from 6.14 per cent to 4.65 per cent of the teeth examined (Grilletto 1973). Because many teeth had been lost both ante- and postmortem, these figures may not be accurate. The postmortem tooth loss in the examined skulls has been found to be mainly in the anterior segment of the dentition because these teeth have single, conical roots and, once the periodontal ligament disintegrates, they are easily dislodged. As these teeth are also the least susceptible to caries, the percentage of teeth affected may be less than the previously recorded figures.

Soluble toxins from bacteria, which are present in carious lesions, disperse through the dentinal tubules and cause the inflammation of the pulp even before the secondary dentine barrier has been breached by caries. When the pulp chamber has been penetrated by attrition, it is specifically the bacteria that cause the pulpitis (inflammation of the pulp). The blood vessels dilate and inflammatory oedema develops; this compresses the circulation and the pulp becomes necrotic.

Suppuration occurs with the breakdown products of leucocytes and bacteria, and the pus is forced through the apex of the tooth and causes a periodontitis (inflammation of the periodontium). If the suppuration continues, the abscess will enlarge, track through the cancellous, alveolar bone, and eventually penetrate the dense cortical bone that covers the jaw. In the ancient Egyptian skulls, this is what is sometimes seen as well-defined, circular holes at the apex of the roots, and which has been previously described as conclusive proof that this was the result of dental treatment.

PERIODONTAL LESIONS. It is necessary to distinguish between the periodontal changes that occur as the result of disease and the physiological changes caused by ageing. Periodontal disease is initiated by gingivitis, which is caused by microbial plaque left lying around the neck of teeth. As nothing is known about the oral hygiene habits of the ancient Egyptians, except for their use of natron masticatories for purification of the mouth for religious and social reasons, it is likely that the plaque around the cervical margins might have adhered undisturbed for a considerable period of time.

FIGURE 15. *Caries in the cervical area plus a large interproximal cavity in an ancient Egyptian dentition.* One interesting finding was that the buccal cavities, which arose in the fissures of the lower molars, did not occur very often. Before a large cavity could form, the wear would reduce the height of the tooth below the level of the developing cavity. *Credit: Judith Miller.*

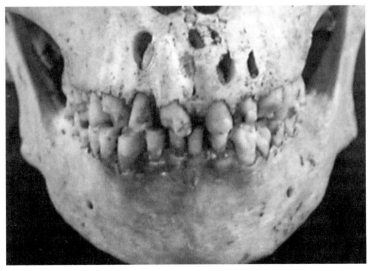

FIGURE 16. *Periapical destruction.* This resulted from the wear shown in Figure 14, caused by the pulp exposure. *Credit: Judith Miller.*

The plaque becomes mineralised by calcium phosphate that occurs in the saliva when the pH is alkaline. This forms calculus and the sites where this is found are closest to the submandibular salivary gland, behind the lower anterior teeth and at the cheek sides of the upper molars, beside the duct from the parotid gland. First, there would be acute inflammatory changes, such as vasodilation, resulting in the exudation of fluid in the crevice between the gingival tissue and tooth. This fluid contains polymorphs and immunoglobulins, which initially would help to control the effects of the gingival infection (Soames and Southam 1998). Eventually, it would result in the destruction of the attachment of the gingiva to the enamel, allowing the deposition of subgingival plaque and further apical movement of the attachment and loss of the supporting bone.

There are two kinds of periodontal bone loss that are noted in the skulls – horizontal and vertical. In the initial stages, the horizontal bone loss may be easily confused with the apparent bone loss seen in the skulls, which is the result of the continuous eruption of the tooth. This is partly the physiological response to the rapid wear by the deposition of cementum at the apex of the roots.

Generalised periodontal disease, initiated by plaque retention, is eventually responsible for the loss of most of the buccal wall of the alveolar bone and the tooth may become so mobile that it exfoliates. In the early stages it can be recognised by the presence of pitting in the compact bone of the alveolar crest.

Because of the condition of the mummified tissue, it is impractical to evaluate the soft tissue; however, because large collections of skeletal remains are available for study, it is possible to assess the skeletal destruction caused by periodontal lesions.

Although the aetiology of periodontal disease relates to the presence of dental plaque, there are other factors that influence the progress of disease, such as nutritional deficiencies and systemic disease (Soames and Southam 1998). In ancient Egypt, nutritional variations were caused by drought and flooding. There is also evidence of diseases such as diabetes mellitus and blood dyscrasias such as anaemia (Estes 1993), which cause gingival inflammation and could therefore result in bone loss and periodontal destruction.

The dental practitioners

One outstanding question is whether the ancient Egyptians, who had sophisticated medical care and treatment, also practised active dentistry. Herodotus (Book II: para. 85) (Selincourt 1972) is quite explicit on this

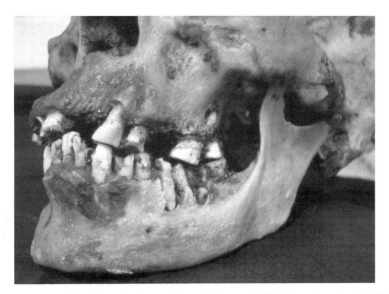

FIGURE 17. *Dentition showing periodontal disease – both horizontal and vertical.* Vertical bone loss is very different in appearance and is the result of an acute periodontal infection, which has resorbed the alveolar bone unevenly. *Credit: Judith Miller.*

matter, stating that medicine was divided into a number of specialisations, and consequently, there were many doctors who dealt with different areas of the body, including diseases of the eyes, head, teeth, and so forth.

From the skeletal evidence, it cannot be disputed that the ancient Egyptians suffered extensive and severe dental disease. Since the advent of forensic Egyptology, it has been a matter of dispute whether any interventional dentistry was performed in ancient Egypt or if the practice of dentistry was limited to the use of the prescriptions in the medical papyri (Nunn 1996).

The title of dentist

As the title of 'dentist' was used in the Old Kingdom and extant medical papyri exist from the Middle Kingdom onwards (see Chapter 12), it is astonishing that there is no significant evidence that the Egyptians applied the advanced technical skills that they had developed in other fields, for the relief of pain and the restoration of function and appearance in the ravaged dentition. The need for dental treatment surely had not lessened by the later periods. Therefore, what is the explanation for this? Are there more 'dentists' to be discovered in the texts or has there been a misinterpretation of the term that Egyptologists currently translate as dentist? At present, there are no satisfactory answers to these questions.

Almost a hundred medical practitioners have been identified to date, and seven of these had the title of dentist (Ghalioungui 1987). Several titles were used, and although they differ from each other, they all define the role of a dentist. In their textual contexts in ancient Egyptian writings, the titles refer to someone who was subordinate to a physician. The most senior title that has been discovered is the 'Chief Dentist of the Palace.'

Of the seven named dentists, six date to the Old Kingdom, and only one is known from a later era, the twenty-sixth Dynasty in the Late Period, which indicates that this title was not in use for almost 1,700 years. Because this seems unlikely, more examples may yet be discovered.

Dental prescriptions that have been found in the papyri

Of the ten medical papyri so far discovered (see Chapter 12), five (Kahun, Edwin Smith, Ebers, Hearst, and Berlin) contain dental prescriptions. In addition there is the Rylands Papyrus, which is not strictly a medical papyrus.

The Kahun Papyrus (c. 1825 B.C.) is predominantly concerned with gynaecology but it includes two cases that mention teeth – the earliest extant dental references from ancient Egypt (Stevens 1975).

Case No. 5 specifies treatment for a woman who is afflicted in her teeth and gums and cannot open her mouth. The text states: 'This is acute pains of the womb,' and recommends that she is fumigated over a bowl containing oil and frankincense and that the urine of an ass is poured into her vagina.

As this is a gynaecological document, the patient was probably of child-bearing age – the period in which a third molar might be erupting. Inability to open her mouth might be due to pericoronitis around the crown of a partially erupted tooth, causing oedema and resulting in trismus. Another cause of trismus or 'lock jaw' might be tetanus. This is a neuromuscular disorder that may follow trauma; it is caused by an exotoxin of *Clostridium tetani* penetrating an open wound. Spasm may occur in the muscles near the injury (Cecil and Loeb 1959).

Case No. 33 describes a prescription to prevent toothache in a woman who has conceived, and includes beans ground up with another substance that could possibly be *tjeret* (willow), which is the precursor of aspirin.

The Edwin Smith Papyrus (c. 1550 B.C.) is a surgical treatise of cases that are arranged in order from injuries of the head down through the body. Two cases are of interest to the dental surgeon.

Case No. 24 provides instructions concerning a fracture in the patient's mandible. The injury is compounded by a wound over the fracture and a fever. Breasted (1930) suggested that words missing from the text may have described the injury in more detail and because of the fever no recovery was likely. The injury may have been a compound fracture and because of the introduction of secondary infection the patient would have died as the result of septicaemia.

Case No. 25 is concerned with dislocation of the patient's mandible, and provides instructions for manipulation and reduction of the dislocation that are still in use today. As further treatment, the Edwin Smith Papyrus recommends binding the mandible with *vmrw* and honey every day until the patient recovers.

The Ebers Papyrus (c. 1534 B.C.) is the best preserved and largest of the papyri; the Berlin Papyrus (c. 1200 B.C.) has similar prescriptions. One of only two printed copies of an unpublished translation of the Ebers Papyrus made by Ghalioungui (1987) was given by his widow to Dr. Benson Harer, who has generously provided the author with a photocopy of the dental prescriptions.

Some prescriptions are relevant to oral and dental conditions. One (Column 86), to expel illness of the tongue, recommends: 'milk, rinse the mouth and spit out.' There is no list of symptoms, but a diagnosis is given although it is difficult to identify the exact nature of the problem. The milk could have been used to soothe the tongue if it had been burnt.

Another remedy for the tongue consisted of 'frankincense, cumin, yellow ochre, grease of goose, honey, water, rinse the mouth for nine (days).' This mixture combined a fragrant resin (frankincense), iron oxide (yellow ochre), a vehicle for active drugs (goose grease), and honey, which has been found to have an antibacterial effect as it is hypertonic and dehydrates the bacteria by osmosis, and would have reduced inflammation in swollen, infected gingivae. It contains propolis from the nectar that until the end of the nineteenth century A.D. was used as an antiseptic after surgery. Other constituents of honey that have antibacterial properties are gluconic acid and hydrogen peroxide.

Eleven dental remedies are given in Column 89, including two prescriptions to 'fasten a tooth.' The first recommends filling the tooth with a mixture of powder of *ammi*, yellow ochre and honey and 'scrapings of millstone, yellow ochre and honey.' *Ammi* is an aromatic herb (but Ghalioungui translated the word as 'emmer seed,' which is wheat) and millstone scrapings were used for superficial injuries. These substances were mixed into a paste that would probably set and act like a splint.

The second prescription recommends that a mixture of frankincense, yellow ochre, and malachite are pounded and applied to the tooth. The papyrus also provides a remedy for treating a gum ulcer: the mouth should be rinsed for nine days with a mixture of cow's milk, fresh dates, and manna.

The Hearst Papyrus (c. 1450 B.C.) has one prescription of dental interest, in Column 1, line 7, which has been translated as: 'which has fallen downwards; *mm* one portion; *aam* one portion; gum one portion. Apply to the tooth' (Quirke 1999, personal communication).

The Ebers Papyrus has a similar prescription 'to consolidate' a tooth, which Reisner (1905) translates as a treatment for a tooth that has fallen out (probably loosened due to periodontal breakdown). *Mm* is *ammi*, which is translated by Ghalioungui as 'emmer seeds,' but I have not found a translation for *aam*. Gum is a viscous secretion from plants that becomes firm when it dries and it may have held the tooth rigid in a splint.

THE RYLANDS GREEK PAPYRUS. This later medical document is in the John Rylands University of Manchester Library, Manchester (Hunt 1911). Case No. 29a is a prescription for a tooth powder (translated by Murphy 1998, personal communication). Unfortunately, many words are missing from the fragment, but it is evidently a treatment for scabs in the mouth that involved rinsing out the mouth and using various ingredients, including stavesacre (*staphisagria* or wild dry grapes, usually known as larkspur, which may have an antiseptic effect) and smooth Egyptian beans (a remedy for skin and musculoskeletal disorders [Estes 1993]). For diseased uvulas, the text prescribes: 'wheaten flower – smooth like granules – having rubbed in.' Acacia, which has astringent properties, is also recommended.

Concepts associated with dental disease

The use of dental titles and the presence of dental prescriptions in the papyri confirm that, at least from the Old Kingdom, there was an acknowledged need for dental intervention. This is also apparent from the evidence of severe dental disease that can be seen in the mummies and skeletal material from this early period. Previous research has documented dental conditions such as caries, attrition, hypoplasia, periodontal disease, periapical lesions, and osteomyelitis and osteoarthritis of the temporomandibular joint.

The ancient Egyptian physician realised the importance of air and water for survival. He thought that air travelled directly into the heart and entered the blood stream. Various afferent channels then carried it to the organs.

These channels were called *metu* (see Chapter 12), and a set of efferent *metu* carried the waste products from these organs to the surface. The *sunu* (physician) did not distinguish arteries from veins or nerves.

The *whdw* (waste products) were of great concern to the ancient Egyptian. In the Ebers Papyrus, there is a chapter about 'expelling the *whdw*.' The physician thought that the *whdw* were putrefying faeces, which would enter the *metu* and infect the heart and organs, thus causing disease. One of its manifestations was considered to be dental disease. The term 'Blood-Eater' appears in the medical texts and was thought to be the effect of *whdw* (pus) on the blood, resulting in the clotting of blood. In Chapter 89 of the Ebers Papyrus there is a prescription to treat 'blood-eating in a tooth.' This clotting was understood to be pathological and not part of the healing process, and the physician tried to prevent the formation of a scab so that the *whdw* could escape.

Evidence of dental treatment

Dawson (1929) commented that, although it was often claimed that dental surgery was practised by the ancient Egyptians, he could identify no evidence of tooth-stopping or any other dental technique. Confirmed by his own examination of human remains, Leek (1984) agreed that evidence was not forthcoming to support the claims of some archaeologists and philologists that an organised dental profession had existed during the period of the Old Kingdom. Indeed, it is difficult to imagine what kind of practical dentistry could have existed, in view of the lack of evidence seen in the many thousands of skulls that have been examined.

Some evidence has been put forward to support the claim that practical dentistry existed. The first example, found by Junker in 1914 in a *mastaba* tomb at Giza, dates from the late fourth or early fifth Dynasty. He conjectured that during mummification, the embalmers had made a 'bridge' in the mouth (Leek, 1984), consisting of a length of gold wire (Weinberger 1947, Leek 1967a) that united an upper second and third molar. The third molar is reported to show more 'attrition' than the second and its roots have been almost completely resorbed.

Professor Euler, the Director of the Breslau Dental Institute who examined the teeth for Junker, believed that the teeth had belonged to the same individual because of the similarity in their colour and anatomical form. He considered that the third molar had become mobile because of its pathological condition and was held in place by attaching it to the second molar by using a method that he said was still performed in 1928 when the teeth were examined. He also stated that 'tartar' on the wire proved that the procedure had been performed in the mouth of a living person.

The photographs show the teeth wide apart; however, Weinberger (1947) wrote that, in Junker's report, both teeth were said to be close together, as is usually found in the mouth. Ghalioungui (1973) also cites the 'bridge' as evidence of dental treatment. Leek (1967a) was sceptical about Euler's conclusions. He had, however, only examined the photograph and had not seen the appliance. Leek reported that the only method by which the concretions on the wire, which were called 'tartar,' could be verified was if the sample were to be examined microscopically.

He explained that there was often an accumulation of material, resembling calculus, on bones that had been buried over a long period. The prosthesis must have been interred separately as there was no evidence of a skull present in the *mastaba* tomb and so the 'bridge' was unlikely to have been in its owner's mouth at death. The wire is tied between the teeth; however, the most convenient position to tie the wire in the oral cavity would have been mesial to the second molar. The wear is much greater on the third molar than on the second molar. This would be unlikely in the mouth as the third molar would have erupted approximately six years after the second molar and would not have been subjected to as much wear because of its age and anatomical position.

Another bridge is discussed by Harris *et al.* (1975). This bridge was found in 1952 by Farid in a *mastaba* that dated to the fourth Dynasty. The bones of the skeleton were almost completely crushed by a fall of stone. The specimen consisted of the upper right canine, with an intact root, which has a double wire wound around its neck and tied at the distal aspect. The authors considered this to be the abutment.

Adjacent to the abutment is a lateral incisor with a groove cut into the labial surface to accommodate the wire, which was then tied around the tooth. The root appears to have been modified intentionally as it is both shortened and narrowed. The central incisor also has a labial groove with a hole drilled mesiodistally to accommodate the wire. The root of this tooth also appears to have been altered. It is suggested that this was attached, in vivo, to the left, central incisor, which was the second abutment to the bridge.

Again, Harris et al. found calculus on the canine and lateral teeth that they considered confirmed that the bridge had been worn for a long period of time. Weeks (1980) alleged that the cemetery had been reused in Ptolemaic times and so the date of the bridge was speculative, possibly advancing the date of the construction of the bridge by 2,000 years.

FIGURE 18. *Example of teeth that could be removed by digital manipulation. Credit: Judith Miller.*

Another specimen, found in Phoenicia (modern Lebanon), has gold wire tied around the gingival margins of the lower incisors and canines to support these teeth. There is also a Roman appliance, made of rolled gold, extending from the lower left lateral incisor to the lower right canine. It is 3 mm in height and is contoured to the gingival margin. Weinberger (1947) suggested that these later examples were probably of Egyptian construction.

Others have proposed that root canal treatment may have been performed in ancient Egypt. Zias and Numeroff (1987) examined skulls from a mass grave in the Negev Desert that dated from the Graeco-Roman Period (c. 200 B.C.). One skull had a discoloured, stained green, right maxillary lateral incisor. A radiographic examination showed that the root canal had been widened and a 2.5-mm bronze wire was inserted into the canal. It was suggested that this had been placed in the tooth to prevent the penetration of 'tooth worms,' which were considered to be the cause of dental pain. Another theory is that it had been placed there to help to drain the large apical cyst. Zias and Numeroff also suggested that because bronze has a similar colour to gold, it may have been substituted fraudulently.

There has also been much controversy about whether there was surgical intervention to extract teeth or to drain apical abscesses. Because of the loss of supporting bone caused by periodontal disease and periapical destruction resulting from pulp death due to attrition, there are many examples of teeth that would have been so mobile that they could have been removed by digital manipulation. These have been left in situ.

Dawson (1929) quoted from the Coptic medical papyrus of Meshaikh from the ninth century A.D. (during the Roman era in Egypt): 'A tooth to be extracted with instruments. Hellebore of good quality and gall; apply to the region of the cheek where the molar is that you wish to extract, and you will be astonished.'

Leek (1967b) stated that he had never identified any interruption of the pathological sequence, and he reached the conclusion that only magical spells were used to treat dental disease. Nevertheless, he accepted that the existence of a method of removing teeth could not be entirely discounted.

This very dismissive conclusion about possible historical dental intervention has to be assessed in the light of the evidence provided by the dental prescriptions in the medical papyri. These were not exclusively magical incantations; some may have been effective as antiseptics and others may have supported mobile teeth when the medicaments set to form a splint.

Evidence for the drainage of abscesses has also been considered. In the foreword to his facsimile of the Edwin Smith Papyrus, Breasted (1930) said that the treatise mentioned the use of the 'fire-drill' for cauterisation. He suggested that this might have been used in a fourth Dynasty mandible to drain an abscess under a molar tooth. He identified what he thought was a drill hole in the mental foramen that he surmised had been made with a bronze drill.

Although this technique was not mentioned in the papyrus, Breasted suggested that the technique must have been taken for granted by the author of the papyrus! Weinberger consulted Thoma and Hooton (who had originally examined the mandible), and they affirmed their original opinion, leading him to claim (1947) that this 'evidence' proved that this operation had been performed in ancient Egypt.

Ghalioungui (1973) agreed with Breasted that holes were drilled to relieve abscesses. Leek (1967b), however, attested that it was not necessary to drill a hole in the bone to drain an abscess because the expansion of the pus, under pressure, forms a sinus and perforates the compact bone of the alveolus.

Some studies have sought evidence that the ancient Egyptians filled teeth. Ghalioungui (1973) suggested that teeth were filled, and he quoted translations of the Ebers Papyrus in which he said that resin, Nubian earth and chrysocoll, or Nubian earth and honey were used. In his unpublished work (1987), he translated these as substances to be used to 'consolidate a tooth.'

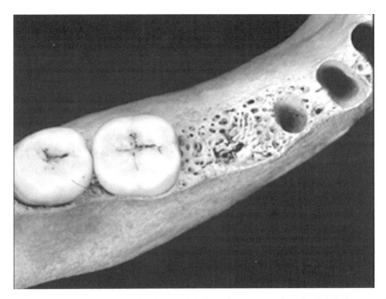

FIGURE 19. *The only example of a possible dental extraction found in Miller's survey* (1997). There is no indication of periodontal disease in the second and third molars and the site of the missing first molar shows bone regeneration and no evidence that this tooth had exfoliated because of disease. *Credit: Judith Miller.*

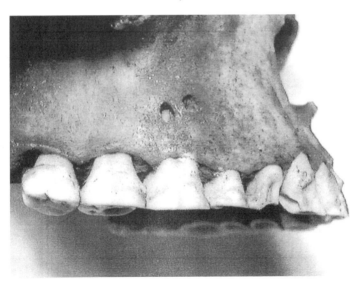

FIGURE 20. *Maxilla showing two nonphysiological defects.* This shows the typical sinuses found penetrating the cortical bone at the apex of the roots. In the past, these have been interpreted as surgical interventions but they are the result of periapical infection. There are many examples of these holes, but no evidence has ever been found of any suitable instrument, such as a right-angled drill, which would be necessary to make the hole surgically. *Credit: Judith Miller.*

No verification of this has been reported either in dental evidence or alternative interpretations of the papyrus.

From the balance of the evidence provided by all research undertaken to date, it must be concluded that dental treatment only became a reality during the Graeco-Roman Period.

CHAPTER 6

Slices of mummy: a histologist's perspective

John Denton

Introduction

The technique of histology has been used for more than a century throughout the world. It is still the basis of modern day pathology for the diagnosis of
plant, animal, and human diseases. Histology is also known as microscopic
anatomy. The word 'anatomy' comes from the Greek *ana-* meaning 'up' or
'through' plus *tome* meaning 'a cutting.' Thus, at first, the term 'anatomy'
meant a 'cutting up' procedure because the structure of the body was originally learned through dissecting it with knives.

The word 'histology' comes from the Greek *histo-* meaning 'tissue' plus
logos meaning 'treatise.' Therefore 'histology' is a treatise about the tissues
and cells of the body. When applied to mummified tissues, it is generally
known as 'palaeohistology,' a term first used by Moodie (1920). Whereas
modern day histology is a diagnostic tool, very different information is sought
from the histological examination of the ancient tissues. For example, it is
always necessary to identify the type of tissue and its state of preservation.
In addition, it is sometimes possible to diagnose diseases and assess the
nutritional status of the individual from whom the tissue was taken.

The histology of ancient Egyptian tissues

Techniques of rehydration and fixation

Essentially histology is the production of thin sections of tissue that can
be stained and examined with a microscope. The major disadvantage
of histological investigation of ancient tissues is that the samples examined are destroyed and can never be returned to the body. The resulting
information is, however, often invaluable and can only be gained by this

destructive technique. Another frequently encountered problem is that of misidentification of the tissue when removed from the mummy. It is often the case that tissues are typed solely on the anatomical site from which they were removed and not on specific pathological identification criteria. Only histology has the capacity to identify the tissue type and degree of preservation. Unless histology is performed in parallel with other methods, such as the more modern molecular techniques, the validity of some of the results may be suspect because the specific tissue type has not been identified.

Ancient tissues have many intrinsic problems that must be taken into consideration before histological techniques can be applied. The universal problem is that the tissue is desiccated and crisp, unlike contemporary tissues that are wet and soft. In this condition, it is impossible to section the samples using the conventional techniques that are applied to freshly surgically removed tissues. To allow subsequent processing, and in particular sectioning, it is necessary to soften the mummified tissues by rehydrating them. This rehydration step has two main purposes: first, rehydration will allow the tissue to regain its normal hydrated architectural and cell structural form, and second, following embedding, it will permit sectioning.

Czermack (1852) was the first person to attempt the histological examination of mummified tissue when he teased out tissue in a sodium hydroxide solution and microscopically examined the resulting fibres. It was Ruffer (1909) who devised the first true tissue rehydrating protocols. He used an alkaline sodium carbonate solution to soften the tissue and then formalin or an alcohol solution to harden the tissue prior to processing. Sandison (1955) further refined the technique originally described by Ruffer.

Some twenty-six years later Turner and Halton (1981) used a commercially available laundry fabric softener (Comfort®) to soften pieces of mummified tissues. One of the problems with using commercially available materials is that the manufacturer often changes the formulation of the product and so standardisation of the technique is impossible. Comfort has the particular problem that, as it is designed for a laundry purpose, it contains optical brighteners to give a 'cleaner wash,' and these optical brighteners also attach to the mummified tissues, changing staining patterns and preventing subsequent immunofluorescent examination.

A comprehensive account (Mekota and Vermehren 2005) reviews the many attempts to refine the original rehydration techniques. Currie (2002), working from basic scientific principles, devised a solution of 1 per cent sodium laureth sulphate (a detergent) in formol saline for the rehydration of tissues, and this is now our preferred technique. All rehydration solutions must have the capacity to kill or at least inactivate bacterial and fungal organisms that would lead to putrefaction of the mummy tissues during the process.

Following rehydration, it is necessary to fix the tissue. Fixation involves a complex series of chemical changes that stabilise the tissue, retaining the tissue architecture in as lifelike a state as possible; it must also allow subsequent processing. It is interesting to note that the ancient Egyptians accidentally discovered fixation many years before the modern histological techniques were described, as they used natron as a fixative to preserve the body as part of the mummification process.

Usually, the rehydration and fixation steps are performed in the same solution, as in the case of formalin and detergent. The rehydration and fixation steps are used for both soft tissues and bone, but in the case of bone, further decisions have to be made about the subsequent processing steps. Trabecular bone (found, for example, in the vertebra and the ends of the long bones) is very difficult to section without first removing its mineral content. Cortical bone (which, for example, forms the shafts of the long bones such as the femur) is impossible to section unless a decalcification step to remove the mineral hydroxyapatite is first performed.

There are two main types of decalcification, acid and chelation, but the most common is the use of an acidic solution to breakdown the hydroxyapatite into the soluble salt of the acid that then diffuses from the bone into solution. The mode of action of chelation is different from acidic processes as it takes place at neutral pH. The most common chelating agent is a solution of ethylene diamine tetraacetic acid (EDTA). The crystal of hydroxyapatite is made unstable by the irreversible capture of a calcium atom from the surface of the hydroxyapatite crystal by the chelating agent, which destabilises the crystal, resulting in the subsequent release of a phosphorus atom; the consequence of this is the dissolution of the crystal.

Many different solutions have been used but it was not until recently that Williams (2006) comparatively determined the optimum mode of decalcification when applied to ancient bone. Through a comparison of the controllability, damage, effectiveness, and subsequent staining of the bone tissues with decalcification by nitric, formic, acetic, and hydrochloric acids and EDTA, she came to the conclusion that a 12 per cent formic acid/sodium citrate solution at room temperature with constant slow agitation was the optimum solution for ancient bone.

Embedding and sectioning the mummified tissue

Mummy tissue is often contaminated by the presence of sand, which can make the tissue difficult or impossible to section; however, the sand is easily removed from the tissue prior to processing by immersion in 2 per cent hydrofluoric acid (extreme caution) with little or no damage to the tissue. The technique was originally described (Denton 1998) not for mummy tissue but for the removal of silica-containing deposits from human female breast tissue in an investigation into failing silicone breast implants.

Following the previous steps of rehydration, fixation, and/or decalcification, prior to infiltration with the final embedding medium, it is necessary to remove any water present in the tissue because the final embedding media are not miscible with water. This stage, known as the dehydration step, generally involves the removal of water by the immersion of the wet tissue in many changes of alcohol until all water is removed. The time taken for this procedure depends on the size and density of the tissue. The media used for the final embedding are generally not miscible with alcohol, and so another step of processing has to be taken. This step, which uses a reagent that is both miscible with alcohol and the embedding media, used to be known as 'clearing the tissue.' This term came about because oils such as cedarwood and sandalwood were used that made the tissue almost transparent; in modern practice, synthetic, cheap hydrocarbons such as xylene are used.

There are two main embedding procedures: either with paraffin wax or with plastic resin. Paraffin wax embedding of tissues has been performed for at least 100 years and it remains the most widely practised embedding technique in modern day histology laboratories. It is especially useful for soft tissues, as it sections easily with standard equipment and knives and has the advantage that it is easily removed with solvents.

For harder modern tissues such as bone, plastic resin embedding has largely replaced wax as an embedding medium. The disadvantage of this form of embedding is that it is more expensive, and requires complex equipment and either tungsten carbide–tipped steel knives, glass knives, or even diamond knives to cut the sections. Well-rehydrated mummy tissues can be embedded in wax and successfully sectioned; however, it is often the case that because of their inherent hardness, mummy tissues require plastic resin embedding.

Karlsen (2006) performed a critical, comparative, evaluation of the embedding of decalcified and nondecalcified ancient bone samples in four embedding resins commonly used for modern day samples. These were Araldite®, Spurr, methylmethacrylate, and LR White resin™. In the study he compared the preservation, ease of embedding, sectioning, and staining of the bone sections. From a staining and sectioning perspective, methylmethacrylate embedding was the preferred embedding type for ancient bone; however, polymerisation of the monomer was very problematic and not controllable most of the time. Karlsen finally concluded that because of the control and sectioning quality, LR White embedding was the preferred medium for ancient tissues.

As mummified tissues are so often exceptionally difficult to section, embedding in one of the plastic resins is the only way, even for soft non-calcified tissues, to be sectioned. Sections are cut at between 5- and 10-μ thickness on machines known as microtomes. These machines often simply consist of a block holder and knife in which the block is passed under the knife and a section is cut; the block advances on the return stroke and the process is repeated. For modern tissues, the knife is generally of the disposable type; however, the fragile edge of the knife is easily damaged, and for mummified tissues it is normal to replace the disposable knife with one that has a hardened edge or even one that has a tungsten carbide tip.

Once cut, the section is mounted onto a glass microscope slide for support and to enable the staining process to be performed. Because the majority of staining techniques take place in an aqueous environment, the wax has to be removed from the section before staining. This is normally a simple matter of reversing the sequence of the processing reagents by soaking the slide in xylene followed by alcohol, and finally immersing the section in water. This is often referred to as the 'section to water' step prior to staining.

The staining process

The whole purpose of embedding and sectioning is to have a section, usually 5 μ thick, that is thin enough to be examined microscopically. Unfortunately, due to the thinness and transparency of the sections, staining is required so that individual tissues and components that have no intrinsic contrast or colour can be visualised.

Thousands of stains are used for histological purposes but many are just minor variations of each other. Only the types of staining and the results are described here as there are many other available sources for specific staining reactions to which the reader can refer. The main reactions are designed to specifically demonstrate individual properties or cellular configurations of the tissue in different colours, such as the common haematoxylin and eosin (H&E) technique that stains cell nuclei blue and the rest of the tissue shades of pink. Some stains are less specific and just stain all components of the tissue in the same colour but with varying intensity, such as the toluidine blue technique.

Before embarking on staining the tissue, it is necessary to identify the required outcome, for example: 'Do I need to see just a global view of the tissue?' or 'Is the information that I require of a very specific nature?' Each question will need to be answered by a different staining technique, and possibly by many techniques. In palaeohistology, the questions are often quite simple, for example: 'Is the tissue what I think it is?' or 'Is it well preserved?' These simple questions, however, sometimes pose complex problems.

Customarily, staining techniques that rely on differing mechanisms of action are used, so that problems of preservation that may preclude successful staining with one stain can be overcome by another, in order that the common features of the tissue can be identified. These objectives can often be achieved by the use of a single stain such as toluidine blue, which is a general stain of matrix, nuclei, and microorganisms. Toluidine blue staining in mummy tissues is simple and rapid, as staining takes one minute with a 0.05 per cent aqueous solution of the dye. The drawback to this stain is that all components including the nuclei are shades of blue, and it is necessary to have prior knowledge of tissue structures so that they may be identified by morphology alone.

Pathologists have overcome this barrier by using two stains in sequence to give a differentiation between the two essential components of tissues: the nuclei of cells and their cytoplasm. The natural stain haematoxylin in combination with the dye eosin (H&E) is the most common staining procedure in histology laboratories throughout the world. It is the basis of all diagnostic histology applied to surgical tissues where it stains nuclei blue and other parts of the tissue varying shades of red. When the H&E stain is applied to ancient tissues, the results are mostly disappointing due to the degradation of the tissue, resulting in the loss of nuclear staining and of the contrast to the eosin stain. This problem can be minimised by using the other staining techniques that rely on other mechanisms of staining.

As connective tissues are often the only ones remaining on the body, it is important that their presence can be demonstrated histologically. Fortunately, staining reactions have been designed that separate the various tissues, including the connective tissues; these show different colours when applied in sequence. This type of staining technique is often called after the number of stains used in the technique; for example, when three dyes are applied in sequence, this is known as a trichrome technique.

Following staining, the final step before microscopic examination is the process of encapsulating the stained section. This is performed by dehydrating the glass slide containing the section with alcohol, replacing the alcohol with xylene, and applying a small quantity of mounting medium followed by the application to the surface of a thin glass coverslip. The mounting medium is often a solution of the plastic polystyrene in an organic solvent. It is designed to have the identical refractive index as that of the slide and coverslip glass, providing a transparent pathway for light and minimising refraction that is a cause of microscopic resolution loss.

Tissue identification

The identification of tissue can be problematic. For example, visual inspection of this specimen from a Canopic jar tentatively indicated that it was a sample of liver (Plate I). To the surprise of the researcher, however, when the specimen was examined by histological techniques and stained, it was identified as a leaf. This finding illustrates the point that it cannot be assumed that visual identification is conclusive. Without correct identification, this material may have been used for more sophisticated analytical or molecular techniques, which would have given erroneous results and wasted the material.

Identification of bacteria and fungi

When mummified tissues are histologically examined, microorganisms such as bacteria and fungi can often be seen in the section. They are generally present as a result of continuing putrefaction of the tissues. These microorganisms are best seen in the toluidine blue staining reaction in which the whole tissue is stained a shade of blue but the bacteria stain the darkest.

Bacteria are divided into two main groups on the basis of their staining by the Gram technique. In this technique, bacteria that are said to be Gram-positive stain blue and bacteria that are Gram negative stain red. Pathogenic bacteria that have caused an abscess in the individual before death most often produce a pus-filled cavity in the tissues, which would be full of bacteria; this would leave evidence of a cavity in mummified tissues. In contrast, bacteria that are starting to invade the tissues as part of the putrefaction process use the route of least resistance, which is normally along and between fibres (Plate II).

Fungi of various types are often seen in ancient tissues; these are a result of poor storage of the specimen (see Chapter 16). Histology allows conservators to identify the fungus on morphological grounds and to assess the effects of the organism on the tissue. A problematic fungus that is encountered is *Serpula lacrymans*, more commonly known 'dry rot.' Conservators normally limit the humidity in the air surrounding the exhibit to control the fungi and bacteria, but unfortunately, dry rot fungus is adept at circumventing this measure by producing its own water as a metabolic byproduct, thus allowing further growth. So even if the mummy is placed in a dry environment, this does not inhibit the growth of the fungus, which proceeds to use the bone as a food source.

In addition to water, the fungus produces oxalic acid as another metabolic byproduct, which can be a problem, particularly for bony structures. The acid acts in a similar way to the acids in the decalcification process but in this case, instead of producing a soluble salt, the oxalic acid produces an insoluble calcium oxalate compound that forms clusters of crystals in the tissues. These crystals are best viewed by the technique of polarising microscopy in which the birefringent properties of the crystal give bright white or coloured crystals on a black or magenta background (Plate III).

Polarising microscopy

Polarising microscopy can also be used to visualise crystals that were deposited during the individual's life as a result of pollution in ancient Egypt. This can be seen in Plate IV in which crystals and soot have been deposited in the pleura, the sac surrounding the lungs. Deposits of this type are accumulated throughout life when the individual is inhaling air containing sand and other particles.

The contents of the deposit are a reflection of the pattern of particulate inhalation throughout the person's life and are nearly always a mixture. It is common to find sand in lungs from the inhabitants of these desert areas, and this type of soot is often the result of burning fats used for illumination in a confined space such as a tomb, mine, or even the home. Mixed particles are sometimes seen in the lungs of smelters and potters, reflecting the dust and smoke that they have inhaled in the course of their daily working lives.

Histological examination of mummified cats

Preservation of tissues is optimally achieved by rapid desiccation of thin, exposed structures that include, for example, the extremities of limbs and protruding thin structures such as the ears. This is well demonstrated by this section of a cat's ear (Plate V). The section shows that there is excellent cellular preservation: even cell nuclei, which are normally one of the first casualties of degradation processes, are present. By examining and identifying the different types of tissue that make up the ear, it can be seen that there is a large band of cartilage running through the centre of the tissue.

Cartilage of this thickness would give the ears a great degree of stiffness, and from this it can be assumed that the ears of the cat were quite stiff and erect. Cats of this type are described and pictured in wall scenes in Egyptian tombs.

Histological examination of plant remains

Histology can also be used to examine ears of wheat. The seed capsule is designed to resist dehydration and remain in a viable condition for a long period of time and is normally harvested in a dried condition. Because of this dried state, the seed is often very well preserved and has resisted attack by microbial agents. Histological examination of the seed allows a comparison to be made between the emmer types of wheat grown in ancient Egypt and the more modern crops grown today. The morphology of the wheat seed and the starch contents demonstrate excellent preservation even after 2,500 years and show a remarkable degree of preservation (Plate VI).

The effects of oxidation and putrefaction

Oxidation and putrefaction can have profound effects on the staining of tissues, in some cases even reversing the normal staining pattern that would be expected by the individual stain on contemporary tissues. Some staining techniques are unaffected by reversal of the normal staining pattern, but the staining techniques that rely on the fact that the molecular pores are filled by dyes having specific molecular sizes are often affected. It is common in this type of technique to have three dyes that are applied in sequence to the section.

The first and largest molecular size dye fills the largest size pores, and this is then followed by the smallest molecular size dye, which can only fill the smallest pores because it is not large enough to fill the intermediate size pores. When the largest and smallest pores are filled, the rest are finally filled with the last dye. Each of the dyes is of a different colour and become localised in different tissue types, allowing them to be separated on the basis of colour alone. This effect is sometimes demonstrated in partially damaged tissue in which only the surface of the tissue is affected, giving a reversal of the normal staining pattern.

Putrefaction often destroys the evidence of pathological conditions in ancient tissues, particularly in softer tissues such as liver (Plate VII). The skeletal tissues are quite resistant to these changes and can sometimes provide much information, as they retain and lay down evidence within the structure of the bone, similar to the way in which the annual rings in a tree are indicative of time and seasons.

The contribution of skeletal material

Skeletal connective tissue remains in mummified bodies are a valuable biological indicator for understanding lifestyle in antiquity and individual nutrition. They can show very complex histories that have been archived in the structure, and these can be revealed through histological examination. An understanding of the basic biology of bone is essential to understand any of the changes that may be expected to appear.

Bone is a highly active calcified connective tissue that is the articulating framework to which the muscles via tendons are attached; it is also the main depot of calcium vital for homeostasis. There are three formations of bone that have different configurations but are essentially composed of collagen fibres, which are calcified with hydroxyapatite. The first type of bone is known as compact bone; this is the type of bone that forms the shafts of the long bones (e.g. femur), and the surface of the trabecular or spongy bone (e.g. vertebra). It is composed of a complex of tubes that are stress bearing due to their shape, and have haversian canals or nutritional channels running through the centre of most tubes.

The second type of bone is known as trabecular or spongy bone; it forms the centre of the ends of the long bones and is the main type of bone in the spine and pelvis. It is composed of an interconnecting mesh or spongelike fingers of bone, which are themselves formed of lamellar or layered collagen fibre structure. In addition, between the bone structure, there is the almost liquid, blood-cell forming, haemopoetic marrow. The third type of bone is formed at sites of damage, and is termed woven because of the relative random structure of the collagen fibres.

As a living, dynamic tissue, bone is not dead or static; it adapts to changes in body demands, either for support or as a result of a disease state. Bone is formed and adapts to these influences through the balance achieved between three different types of cells. Bone is formed by cells known as osteoblasts, which lay down a precursor of bone called osteoid; some days later, this becomes mineralised with the complex calcium phosphate known as hydroxyapatite. So that bone can be removed to change its configuration, either simply to renew it or as a direct result of pathological conditions, a cell known as an osteoclast attaches itself to the surface of bone, where it secretes acid and collagen-degrading enzymes. This results in the specific removal of bone, leaving hollows or pits and a scalloped surface.

Following removal, the bone is replaced where necessary by the bone-forming cells (osteoblasts), which first lay down the nonmineralised osteoid that then becomes mineralised. It is this relationship of osteoid and mineralised bone that is destroyed when the mineral is removed through the decalcification process. If the relationship is needed, then the bone must not be decalcified. Although the section is much more challenging to cut, the diagnosis of rickets and adult osteomalacia can be made.

Telltale changes in the orientation of the collagen fibres occur at the point at which osteoclasts finish bone removal and when osteoblasts start new bone formation; there is also a stainable line known as a reversal line that is produced at the junction of the old and newly formed bone. The whole process continues throughout life to maintain the biological and biomechanical properties of bone. Problems occur within the skeleton, either locally as in the case of a fracture or systemically as in the case of osteomalacia (in children known as rickets) and osteoporosis. In contemporary bones, the difference between osteoid and mineralised bone can be demonstrated, enabling the ratio of mineralised bone to osteoid to be measured and compared with normal. If this relationship is to be investigated, the bone cannot be decalcified and must therefore be embedded in plastic resin.

In ancient skeletal tissues, the presence of osteoid cannot often be estimated because it is removed as part of the bacterial and fungal putrefaction process that causes all soft tissues including osteoid to be lost; therefore, the diagnosis of rickets or osteomalacia cannot be made. In cases of this nature, the diagnosis of osteomalacia is impossible; however the diagnosis of osteoporosis can be made because this simply involves the measurement of bone volume and its comparison with an age- and sex-matched normal control.

Despite putrefaction, residual detail always remains in the bone. In the following case (Plate VIII), this has facilitated the reconstruction of a very specific individual history. A histological section from a Nubian female of childbearing age was examined and an unusual pattern of staining was noted. The pattern demonstrated severe bone removal by osteoclastic resorbtion, leaving a scalloped surface; this then came to an end but was followed by a healing phase when new bone formation occurred over this old surface. This pattern was then repeated, but this time, the resorbtion occurred through the new bone and into the old bone. This process then suddenly came to an end, and no new bone was formed.

Such rapid removal of bone is often associated with the nutritional demands of pregnancy in which the maternal skeleton is eroded by foetal demands for calcium. During pregnancy, the demands for calcium are approximately 300 mg per day, but during lactation, the demand is in the region of 3,000 mg per day, most of which comes from the maternal skeleton. If this is compounded by a poor diet, which was probably common in ancient Egypt, then this can produce the episodic removal, healing, and subsequent removal observed in this woman.

Thus, the abnormalities in the section of bone shown in Plate VIII can be explained by piecing together a timeline of events: a normal woman with normal healthy bone (HB) becomes pregnant and delivers a healthy child whom she breast-feeds. This leads to massive calcium demands that result in bone removal (evidenced by the old resorbtion line [OR]). She then stops breast-feeding and has a period of normal health that allows her bone to heal by formation of new bone on the surface of the old bone (NB).

The woman then re-enters the cycle of pregnancy and lactation, which again results in bone removal by osteoclasts, but this now occurs through the bone laid down between the two pregnancies and into the original old healthy bone (NOC). This cycle then stops suddenly, demonstrated by the resorbtion and lack of new bone formation. This abrupt halt was almost certainly due to the woman's death. This example demonstrates how histological examination of a small sample of bone can produce detailed information about the months or years of the person's life prior to death.

Textile studies

Egyptian mummies are often wrapped with cloth bandages, as are sometimes the individual organs in the Canopic jars. It is therefore not unusual to have pieces of bandage included with the tissue to be examined histologically.

At the microscopic level, it is usually possible to provide a positive identification of the structure of the cloth and the type of fibre of which it is composed (Plate IX).

In conclusion, histology was one of the earliest scientific techniques to be used for the investigation of ancient human, animal, and plant remains. It is still the only technique that can identify specific tissues at a cellular level and allow the pathological diagnosis of disease states.

CHAPTER 7

Palaeopathology at the beginning of the new millennium: a review of the literature

Maria Jeziorska

Introduction

> The attempt to study the significance of disease in prehistoric and early historic people is challenging and somewhat analogous to reconstructing the plot of a feature length motion picture from a few frames. – Miller et al. (1996)

Human palaeopathology can be defined as the study of disease in ancient populations by the examination of human remains (Aufderheide and Rodriquez-Martin 1998). It has changed from a description of isolated cases of interesting findings during archaeological excavations to a fascinating branch of science offering insights into the past with clues to understanding the present. In most of the cases, it is now no longer a solitary task of a single researcher but an effort of a multidisciplinary team. In many cases, work on mummified remains from one location is continued over several years, building a complex interpretation of the cause and circumstances of death of particular individuals and their place in the society.

This is a review of publications on the issues of palaeopathology published in the last decade, but mostly after the beginning of the new millennium. It may seem a short period of time, but the number of publications is quite substantial so the decision to limit the scope of this review to those years was made because the earlier publications were exceptionally well presented in two books by Aufderheide and Martinez (1998) and Aufderheide (2003).

This review is presented from the point of view of a pathologist. Palaeopathology is a fascinating subject for any pathologist. It is challenging, baffling, and occasionally humbling to those who are confidently dealing with contemporary tissues.

Studying ancient human remains presents many challenges. One of the most difficult situations is when the researchers encounter badly damaged human remains with a rarely occurring variant of disease or when the individual suffered from concurrent diseases that caused superimposed tissue changes. Such situations can easily lead to misdiagnosis.

Nevertheless, the scientific investigation of mummies and skeletons provides considerable data for the reconstruction of the living conditions and diseases of past populations (Nerlich 2002). Ancient human remains occur either in skeletal form or with soft tissues preserved due to natural or artificial mummification. The most crucial factor for any kind of scientific assessment is the state of preservation. It is now understood that both soft tissues and bone are affected by the mummification process, and the quality and type of information gained from studying ancient remains depend greatly on the substances used.

Mummification and materials used for mummification

The favourable environmental effects (hot and dry climate, or the opposite – ice and snow – alternately desiccating or freezing the tissues) may preserve the bodies in a mummified state without human intervention (see Chapter 16). Anthropogenic (artificial) mummification is a deliberate act of preservation of the body after death. It is generally believed that the reason for intentional mummification was a system of religious beliefs that eventually evolved into cultural practices. Whatever the reason for its use, mummification was applied to the bodies to arrest the inevitable decay starting after death. In ancient Egypt the most effective method of mummification was evisceration of the corpse, which involved removal of the gastrointestinal tract containing the greatest source of bacteria (see Chapter 2).

Desiccation and preservation were achieved by surrounding the body with natron, a naturally occurring mixture of sodium salts that removed water from the tissues, thus stopping enzymatic activity of both the body's own enzymes and those from invading microorganisms. There are indications that, in certain circumstances, natural mummification preserves tissues as effectively as the artificial process (Shin et al. 2003; Jeziorska et al. 2006).

Chemical components used in mummification
and their effects on tissue preservation

Resins and bitumen

With the wider use of established methods such as gas chromatography (see Chapter 10) in combination with other techniques, there is a renewed interest in identifying the components of embalming fluids. Mastic resin, vegetable oil, beeswax, and bitumen were found in the oldest mummies (seventh century B.C.) but the younger samples (second century B.C.) showed more variation in the components used (Colombini et al. 2000).

The embalming materials from the Roman Period mummies were analysed for the soluble lipid components to determine the source of embalming material. The results indicated the presence of plant material (coniferous resin and possibly beeswax) and bitumen, resembling Dead Sea asphalt (Maurer et al. 2002). Recent investigations of molecular signatures of oil seeps from the Gulf of Suez showed that they were used by ancient Egyptians for embalming (Barakat et al. 2005).

Borate

Weser and Kaup (2002) assayed mummification salts and mummified bones for borate and the reactivity of this compound on bone alkaline phosphatase, which is known to survive mummification for more than 4,000 years. Further investigation showed the elevated borate contents in both mummification salts and ancient bone samples. The experimental work showed that borate stabilises alkaline phosphatase molecules (Kaup et al. 2003).

Arsenic

Arriazza (2005) recently offered an interesting hypothesis on the origin of the earliest form of mummification. He proposed that a natural phenomenon of highly toxic water from a local river that contained a hundred times the contemporary level of arsenic caused an extremely high spontaneous abortion and preterm birth rate in an ancient population of the Chincorro people who were also apparently the first people in the world to practise intentional mummification. This author proposed that the Chinchorro mortuary practice began as a cultural response to an environmental phenomenon.

In much more recent times, c. early 1600 A.D., arsenic was introduced in Europe for the preservation of birds used as decoys or exhibits (Schulze-Hagen et al. 2003). In 1835, Giuseppe Tranchina described a method of injecting the blood vessels of a corpse with an arsenic–mercury solution. This method was used in 1836 A.D. on the corpse of a prisoner who died of pleurisy. His mummified body remained in an excellent state of preservation and was recently examined by computed tomography (CT), with which the historic case notes indicating pleurisy were confirmed; the pleurisy was most probably caused by tuberculosis (Ciranni et al. 2005).

Cedar oil: 'cedrium'

The examination of unused ancient Egyptian embalming material dated c. 1500 B.C. revealed the presence of phenols, guaiacols, naphthalenes, and sesquiterpenoids (Koller et al. 2003, 2005). These compounds are found in wood tar oil obtained from the true cedar tree by dry distillation or smouldering process. Similar compounds were extracted from a Ptolemaic torso (340 ± 170 B.C.). The authors point to the fact that the examined materials were in striking accordance with Pliny's description of liquid *'cedrium,'* which was used in Egypt for mummification. The most valuable attributes of these compounds are their fungicidal and bacteriostatic properties and their excellent ability to preserve alkaline phosphatase.

Sodium sulphate

Not all the salts detected in the Egyptian mummies enhanced the preservation of all tissue components. Sodium sulphate was found in areas where the degradation of lipid and protein seemed to be higher (Petersen et al. 2003).

Experimental mummification

Each example of human remains that is examined is unique. Even if they are of a similar age and the mummification process and burial circumstances were alike, the subsequent fate of each body is unique. Experimental studies help to explain on a molecular level what happens to the tissue during mummification and shortly after mummification (Jeziorska et al. 2005a). Experiments on animal carcasses shed some light on the influence of different conditions of burial on decomposition and the rate of water loss.

Koller et al. (2003) used four selected embalming compounds that were found in resins and wood tars used for embalming in Egypt to experimentally embalm porcine ribs before air-drying them. The level of alkaline phosphatase present was used as a measure of preservation of the bone tissue. Guaiacol was the most effective in retaining alkaline phosphatase activity. Experimental desiccation of mice showed that even DNA material that is highly susceptible to degradation can be identified in the tissues (Terra et al. 2004).

Methods of rehydration

Desiccated, mummified, or embalmed tissues need to be rehydrated to resemble contemporary material (see Chapter 6). Each sample changes its consistency differently, depending on its histological content, mode of mummification, and preservation, so individual processing of samples under close macroscopic inspection is essential (personal experience, Jeziorska et al. 2005b). Some samples may even appear to dissolve in the rehydrating/fixing solution. This is caused by the destructive action of bacteria invading the tissue some time after death.

Methods of investigation

There are some well-established methods used for the investigation of ancient human remains.

Gross examination

A thorough macroscopic description of the mummy or its fragments is an essential part of the scientific assessment. Much valuable medical information may be gained from this process. Great care must be taken not to damage the mummified remains for both ethical and scientific reasons. For a long time, mummies were treated as 'curios,' unwrapped for entertainment, or used for medicinal purposes, following a bizarre belief spreading in the eighteenth and nineteenth centuries A.D. that powderised mummy tissue could cure various ailments.

Recently, complex ethical, cultural, and legal issues have been raised (see Chapter 15) and now great care is taken to use minimally invasive and least-damaging methods of investigation and sampling. In cases in which the mummified body is partially dismembered or if an endoscopic procedure can be performed (see Chapter 4), this may often give valuable information about the state of the body cavities, enabling some diagnoses to be made, similar to contemporary postmortem examination. Removing small fragments of tissue from carefully targeted areas that are anatomically well defined and in which the tissue looks best preserved can often form the basis for good histological study.

Light microscopy

Light microscopy of the histochemically stained sections is the oldest method of investigating mummified tissues. It remains a very important technique.

Light microscopy using polarised light has an exceptionally high value for the differential diagnosis of changes found in dry bones. Using thin-ground sections of nondecalcified bone allows for detailed examination of bone and periosteal changes on the bone surface in different pathological conditions (Schultz 2001).

Infrared microscopy

The state of conservation/degradation of mummified remains can be inferred from their biochemical composition, as well as from the secondary structures of proteins (see Chapter 16). Examination of the skin of an Egyptian mummy by using synchrotron infrared microscopy enabled the main degradation products to be identified as adipocere and calcium oxalate (Cotte et al. 2005).

Electron microscopy

This technique was quite often applied to mummified tissues in the past, but in the last few years it has been used very rarely. Transmission electron microscopy (TEM) facilitates the study of subcellular details of the tissues, and therefore is rarely successful in heavily damaged mummified tissues. Scanning electron microscopy (SEM) is more promising, especially for bodies that are not desiccated (Shin et al. 2003).

Molecular pathology

Molecular pathological methods used in contemporary research were recently successfully applied to the investigation of mummified tissues. They produce particularly good results in palaeomicrobiology (see below, *Tuberculosis*).

Infectious diseases

Tuberculosis

Tuberculosis is a re-emerging threat in the contemporary world, which is why studies of evolution of the disease are being actively pursued. In recent years, there has been a rapidly growing number of publications about tuberculosis, especially in the field of molecular pathology, so it is possible to mention only a few.

Previous macroscopic reports on tuberculosis in pre-Columbian skeletal remains from South America causing severe destruction, collapse, and fusion of spinal lesions were confirmed by the molecular evidence. Daniel (2000) presented an overview of the evolving views on the spread of tuberculosis. For those with deeper interest in tuberculosis in ancient populations the book by Roberts and Buikstra (2003) was hailed as the first all-encompassing work on the history of the disease.

Leprosy

This entity is a chronic infectious disease that affects peripheral nerves, skin, and in later stages, the skeleton. The disease is not fatal and if there are no other concomitant diseases worsening the prognosis, the sufferers have a long life expectancy. Disfiguring and mutilating aspects of the disease led to ostracism and segregation of the affected individuals from the rest of the society. Mark (2002) offered a new suggestion as to how leprosy spread around the Mediterranean. He pointed out that ancient ships are seldom mentioned in the literature as conveyors of disease, but they undoubtedly were. He proposed that cargo ships with slaves being taken from India to Egypt could have easily spread the disease.

A skeleton dated fourth to third century B.C. from a Celtic necropolis in Italy shows probable lepromatous changes and if the planned DNA investigation is successful, it might prove to be the earliest case of leprosy in Europe (Mariotti et al. 2005). The presence of *Mycobacterium leprae* DNA was successfully confirmed in a tenth century Hungarian skull (Haas and Zink, 2000). There are only a few reports that concentrate on the health status of ancient populations from Central Asia, but the investigation of one of the kurghans from Uzbekistan showed lesions that were probably due to lepromatous leprosy (Blau and Yagodin 2005).

Finally, an interesting work by Bolsden (2001) goes beyond descriptive approaches and uses modern epidemiological methods to address the prevalence of leprosy in medieval Denmark. In this study, the author set out to define the osteological scoring system for leprosy and assess the sensitivity and specificity of seven leprosy-related osteological changes and the frequency of leprosy at death in three different medieval burial sites (leprosy institution and urban and rural cemeteries). The statistical approach and methodology used in this paper show a new critical approach to palaeopathology.

Treponematoses

There are four treponemal pathogens that affect humans: *Treponema pallidum* subspecies *pallidum* (causing syphilis), *T. pallidum* subspecies *endemicum* (causing endemic syphilis or bejel, found in temperate and subtropical areas), *T. pallidum* subspecies *pertenue* (causing yaws, found in tropical/subtropical regions), and *T. carateum* (causing pinta).

Bejel and yaws are contracted through nonsexual contact but venereal syphilis is transmitted during sexual contact or transplacentally from mother to the foetus. The first three pathogens cause skeletal lesions, so evidence of infection is detectable in skeletal remains. A heated debate on the origin of European venereal syphilis led to the formulation of three hypotheses: Columbian (maintaining that venereal syphilis was introduced to Europe upon return of Columbus and his men from the New World in 1493); pre-Columbian (claiming that it was present in Europe before 1493); and a unitarian hypothesis (claiming that treponemal diseases had long been present in both Old and New World but manifested differently due to different ecological and social conditions).

Recently, there have been some new reports suggesting the presence of treponemal infections in Europe preceding 1493 A.D. Rothschild (2005) presents a critical review of the European pre-Columbian cases, arguing that all of them were caused by taphonomic changes, inflammatory conditions, or at best other treponematoses, such as yaws or bejel.

His view is that treponematoses originated in Africa in the form of yaws, passed through Asia forming bejel, and then both forms were transmitted to North America where another mutation initiated syphilis, which was spread to continental Europe with the return of Columbus's men. Nevertheless, the most recent report from Europe (based on four skeletons from Hull, England, dated between 1300 and 1450 A.D.) described microscopical changes consistent with venereal syphilis, so the diagnosis of this disease is most likely unless those individuals were migrants from other parts of the world (von Hunnius et al. 2006).

Plague

The epidemics of plague were estimated to have killed millions of people, but obtaining irrefutable evidence of the presence of *Yersinia pestis* was very difficult. Drancourt et al. (1998) used unerupted teeth from skeletons excavated from sixteenth and eighteenth century French graves of individuals thought to have died of plague, thus obtaining sterile samples of dental pulp. They were able to show a nucleotide sequence indistinguishable from modern day bacteria, and later they demonstrated that *Yersinia pestis* was the aetiological agent of the European Black Death in 1347 A.D. and the two additional outbreaks in 1590 A.D. and 1722 A.D. in southern France (Drancourt et al. 2002).

There is a strong suspicion that peoples of America were infected with Old World diseases prior to the founding of the first mission in 1769 A.D. but it is a controversial view and not widely accepted (Preston 2002). This author quotes numerous publications detailing evidence that much of North America was devastated by a catastrophic disease prior to Euro-American occupation, but there is a lack of irrefutable archaeological evidence, so only a compilation of historical, ethnographic, archaeological, and biological information taken together could indicate the high probability of plague.

Viruses

Many researchers doubted the possibility that confirmation of viral infections in historic material could ever be obtained. Simmonds (2000) discussed virus archaeology and evolution and stated that the direct evidence for virus infection by isolation or by polymerase chain reaction is very rare in material older than thirty years, but the archaeological evidence for virus infection has been found. He recalled the discovery by Wells (1964) of skeletons from the Neolithic and Bronze Age periods with deformities similar to present day poliomyelitis indirectly implicating viral infection. The best example of a virus whose existence can be determined from descriptions of epidemics is smallpox (Simmonds 2000).

The artificially mummified body of a sixteenth century Neapolitan noblewoman showed the presence of a large papillary skin lesion in the paravulvar region. The DNA was extracted from the lesion, amplified, cloned, and sequenced. The diagnosis of condyloma acuminatum, a lesion caused by human papilloma virus (HPV) was established (Fornaciari 2003). This report followed an earlier discovery by the same group of the presence of a smallpox virus in a sample of mummy skin (Fornaciari 1989). These findings are very encouraging for renewed efforts for direct confirmation of viral infections in ancient material.

Palaeoparasitology

Palaeoparasitology is the study of parasites in archaeological material. Parasite remains in archaeological sites were sporadically reported for many years and almost all known human parasites have been found in ancient faeces. An excellent and comprehensive review of the topic was recently published (Goncalvez et al. 2003). The authors also present their new data confirming human ancylostomids, *Ascaris lumbricoides* and *Trichuris trichura*, in pre-Columbian times.

Chagas' disease (American Trypanosomiasis)

Mammals infected with *Trypanosoma cruzi* and the insect vector seem to be well adapted for coexistence and survival, but for humans, Chagas' disease is a purely accidental occurrence and results in a much more serious disease (Aufderheide et al. 2004, 2005).

Fasciola hepatica

Liver fluke eggs are a rare finding in palaeopathological material (Araujo et al. 2000), but one such case reported recently describes both human and cattle hosts involved in the infection cycle (Dittmar 2003).

Trichinellosis (oxyuriasis)

Trichinellosis in an Egyptian mummy was described in the early nineteenth century A.D., but it has been occasionally reported in Europe, resulting in outbreaks that have a deadly outcome. For example, a very serious infestation was reported in Germany (1860–1880 A.D.) that resulted in more than 500 deaths (Blancou 2001).

It is a rare but increasingly frequent occurrence that findings about past diseases can have a bearing on understanding the contemporary manifestations of particular ailments. This is particularly true in relation to parasitic diseases (Araujo 2000).

Cancer/neoplastic diseases

There is no evidence of true neoplastic diseases other than in vertebrate animals (Capasso et al. 2005), but humans are by no means the first to suffer from cancer. Rothschild et al. (2003) have recently published their findings from the examination of a staggering number of over 10,000 specimens of dinosaur vertebrae by using fluoroscopy as a screening technique. They found evidence of hemangioma, desmoplastic fibroma, osteoblastoma, and metastatic cancer but only in Cretaceous hadrosaurs (duckbilled dinosaurs), leading them to the conclusion that the predilection of hadrosaurs to tumours is unprecedented and unique.

The prevailing opinion in the literature is that the occurrence of malignant neoplastic diseases in humans is greatly influenced by environmental factors and blamed on worsening living conditions caused by pollution. Over the years, there have been numerous examples of neoplastic diseases found in the ancient human remains but the frequency of malignant tumours in ancient populations cannot be inferred from the reports of single cases.

The examination of a large necropolis gives much better insight into the frequency of cancer in ancient populations, even though there is a large time-span between the earliest and latest burials, and the investigation is mainly limited to the skeletal remains. Zink et al. (1999) examined 415 mummified individuals from the necropolis of Thebes-West in Upper Egypt and found that among 325 adults there were at least four cases of malignant tumours with osseous manifestation.

The attempted age and sex adjustment and comparison to contemporary populations showed an astonishing result: namely, that the frequency, albeit lower than in a comparable present day population, was higher than in an English population from 1901 to 1905 A.D. This finding led the authors to conclude that important factors affecting malignant tumours were effective even in historic populations.

A recent review on the antiquity of cancer (Capasso 2005) summarised the complexity of palaeooncology and the difficulties in diagnosis and interpretation. The author also offers a critical analysis of the fossil record of neoplasms and a detailed review of the literature on cancer in human populations, as well as his views on why cancer in ancient human populations is rare. The problem of differential diagnosis between primary and metastatic bone tumours encountered in contemporary material is even more accentuated in the ancient remains (Rothschild 1998). For further reading on the subject, there is an excellent review by Halperin (2004).

Diet/palaeonutrition/vitamin deficiency

Danforth (1999) touched on a philosophical question relating to the interrelationship of diet, nutrition, and political organization by using the examples of prehistoric North American and Mesoamerican societies. Although nutrition is only indirectly reflected through the osteological record, it nevertheless reveals certain patterns, showing that from egalitarian to chiefdom-level groups there was little difference between members of the same society. This suggested that to remain in power, the elite still had to share resources.

In state-level societies, the gap in health status between high- and low-status individuals is readily apparent, and it widens over time. Recently, it has been suggested that a low-diversity diet consumed by Neanderthals put them at a disadvantage and eventually caused the demographic shift towards the anatomically modern *Homo sapiens* who consumed a slightly more diversified diet, allowing for a lower maternal and fetal-to-infant mortality (Hockett and Haws 2005).

Anaemia

Cribra orbitalia is a lesion in the bone forming the roof of the orbit; for a long time, this was generally accepted as a proof that the individual suffered from anaemia. It is true that the lesion is seen in cases of hypertrophy of the red bone marrow, which may occur as a result of anaemia, but there are other conditions, such as inflammation or osteoporosis that result in formation of cribra orbitalia.

Wapler et al. (2004) examined 333 skulls from a Nubian population and found that there were histological features indicating anaemia in less than 50 per cent of cases with evident cribra orbitalia, proving that cribra orbitalia is not synonymous with anaemia. Nevertheless, such findings do not diminish the value of numerous previous reports on the prevalence of cribra orbitalia in ancient populations, as discovery of this feature indicated a pathological condition, even if not necessarily anaemia. It is probable that cribra orbitalia found in children is more likely to be a reflection of anaemia.

Childhood mortality in individuals with cribra orbitalia was higher when tuberculosis or tuberculosis-like conditions were present (Blom et al. 2005). Recent advances in multislice computed tomography, with three-dimensional reconstruction used to image rare cases of cribra orbitalia in contemporary population, may offer some help in assessment of historic skulls (Exner et al. 2004).

Scurvy

This entity is caused by the lack of ascorbic acid in the diet. Brickley and Ives (2006) pointed out that the diagnosis of infantile scurvy based on changes in the sphenoid bone may be misleading and result in false-negative reports of the occurrence of this condition. Taking into account changes in cranial bones and scapulae gives a more realistic reflection of the incidence of infantile scurvy, which can be linked to recorded periods of potato blight in the investigated region of Birmingham.

Occupational diseases

Heavy metals

Mercury was mined in Peru in pre-colonial times on a relatively small scale as cinnabar (mercuric sulfide) and used mostly in cosmetics. In colonial times, it was used to amalgamate and refine silver ores, so there was a great demand for it. The toxic nature of mercury combined with respiratory diseases, mining accidents (mostly broken limbs), and work at high altitude made those mines exceptionally dangerous places with a high mortality rate and constant demand for new workers, which could only be achieved by forced labour, causing depopulation of surrounding provinces (Brown 2001).

Bone and joints

Recognising periosteal reaction and distinguishing it from postmortem bone damage (taphonomy) is one of the most difficult diagnostic challenges faced by palaeoanthropologists. New methods offer some hope but have yet to be tried and tested on large numbers of skeletal samples. One such method is an assessment of heat dissipation through the normal bone surface, which is different from the bone with taphonomic changes (Rothschild et al. 2003). Rheumatoid arthritis (RA) in Europe and in the New World has been the subject of many publications.

Recently, more examples of descriptions and representations of a symmetric chronic polyarthritis with characteristic deformities were found in ancient Rome and India, with the first clinical distinction between RA and gout published in Mexico in 1578 (Aceves-Avila et al. 2001). The authors searched for descriptions of symmetric chronic polyarthritis and characteristic deformities seen in contemporary RA and concluded that it had existed in America since 8,000 B.C. and in Europe since the seventh century A.D.

A comparison between morphology and radiology, as seen in ancient skeletal remains, enables a unique appraisal to be made of osteoarthritis and RA in the advanced stages of those diseases (Lagier 2006). Until fairly recently, osteoarthritis was considered a wear-and-tear disease and a disease of the modern age. The examination of large numbers of the spinal columns of Neolithic ancient Chinese revealed a slightly higher prevalence of calcification of the posterior longitudinal ligament than found amongst the modern populations of Japan, Korea, Taiwan, Hong Kong, Philippines, Malaysia, and Singapore (Hukuda et al. 2000). There are striking similarities in localization (hand, shoulder, knee, and hip) between ancient and contemporary cases, but the elbow joint was more frequently affected than it is today (Crubezy 2002).

Traumatic injury seems to be the most common cause of bone pathology besides arthritis. In the past, there was ample evidence of healed fractures in animal and human skeletons. Signs of trauma are comparatively high in most reports on material from ossuaries. Bone tumours have been mentioned in the section on Cancer/Neoplastic Diseases.

Circulatory system

Atherosclerosis

Atherosclerosis has been quite frequently diagnosed in Egyptian and South American mummies. In the last decade, Fornaciari (1999) found evidence of atherosclerotic lesions when studying Italian Renaissance mummies. Miller et al. (2000) described the astonishing discovery of molecular evidence, obtained using a sensitive and specific assay for cardiac troponin, of cardiac infarction in mummified tissue.

The most recent report on congenital cardiovascular disease was that of aortic coarctation in a skeleton (sixth to fifth century B.C., Etruscan population), which showed typical indentations on the surface of the ribs, characteristic for collateral circulation caused by narrowing of the aorta (Ciranni et al. 2006). A very famous case of hyperlipidemia (or only a suspicion of it) is quoted below in the section on Palaeopathology in Art.

Reproductive and urinary systems

Soft tissues of the body, especially those in the pelvic region, are not easily accessible for investigation, even with the use of modern endoscopic techniques; this is probably partially the reason why only two cases of prostatic hyperplasia have been described in ancient material. The condition was reported in the mummified body of an Italian prince, Pandolfo III Malatesta, who died in 1427 A.D. X-ray investigation showed foci of calcifications and macro- and microscopic evaluation was typical for nodular hyperplasia (Ciranni et al. 2000; Fornaciari et al. 2001). The second case of prostatic hyperplasia was diagnosed in a natural mummy found in a friary in central Italy (Fornaciari et al. 2001).

The urinary system lies beyond the confines of the peritoneum covering the inner layers of the abdominal wall, so the Egyptian embalmers left the kidneys inside the mummified body. There is little information in the literature about examination of the kidneys in mummified human remains but the investigators of the mummy of Pandolfo III Malatesta found a staghorn calculus (calcium urate) in his left kidney (Ciranni et al. 2000).

Nervous system and palaeoneurology

Mummified brain tissue is very rarely available for investigation. The largest and so far the only systematic investigation of naturally mummified brain tissue was performed on the contents of fifteen skulls excavated from the Atacama Desert in Chile (1000 B.C.–1500 A.D.) (Gerztein et al. 1995).

There has been even less investigation of the peripheral nervous system, but an interesting approach was used by Appenzeller et al. (2001) who studied about 200 mummy portraits from the beginning of the first millennium. The portraits and several skulls were measured and their right/left ratio was assessed. In four cases, clinical diagnoses of neurological disorders were proposed (e.g. progressive facial hemiatrophy), from which it is possible to predict the symptoms with which those individuals presented during life.

Skin

Skin is easily damaged during the mummification process when natron is used: the epidermis, especially on large flat surfaces, is easily undermined with escaping moisture and sloughed off, exposing underlying connective tissue. The places where some patches of undamaged epidermis may survive are in the natural creases of the skin, such as behind the ears and at the flexor side of the joints. Infrared spectroscopy is another new method which can help in the investigation of the skin, hair, and various soft tissues (see Chapter 10; Kupper et al. 2001; Petersen et al. 2003).

Statistical approach to palaeopathology

The bayesian statistical method interprets probability as a measure of one's degree of uncertainty about an event. Probability lies in the mind of the observer and may vary for people having different information or different past experiences. Inference is performed by evaluating the probability of a hypothesised model, given observed data (Bullard 2001). Byers and Roberts showed how Bayers' theorem could be practically applied to palaeopathology by using an example of prehistoric rib lesions and the probability of tuberculosis (Byers and Roberts 2003). Another example of using statistical methods in palaeopathology is mentioned in the section on Leprosy.

Medical conditions recorded in art/palaeopathology in art

By studying the pictures of the New Kingdom pharaoh Amenhotep IV (*Akhenaten*), Cattaino and Vicario (1999) concluded that he may had been affected by myotonic dystrophy (MD) which is an example of mendelian inheritance in man. The surviving images of Akhenaten are unusual in their departure from idealised representation of the pharaoh and show some physical attributes that may support the diagnosis of myotonic dystrophy (e.g.

distal lower hypotrophy of the lower limbs). The authors have also suggested that this disease might have caused the end of the eighteen Dynasty.

Conclusions

Palaeopathology makes a very valuable contribution to our general knowledge of disease, both in antiquity and the modern day. The introduction of a more systematic approach and the use of new technologies and techniques allow an insight into the nature and epidemiology of diseases in ancient societies.

We find evidence that some of the diseases thought to be a scourge of the modern industrialised world were in fact encountered in the past, proving that their underlying causes are much more complex than originally thought. Examination of demographics, the anatomical distribution of changes, the spectrum of manifestations for each disease, and their discriminating characteristics in ancient populations may offer a multilayered and much needed perspective for the understanding our heritage.

CHAPTER 8

The use of immunocytochemistry to diagnose disease in mummies

Patricia Rutherford

Foreword

An epidemiological study of schistosomiasis at the University of Manchester in the United Kingdom (see Chapter 1) indicated a need for diagnostic tools that could be applied to large numbers of ancient Egyptian tissues. This chapter discusses the successful application of immunocytochemistry to both modern and ancient tissues. This was acheved in an initial investigation in which tissue samples from fifty Egyptian mummies were studied with a view to establishing protocols that are now being applied to a larger epidemiology research project.

Using an indirect fluorescence staining protocol with antisera directed against *Schistosoma mansoni* and *Schistosoma haematobium* antigens, positive staining to S. *mansoni* and S. *haematobium* antigens in modern tissues, a fifty-year-old tissue sample from an Egyptian cadaver, and ancient Egyptian tissues has been achieved. Immunocytochemistry has proven to be cost effective and easy to perform, and is now a preliminary to other tests.

Although the enzyme-linked immunosorbent assay (ELISA) and other tests such as histology, enzyme immunotransfer blots (EITB), and DNA analysis have also been explored to reinforce the initial immunostaining results, this chapter will focus on the use of immunocytochemistry to diagnose ancient disease. The definition of an immunoassay and the principles of immunocytochemistry are briefly outlined, followed by details of the development of immunocytochemistry as a diagnostic tool for schistosomiasis in ancient tissues. This chapter highlights how experimental principles have been adapted when working with ancient dehydrated samples.

Terms and techniques

Immunoassays

'Immunoassay' describes a technique that measures the presence of a substance by using an immunological reaction that would naturally occur in the body. When the immune system detects a foreign substance within the body, commonly known as an antigen, it responds with a proliferation of cells; some directly attack the invading organism (T cells), and others produce specialised molecules called antibodies (B cells). The molecules on the surfaces of viruses, bacteria and other pathogens such as parasitic eggs stimulate such an immune response. Antigens are usually large molecules and the majority are proteins or large polysaccharides that are present as outer components of the invading pathogen.

The antibodies that are stimulated are specific and bind to antigenic determinants of the invading pathogen to mark them for destruction by other cells such as macrophages and T cells. Antibodies do not recognise antigens as a whole but only localised regions on the actual antigen surface, consisting of seven to fifteen amino acids and sugar residues, commonly known as epitopes. Antibodies are so specific that, if only one amino acid is changed, it does not bind as well, or not at all. If an antigen is large, many different antibodies are produced, each type binding to specific antigenic determinants. An immunoassay exploits this reaction between antibodies and antigens, especially as antibodies raised by infecting laboratory animals with the disease of interest can easily be isolated and conjugated to a tag that can be visualised directly or under a certain ultraviolet wavelength.

Immunocytochemistry

Immunocytochemistry is a laboratory technique that has been utilised for nearly fifty years to perform research and diagnosis. It unites the use of microscopy and immunology and can be easily performed with routine microscopy equipment. Immunocytochemistry demonstrates antigens in tissue sections or smears by using antigen/antibody interactions. As smears are not available for analysis from ancient samples, this chapter will focus on immunostaining of dehydrated tissue samples.

Any biological macromolecule, such as proteins, carbohydrates, DNA, lipids and even cell constituents such as collagen, is capable of stimulating antibody production. Antigens can be anything of interest, not just disease-causing pathogens, and can be present anywhere in a sample. For example, cells secreting antigen can be distinguished from nonsecreting cells.

Reagents used

There are two types of antiserum, polyclonal and monoclonal, and each has negative and positive characteristics when used for immunostaining. Polyclonal antiserum is a mix of high-affinity antibodies that have been stimulated by all antigenic sites (epitopes) present on the surface of an invading pathogen. The antiserum will also contain antibodies to any impurities present with the immunogen and these may bind nonspecifically to tissue components, causing background staining. These often have a low titre and affinity, and can be diluted out through columns to zero activity before use. In contrast, monoclonal antiserum only targets a single epitope on an antigen and is so specific that nonspecific background staining is often eliminated. Monoclonal antisera are produced using a more time-consuming procedure, thus making them a lot more expensive to produce. Also, apart from the added expense, the epitope in question may be lost during tissue preparation, as antigens are susceptible to destruction during tissue fixation. This can occur, as fixation may be used to stabilise cells against dehydration, embedding, sectioning, and staining, but unfortunately it also denatures proteins.

An array of polyclonal antisera have been used in this study but they are monospecific and thus very specific towards schistosome epitopes.

Schistosomiasis

Schistosomiasis is endemic today, infecting more than 300 million people, mainly in the developing world. The disease is caused by a trematode of the genus *Schistosoma*, which lives and feeds on the cells, blood, mucus, and tissue fluids of its primary host. Although most *Schistosoma* only infect animals, humans are also infected, the three main species responsible being *S. mansoni*, *S. haematobium*, and *S. japonicum*.

The *S. mansoni* and *S. japonicum* live primarily within the veins of the hepatic portal system, which drains the intestines, whereas *S. haematobium* mainly occupies the veins draining the bladder. Schistosomes can live in humans for more than twenty years, continually breeding and producing thousands of ova. Half of these are released back into the water via faeces or urine, depending on the worm's location in the body, while the other half remain in the body, causing continuous mechanical, immunological, and pathological damage such as inflammation, fibrosis, cirrhosis, abdominal distension, and haemorrhaging (Cheever 1969).

Evidence of schistosomiasis in ancient times

Studies of ancient literature, artistic representations, and physical remains have suggested that schistosomiasis is an ancient disease. It was present in ancient Egypt, with one of the classic symptoms, blood in the urine, being described in the Ebers Papyrus (see Chapter 12) as the *aaa* disease (Farooq 1973; Contis and David 1996). The ancient Egyptians also wrote that boys became men when blood was seen in their urine, and likened this to the young female's first menstruation (Despommier et al. 1995).

Scientific evidence also supports the presence of schistosomiasis. Ruffer (1910) saw one of the first examples in mummified remains, and subsequently other researchers have corroborated this with histological evidence (Millet et al. 1980). More recently, work performed by Deelder et al. (1990) has confirmed the presence of *Schistosoma* circulating anodic antigens (CAA), regurgitated from the worms' gut, in ancient Egyptian samples. This was achieved by means of ELISA. The oldest example was seen in tissue taken from the shin of a 5,000-year-old predynastic mummy (BM32753), making this the earliest diagnosis of schistosomiasis to date.

Radiology has also suggested the presence of schistosomiasis in ancient remains, by revealing one of the classic symptoms of *S. haematobium*, calcification of the bladder (Isherwood et al. 1979; Adams, personal correspondence 2000). It is therefore clear that methods such as histology, radiology, and ELISA (Miller et al. 1992, 1993) can be readily adapted for the diagnosis of schistosomiasis in ancient tissues.

Some of these diagnostic tools can be impractical when working with ancient tissues on a large scale because they may be very expensive (radiology and ELISA) or low in sensitivity (histology). Although histology would be the obvious choice for detecting ova in bladder and viscera samples, previous research has shown histology to produce inconsistent results (Tapp 1979, 1984; Tapp and Wildsmith 1992). An alternative test was therefore sought that would be cost effective, reproducible, and sensitive. Immunocytochemistry meets all the aforementioned criteria, and has been successfully applied to both modern and ancient tissues (Rutherford 1997, 1999, 2000, 2002, 2005).

The development of immunocytochemistry for ancient samples

Today, immunocytochemistry is frequently used to diagnose many diseases, as it is a powerful, sensitive, diagnostic tool. It is not considered, however, to be an efficient way of diagnosing schistosomiasis in modern samples as it may obscure the distinctive ova shapes when sections are cut. Therefore, the application of immunocytochemistry to ancient tissues often only reports the demonstration of cellular components (Wick et al. 1980; Horton et al. 1983; Krypczyk and Tapp 1986; Fulcheri et al. 1992; Nerlich et al. 1993). In most studies ancient samples are embedded in paraffin wax, a type of tissue preparation that has been successfully performed for many years, predominantly for histological purposes (see Chapter 6; Ruffer 1910; Tapp 1979). In contrast, in this study both modern and ancient tissues are embedded in an alternative medium called 2-hydroxyethyl methylacrylate (Taab, UK) to detect *Schistosoma* antigens (Rutherford 1997, 1999, 2000, 2002, 2005; Lambert-Zazulak et al. 2003).

This resin was chosen because preparation in hot wax often has deleterious effects on the tissue, causing diffusion, loss, and even chemical alterations to the antigens of interest. As the ancient *Schistosoma* antigens will already be degraded and only present in very small quantities, such high temperatures are avoided when resin, which polymerises at 4°C, is used. The hardened resin also allows much thinner tissue sections to be cut (2 μm), which enhances the sensitivity of the test, often producing intense reactions (Heryet and Gatter 1992).

Experimental designs for the ancient samples were approached cautiously and previous research taken into account. For example, in previous histological studies of ancient mummified tissues, the rehydrating solutions used most frequently were those developed by Ruffer (1921) or Sandison (1955). A comparative study done by Turner and Holtom (1981) has shown that these solutions do not always produce suitable tissue samples for sectioning, when compared with the use of a fabric conditioner trade-named 'Comfort' (Lever Bros) (see Chapter 6). In response to this study, several researchers now use some type of conditioner to rehydrate the sample (Tapp 1984; Tapp and Wildsmith 1992; Rutherford 2002).

Because the types of experiments undertaken in this study are predominately immunological, the colour, preservatives, and perfumes found in the 'Comfort' fabric conditioner are unacceptable, as they may interfere with the immunocytochemistry in some way. An alternative conditioner (Surfacem, UK), which contains no perfume, preservatives, or colour, was therefore selected.

It is the opinion of some researchers that once water has been put back into the tissue, it will begin to degenerate unless fixed; however, not all researchers fix the sample with classic fixatives such as formalin (Sandison 1955; Rutherford 2002), regarding it as unnecessary. In particular, I do not use formalin as it causes cross-links between molecules, and if samples are to undergo both histology and immunocytochemistry tests, such cross-linking may interfere with the immunological reactions. Therefore, the samples are placed into increasing strengths of alcohol, which slowly fixes the tissue whilst killing any spurious bacteria and fungi. Furthermore the damaging enzymes that need water to function are probably too degraded, or not present (as they are modified proteins), to be reactivated by the addition of water.

HYDROFLUORIC ACID PREPARATIONS. As immunocytochemistry was predominately dependent upon the successful sectioning of both the modern and ancient tissues, the preparation of the tissue prior to sectioning was very important. Although there were no problems cutting the modern and ancient unembalmed tissues, the presence of resins used in the mummification process and silica particles enmeshed within certain ancient tissues made sectioning difficult. It is not known whether the silica (sand) particles are contamination from the natron used to desiccate the body, or whether they are from the desert environment.

To overcome such problems, tissues were soaked in a very dilute solution of hydrofluoric acid (2.5%). This option was chosen after other acid preparations such as nitric and hydrochloric acid were unsuccessful in removing the sand. As palaeobotanists use hydrofluoric acid to decalcify ancient petrified seeds and plant material without damaging the delicate specimen, it was thought that, if dilute enough, the acid would only dissolve the silica present in the tissue without damaging the tissue itself (F. Barnett, personal correspondence 1997).

An excellent example of such work, using hydrofluoric acid, is provided by Professor Stein at Binghamton University in the United States. He used diamond tip saws to cut through rock specimens to reveal fossilised plant material within. After the fossils had been honed into thin slices, the fossilised plants were removed from the ancient sediment by placing the rocks into hydrofluoric acid. Although this treatment seems harsh, Stein states that 'the fossilised plant material cannot be destroyed because it consists of carbon and is not subject to degradation by the acid' (Dowling 2002).

This principle seems to be true for tissue samples also, as experiments with both modern and ancient tissues have shown that at the correct dilution, the acid does not disrupt the antigenic epitopes, as positive staining still occurs. It does however enable the ancient tissues to be cut easily after the silica has been slowly dissolved. Although unembalmed tissues are preferable, if silica and resins are present, this acid treatment is now an option in future studies.

OTHER REINFORCING TESTS. Although immunocytochemistry is now used on samples thought to harbour the ova and worms, other diagnostic tests have also been investigated, namely the ELISA. As the ELISA target is a CAA regurgitated from the worm's gut, it should be present in all vascular tissues of the body, in contrast to the ova and worms that are only found in specific sites. The ELISA was therefore initially used to both reinforce immunostaining results and to increase the sample number, as it could be applied to the many body parts present in collections around the world. The test, however, does have limitations, as the CAAs are only present during the occurrence of an active infection, because they are degraded each day by the liver (Deelder et al. 1990).

If the immunostaining results were positive, then additional techniques such as histology, EITB (Al Sherbiny et al. 1999), and DNA analysis (Rutherford 2002) were also explored. Histology was used to show the general morphology of tissue samples, whereas the EITB targeted antibodies rather than antigens in the tissue. Although histology remains a viable, regularly used technique, the EITBs were quickly discarded from the study as these targeted antibodies rather than antigens in the samples. The drawback of testing for antibodies is that their presence does not necessarily indicate the presence of an active infection. This is because antibodies can be present in the bloodstream for up to one year after any infection (Neva and Brown 1994), and therefore it can only be concluded that the individual suffered from an infection, but it may have been in the past. In modern patients, this is not the case as other symptoms manifest at the time of testing, but unfortunately, these are not present in ancient mummies.

The results of the immunostaining also dictate whether DNA analysis is performed. Although such analysis could identify the actual species that had caused the infection, the decision to destroy finite samples is always approached with caution, not only from an ethical point of view but also because considerable problems occur when analysing ancient DNA (Pääbo 1989; Hoss and Pääbo 1993; Hummell and Herrmann 1994). Again, the availability of suitable samples is also a factor, as the ancient schistosome DNA can only be extracted from tissue that harbours the ova and worms. Therefore, only a few selected mummy tissue samples available for testing in the schistosomiasis study have been investigated for the *Schistosoma* parasite at the DNA level.

Materials and method

A protocol had to be established using modern samples infected with *Schistosoma*, before irreplaceable ancient samples could be investigated. Once procedures were established with the modern material, these positive and negative samples then served as controls, which could be directly compared with the ancient samples also being tested. To limit unnecessary sampling of ancient tissues, an interim step ascertained whether antisera would react with infected tissues that had been blocked in wax, and then badly stored. Bladder tissue taken from an Egyptian cadaver more than fifty years ago was used for this purpose. If positive results could not be achieved with this sample, then it would be unlikely that antigens would be present in the ancient samples.

The following methods are as already outlined by Rutherford (1997, 2000, 2002, 2005).

MODERN TISSUES. Samples for this study were provided by Professor M. Doenhoff (University of Bangor, UK). The liver of both *S. mansoni* infected and uninfected mice, and *S. haematobium* infected and uninfected hamster livers were used as positive and negative controls. Both *S. mansoni* and *S. haematobium* worms were also used. The bladder sample taken from an Egyptian cadaver more than fifty years ago (provided by the University of Manchester), and known to be infected with *S. haematobium*, was also used as an interim sample.

MUMMIFIED TISSUES. When trying to detect the *Schistosoma* ova and worms in ancient tissue, the probable location of such parasites within the body dictates which samples are worth investigating. The worms live in the veins that drain the bladder or liver and their ova are more prevalent in certain areas of the body than others. Therefore, bladder, liver, and visceral samples were the preferred target. Tissues that may harbour schistosome ova and worms and could be obtained with little or no destruction were the optimal specimens. The source of these samples included whole mummies, from which small sections of bladder, liver, intestines, and pelvic tissue were taken. Several of the samples had no provenance but this was not relevant at this point in the research process, as the main aim was to perfect and establish research guidelines for the large-scale study.

The initial fifty samples were chosen simply so that it could be established which experimental formats were most appropriate. Thus, the samples varied greatly in condition and appearance, although the size of the samples required for each test did not. A sample as small as 2 mm³ was acceptable for immunocytochemistry and histology. In contrast, 150 mg of tissue was required for the ELISA and 100 mg for EITB and DNA analysis. As bladder, liver, and visceral samples were the preferred target for immunocytochemistry, only twenty-four of the fifty samples were suitable for immunostaining. Once standard procedures had been established, sample collection then concentrated exclusively on provenanced samples that could be mapped to a certain place and time. Thus, the samples currently being studied are provenanced and represent burial groups found in the Sudanese Desert and the Dahkleh Oasis (see Chapter 15).

ANTISERA/SERA. Several polyclonal antisera directed towards an array of epitope sites found on S. *mansoni* (raised in rabbit) and S. *haematobium* (raised in hamster) antigens were used. Rabbit and hamster sera taken from unimmunised rabbits (Sigma Diagnostics, UK) were also used to ensure the reactivity of the antisera. As an indirect immunostaining protocol was used, the secondary antibody was conjugated to biotin (i.e. donkey biotinylated anti-rabbit, Amersham UK; and goat biotinylated anti-hamster, Jacksons, USA). To visualise the reaction, the protein streptavidin conjugated with fluorescein isothiocyanate (Amersham, UK), was used. All dilutions were done with 0.1 M phosphate-buffered saline (PBS), pH 7.4. Before any antiserum was applied to the sections, a blocking serum was applied (10 ml PBS, pH 7.4, 0.05 g bovine serum albumin, 150 µl donkey serum (S. *mansoni*) or goat serum (S. *haematobium*), 50 µl Triton-X).

PREPARATION OF MODERN AND ANCIENT TISSUES FOR BLOCKING IN IMMUNOGENIC. The modern tissue samples were prepared according to the manufacturer's instructions (Taab, UK). In contrast, small pieces of ancient tissue, approximately (0.2 cm^3), were placed into one part conditioning solution (Surfacem, UK) to ninety-nine parts distilled water, which completely immersed the tissue. This was then stored at 4°C for seven days. If the tissues retained their form, the conditioning solution was decanted and the tissues were gently rinsed three times with distilled water.

After the third rinse, the tissues were left to soak in distilled water for a further two days at 4°C. The distilled water was decanted and replaced with 50 per cent alcohol in which the samples were left to soak for a further five days at 4°C. This was decanted and replaced with 70 per cent, and then 90 per cent alcohol for thirty minutes each time. The 90 per cent alcohol was replaced with acetone, in which the samples were left to soak overnight at 4°C. The acetone was replaced with fresh acetone in which the samples were left to soak for a further eight days at 4°C. The acetone was then replaced with immunoresin and left to soak for three days at 4°C. The immunoresin was replaced with fresh immunoresin three times, and left at 4°C for three days each time.

Tissues impregnated with sand and resin proved difficult to section unless the conditioning solution was replaced with a dilute solution (2.5 per cent) of hydrofluoric acid (Sigma, UK). The samples were left to soak at room temperature for four weeks. Once removed from the acid, the samples were washed carefully with distilled water, and then placed into 50 per cent alcohol. The remainder of the aforementioned protocol was followed from this point.

PLACING TISSUES (MODERN AND ANCIENT) INTO IMMUNORESIN BLOCKS. Placing the tissues into immunoresin blocks entailed following the manufacturer's instructions (Taab, UK). After polymerisation had taken place at 4°C, a Perspex block holding the embedded tissue was secured onto a semithin LKB Historange microtome and sections ranging from 2 to 3.5 μm thick were cut with a glass Ralf knife. If the samples were gritty, a diamond knife was used (Taab, UK).

IMMUNOSTAINING. An indirect immunostaining protocol was followed: 100 μl of 0.1 M PBS, pH7.4, was applied to each section and left on the tissue sections for fifteen minutes. After three washes with PBS buffer, 100 μl of blocking serum was put onto each section and left to incubate at room temperature for thirty minutes. After thirty minutes, the excess was shaken off. The actual section was not washed with PBS, as the blocking agent must remain on the section to compete with the primary antibody. One hundred microliters of the chosen primary antibody was then applied to each section. The primary antibody was then left to incubate on each section overnight at 4°C. Each section was gently washed three times (five minutes each time) with PBS to remove unbound antibody.

One hundred microliters of secondary antibody (biotinylated goat anti-rabbit immunoglobulin, dilution 1:200, Amersham Pharmacia Biotech, UK; or biotinylated donkey anti-hamster immunoglobulin, dilution 1:200, Jacksons, U.S.) was then applied and incubated at room temperature for one hour. Following washing in PBS, 100 μl of fluorescein isothiocyanate–conjugated streptavidin (1:100) was applied to each section, and left to incubate at room temperature for forty-five minutes.

An optional step, to stain any DNA present in the tissue sections, was also performed while the tertiary streptavidin was incubating on the sections. This was achieved with the application of 100 μl Hoechst – bisbenzimide stain (Sigma, UK), which intercalates with the A and T residues of DNA. This was diluted 1:2,000 and was applied to each section two minutes before the streptavidin was due to be washed off. The slides were carefully mounted using the aqueous mountant, gelvatol, and placed between light protective wooden trays. The slides were then left to dry at − 20°C for at least twenty-four hours. Once dry, they were viewed on the fluorescent microscope and the results were photographed and noted.

Results

Although positive results have been seen in the provenanced samples collected from the Sudanese Desert and the Dakhleh Oasis, the results presented below represent the initial sample group used to establish ideal protocols.

REACTION OF ANTISERA UPON MODERN SAMPLE. The antisera produced excellent immunostaining results on S. *mansoni*–infected mouse liver, (Plates X and XI), S. *haematobium*–infected hamster liver (Plate XII), the 1950s bladder and both species of worms. The presence of lateral spines can clearly be seen on the S. *mansoni* ova, if the sections are cut in the correct orientation, whereas the S. *haematobium* ova do not display the distinctive spines (Plate XII).

It is worth noting that Plate XI also shows that the classic oval shapes associated with such ova are not always seen, and some distortion due to the orientation of the ova may produce obscure results. Immunostaining of the 1950s bladder confirmed that epitopes were still present after many years of exposure to fluctuating temperatures and conditions. The ova size is smaller than those seen in the mouse and hamster liver, suggesting that they may have undergone some shrinkage during the past fifty years. Any ova present in ancient tissues may therefore be even smaller or totally collapsed, not resembling ova shapes at all, after thousands of years.

Such positive results towards epitopes that have undergone fluctuating temperatures and conditions suggest that they may still be present in ancient samples. Paradoxically, although older, the ancient samples may have been in more stable, static environments. Positive samples were also assessed for DNA content to pursue genetic analysis.

The DNA-specific Hoechst stain bound strongly between the A and T residues within the nuclei of the modern tissue, ova, and worms. All these results served as good comparative samples to the ancient tissues. The Hoechst stain also produced positive staining, albeit paler upon the tissue sections from the modern Egyptian cadaver bladder.

REACTION OF ANTISERA ON THE MUMMIFIED TISSUES. Immunocyto-chemistry was used to test twenty-four different mummy samples for schistosomiasis. Of these, six (25 per cent) have displayed positive results for schistosome antigens. The DNA-specific stain (Hoechst) also bound in the same areas as the antiserum, which warrants DNA analysis.

(1) *Manchester mummy 7700/1766, c. 1800 B.C., Fayoum Oasis (Middle Egypt), Bladder tissue.* Immunostaining of the calcified bladder tissue has shown discrete staining to both ova and worms. The fluorescent shell and lateral spike can clearly be seen, with the green fluorescence mainly bound to the inside of the ovum in Plate XIII.

In contrast, the ova seen in Plate XIV do not display spines and resemble distorted *S. haematobium* ova seen in Plate XII. Positive immunostaining of worms has also been achieved, and although most are distorted in shape, some of the features could clearly be seen, and show clear similarities to the modern schistosome worms. Experts at the Egyptian Organization for Vaccine and Biological Production (VACSERA), Cairo, assessed these results and confirmed them to be *S. haematobium* ova and worms (Al Sherbiny 1999, personal correspondence). The ELISA supports these results, indicating a positive result for CAA (80 ng/ml).

(2) *Leicester Museum 528/1981.1885, mummy 1, c. 2700 B.C., Akhmim (Middle Egypt), Pelvic tissue.* Positive staining to small clusters of ova was seen. As with the 7700/1766 bladder samples, the staining was more prominent to the inside of the ova; however, the chitin shell can clearly be seen. DNA analysis has amplified a small fragment of the *S. haematobium* cytochrome oxidase C subunit 1 (COI) from this sample (see Chapter 9).

(3) *Leicester Museum 528/1980.1882, mummy 2, c. 2700 B.C., Akhmim (Middle Egypt), Pelvic tissue.* Positive staining to clusters of ova was achieved. This is unlike the solitary ova and worms found in other mummy samples. The pattern of ova distribution resembles the 1950s *S. haematobium* infected bladder.

(4) *Manchester Museum 7700/1777, Asru, c. 2750 B.C., Luxor (Upper Egypt), Bladder tissue.* Discrete immunostaining was found in these bladder sections. Again, the immunostaining is precise to oval bodies thought to be ova, with very little background staining. No positive results were found in the intestinal material, even though Tapp (1979) had shown the presence of some type of ova. The ELISA showed that the intestinal tissue was positive for CAA (455 ng/ml) and the (EITB) showed a pale positive reaction for *S. haematobium* antibodies.

(5) *Manchester Museum 7700/13010/5, no provenance, Bladder tissue.* Discrete staining to several oval shapes, with little or no background staining,

was seen. Although oval shapes are present, no worms have been found. In this study, all sections taken from the bladder of this mummy have been consistently positive, suggesting that the bladder had a high yield of deposited *Schistosoma* ova.

(6) Manchester Museum 7700/9430, no provenance, Canopic jar material. Positive staining to clusters of oval shapes, resembling ova, was achieved. These results were positive to varying degrees, as there was variation in the quality of the sections from this sample because degradation was not uniform throughout the sample. This inconsistency has been noted for future studies. ELISA results supported this by showing a positive result for CAA (22 ng/ml).

Discussion

A marked difference was noticed between preparations of modern and ancient samples for immunocytochemistry. Unfortunately, only a few ancient samples were prepared with the same ease as the modern tissues. In samples from the early dynasties, such as the liver tissue from the Canopic jar associated with the mummy of Nekht Ankh (twelfth Dynasty), no debris or resins were present. This easily sectioned tissue showed good tissue integrity, and supported other researchers' results (Tapp 1979).

The remaining ancient samples contained varying amounts of mummification resins and gritty silica particles. A dilute solution of hydrofluoric acid was used to remove the particles, enabling very thin (2 μm), flat, intact sections to be cut with ease. Although this pretreatment is now an option, because of its hazardous nature, tissues without resin or sand are sought first, but if they are not available, any samples with sand present can be soaked in an acid solution.

The fragile state of the ancient samples benefited from the use of immunoresin as it provided a more supportive medium than wax, and can also be prepared and kept at 4°C, thus preserving epitopes of interest. Such epitopes were visualised by precise staining on both the modern and ancient samples, thus showing that the antisera used throughout this study are very specific and are of the highest quality.

As one of the aims of this study is to identify ancient schistosome ova and worms in ancient Egyptian tissues, their morphology was studied in modern samples. Cut at different orientations, the ova and worms did not always display the classic shapes. Such distorted images served as excellent comparisons when analysing the ancient samples. Although the ova and worms present in the ancient samples were often distorted in shape, this is not surprising, as most of the samples were more than a thousand years old.

Positive reactions, however, still occurred, suggesting that *Schistosoma* antigens are present after many centuries. The DNA-specific Hoechst stain indicated that DNA was still present to some degree in the ancient tissues, particularly within the immunostained ova. Further research is being pursued to investigate the hypothesis that the chitin shell had played some role in protecting the DNA within the ova.

Although the results reported in this chapter confirm the presence of schistosome parasites in both Upper and Middle Egypt, no real pattern can be seen (Rutherford 2005:82). So far, the only conclusion that can be drawn is that the *S. haematobium* parasite was present in Middle Egypt more than 2,700 years ago at Akhmim, as demonstrated in the pelvic tissue samples taken from the Leicester Museum mummies. Leicester mummy 1, known as Bes-en-Mut, was a priest in the Temple of Min, whereas Leicester 2, named Ta-Bes, was a teenage girl. There was a considerable divergence between the amount of ova found in these two mummies: the teenage girl had a high distribution whereas the priest had only small clusters. This mirrors the patterns seen in patients today, where children and teenagers are heavily infected because their activities often entail more contact with water, and acquired immunity is thought to occur with adulthood.

The *S. haematobium* species was also present in the Fayoum Oasis 1,800 years ago, as seen in the bladder tissue of 7700/1766, and the mummy of Asru (No. 1777) confirms the presence of *S. haematobium* in Luxor (Upper Egypt) some 2,700 years ago. Today, *S. haematobium* is still prevalent in both Middle and Upper Egypt, whereas *S. mansoni* is almost absent in the upper region. As the EITB results display only a pale band for *S. haematobium* antibodies, further tests at the DNA level are needed to reinforce which species is present in Asru's bladder.

The positive results seen in mummy 7700/13010/5 and in the Canopic jar material (7700/9430) have limited impact regarding the epidemiology study, because the only historical information we have about each sample is that mummy 7700/13010/5 may have been a scribe, and an inscription on the Canopic jar confirms that its owner was a priest. Overall, the results highlight the fact that, in contrast to today when schistosomiasis mainly affects poorer, rural village communities, in antiquity, there was probably no marked difference in the incidence of the disease between the various social classes, as everyone would have bathed in the river or in garden pools fed with infected water from the canals.

Now that standard procedures have been established, the context of sample collection has moved to provenanced-only samples that can be mapped to a certain place and time (Chapter 15). Such samples form the basis of the author's continuing work: medieval samples collected from Sudanese Nubia (c. 1500 B.C.) have been immunoassayed, and two samples that have shown positive results are being investigated further.

In addition, preparations are in hand for immunocytochemistry tests to be performed on a large group of samples from forty-eight Graeco-Roman mummies found in the Dakhleh Oasis. This particular group is an excellent source of material as many of the samples have been taken from the liver, colon, intestines, and coprolites, all of which harbour both the schistosome worms and ova. Once a substantial number of provenanced samples have been tested, a distribution pattern should emerge, which will contribute valid information to the field of anthropology (Rutherford, 2005:82).

From an immunological point of view, the detection of antigens rather than antibodies would appear to be the preferred method for diagnosing disease in ancient samples, as antigens seem to be hardier than antibodies and may therefore still be present in samples more than a thousand years old.

Because of the weak reactions seen in the EITB tests performed on a few samples, the detection of *Schistosoma* antibodies rather than antigens is no longer regarded as a diagnostic option in this continuing study. This decision has also been reached because the presence of antibodies does not always indicate an active infection, and the total destruction of the sample necessitated by this technique conflicts with an ethical approach which attempts to keep destruction of material to a minimum.

Combining results from several tests can provide an overall picture of the state of health in the case of each mummy. An excellent example of this is the bladder samples taken from mummy 7700/1766. Here, immunocytochemistry has clearly demonstrated the presence of schistosomiasis, especially as the (EITB) dipstick test for GP23 antibodies and the ELISA test for CAA were positive, and calcification of the bladder was also evident, suggesting that chronic schistosomiasis may have been present for several years.

Although DNA-specific Hoechst staining also showed that DNA was still present for analysis, amplification of *Schistosoma* DNA was unsuccessful, perhaps because the DNA of interest was only present as a minute quantity or because there were no worms or eggs present in the selected tissue sample. After these initial attempts had been unsuccessful, it was eventually decided not to use a second sample of bladder because of ethical considerations about destroying further samples. The overall results obtained for mummy

7700/1766 provide sufficient evidence to conclude that, when alive, this person suffered from chronic schistosomiasis caused by S. *haematobium*. As tissue samples that contain S. *haematobium* worms and eggs are already blocked in immunoresin, in situ hybridisation may be a better option when less harsh pretreatments are available.

Conclusion

Combining the contributions of science and Egyptology can provide researchers with insight into a particular disease; however, they must always be aware of ethical considerations surrounding the destruction of finite mummy tissue, and any destructive methods they use should be performed conservatively. Studies on the distribution patterns of any infection such as schistosomiasis require access to provenanced samples, but this information is not available for many mummies or body parts held in museum collections. Nevertheless, the collection of provenanced samples will be an essential factor in any future, large-scale epidemiology studies, as it is pointless to destroy ancient tissues that can provide scientific results which cannot be placed within particular chronological, geographical, or sociological contexts (see Chapters 15, 17).

In this study, testing the initial fifty samples has provided many answers and highlighted several problems that may occur in a wider context. For example, some tests initially considered to be appropriate for this study (the use of EITB dip sticks for targeting antibodies) have now been discarded or limited. Positive samples will continue to be analysed at the DNA level, as it is thought that DNA can yield more information than the detection of an antibody, such as, for example, which species has infected the host. Ultimately, this should provide the means of mapping the occurrence of both S. *mansoni* and S. *haematobium* infections in ancient times.

With the current study, results have been obtained using several methods of investigation rather than relying on one line of enquiry (Rutherford 2002). Immunocytochemistry has made a major contribution to this work, and will undoubtedly provide a valuable diagnostic tool for other projects. The techniques used to investigate schistosomiasis can be easily adapted for research on other diseases present in antiquity. For example, under the author's supervision, master's students at the University of Manchester (UK) (see Chapter 17) have mirrored the outlined procedures with respect to diagnosing malaria (Marmion 2003; Bratcher 2006), and several of the liver samples tested from the Dakhleh Oasis group have shown positive results. These positive samples are now being investigated at the genetic level (Bratcher 2006).

The Tissue Bank was originally developed to collect tissues for the schistosomiasis research project (see Chapter 15), but it now facilitates other studies which, in due course, will produce data that can be used to reconstruct the living conditions and diseases of the past.

CHAPTER 9

DNA identification in mummies and associated material

Patricia Rutherford

Foreword

Molecular analysis such as serological tests were conducted by Boyd and Boyd (1934) when they tested the blood groups of 300 Indian and Egyptian mummies, and by Candela (1936) who used a modified version of this procedure to test eleven mummies. Initially, it was hoped that such tests would show not only evidence of migration on a large scale but also family relationships and diseases.

Serological tests were, however, soon discarded as a valid test. One of the main problems was degeneration, because the A and B antigens targeted in such blood tests are made up of simple sugars that can degrade over time (Harrison and Connolly 1969). Contamination is also a major problem when working with ancient samples, especially mummies that have been subjected to various herbs and spices during embalming (Flaherty and Haigh 1984, 1986). Such degradation and contamination hindered Harrison and Connolly's (1969) study when they attempted to show kinship between Smenkhkare and Tutankhamun.

Today, population and sibship studies follow the mitochondrial DNA line, which is inherited maternally, as studying the ancient DNA molecule can yield far more information than serology tests as it codes for all proteins in the body. To date, ancient DNA has been successfully extracted from teeth (Drancourt et al. 1998; Merriwether et al. 1994), bone (Cipollaro et al. 1998), soft tissues (Rutherford 2002), hair (Wilson et al. 1995), faeces (Loreille et al. 2001; Pioner et al. 2003), plant material (Brown et al. 1994; Harper 2003; Bzdega 2006), insects (Cano et al. 1993), and fossils (Goldenberg et al. 1990) that are seventeen to twenty million years old, although it has still not been proven how long a DNA molecule can survive. The targets have been both organellar (chloroplast and mitochondria) and nuclear DNA.

DNA analysis has its own limits. This chapter discusses the possibilities and limitations of working with ancient DNA and describes the methods the author has adapted to amplify and sequence ancient *Schistosoma* DNA fragments. Several other projects that have been successfully conducted using these established protocols are presented, and future possibilities within this field, and the potential contribution to Egyptology and palaeopathology, are also considered.

Possibilities and limitations of analysing ancient DNA

There are three stages to analysing ancient DNA: extraction, amplification, and either sequencing or restriction site analysis. Each stage poses considerable problems as only 1–2 per cent of the DNA yield that is expected from modern samples is extracted from ancient tissues (Pääbo 1989, 2004). Therefore, many researchers concentrate on targeting mitochondrial (mt)DNA, as there are several hundred copies of this genome per cell in contrast to two copies of each gene locus in the nuclear genome (Stone et al. 1996; Hauswirth et al. 1994; Rutherford 2002; Smyth 2005). Mitochondrial DNA also has the advantage of being inherited exclusively through the maternal line and is therefore used in sibship studies (Smyth 2005).

Another advantage is its circular structure, which is supercoiled, in contrast to the linear nuclear DNA that is easily degraded. This supercoiling seems to protect the mtDNA from excessive cleaving, thus producing fragment lengths between 100 and 500 base pairs (bp) (Hagelberg 1994; Pääbo et al. 2004). In general, only small fragments of ancient DNA survive, even from the nucleus or organelle, the average size being about 200–300 bp (Kaestle and Horsburgh 2002).

A recent study by Binladen et al. (2005) has also shown that similar damage is found in both the nuclear DNA and mtDNA because the same amount of miscoding occurs. Therefore, despite mtDNA being present in high copy numbers, the amount of damage is the same. Perhaps the histones present in the nucleus serve to protect the DNA wrapped around them (~200 bp), in the same way that supercoiling protects mtDNA, and therefore the only real advantage of working with mtDNA is its abundance.

The method that revolutionized ancient DNA analysis

Despite the difficulties posed by working with such small fragments, studies began in the 1980s and have progressed slowly ever since. The earliest work, undertaken by Higuchi et al. (1984) and Pääbo (1985), involved cloning the ancient DNA into bacteria to amplify the extract. This had many problems; for example, a large part of the extracted DNA was heavily modified (Pääbo 1989), which meant that cloning artefacts were introduced during replication of the DNA in bacteria. In contrast, the polymerase chain reaction (PCR) protocols devised by Mullis and Faloona (1987) for modern DNA amplification means that small intact copies of DNA can be amplified alongside the badly degraded molecules, and this eliminates the modification problem.

The principle of the PCR is quite simple: it mimics DNA replication in vivo. As DNA is a double-stranded molecule, and each strand complements the other (i.e. the adenine [A] residue binds to the thymine [T] residue, and guanine [G] binds to the cytosine [C]), if one sequence is known, then the complementary strands sequence can be worked out. The bonds between these residues are easily broken using heat, which separates the strands. Once cooled, these complementary strands anneal to each other again. The structure of the DNA molecule allows for it to be amplified using different temperatures, adding small primers and the nucleotide residues A, T, C, and G and an enzyme, to read the template and make a complementary strand with the free nucleotides. Today, molecular biologists use this method routinely, as it can now be reproduced in vitro.

The PCR method selectively and repeatedly replicates defined DNA sequences from a whole DNA mixture. A pair of oligonucleotide primers some 20 bp long flank the DNA sequence of interest as they complement the template sequence. Information about the DNA code is needed before a complementary primer can be synthesized synthetically. Today, millions of DNA sequences are accessible from the Internet; for example, the *Schistosoma* mitochondria sequences targeted in the schistosomiasis study were accessed from GenBank, National Center for Biotechnology Information (Rutherford 2002).

Polymerase chain reaction has, therefore, given ancient DNA work more momentum, as it has enabled the specific targeting of informative sequences. These are often no longer than 200 bp in length, however, and such targets should be chosen carefully to ensure that the optimum yield of information is gained. Although the PCR method combined with sequencing is routinely used for diagnosis of diseases, genetic screening, and population analysis in modern humans, it has received more media coverage for its potential use in the study of ancient DNA molecules.

Overview of ancient molecular work

Initially, DNA was extracted from animals such as the Quagga (Higuchi et al. 1984), mammoth (Johnson et al. 1985), insects (Cano et al. 1993), and plant material such as a magnolia leaf from the Miocene period (Goldenberg et al. 1990). Pääbo (1985) was first to extract human DNA from ancient Egyptian mummy tissue.

More recently, some of the above-noted results have been questioned. For example, the sequenced magnolia DNA was 790 bp in length; when Pääbo and Wilson (1991) repeated these experiments but only amplified bacteria, they concluded that the initial results were probably due to contamination rather than ancient magnolia DNA. Furthermore, there is scepticism about the early date that Goldberg et al. (1990) claim for the magnolia leaf DNA because studies performed by Lindahl (1993) regarding the rate of DNA degradation suggest that DNA cannot survive for millions of years.

Racemisation studies by Poinar et al. (1996) have also raised questions about the age limit of DNA molecules, suggesting that the rate at which the amino acids racemise correlates to DNA survival. Data suggest that some of the studies on samples in excess of 10 million years old are questionable. Enthusiasm also began to wane as it became clear that there were fundamental problems with the high failure rate for amplification and it was realised that modern DNA was a prevalent contaminant.

Limitations

Nearly twenty years after extracting DNA from mummified Egyptian remains, a recent review by Pääbo et al. (2004) shows that serious concerns still remain regarding degradation, contamination, and authentication. In particular, degradation is constantly being reviewed in detail (Pääbo et al. 2004: Hofreiter et al. 2001; Handt et al. 1994; Lindahl 1993). Although the structure of DNA makes it a stable molecule, postmortem diagenetic changes occur over time, thus damaging both the double helix and the nucleotide chains (Poinar et al. 2003). Examples of such damage are denaturation, in which two DNA strands separate and the single strands degrade further.

Hydrolysis and oxidative damage are the two main degradative processes (Lindahl 1993; Pääbo et al. 2004). Oxidation, which is often due to ionising radiation producing free radicals, leads to modification (oxidised pyrimidines and sugar residues), distortion of the helix, and even the loss of bases. Furthermore, the C and T are oxidised to hydantoins, which are PCR inhibitors (Pääbo 1989; Hoss et al. 1996). Hydrolysis also breaks the phosphodiester bonds between sugars and phosphates due to the breakdown of the N-glycosyl bond in the presence of water (Hoss et al. 1996). Although such degradation occurs continuously in vivo, it is constantly repaired, but such repair mechanisms cease postmortem and damage accumulates.

Degradation and modifications of ancient DNA are not the only problem to consider when trying to amplify the DNA of interest by means of PCR. Unfortunately, PCR is so sensitive that other components extracted along with the DNA often inhibit the reaction. Such contamination is derived from soil components, which several researchers have reported when extracting DNA from bone and tissue (Krebs et al. 2000).

A variety of organic and inorganic substances may be extracted, such as salts, heavy metals, and even DNA from soil-dwelling bacteria and fungi. Krebs et al. (2000) and Tuross (1994) have reported the presence of fulvic and humic acids and these phelonic products inhibit the polymerase (*Taq*) enzymes used in the PCR reactions because they are similar to DNA. It is therefore important to remove such contaminants before PCR is attempted. Krebs et al. (2000) have reportedly overcome this by using high-performance liquid chromatography.

Different innovations have been introduced in individual laboratories, although many are derived from the protocols developed by Pääbo et al. (1989). Many researchers have tried different solutions to enhance ancient DNA extraction, for example, Chelex (Woodward et al. 1994) and guanidine thiocyanate (Boom et al. 1990; Hoss and Pääbo 1993; Pääbo 1994). Chelex and guanidine thiocyanate were explored along with the standard phenol extraction methods by Rutherford (2002). The standard phenol extraction, repeated twice, seems to clean the extract enough for amplification to be achieved. Many researchers have used silica beads to clean preparations (Hoss and Pääbo 1993). If dealing with a very low yield of DNA at the outset, the extract may be totally lost, and for this reason, the author does not use silica beads.

Inhibitors are always present to some degree and, as it is not always possible to eliminate these totally, several strategies are often used to decrease the chances of inhibiting contaminants. One option is to dilute extracts with deionised, distilled water as this reduces the concentration of contaminants, making the primers more specific to the ancient DNA than to the contaminants. An increase in the ratio of the polymerase enzyme to the sample DNA may also be helpful, or the additions of bovine serum albumin to the PCR mix (Pääbo 1989).

Environmental effects on ancient DNA

The environment from which DNA is retrieved has a significant influence on its quality (Burger et al. 1999). Several biological, physical, and chemical factors affect DNA preservation. For example, a very low temperature can preserve DNA, and research performed by Hoss et al. (1996) showed that a 20°C decrease in temperature reduces DNA degradation by ten- to twentyfold. Although low temperatures alone are not sufficient to preserve all specimens (Smith et al. 2001), postmortem degradation is significantly slowed by cooling.

Humidity provides moistness that aids the action of nucleases. Desiccated mummies are therefore often well preserved because of the lack of moisture. An alkaline environment, such as the one provided by mummification in alkaline natron, is also beneficial to the survival of the acidic DNA molecule. Desiccation, freezing, or high salt concentrations inactivate the nucleases before significant damage is done. Therefore, rapid desiccation, particularly of the skin of a mummy, may result in consistently good preservation.

Research conducted by Bibby (2005) under the author's supervision showed good preservation of mummified skin samples, thus supporting Pääbo's (1986) hypothesis that overall preservation is directly related to the rate at which water is removed. Thus, because the skin is dehydrated first, it could be expected to have a better DNA yield than the internal organs.

The airtight tombs in which many Egyptian mummies are found will inhibit aerobic conditions where oxygen enables chemical reactions and decomposition by microorganisms to occur. Researchers often speculate about DNA survival in ancient mummified tissue, but not all sources of DNA are equal: muscle tissue contains innumerable mitochondria and is therefore likely to provide more mtDNA than other tissues. Conditions inside the tombs need to be considered rather than the outside environment, as these differ substantially. Low temperatures and dry air in the tomb and desiccation and alkalinity of the natron used in mummification provide ideal preservation conditions for the DNA molecule. Therefore, some researchers have claimed that 'a DNA investigation in pharaonic mummy tissue samples is indeed not senseless' (Zink and Nerlick 2003: 109).

Marota and Rollo (2002) disagree that such conditions are beneficial and argue that ancient DNA cannot be recovered from ancient Egyptian mummies. Their study was based on degradation rates in papyri, combined with racemisation data, and not on tissue samples; thus, it is more theoretical than practical. Interestingly, Professor Cooper at the University of Adelaide, Australia, has recently targeted piles of dung in Australia for his next ancient genetic project on the basis that because the dung is so dry, it does not decompose, and a hot dry climate is one of the best environments for ancient DNA (Salleh 2005). Some studies can benefit from other types of environment. For example, at Windover, Hauswirth et al. (1994) were able to analyse samples from bodies that had been in an aqueous environment.

Sibship studies

In the study by Hauswirth et al. (1994), although mtDNA is often the chosen target, nuclear DNA was also targeted here to establish family relationships. Research undertaken at Windover is important because it was possible to determine that a variety of genetic markers (i.e. nuclear human leucocyte antigens (HLAs), nuclear microsatellites, and mtDNA) could be examined. Hauswirth et al. argued that although the samples spanned a thousand years, DNA analysis showed results that indicated a homogeneous population. Such results suggest that the same type of analysis could be conducted on any large number of ancient bodies, particularly Egyptian mummies found within one burial site, thus providing the opportunity to confirm relationships.

Other sibship studies have been performed by Evison et al. (1998) and Elles et al. (1993) by using analysis of HLAs. The HLA genes are found on the short arm of chromosome 6 and they are the most variable (polymorphic) gene cluster in humans. The genes code for the proteins that span cell membranes, and these proteins enable humans to make the distinction between self and foreign.

Therefore, the proteins are an integral part of the immune system and must match when a transplant organ is received from a donor. Matches are invariably found within a family unit, but only rarely in unrelated individuals. Allelic variants of the HLA are also associated with disease and resistance to disease. The HLA differences are now well documented and differences across the world are known (Charron 1997). When combined with sexing analysis, the results may provide information about biological relationships in burials, population movements, evolution of disease, and immunity.

One study by Elles et al. (1993) analysed tissue samples from five bodies found in a previously undisturbed, communal tomb at El-Hagarsa, Middle Egypt, to attempt to sex the mummies and match the findings to the evidence on the coffins and face masks (see Chapter 1). The archaeologists also questioned whether the mummies all came from the same family, as indicated by the inscriptions. Primers were designed for both the HLA DRB1 and the repetitive sequence (DYZ1) found only on the Y chromosome.

The sexing experiments produced contradictory results: for example, the genetic evidence showed that one of the mummies was male, although its associated face mask and inscriptional evidence indicated that it belonged to a female. The HLA results demonstrated that two of the mummies had a DRB1-1001 allele, which is rare in Caucasians (2.1 per cent) and more prevalent in Middle Eastern populations. Although the remaining results suggested that this was a family group, this could not be clarified because the researchers were unable to gain access to more tissue samples for further analysis.

Diseases

There have been many reports of human, animal, and plant DNA being extracted and amplified. There are fewer reports of extracting DNA from disease-causing parasites, bacteria, and viruses, although such studies are important as they can have an impact on modern studies of disease (see Chapter 7). Work in this field includes the report by Sallares et al. (2000) that they had amplified part of the 18s ribosomal DNA specific for *Plasmodium falciparum*, which causes the disease malaria. Here, the DNA of interest, amplified from skeletal human remains excavated from a fifth-century A.D. Roman cemetery in Italy, was more than 1,500 years old.

Another report by Guhl (1997) states that 330 bp of *Trypanosoma cruzi* DNA were amplified to confirm the presence of Chagas' disease. In tests on a total of twenty-seven samples from skeletal remains that included viscera, heart, and oesophagus, he found that seven had the target DNA. These results correlate to the 10–15 per cent of people who are infected today.

More recently I have amplified 236 bp of the *Schistosoma haematobium* cytochrome oxidase C fragment from the bladder tissue of an Egyptian mummy in the Leicester Museum (UK) (see Methods and Materials and also Chapter 8). Modern genetic techniques have also identified other ancient diseases such as plague (Drancourt et al. 1998), leprosy (Haas et al. 2000; Montiel et al. 2003), and tuberculosis (Donoghue et al. 1998). In addition, Ascaris DNA found in coprolites by Loreille et al. (2001) has been sequenced.

Limited research into viral DNA has also been conducted. Li et al. (1999) have identified the DNA of the human T cell lymphotropic virus (HTLV)-1 in an Andean mummy. HTLV causes T cell leukemia and may have originated from paleomongoloids who migrated to Japan and South America more than 10,000 years ago. The researchers studied 100 Andean mummies excavated from the Atamaca Desert. Because of the salty, arid conditions in this rainless plateau, the mummies buried there more than 1,000 years ago were well preserved. The group extracted DNA from bone marrow and successfully isolated the viral DNA from one mummy.

Ancient bacterial DNA has also been found in the digestive tract of human remains. For example, Cano et al. (2000) demonstrated the presence of Vibrio from the gut flora of the Tyrolean Ice Man, and *Escherichia coli* has been genetically identified in the Lindow Man (c. 300 B.C.) by Fricker et al. (1997).

Research has been undertaken on various types of archaeological remains, and many genetic results have been achieved. The ethics regarding total destruction of samples should always be addressed, as there is often no material left for replication of results. To simply destroy a sample for a meagre 200–300 bp of DNA seems extreme. The author (Rutherford 2002) and other researchers believe that alternative methods should always be considered first, and for this reason, only a select few of the mummy tissue samples available for testing in the Manchester schistosomiasis study have been investigated for the *Schistosoma* parasite at the DNA level (see Chapter 8).

The Schistosomiasis project – methods and materials

The finite samples of mummified material were assessed for DNA content before any destructive analysis was conducted. As already discussed in Chapter 8, the DNA-specific Hoechst stain, which intercalates between the A and T residues of DNA, was used to assess the presence of DNA. It reacted strongly with both modern and ancient tissue samples. The stain often bound to the same areas as the antiserum, suggesting DNA analysis was warranted. Other assessments of DNA content were not used, such as racemisation (Pioner et al. 1996), because it is a destructive method and inappropriate for the small samples that are usually available for testing.

At first, amplification of ancient DNA followed the same protocols used for modern DNA; however, new methods have subsequently been developed. Parr et al. (1996) substituted the polymerase *Taq*1 enzyme used for modern DNA work for Deep Vent (exo-) polymerase (New England Biolabs) because it has several qualities that suit the amplification of ancient DNA. These include a greater sensitivity for deoxyribonucleotide triphosphates (dNTPs), and a longer halflife at high temperatures, which results in prolonged amplifications (i.e. forty cycles instead of the normal thirty), thus increasing the chances of amplification of any ancient DNA that may be present. Also, the Deep Vent (exo-) polymerase does not appear to cause 'jumping PCR,' a problem reported by Pääbo et al. (1990) who described this as a phenomenon where the *Taq* 1 enzyme places an adenosine (A) residue at damaged sites and then jumps to another template, producing chimeric products.

Before ancient samples could be analysed, protocols had to be established for modern samples. *Schistosoma mansoni* and *S. haematobium* worm, cercaria and egg DNA were obtained from Christies Hospital, Manchester (UK) to use as positive controls. Negative controls were also incorporated into the study, that is distilled water and reagents only.

The usual guidelines for ancient molecular work were followed. Positive controls were amplified and extracted in a separate area from the ancient samples. The ancient samples were studied in a separate laboratory where PCR was not performed. All steps were conducted under sterile conditions. If possible, experiments were also repeated to confirm the results.

Extraction of genomic DNA from mummy tissue

Extraction of mummy DNA was performed using proteinase K buffer followed by phenol, based on published methods by Sambrook et al. (1989). Each crushed tissue sample (~200 mg) was placed into 1,000 μl proteinase K buffer and 50 μl proteinase K stock solution (10 mg/ml). Incubation times were often increased to ensure proper digestion had occurred. Digestion of tissue samples was variable, according to tissue type and condition. As each sample was unique, no standard time limit was set. Adequate digestion was achieved once the tissue had totally merged with the solution. After digestion a standard phenol extraction was performed.

Extraction of DNA by using DNAzol

Approximately 500 mg of mummy tissue or 50 mg of modern liver tissue was homogenised in 1 ml of DNAzol, a guanidine detergent lysing solution (Helena Biosciences, UK), and then left at room temperature for ten minutes. The homogenate was sedimented by centrifugation for ten minutes at 10,000 G. The protocol then followed the manufacturer's guidelines. The extracted DNA was resuspended in 8 mM NaOH, pH 7.8.

Extraction of ancient DNA by using instagene matrix

Approximately 200 mg of ancient tissue was crushed with a pestle and mortar and placed into a sterile Eppendorf tube. One milliliter of 1 X trypsin/ethylenediamine tetraacetic acid was added, gently mixed, and left to stand at room temperature for thirty minutes. The extraction then followed the manufacturer's guidelines (Chelex, BioRad, UK). Twenty microliter aliquots were used for PCR.

Amplification of S. haematobium *and* S. mansoni *DNA from modern and ancient samples*

The author optimised the PCRs, using information from a range of published methods (Pääbo 1989; Sambrook et al. 1989) and recommendations from Promega (UK). Primers were designed by the author to amplify 236 bp of S. *haematobium* cytochrome oxidase C and S. *mansoni* cytochrome C DNA. These were:

1. S. *mansoni* 1 5′ TCTAAGGAATAAAGATTCG 3′
2. S. *mansoni* 2 5′ CATACCACAACTATTCAAC, 3′
3. S. *haematobium* 1 5′ GATAAGTAATAATGATTCATC 3′
4. S. *haematobium* 2 5′ GACCCACAGCTTTTAAG 3′.
   Primers 1 and 2 were designed from Accession No: SHU22162 (Bowles et al. 1995).
   Primers 3 and 4 were designed from Accession No: SHU82266 (Blair et al. 1997).

A range of experiments, using different temperatures, amounts of magnesium (i.e. 2 mM–8mM), the enzyme Deep Vent (exo-) *Taq* polymerase (New England Biolabs, UK, 2 U–4 U), and DNA templates (1 µl–20 µl) have been conducted. The optimum 100-µl reaction contained: 4 U of (exo-) *Taq* polymerase, 200 µM dNTPs, 4 mM MgSO4, 1 µM of each primer, made up to 90 µl per reaction, with ×1 ThermoPol buffer (supplied with [exo] *Taq* polymerase). Ten microliters of either the ancient or modern DNA extract was added. Two controls of reagents only and distilled water were also included.

The reactions were then amplified in a thermal cycler (Cyclone, Techne) as follows: First cycle –94°C for 5 minutes, 50°C for 2 minutes, 72°C for 3 minutes; followed by 28 cycles of –94°C for 1 minute, 50°C for 1 minute, 72°C for 1 minute; and a final cycle of –94°C for 1 minute, 50°C for 2 minutes, and 72°C for 10 minutes.

The ancient samples were amplified for 38 cycles as opposed to the 28 cycles used for the modern samples. Ten microliter aliquots of the amplified DNA were viewed on a 1 per cent agarose gel stained with 2 µl of ethidium bromide.

Sequencing and precipitation of sequenced DNA

The PCR products were purified to remove dNTPs and primers by using the Qiquick Gel Extraction Kit (Qiagen, UK). After quantitating the amount of DNA present after amplification and purification, a sequencing reaction for each sample was set up as follows: To a 1-ml Eppendorf tube, 1 μl (10 ng) of DNA template was added, plus 4 μl of terminator ready reaction mix, 1 μl (5 pmol) of primer 1 or primer 2 to ensure that both forward and reverse sequences were obtained. Fourteen microliters of deionized water was also added to make the total reaction up to 20 μl. After gentle mixing, the tubes were placed into a thermal cycler (Cyclone, Techne). Twenty-five cycles were run at the following temperatures and times: 96°C for 10 seconds, 50 °C for 5 seconds, and 60°C for 4 minutes. Precipitation of the DNA followed the methods outlined by the manufacturer (ABI, UK). The precipitated DNA was then passed to the 'in house' sequencing department.

Results and discussion

DNA extraction results

The average yield of DNA extracted from modern eggs, worms, and cercariae by using phenol was in excess of 1 mg/ml, with a purity of 93 per cent.

Extracting DNA from 0.2 g of ancient tissue by using DNAzol (Helena Biosciences, UK) produced an average yield of 393 μg/ml, with a purity of 61 per cent; however, amplification was unsuccessful, even after several different amounts of ancient DNA template, *Taq* enzyme, and magnesium were added. Amplification of DNA extracts obtained from incubation with Chelex (BioRad, UK) was also unsuccessful.

The supernatant containing the DNA was very dark and could not be assessed by spectrometry. Therefore, aliquots of the extracts were assessed by electrophoreses, which showed that the Chelex extractions did not produce clean preparations, as excessive smearing could clearly be seen. Such contamination inhibited amplification of both modern and ancient samples. Therefore, this type of extraction will no longer be used in future studies.

The DNA extracted from 0.2 g of ancient tissue by phenol X 2 (Sambrook et al. 1989) produced an average yield of 1,113 μg/ml, with a purity of 57.5 per cent. Although the purity was not markedly high, the average DNA yield was approximately four times greater than that extracted when using guanidine thiocyanate (DNAzol). It was the DNA extracted with phenol that was successfully amplified from pelvic tissue taken from Leicester Museum mummy No. 1.

When extracting DNA from a modern sample, visual assessment of the sample plays an important part in obtaining a clear, uncontaminated extract. When working with ancient mummy tissues, this is very difficult to achieve as the mummification resin, dirt, and salts present are released into the solutions being used.

Working with dark brown solutions hinders the preparation markedly, and therefore, several centrifugation steps were sometimes necessary. Even after this, the preparation was often still slightly brown. This colour often obscured spectrometry readings and, therefore, before assessment could be performed, the sample had to be relatively clear in colour. The use of silica beads was considered, but there is often a loss of DNA with such beads (Hoss and Pääbo 1993); therefore, as only 1 to 2 per cent of DNA may still be present, it was decided not to pursue this option.

After extraction from modern samples, the DNA is often visible as small strands; however, it is often not visible in ancient extracts because of the discoloration of extraction solutions. Therefore, caution was always taken when separating the organic and inorganic phases with pipettes. The only sample in which the ancient DNA was visible after extraction had been taken from the liver of a twelfth Dynasty (c. 1900 B.C.) mummy, Nekht Ankh. This was not surprising, because, once treated with conditioning solution, this sample resembled modern liver.

Amplification of modern and ancient DNA

An amplification procedure for modern schistosome samples was established before an attempt was made to amplify any ancient samples. After several attempts in which different concentrations of the reagents were used, amplification of both S. *haematobium* and S. *mansoni* DNA fragments was achieved. The primers for each species were used on their respective DNA extracts, and on each other. This was done to establish the specificity of each primer. Each set of primers did not amplify the other species' DNA. The best results were achieved using 4 mM of $MgSO_4$ and 2 U of *Taq*, and thereafter, this was used for both modern and ancient DNA amplifications. The main variable changed in the ancient DNA amplification was the amount of ancient DNA template. After several attempts, it was established that 10 μl of the ancient DNA extract was the optimum amount to use.

The only ancient sample that produced an amplified DNA fragment over 200 bp in length was from the bladder of Leicester Museum mummy No. 1. Sequencing confirmed that the fragment was 209 bp of S. *haematobium* cytochrome oxidase C subunit. Amplification and sequencing were time-consuming and there were many failures. If unsuccessful, the finite samples cannot be retested indefinitely, and therefore, false negatives and positives are often the only results available from a first or second attempt.

Initial immunostaining tests suggest that Leicester Museum mummy No. 1 was infected with schistosome worms and eggs; however, distorted egg shapes, combined with nonspecificity of the polyclonal antiserum for a particular species, meant that the species type had to be investigated at the DNA level. Successful amplification and sequencing of the S. *haematobium* species cytochrome oxidase C sequence has now enabled the actual species to be identified.

This identification ensures that for the ancient epidemiology study, it should be easier to distinguish between the two species, S. *mansoni* and S. *haematobium*, that are present in modern Egypt. Until now, S. *mansoni* DNA has not been amplified or sequenced in the ancient samples, thus supporting the theory that only S. *haematobium* existed in ancient Egypt.

Other studies

The Manchester research has added to knowledge about the practicalities of ancient DNA work. Several protocols commonly used in molecular work have proved to be impractical, whereas others have proved to be effective. More recently, this knowledge has been successfully applied to several other ancient DNA projects (see Chapters 15 and 17) performed by Master of Science students at Manchester, under the author's supervision (Harper 2003; Parker 2003; Bibby 2005; Schrieber-Goshe 2005; Smyth 2005; Bratcher 2006; Bzdega 2006).

Harper's study involved the extraction, amplification, and sequencing of DNA from ancient barley and wheat seeds. Attempts to amplify 822 and 162 bp of chloroplast DNA were only partly successful. The amplification of the 822 bp would have supported the theory of Goldenberg et al. (1990) that ancient DNA can be present in excess of 500 bp, but unfortunately, only 162 bp were amplified. Interestingly, when one seed was sterilized and placed onto plant growth media, a callus formed for a limited period, suggesting that part or all of the DNA responsible for cell division was still intact. Eventually, the callus collapsed and the seed was sectioned and plated onto several separate growth media.

The collapsed seed and callus have now been analysed by Bzdega (2006), using a comparative study of Rutherford's established protocols and commercial kits. It was hoped to amplify the larger fragment (822 bp), which may have indicated new cell and DNA generation, but unfortunately, only 162 bp have been amplified. The addition of the enzyme Restorase (Sigma, UK) was also explored, but no extended DNA fragments were amplified, suggesting that the template is beyond repair. This particular seed is approximately

4,000 years old and may therefore be too degraded for Restorase to have any effect. The commercial kit for general PCR made the experiments less time-consuming, as it entailed a one-step preparation, but apart from this advantage, the final results were not improved.

Another project (Parker 2003) addressed the issue of identifying ancient remains. A collection of mummified cats and cat remains in the Manchester Museum has been catalogued as specific breeds. For example, one particularly large detached cat head, covered with black fur, was recorded as the head of a *Felis Silvestris*, on the basis that this is a large breed. Successful DNA amplification and sequencing has now confirmed this visual identification; this conclusion is based on the amplification of a small sequence of 301 bp, which has a 97 per cent match to modern *Felis Silvestris*.

These established protocols were utilized in three further studies. One project established the gender of a mummy (Bibby 2005), another focused on sibship studies relating to the mummies of the 'Two Brothers,' Nekht Ankh and Khnum Nakht, in the Manchester Museum collection (Smyth 2005), and the third analysed samples from the mummy Asru for the presence of the cancer-causing gene BRCA1, as previous research by Tapp (1984) had suggested the presence of a cancerous growth (Schrieber-Goshe 2005).

Apart from the sibship study, both nuclear and mtDNA were targeted. Not surprisingly, the nuclear DNA was not successfully amplified, but all three mummies yielded mtDNA fragments from the hyper variable region 1 (HVR1), which enabled Smyth (2005) to conduct a genetic statistical analysis on the sequenced results by using a forensic population database. The results suggest that it is 185 times more likely that they are related than unrelated.

Finally, molecular analysis has been performed on liver samples taken from mummies from the Dakhleh Oasis to identify the presence of *P. falciparum*. Because an immunostaining method (Rutherford 1997, 1999, 2000, 2002, 2005) performed by Marmion (2003) had already yielded tentative positive results, Bratcher (2006) undertook further immunoassaying and genetic analysis to reinforce this work

Many of the above-noted projects were repeated more than once, and were independently amplified and sequenced by the separate sequencing laboratory at the University of Manchester. To reinforce such results, the findings should also be replicated at independent laboratories, but unfortunately, because of the scarcity of tissue samples, it is not always possible to repeat the tests. Nevertheless, there is a significant difference between this current research and the first schistosomiasis study, in that the amount of tissue now required is as little as 20 mg. Thus, it is more likely that it will be possible to repeat tests in future work.

Conclusion

Scientists in this field have faced many challenges, but innovations have been introduced as the number of investigations has increased. For example, the extracted inhibitors once common in amplification experiments are now often eliminated by the use of GuScn and silica beads (Hoss and Pääbo 1993). Also, coextractions of bacterial and fungal genomes are now no longer amplified, as the great care taken in designing primers that are species specific (i.e. human or schistosome) eliminates the mispriming of these exogenous DNA templates which may yield small spurious PCR products.

The problems relating to contamination with contemporary DNA have also inspired the establishment of facilities such as the Ancient Biomolecules Centre, housed in the Museum of Natural History, Oxford University (www1). This enables sterile studies to be undertaken, as the environment is reportedly free from contaminants such as skin flakes and exhaled cells. To eliminate these contaminants, the building is provided with positive air pressure and HEPA filtering systems, and the researchers are required to remove clothing and to be cleansed by means of air-showers, before entering the centre.

Although future research undoubtedly holds many answers, there will always be limits. One of the main limiting factors is the natural degradation of the DNA molecule, and researchers are now resigned to the fact that most ancient DNA is preserved in fragments no longer than 300 bp (Pääbo et al. 1989; Kaestle and Horsburgh 2002; Rutherford 2002). This problem is now being addressed by designing primers that amplify small fragments of the genome and specific regions that are connected to family traits and diseases.

As mitochondrial DNA is inherited exclusively from the mother, targeting the mtDNA can follow the maternal line. In contrast, targeting nuclear DNA fragments that are inherited within family groups, such as short tandem repeats (STRs), variable number tandem repeats (VNTRs) and human leocyte antigens (HLAs), can show family relationships and perhaps migration patterns. Nuclear point mutations such as a single base pair change may also highlight the presence of diseases such as cystic fibrosis and sickle cell anaemia. However, the majority of primers that are designed to highlight the presence of disease target mitochondrial DNA for reasons already discussed. Primers have been successfully designed for detecting diseases such as schistosomiasis (Rutherford 2002), syphilis (Fornaciari 1989), Chagas' disease (Fornaciari 1992; Guhl 1997; Guhl et al.1999), and malaria (Salleres et al. 2000). The diagnosis of other diseases, using similar methods, will inevitably follow the same path.

There is also no direct correlation between the age of a sample and its DNA preservation, and even if similar in age, remains from different environments may yield different amounts of DNA (Haynes et al. 2002). Neither, according to Hoss et al. (1996), is there any correlation between preservation and tissue type, although bones and teeth provide better protection for ancient DNA because the DNA binds to the hydroxyapatite in the bone matrix. An individual assessment should be undertaken of any remains because no two samples are the same. The environmental factors for each will be different, even if the material has been excavated as a group from one burial ground, because the same degradation factors may not have been present in all the burial sites.

The debate continues regarding whether ancient DNA is present in many samples, particularly dehydrated tissues. Some researchers have concluded that high temperatures are detrimental to DNA survival and that permafrost is the ideal preservation medium. It is the author's opinion that one of the main factors is the removal of water. In ten years of working with ancient mummified tissues and seeds, only mtDNA has been amplified from several different samples. Some researchers insist that nuclear DNA is too degraded and therefore any positive results are merely contamination, but this would be disputed by the many groups who are now regularly targeting nuclear DNA. This is still a very new field, and in future, the use of sophisticated methods of analysis such as Stingray, Fourier transform infrared, mass spectrometry, and even in situ hybridisation may help to provide some of the answers.

CHAPTER 10

An introduction to analytical methods

Andrew P. Giże

Introduction – organic methods

Currently, the integration of organic analyses and interpretations with archaeology promises an exciting future. Some of the results obtained in studies undertaken in Manchester on pharmacological applications in Egyptology are discussed more fully in Chapter 13.

The objective of this review, however, is to introduce selected analytical methods to study organic matter in archaeological sites and materials. It is not a comprehensive guide to all techniques. The underlying theme is to guide the interested reader with an idea to be solved towards an appropriate analytical strategy. Following an introduction to sample preparation, the remainder of the chapter summarises general and spectroscopic methods that provide a general indication of organic composition, followed by physical techniques that ultimately yield detailed information at a molecular scale.

This review is based in part on an organic geochemical review by Simoneit and Giże (2000), in addition to those by Silverstein et al. (1974), Banwell (1983), and Peters and Moldowan (1993). Additional inorganic analytical reviews include Pollard and Heron (1996) and Gill (1997). An invaluable laboratory techniques text is *Vogel's Textbook of Practical Organic Chemistry* (Furniss et al. 1989). Essential data sources are *The Merck Index* (Budavari et al. 1989), *The Chemical Rubber Company Handbook of Chemistry and Physics* (Weast 1976), and Internet resources such as National Institute of Standards and Technology and Merck.

All organic analytical methods are constrained by organic matter properties, such as phase (solid, liquid, or gas), molecular structure (individual molecules or polymers), and molecular weight (to identify a molecule). Consequently, part of the analyst's aim is to render the organic material from an archaeological source into a form that can be analysed, without losing the information sought.

Organic matter in archaeological material is derived predominantly from biological precursors (e.g. flower wreaths, beeswax, and animal hides), as is organic matter from geological sources (e.g. bitumens). Biochemical synthesis is enzymatically controlled, resulting in relatively few compounds being synthesised. This helps the analyst because natural product chemistry forms a basis for interpreting data.

The organic analyst is usually concerned with carbon, as well as hydrogen, oxygen, nitrogen, sulphur, and phosphorus. The Group IV elements are unusual in that an atom of an element can bond to another atom of the same element or catenate. Carbon catenates to a greater extent than any other element, resulting in a major analytical consideration, isomerisation. If atomic absorption spectroscopy, for example, indicates the presence of arsenic, there is no other element with the same characteristic absorption lines as arsenic.

Identification of arsenic automatically fixes the atomic weight. Infrared (IR) analysis of an organic material will indicate bond energies, from which a structure can be deduced, but not the molecular weight. Alternatively, MS of the organic material may provide a molecular weight of, for example, 58 D. This fixes the hydrocarbon composition as C_4H_{10}, from which the isomers n-butane and methyl propane can be deduced (Figure 21), as well as other heteroatom compositions (i.e. C_3HgO and $CaHgS$). To unequivocally identify which isomer is the correct structure, an alternative analytical method, such as IR spectroscopy or GC, must be used. Although the inorganic chemist may have to use two independent analytical methods (e.g. x-ray crystallography to identify $CaCO_3$ polymorphs), the organic analyst must always use two independent methods before a molecular structure can be assigned.

A final organic analytical issue is determining the three-dimensional shape of the molecule or its stereochemistry. A small difference between two molecules in their stereochemistry can result in different interpretations. Figure 22 shows the structures of 5α(H)-cholestane and 5β(H)-cholestane. The two molecules differ only in that the hydrogen at the carbon-labelled 5 is directed away from (5α) or towards (5β) the reader. The 5α(H)-cholestane is derived from the ubiquitous cholesterol, and is common in recent sediments. The 5β(H)-cholestane, however, is derived from the faeces of carnivores (including humans), and can be used as a marker of carnivores.

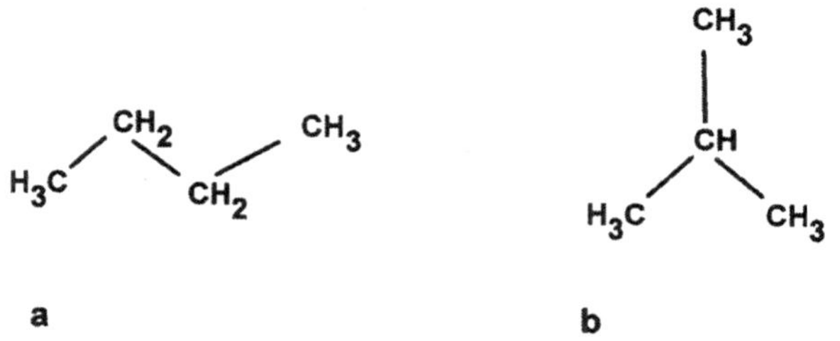

FIGURE 21. Isomers of $C_4 H_{10}$. a: butane. b: methyl propane. *Credit: Andrew Gize.*

Sample preparation

Sample preservation should be considered at the site, with immediate protection from contamination sources, including suntan protection and vehicle exhausts. Museum samples may already be irreversibly contaminated, for example, from nicotine from cigarettes. Samples should be wrapped in aluminium foil (previously baked at >300°C to remove manufacturing oils) or sealed in Teflon or laminated polycarbonate-polyethylene (Kapak) bags. Printer inks in newspaper can cause contamination. Other plastics

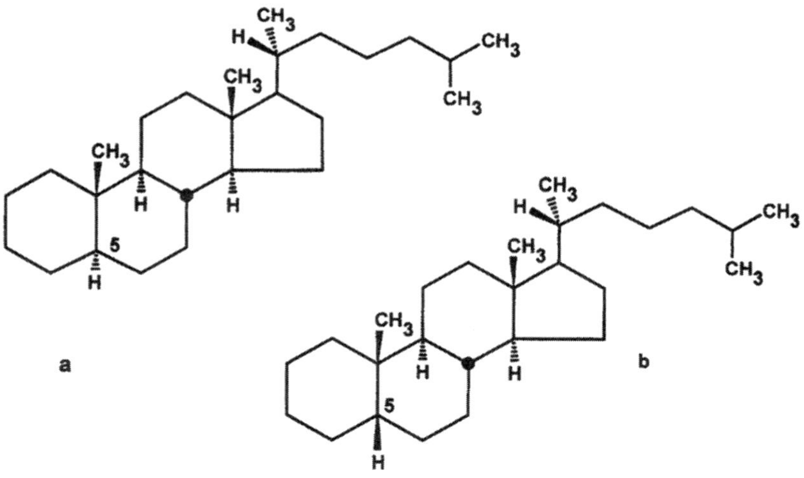

FIGURE 22. Diastereomers of cholestane. a: The hydrogen on carbon 5 is depicted as away from the reader (5). b: The hydrogen on carbon 5 is depicted towards the reader (5). *Credit: Andrew Gize.*

(polyethylene, plastic wraps, etc.) are renowned sources of contamination by plasticisers (phthalate esters).

In the laboratory, samples and extracts must not be exposed to direct sunlight because organic compounds can be photosensitive. Sample trimming should be done with a water-cooled saw without any organic-based antirust. Organic concretions (e.g. resin and bitumen) can be hand picked for analysis by using a dissecting kit.

Organic matter can be extracted from a sample either by a Soxhlet apparatus or ultrasonic extraction (Furniss et al. 1989). In Soxhlet extraction, the sample is placed in a preextracted cellulose or quartz thimble, and the organic matter is extracted with a negative azeotrope (e.g. toluene-methanol) or single solvent (e.g. dichloromethane) for a specified time (e.g. twenty-four–forty-eight hours). The extracted organic matter is obtained after evaporation of the solvent under reduced pressure in a rotary evaporator.

In ultrasonic extraction, the sample is placed in solvent and sonicated with a sonic probe in the sample. An ultrasonic waterbath is an inadequate alternative, resulting in poor extract yields. Soxhlet extraction provides higher yields, but with some loss of semivolatile compounds. Supercritical CO_2 is an alternative extraction technique (Schneider 1978; Hopfgartner et al. 1990) but the yields tend be less than other methods. The organic sample after extraction is the crude extract.

Chromatography

The crude extract can be analysed directly, but further separations are usually advisable to maximise the information available using the analytical methods available. Simplifying a complex mixture into compound classes, for example, focusses interpretation directly on a compound class, without ambiguities resulting from peak overlaps. Chromatography is the standard separation technique, being based on different partitioning of compounds in a complex mixture between two phases (solid-liquid, solid-gas, and liquid-gas).

Column chromatography (liquid chromatography) is a routine technique for separating organic compounds into compound classes by polarity, typically using a burette as the column. Using, for example, Al_2O_3/SiO_2 as the column stationary phase, the crude extract is separated into compound classes (e.g. saturated and aromatic hydrocarbons, and polars) by eluting with a series of mobile solvents with increasing polarity (e.g. hexane to methanol).

In thin-layer chromatography, the solid phase (e.g. silica and cellulose) is on a glass plate, and the mobile solvent moves up the coating. After sample chromatography, the separated bands are visualised under ultraviolet (UV) light or by application of iodine vapour or a dye. Fractions corresponding to the elution region of standards (e.g. hydrocarbons, aromatics, ketones, esters, and alcohols) are removed from the plate, extracted, and concentrated for further analysis. High-pressure (performance) liquid chromatography is a powerful separation technique for polar, nonvolatile, or thermally unstable compounds that are otherwise incapable of separation by other chromatographic methods.

Chromatographic separation will provide concentrates of a given class of organic compounds that can be analysed directly. Nevertheless, for some compound classes (e.g. saturated or aromatic hydrocarbons, and polars such as carboxylic acids and alcohols), further preparative work may be desirable.

The saturated hydrocarbons are often dominated by high concentrations of normal and isoprenoid alkanes, but the multi-ring compounds (e.g. derivatives of steroids) can be in such low concentrations that analysis is difficult. The molecular shape and size of the molecules can be used for further separation. Zeolite-based molecular sieves are available with various channel diameters. A 5-Å molecular sieve will extract the frequently dominating normal alkanes, leaving an extract containing branched and cyclic hydrocarbons only. Silicalite has larger channels that will accept normal and monomethyl alkanes, leaving a concentrate of cyclic saturated hydrocarbons (Hoering 1981).

Alternatively, urea and thiourea crystals can be grown in the saturated hydrocarbon fractions that will clathrate the normal alkanes and normal alkanes and isoprenoids, respectively. Isomers of polycyclic aromatic hydrocarbons can result in complex mixtures that are difficult to interpret (especially by UV spectroscopy). These compounds can be simplified by gel-permeation chromatography separation according to ring size (Giger and Blumer 1974). Polar compounds, including carboxylic acids, phenols, amino acids, and alcohols present a special problem in GC because of gas phase hydrogen bonding resulting in a broad peak that is difficult to quantify and may hide compounds that elute in a similar retention time. Thicker film and new bonded phases in GC columns have reduced these problems to some degree.

It is analytically more elegant, however, to cover the functional group, which contributes to hydrogen bonding by converting it to a derivative. Prior to analysis, carboxylic acids typically are derivatised to methyl esters, and phenols and alcohols to trimethylsilyl ether derivatives (Murphy 1969;

Pierce 1979). Murphy (1969) provides an introductory review of the separation of organic mixtures by chromatography, followed by molecular sieving, clathration, and derivatisation. Lee et al. (1981: 78–112) review other analytical schemes for aromatic hydrocarbons.

In any analysis, procedural blanks are essential because the concentrations of organic matter in many samples will be small and the potential for significant contamination is consequently greater. Widespread usage of plastics in laboratories results in phthalate esters being probably the most frequently encountered contaminants. In multiuser laboratories, blank solvents should be run first, primarily to eliminate ghost contamination from the previous user. When the extract yields are small (<1 mg), scrupulous care should be taken to eliminate losses by adsorption to glassware. A five weight per cent loss for submilligram samples can occur by adsorption in each stage in an analytical protocol (Giże 1984).

Pyrolysis

Some samples (e.g. ambers and hair) may not readily dissolve using solvent extraction, and have to be rendered into smaller fragments before chromatography. Pyrolysis is the nonoxidative thermal breakdown of a sample. A large molecule (a polymer), which cannot be analysed directly, is thermally broken into smaller fragments (pyrolysates) that are facile to analyse. From the pyrolysates, a conceptual image of the original macromolecule is deduced.

A simple pyrolysis system comprises a vertical quartz tube within a heater set at a determined temperature (e.g. 50–1,000°C), with an inert gas (e.g. helium) passed through the tube. The sample ($\approx$1 mg) is injected on a needle, or falls through the furnace, and is pyrolysed. The pyrolysis time is of the order of seconds, with $\approx$600°C a suitable temperature for many applications. An alternative pyrolysis system is to pass a current, using an inductive coil, through a ferromagnetic material (wire or foil). When the Curie point temperature of that material is reached, its temperature will not increase further.

Curie point pyrolysis is advantageous in the temperature control, but a furnace provides a complete range of temperatures in contrast to those fixed by Curie points. In both cases, the pyrolysates are flushed in the inert gas to a capillary column in a gas chromatograph, where they are cold trapped with liquid nitrogen prior to analysis (Wampler 1999).

Microscale sealed vessel is a mild pyrolysis method (Hall et al. 1999). In both furnace and Curie point pyrolysis, the thermal fragmentation results in artefacts, typically unsaturated fragments. For example, the pyrolysate may yield normal alkanes, but artefacts include mono- and dialkenes. The microscale sealed vessel method does not generate these artefacts. The sample ($\approx$1 mg) is placed in a capillary tube and packed with precleaned silica sand. The sealed capillary and sample are oven heated (e.g. 300°C) for longer times (e.g. forty-eight–seventy-two hours). The capillary tube is then crushed in a heated gas chromatograph inlet to release the pyrolysates, which are cold trapped at the head of a capillary column before analysis.

A major advantage of pyrolysis is the small sample size, whereby virtually negligible samples can be taken from an archaeological artefact, and considerable molecular information can be obtained. The disadvantage is that all the pyrolysate is analysed, and significant compounds in low concentrations are more difficult to detect. Pyrolysis offers a rapid molecular screening technique to identify samples that have the potential to offer more information when using larger sample masses.

Spectroscopy

Introduction

Archaeological material is irreplaceable and consequently nondestructive methods are preferable. Analytical approaches to screen samples should be undertaken before deciding which have the potential to offer the most information by destructive methods. Spectroscopy offers nondestructive methods to provide detailed information on the structure of polymers and individual compounds. Even without detailed interpretation, spectroscopy can 'fingerprint' samples into groups, enabling a preliminary classification. Spectroscopy, however, does not yield molecular weight. Additional introductory sources include Banwell (1983) and Smith and March (2000).

Electromagnetic spectrum

The electromagnetic spectrum is a continuum, but is analytically divided into several regions (Figure 23; Banwell 1983), with each region involving a different electronic or magnetic response of the sample to the incident radiation.

1. UV and visible spectroscopy: the region covers 3×10^{14} to 3×10^{16} Hz, with wavelengths of 1–10 nm. The spectroscopy involves excitation of valence electrons, requiring energies 10^5–10^7 kJ mol^{-1}.

2. IR spectroscopy: the region covers 3×10^{12} to 3×10^{14} Hz, with wave-lengths of 1–100 μm. The spectroscopy involves molecular vibrations that change dipole moments, requiring energies $\approx 10^4$ J mol^{-1}.

3. Radiofrequency spectroscopy: the frequencies involved are used in nuclear magnetic and electron paramagnetic resonance spectroscopy. The region covers 3×10^6 to 3×10^{10} Hz, with wavelengths of 1 cm–10 m. The spectroscopy involves reversal of the spin of a nucleus or electron, requiring energies 10^{-3} to 10 J mol^{-1}.

Ultraviolet spectroscopy

Molecular absorption in the UV (and visible) regions of the spectrum affects the electronic structure of the molecule. The absorption of energy is quantised, resulting in the elevation, or excitation, of electrons from ground state orbitals to excited states in higher energy orbitals. Consequently, two measurements may be made. The intensity of absorption (or transmittance) can be measured versus the frequency of irradiation. Alternatively, the energy emitted in the visible range can be measured as the excited electrons drop back to the ground state.

UV spectroscopy is limited to analysis of conjugate bonds, which are double bonds in sequence stabilised by additional Π-bonding as, for example, in benzene. One aspect of UV spectroscopy is that characteristic UV-absorbing bonds can be recognised in molecules with very different structures. The UV spectra of pure compounds usually show some detail or fine structure. Mixtures of compounds yield spectra in which fine structure is lost or reduced as a result of peak overlap. Consequently, UV spectroscopy is best used in conjunction with other analytical methods, such as GC/MS.

Visible spectroscopy

The visible region of the spectrum can also be used in two ways. One method is the use of colour. The second is the absorbance in the visible spectrum by certain molecular compounds. The visible part of the electromagnetic spectrum can be used for the identification and quantification of ring compounds such as the porphyrins, and pigments such as henna.

Infrared spectroscopy

The IR region is one of the most useful for the organic analyst because it is where changes in dipole moment resulting from bond vibrations are

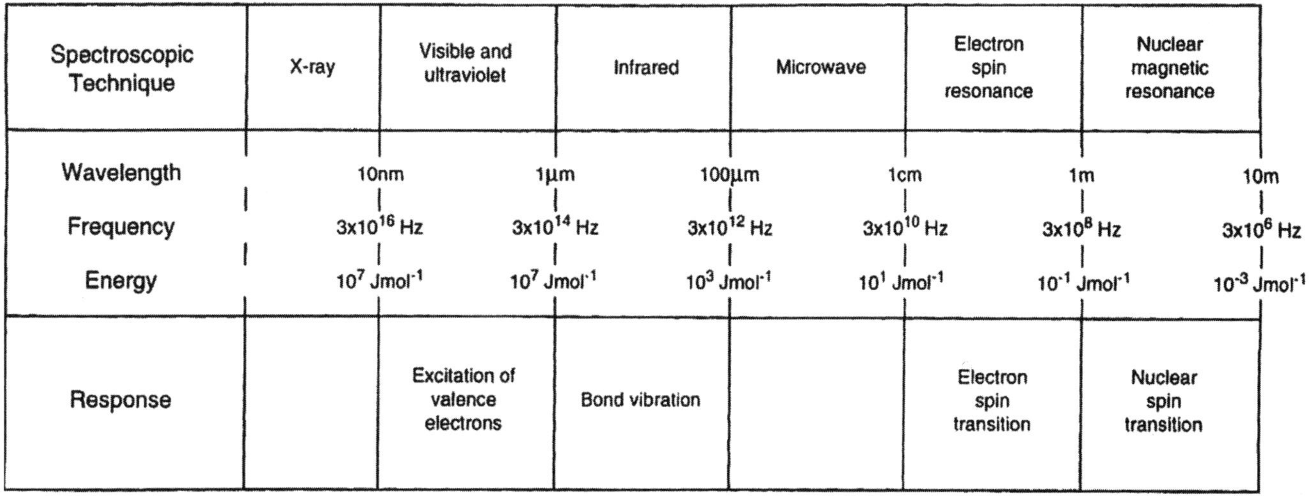

Spectroscopic Technique	X-ray	Visible and ultraviolet	Infrared	Microwave	Electron spin resonance	Nuclear magnetic resonance
Wavelength	10nm	1µm	100µm	1cm	1m	10m
Frequency	3×10^{16} Hz	3×10^{14} Hz	3×10^{12} Hz	3×10^{10} Hz	3×10^{8} Hz	3×10^{6} Hz
Energy	10^{7} Jmol^{-1}	10^{7} Jmol^{-1}	10^{3} Jmol^{-1}	10^{1} Jmol^{-1}	10^{-1} Jmol^{-1}	10^{-3} Jmol^{-1}
Response		Excitation of valence electrons	Bond vibration		Electron spin transition	Nuclear spin transition

FIGURE 23. The electromagnetic spectrum. (after Banwell, C. N. 1983. *Fundamentals of molecular spectroscopy*. 3rd edn. London: McGraw-Hill.) *Credit: Andrew Gize.*

recorded. In the author's opinion, IR spectroscopy provides the best 'finger-printing' method.

IR spectroscopy can be performed on organic products, such as extracts and bitumens. Spectra can be obtained on gases, liquids, and solids. Liquids can be examined in a cell or as smears on salt plates or pellets of silver chloride or potassium bromide. Solids can be examined either as a mull or powdered with potassium bromide and then pressed to make a pellet.

Quantification of chemical groups can be obtained by use of band intensities (Rouxhet et al. 1980) with application of the Beer-Lambert Law and determination of the absorption coefficient, K. When similar materials are studied by IR spectroscopy, K is anticipated to be proportional to the concentration of the chemical groups contributing to the absorption band.

Fourier transform infrared spectroscopy

A development in spectroscopy has been Fourier-transform infrared (FTIR) spectroscopy (for an introduction to Fourier transform, see Banwell 1983). The previous method of collecting spectra was by recording the absorbance at each point of the spectrum separately. Until relatively recently, it was only in the visible and UV regions that the whole spectrum could be recorded simultaneously as a photographic plate. FTIR now provides simultaneous and almost instantaneous recording of the whole spectrum in the IR, microwave, and magnetic resonance regions.

One advantage of FTIR is that spectra can be collected and summed in seconds. With FTIR, 4,000 scans can be obtained and summed in less than an hour. The result of the additions is that noise is eliminated or reduced, and absorbing bands are enhanced. Consequently, FTIR can be used on seemingly opaque material or very small samples.

Nuclear magnetic resonance

Nuclear magnetic resonance (NMR) is another form of absorption spectroscopy, in which a sample can absorb electromagnetic radiation at radiofrequencies governed by the atomic nuclei in the sample. Silverstein et al. (1974) provide an introduction to NMR.

The nuclei of interest in organic chemistry are ^{12}C and ^{16}O, and ^{1}H, and ^{13}C. The NMR signals produced, for example by ^{1}H, will depend upon the bonds present. Originally, NMR could be obtained only on liquids. More recently, it has been possible to obtain high-resolution spectra of solids using cross-polarization magic-angle sample-spinning NMR spectrometry.

Lambert et al. (2002) suggest that NMR is an appropriate method to fingerprint and classify the sources of resins from Africa and the Americas.

Electron paramagnetic (spin) resonance

The primary application of electron paramagnetic resonance (EPR) or spin (ESR) lies in determining if samples have been burnt. For example, Hayes and Schurr (2002) have suggested EPR to be applicable to determining the thermal histories of burnt bones.

Permanent magnetization occurs only in ferromagnetic and ferrimagnetic substances, in which the magnetization persists outside of an external magnetic field. An induced magnetization can occur in the presence of an external magnetic field. When the magnetization is proportional to the applied magnetic field, the material is referred to as paramagnetic or diamagnetic. Electron paramagnetic- (or spin-) resonance (EPR or ESR) spectroscopy is based on the electron spin of free radicals. When the electron of a free radical is placed in a magnetic field, the electron has one of two possible orientations, which have spin quantum numbers of $m = +1$ and $m = -1$. A transition from the lower to the upper energy state is effected by absorption of electromagnetic radiation of a suitable frequency.

Applications of EPR have been reviewed by Marchand and Conard (1980). Initially, the paramagnetic centres in thermally immature organic matter are localised. During thermal alteration, volatile organic groups are broken as free radicals from the parent material ($-CH_3$, $-C_2H_5$, etc.), leaving an unpaired electron on the parent. The residual solid becomes progressively aromatic, with the unpaired electrons remaining delocalised throughout the molecules. With increasing temperature or time, they grow more delocalised as the aromatic domains become larger. At $900°C$, or when time is very long, the free electrons become more numerous until, at the stage when the graphite lattice is formed, the electrons become free to move along the graphite layers.

EPR therefore has been considered as a palaeotemperature index, but should be utilised as such with extreme caution (Marchand and Conard 1980). There is no direct correspondence between the paramagnetic susceptibility and the palaeotemperatures. Time must be considered with temperature. The paramagnetic susceptibility also depends upon the biological source of the organic matter. Therefore, EPR should be used in conjunction with other methods.

Microscopy

The advantage of microscopy is that an immediate visual image is obtained. Spectroscopy offers nondestructive analytical methods to the analyst. When combined with microscopy, a pinhead sample or a few hairs can be removed and returned to an artefact. One key piece of information from microscopy is the extent to which a sample is homogeneous or heterogeneous. Gas chromatography/mass spectrometry, for example, can provide detailed molecular information on a few hair strands, but microscopy alone will give information on whether the analyses apply to unaltered hairs, fungally degraded hairs, or hairs which have been henna coated.

Ultraviolet light microscopy

In UV, or fluorescence microscopy, the sample is irradiated with UV light, ideally filtered to a fixed wavelength (e.g. 546 nm). If the sample contains areas with functional groups in which electrons are excited by UV radiation, then those areas will emit light in the visible spectrum as the electrons fall back to lower energy levels. As an example, hairs from a Manchester Museum mummy are shown in Plate XV.

Visible light microscopy

Microscopes using visible light which is passed through the sample are commonplace in many laboratories, and will not be described further here.

In polarized light systems, light is initially passed through a polar, which limits the plane of light vibration to one direction only (e.g. 0° and 180°). If the plane of light is not changed by passing through the sample, placing a second polar at 90° to the first (e.g. 90° and 270°) will filter out all light, and the viewer will not see any light from the sample. If the sample rotates the plane of polarized light to the left or right, then some light will pass through the second polar to form a visible image. The information obtained on the sample is varied, including whether it is optically active or the crystallography.

In reflected light systems, light can be reflected back from the surface of an opaque sample to give an image of its surface features. Alternatively, light may pass into the sample before being reflected back. If polars are placed with their vibration planes set at 90° to each other, before the light hits and is reflected back from the sample, the image colour seen is usually diagnostic of the material, and is termed 'internal reflections.'

Infrared microscopy (with R. Speak, School of Chemistry, University of Manchester)

IR microscopy is a relatively new nondestructive technique. Rather than using a single detector, the microscopy system uses a detector array (e.g. 64 × 64 detectors). This array provides an IR image of an area of approximately 400 × 400 μm, with a resolution of ≈7 μm. With the advantage of Fourier transform data manipulation, an entire set of 4,096 spectra can be collected and processed in less than five minutes in the range of 4,000–1,000 cm^{-1} with a 16-cm^{-1} spectral resolution.

By cross-indexing the 4,096 spectra, false-colour two-dimensional IR images are produced which relate the chemical content (using the diagnostic vibrational absorbance frequencies of the molecular bonds in the substance) to its location within the object area. For example, the distribution of organic matter within a matrix can be determined by mapping the ~2,900 cm^{-1} C-H stretch band that is characteristic of aliphatic compounds.

Shown in Plate XVI are optical and IR images of a hair from the twenty-fifth Dynasty mummy of Asru, a chantress from the Temple of Amun at Karnak. The lumpy nature of the optical picture, echoed by the average IR picture, is considered to be due to a paste of oils and dyes applied to the scalp and hair. This theory is borne out by the uneven orange colouring on the hair, suggestive of henna.

The active ingredient in henna is hydoxynaphthoquinone, a light yellow crystalline compound when pure. In henna, it complexes and oxidises to produce the characteristic orange colour. The uneven coating on the hair suggests it was applied after death as part of the ritual preparation process rather than as a cosmetic during life, an identical interpretation to that obtained from another mummy (Plate XV). Mapping the 1,600 to 1,700-cm^{-1} C=O and aromatic carbon region produces an image with bright spots roughly corresponding to the orange areas in the optical picture, not inconsistent with the application of the aromatic oil/henna mix.

Molecular analysis

Stereochemistry

Stereochemistry refers to the three-dimensional shape of molecules. An understanding of stereochemistry is required to appreciate not only GC and MS data, but also every aspect of natural product organic chemistry, including biological sources for archaeological and geological materials, reaction mechanisms, and the thermodynamic stability of organic matter. Using GC/MS, information is obtained not only on molecular structure, which supplements spectroscopic interpretations, but the molecular weight is obtained. With this information, highly specific questions can be answered, such as the source of bitumens in mummy wrappings, and agricultural practices.

To appreciate especially the power of coupled GC/MS as an analytical method, a brief introduction to stereochemistry and some terminology is essential. Stereochemical terminology can be initially daunting, as it is partly the result of a need to communicate three-dimensional information on the two dimensions of a book page. It is the author's view that the best method of appreciating stereochemistry is to use commercially available stick-and-ball chemical model kits. Such models immediately teach understanding of bond rotation and symmetry, in addition to providing therapeutic pleasure and office decorations. Stereochemistry is reviewed in most organic chemistry textbooks, including Smith and March (2000).

The electronic structure of carbon can be represented initially as $1s^2$, $2s^2$, with the remaining two unpaired electrons in two of the three $2p$ shells. One arrangement of the $2s$ and $2p$ electrons in bonding is by hybridisation to sp^3. In this instance, the carbon valency is 4, with bonds forming a tetrahedral arrangement with bond angles of 109° 28′. If two or more carbons are linked by sp^3 hybridised bonds, then the molecule (or section of a molecule) is commonly termed saturated. The nomenclature of saturated hydrocarbons is an ending in –ane (e.g. methane). A second arrangement in bonding of the $2s$ and $2p$ electrons is by sp^2 hybridisation. The resultant carbon has three bonds in a plane, with an ideal bond angle of 120°.

Bonds formed by sp^2 hybridisation are commonly termed unsaturated, or double. Such bonds are relatively unstable and are prone to addition of an atom to form a saturated bond. The special exception are the aromatic hydrocarbons, in which carbons linked by conjugate sp^2 hybridised bonds are rendered very stable (and therefore persistent in the natural environment) by electron delocalisation. Unsaturated hydrocarbons end in –ene (e.g. ethylene, benzene). One other possible arrangement of the $2s$ and $2p$ electrons in bonding is by sp hybridisation to form triple bonds. Compounds with sp hybridised bonds end in –yne. In natural environments, sp bonds are usually extremely unstable, and thus can be neglected in the context of this introduction.

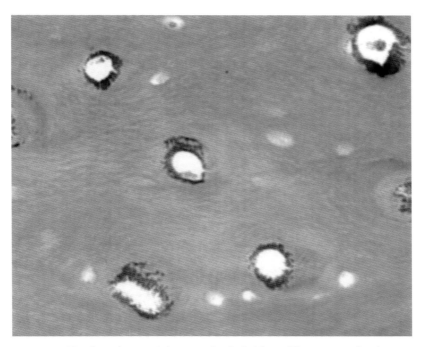

PLATE VII. *Histological section of ancient decalcified bone.* This section of trichrome-stained, decalcified bone demonstrates the edge effect of putrefaction and oxidation. Where the edge of the bone has been degraded, it is red, whereas the normal green stain is evident in the bulk of the bone. This edge effect is particularly noticeable in bone, as the soft tissues commonly show the reversal throughout the tissue. *Credit: John Denton.*

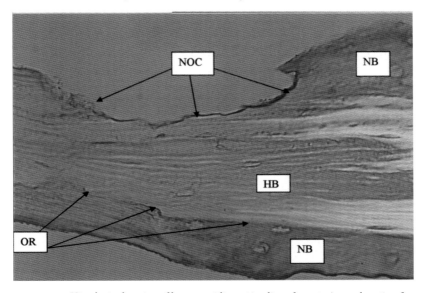

PLATE VIII. *Histological section of bone providing a timeline of events.* An explanation for the abnormalities in this section of bone can be explained by piecing together a timeline of events. *Credit: John Denton.*

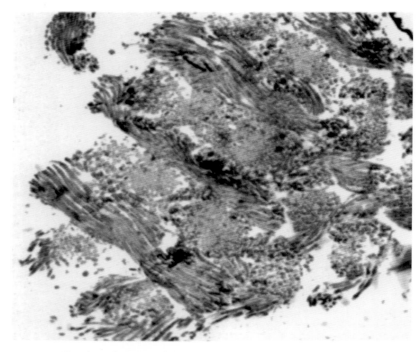

PLATE IX. *Histological section of Egyptian bandage*. This section of bandage from a mummy shows the twisted bundled of flax forming the warp and weft of the linen. At the microscopic level, positive identification of the structure of the cloth, and the type of fibre of which it is composed can be made with a great degree of certainty. *Credit: John Denton*.

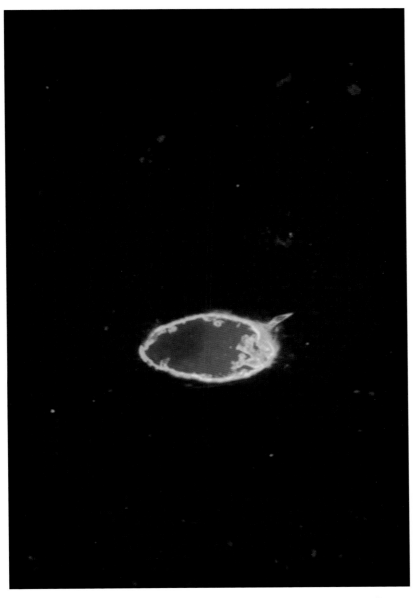

PLATE X. *Positive staining of* S. mansoni *ova within infected mouse liver.* ×100. If cut in the correct orientation, the lateral spike can be clearly seen. *Credit: Patricia Rutherford.*

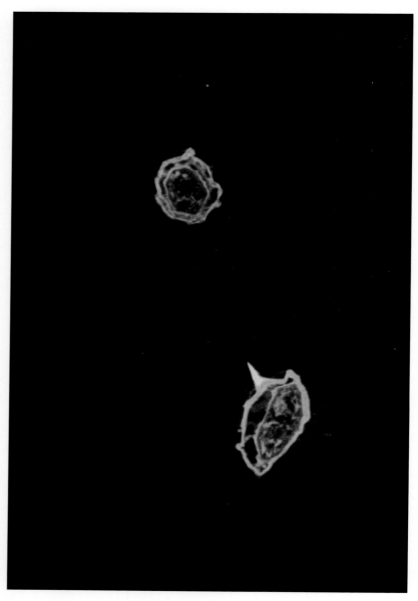

PLATE XI. *Positive staining of* S. mansoni *ova within infected mouse liver.* ×100. The classic oval shapes are not always seen. *Credit: Patricia Rutherford.*

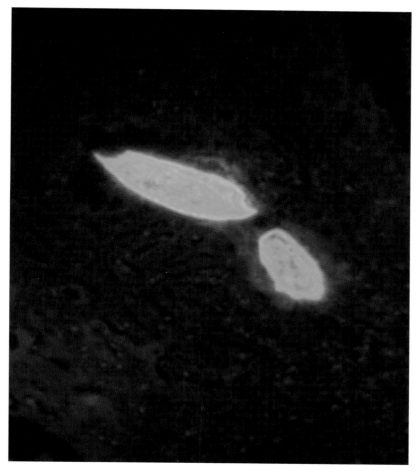

PLATE XII. *Positive staining of* S. haematobium *within infected hamster liver.* ×100. *Credit: Patricia Rutherford.*

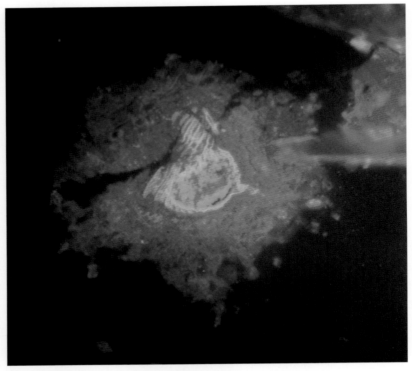

PLATE XIII. *Positive staining of bladder tissue from a mummy.* ×100. Tissue from the bladder of Mummy 7700.1766 (Manchester Museum). The distorted shape of the ova means that species identification is often difficult. *Credit: Patricia Rutherford.*

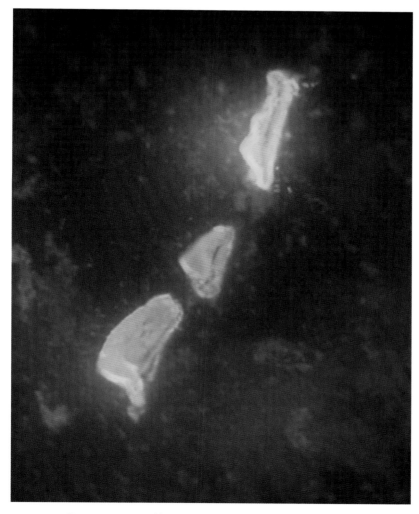

PLATE XIV. *Positive staining of bladder tissue from a mummy.* ×100. The ova in this 2,000-year-old, dehydrated, mummified tissue from the bladder of Mummy 7700.1766 (Manchester Museum) still resemble the modern S. *haematobium* seen in Plate XII. *Credit: Patricia Rutherford.*

PLATE XV. *Ultraviolet fluorescence microscopy of hair taken from the scalp of a mummy.* The hairs are coated with an orange fluorescing material, which developed droplets at the hair ends. The observation is that the hair was cut before the coating was applied. The interpretation is that the coating was not applied as part of a daily cosmetic routine, but is probably connected to mummification rituals. Width of view: 0.8 mm. *Credit: N. McCreesh, University of Manchester, unpublished data.*

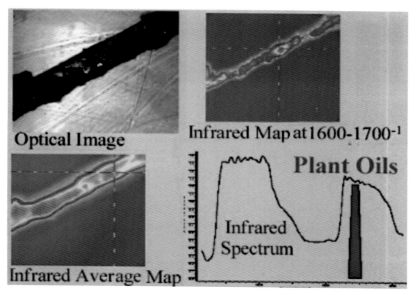

Optical Image

Infrared Map at 1600-1700^{-1}

Plant Oils

Infrared
Spectrum

Infrared Average Map

PLATE XVI. *Visible light and infrared images of a hair from the mummy of Asru.* Top left: hair (colourless) with darker coating. Bottom left: Infrared image over entire infrared spectrum, showing organic material unevenly coating the hair (red colour indicates highest infrared activity). Top right: infrared image over the range 1,600–1,700 cm -1 only, indicative of the concentration of $C = O$ on the hair. Bottom right: Anticipated infrared absorbtion area if hair was coated with plant oils. *Credit: Andrew Gize.*

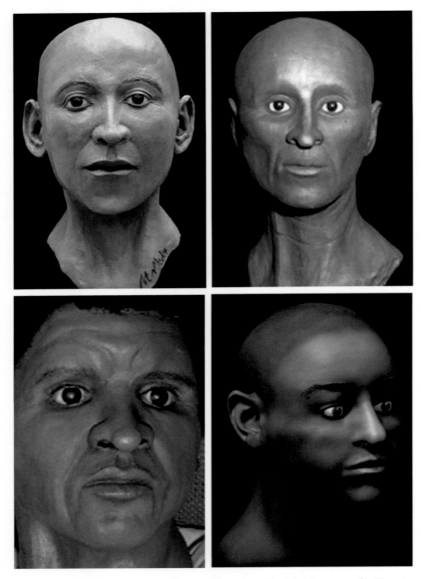

PLATE XVII. *Facial reconstruction of ancient Egyptians.* Top left: Nesperennub – Twenty-Second Dynasty priest (British Museum). Top right: Lady X – unknown mummy found in the tomb of Seti II (Egyptian Museum, Cairo). Bottom left: Janus – mummy of a man (Groningen Museum, The Netherlands). Bottom right: A 3,800-year-old female mummy (Georges-Labit Museum Toulouse, France). Facial reconstructions by Caroline Wilkinson, Dundee University (UK). *Credit: Caroline Wilkinson and University of Manchester.*

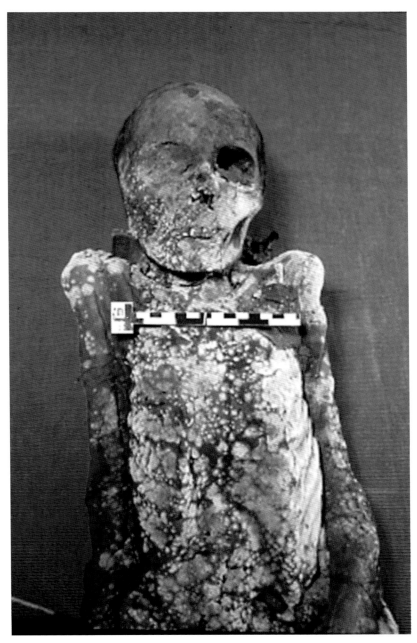

PLATE XVIII. *Mummy covered with efflorescence and mould growth*. Due to inept environmental storage conditions over many years, the partially unwrapped mummy has suffered physical damage. *Credit: Antony E. David.*

PLATE XIX. *Hand and torso of the mummy after conservation treatment.* The wet sterilization method has been used to successfully treat this mummy. *Credit: Antony E. David.*

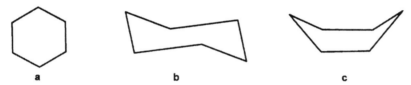

FIGURE 24. Depictions of cyclohexane. a: planar view. b: chair conformer. c: boat conformer. The chair and boat conformers are interchangeable by C – C bond rotation. *Credit: Andrew Gize.*

Isomers are compounds with the same empirical formula, but with different three-dimensional structures. When a molecule contains carbons linked by sp^3 bonds, then rotation can occur on those bonds. Rotation cannot occur between two sp^2-bonded carbons, or in ring compounds formed by conjugate sp^2 carbon bonds (aromatic hydrocarbons). When two different arrangements in three dimensions of a molecule are possible by bond rotation, then the stereoisomers are referred to as conformational isomers (conformers). In Figure 24, cyclohexane is depicted as a planar molecule (A), and then as the chair and boat conformers (B and C, respectively).

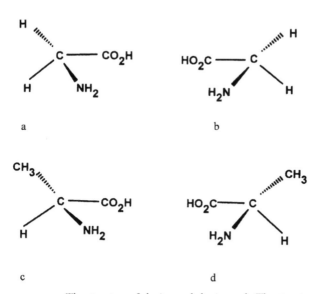

FIGURE 25. The structure of glycine and alanine. a, b: The structure of glycine, in which two mirror images are superimposable. c, d: the structure of alanine, in which the two mirror images are not superimposable. c and d are enantiomers, but a and b are not enantiomers. *Credit: Andrew Gize.*

If two molecules have the same empirical formula, contain the same atoms linked by the same bonds, but have two or more three-dimensional shapes that cannot be obtained by carbon–carbon bond rotation, then they are configurational isomers. Further terminology is then based on the symmetry and asymmetry of the groups attached to each of the carbons in the molecule.

The property resulting in molecular rotation of the plane of polarized light is exhibited by the reader's hands. Held palm to palm together, the left and right hands are mirror images. Placing one hand on top of the other should result in the thumbs sticking out in opposite directions, indicating that one hand cannot be superimposed on its mirror image. The property of nonsuperimposability of a hand or molecule on its mirror image is termed chirality. A molecule that rotates the plane of plane-polarized light is termed optically active and cannot be superimposed on its mirror image.

The majority of amino acids are optically active and are based on one amino group, one carboxyl group, and one hydrogen bonded to a single carbon. The difference between all amino acids lies in the fourth group. In glycine, the fourth group is a hydrogen. In Figure 25, the structure of glycine (A) and its mirror image (B) are shown. Structure (A) can be rotated 180° and superimposed on its mirror image. Consequently, glycine is not optically active.

The structure of alanine, where the fourth bond is to a methyl group, can have two forms (and only two isomers), which are mirror images of each other but which cannot be superimposed on each other (Figure 25). The two isomers are termed enantiomers. The central carbon is the source of chirality, and is termed a chiral carbon (C*). The properties of the two enantiomers of alanine, and any other enantiomeric pair, are identical except for the following two properties.

First, each enantiomer will rotate the plane of plane-polarized light in opposite and equal directions. Consequently, the enantiomer that rotates the plane to the left is the levo-isomer (designated –), and the other is the dextro-isomer (designated +). Second, each enantiomer will react at the same rate with achiral compounds, but at different rates with other chiral compounds. This latter property forms the basis of analytical separation techniques. It is noteworthy that chirality in molecules may have been recognized only because humans consist of chiral compounds such as amino acids.

A molecule can contain more than one chiral carbon, and in extracts derived from geological sources, such molecules are usually ubiquitous. Although there are several isomers for a given compound with several chiral carbons, only two can be enantiomers. The other isomers based on chiral carbons, which are not enantiomers, are termed diastereomers. Diastereomers have very similar chemical and physical properties, but commonly, these properties are sufficiently different for immediate analytical recognition.

The two isomers of cholestane (5α(H)-cholestane and 5β(H)-cholestane) are diastereomers, with 5β(H)-cholestane being diagnostic of carnivores. Identifying the 5β(H) in cholesterol derivatives provided Bull et al. (1999, 2000) with evidence for human and porcine manure in historical sites.

Gas chromatography

Gas chromatography (GC) is a very active aspect of analytical chemistry, with extensive application in natural product chemistry (including archaeology), especially when coupled with MS.

GC is the separation of a complex volatile mixture using an inert gas and a column which can contain a stationary phase (e.g. a solid packing), or a high boiling point polymer or liquid. The sample is introduced to the gas chromatograph through a heated injector (typically $\approx 300°C$), using a syringe, probe, or pyrolyser. A relatively new introduction method, which can also eliminate solvent use, is a needle coated with an organophilic polymer (solid phase microextraction, SPME).

The sample is vaporised and swept in an inert gas (e.g. H_2, He, or N_2) to the head of a column in an oven, which is held at a lower temperature than the injector (e.g. $40°C$, or with a liquid nitrogen cold trap). The sample condenses in as sharp a band as possible at the column head. The gas chromatograph oven is then heated at a standard rate (e.g. $4°C$ min^{-1}) to a final temperature (e.g. $300°C$).

As the boiling point of a compound is reached, it will enter the gas phase and be transported through the column to a detector. As in a complex mixture several compounds will vaporise at the same temperature, further separation occurs between the compounds in the gas phase and the stationary phase. Following separation in the column, the compounds leave the column (elute) to a suitable detector.

The GC column is crucial in analysis. The stationary phase in the column coating should be tailored to the specific analytical problem (Gruschka 1974). For rapid gas chromatographic analyses and separations of high molecular weight compounds, shorter columns (e.g. 15 m) are useful, but these lack the resolution of longer columns (e.g. 30 m). Flexible fused-silica capillaries with bonded phases are now in virtually exclusive use. To separate enantiomers, such as amino acids, the stationary phase must be optically active.

There are many types of detectors, ranging from general to those specific to a compound class (Natusch and Thorpe 1973; Buffington and Wilson 1991). The destructive flame ionisation detector (FID) and non-destructive thermal conductivity detector (TCD) are the two most commonly used. In an FID detector, the column eluate is taken by the carrier gas into the base of a flame.

Simplistically, when a compound burns, it forms ions, and the resistance across the flame will decrease. The resistance change is a function of the number of ions formed (compound composition) and their concentration. When the resistance change is recorded, peak area (or height × width at peak half height) is directly proportional to concentration.

FID is advantageous in that it responds well to hydrocarbons but not to water. Quantitation is either internal or external. In internal calibration, the sample to be analysed is spiked with a compound of known concentration which is not anticipated to be in the sample (e.g. a deuterated aromatic). In an external calibration, a series of analyses are run, using different concentrations of one or several compounds which are expected to be in the sample.

Additional detectors include electron capture (ECD) which is specific to compounds containing electronegative elements (e.g. Cl), the nitrogen-phosphorus detector (NPD), and the flame photometric detector (FPD) sulfur and phosphorus-containing compounds which produce chemiluminescent species.

The absolute identification of a compound requires two independent methods. GC using only one stationary phase is not usually reliable to identify the molecular structure (e.g. which isomer). Identification of the isomer strictly needs the sample to be run on two columns of different polarities, usually with standard (reference) compounds. The alternative route to identifying a molecular structure, which fulfils the requisite of two independent methods, is chromatography-MS.

Mass spectrometry

MS is unique in terms of both the principle on which it is based and the instrumentation required. In the mass spectrometer, molecules are ionised and it is these ions which are analysed in detail. This is an irreversible process and thus MS is a destructive analytical method. The fundamental stages in a mass spectrometer are sample introduction, ionisation to form positive or negative ions from the organic molecules, which are then separated as a function of mass to charge, and a detector for mass analysis. MS has been extensively described (e.g. Biemann 1962; McLafferty 1963; Budzikiewicz et al. 1967; Burlingame and Schnoes 1969; Silverstein et al. 1974; McLafferty and Turecek 1993).

Sample introduction methods include direct insertion using a probe, high-pressure liquid chromatography, and GC. Ionisation methods include thermionic electrons from a filament (electron impact, EI), or softer indirect ionisation using a reagent gas (chemical ionisation, CI). The ions are separated by a variety of 'mass filters', such as magnetic field, quadrupole, ion trap, and time-of-flight (TOF). Additional resolution of the ions can be obtained by tandem MS (MS-MS).

Low-resolution (nominal-mass) mass spectrometric requirements for most organic compounds can be satisfied with magnetic, quadrupole, or time-of-flight mass spectrometers. Electron impact (*EI*) is the commonest method used for sample ionisation. The usual 70 eV ionisation energy is chosen as it provides a balance between extensive molecular fragmentation with a high yield of ions (designated by mass to charge, m/z or m/e) and the detection of parent ions (molecular weight, M^+), and the best sensitivity.

The mass spectrum is a plot of ion intensity *versus* the mass-charge ratio (*m/z* or *m/e*). If the molecule is not fragmented, and has only one charge, then the molecular weight of the compound is the parent (or mother) peak (M^+) in the mass spectrum. When the molecule is fragmented, the original molecular structure results in some fragments being more frequent than others. These more frequent fragmentations will be recorded as higher intensities than the more infrequent fragmentations. Knowledge of the fragmentations a molecule produces can be used to deduce molecular structure.

Mass spectral databases (e.g. the National Institute of Science and Technology [NIST] and the Wiley Registry) are available to facilitate interpretation, but should not be used as the ultimate tool for identification. Mismatches are common in molecules which fragment to produce many ions and a molecular ion (parent ion) of relatively low intensity. Identification should be based on the user first interpreting the mass spectrum using known fragmentation rules, determining the parent ion, and using the mass spectrum and chromatographic behaviour to suggest a molecular structure, facilitated by a mass spectral interpretation program (e.g. AMDIS). The mass spectral databases can then be used to support the user interpretations.

Gas chromatography/mass spectrometry

GC/MS consists of coupled GC and MS, which are two independent analytical methods, in which the GC is the separation technique and the MS analyzes ions from compounds according to their mass/charge ratio. The power of the coupled techniques lies in the separation, followed by structural determination of the typically complex compound mixtures present in most samples. The analyst's approach typically follows three stages: (1) choice of sample introduction into the GC; (2) choice of GC parameters; and (3) choice of MS parameters.

There are numerous examples of the application of GC/MS to archaeological material. Pollard and Heron (1996) discuss the chemistry of resins and tars, using their molecular composition. Lampert et al. (2002) applied GC/MS in a preliminary study of SE Asian resins, and were able to suggest a botanical source. Connan and Nissenbaum (2004) have shown that detailed molecular studies of bitumens can be used to identify their sources, and establish trade routes. Seath et al. (2006) showed that a wax coating a pillow was not derived from beeswax, but geologically sourced (Figure 26).

Introduction – inorganic methods

Inorganic analytical techniques are well established in the archaeological literature. Many of the techniques introduced in the organic section are directly applicable to inorganic analyses, especially spectroscopic methods for the determination of cations and anions in aqueous solutions. Elemental analyses, for example, can be undertaken by using a plasma to ionise elements in aqueous solution before MS (inductively coupled plasma – MS, ICP-MS). Hawthorne (1988) introduces spectroscopic inorganic analyses, and Pollard and Heron (1996) indicate archaeological applications.

In this section, analytical methods focus on x-ray techniques which are largely nondestructive, or require small enough samples to be almost nondestructive. The analytical methods are outlined here, with Reed (1993, 1996) and Potts et al. (1995) recommended for more intensive reading.

X-ray techniques

In 1895, Roëntgen discovered mysterious rays, or x-rays (see Chapter 3). X-rays are short wavelength electromagnetic radiation, with wavelengths (λ) between 10^{-8} and 10^{-11} m. At the same time, it was also realized that crystals had periodic groups of atoms and ions, and were a 3D grating.

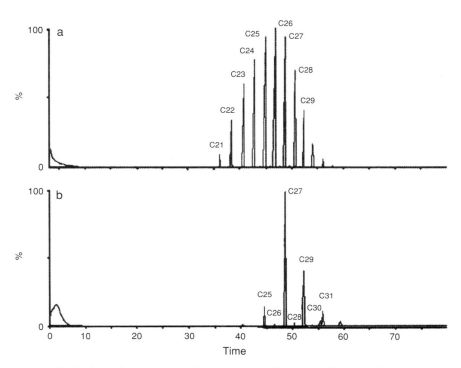

FIGURE 26. Total ion chromatograms of wax coating a pillow (a) and beeswax (b). The very different molecular compositions indicate that the pillow wax was not derived from beeswax, but a geological source. *Credit: Reproduced from Seath, J., Gize, A., David, A. R., Hall, K., Lythgoe, P., Speak, R., Caldwell, S. 2006. 'An atypical ancient Egyptian pillow from Sedment el-Gebel: evidence for migrant worker trading and technology'. Journal of Archaeological Science 33: 549.*

X-ray generation

X-ray radiation is generated when a charged particle is decelerated. When an electron (e) is accelerated through a high potential difference (V), and then stopped, released energy (E) will be in the x-ray wavelength (λ) range.

$$E = eV = h\nu = \frac{hc}{\lambda}$$

hence

$$\lambda = \frac{hc}{eV} = \frac{12398}{V}\text{Å}.$$

A filament generates thermionic electrons in a sealed low-pressure x-ray tube which are accelerated through an applied potential difference and to hit a metal target. The x-ray wavelength generated depends on the metal used in the target. Much of the energy released by the metal target is heat, and it must be water cooled (an advantage of Cu as the target). The generated x-rays pass through a window in the x-ray tube to the crystal.

If the target stops the electron in one step, then the maximum energy, shortest λ, x-ray energy will be obtained. Energy transferred to the target atoms will cause them to oscillate, and lower energy, longer λ x-rays will be generated. Consequently an x-ray wavelength continuum is generated. To filter the required x-ray wavelength from the continuum, a metal foil (e.g. Ni) can be used, or a diffraction beam monochromator.

Powder X-ray diffraction

In x-ray diffraction (XRD), x-rays are reflected by atomic or ionic planes in a crystal lattice. The spacing between the various lattice planes is diagnostic of the crystal. Consequently, an XRD pattern can be used to identify unknown minerals, either singly or in a mixture. In a mixture, a quantitative analysis of the different minerals can be obtained. As the technique is based on a crystallographic lattice, it is not applicable to liquids (including resins) or gases, except liquid crystals. To obtain wavelengths appropriate for XRD from crystals ($\approx$1 Å), V needs to be $\approx$10 kV. A copper target is commonly used, generating $\lambda = 1.5$ Å.

A crystal is built from unit cells, which are the arrangement of atoms in a 3D shape (e.g. a cube, rhombohedron), to develop the crystal lattice. The crystal lattice is the arrangement of atoms as geometric points. The array of atoms defines a plane, or groups of planes. The interplanar distance is the d-spacing. The incoming x-ray from the x-ray tube will hit electrons in the atoms in the crystal. The electrons will emit radiation in all directions. Most of the wavelengths emitted will cancel each other out, except when a certain incoming x-ray vector causes enforcement in one direction. This direction is the 'reflection.'

Braggs Law expresses the relationship between the incoming and reflected x-ray vector (θ), the interplanar distance (d), and wavelength (λ):

$$n\lambda = 2d \sin \theta$$

where n is the order of reflection (frequently 1) (See Reed 1993: 59, fig. 6.1).

Much research has been undertaken on single crystals, but it is recognised that archaeological applications tend to be identification of mineral mixtures in pot fragments, geological samples (e.g. natron), or residues in pots. Consequently, only powder XRD will be discussed further.

SAMPLE PREPARATION. The aim of the sample preparation is to provide a thin mixture of the analyte on a glass slide, covering an area of approximately 1×2 cm, in which the mineral fragments in the sample are randomly orientated. By randomly orientating the mineral fragments, the maximum number of diffraction planes will be utilised, providing the best XRD pattern for interpretation. A few milligrams of sample is sufficient.

The material to be analysed is powdered initially in an agate mortar and pestle, with amyl acetate. The powdered sample is pipetted as a suspension in the amyl acetate onto the glass slide, resulting in a random orientation of material in the amyl acetate suspension on the glass slide. The amyl acetate is evaporated, leaving a dry residue for analysis. If an amyl acetate suspension is not effective (e.g. with platey minerals such as micas and clays), the powder can be mixed with collodion, Vaseline or Apiezon and then smeared on the glass slide. During powdering of the sample, individual grains can become covered with other minerals. It is essential to undertake electron microscopy before powder XRD, as surface characteristics are lost during powdering.

ANALYSIS. The glass slide is placed in the x-ray diffractometer and kept stationary. The x-ray source is moved in an arc around the sample to ensure as many lattice planes are used in the analysis. The reflections are detected. Historically, photographic film was used as the detector. Alternative detectors are now used with computerised systems.

INTERPRETATION. The powder x-ray diffractogram contains three pieces of information:

1. The angular position of the reflection line. This is related to the interplanar distance, d.
2. The intensity of the peak. In a mixture of minerals, the intensity can be used towards a quantitative analysis. In a single mineral, the intensity is related to the arrangement of atoms in the unit cell.
3. The shape of the peak. A sharp peak results from a well crystallised material, whereas a poorly crystalline material will have broader peaks.

In identifying an unknown mineral, the angular position of the three most intense lines are used initially, and searched through the Joint Committee on Powder Diffraction Standards (JCPDS) database. A difficulty is that the relative intensities of the peaks can vary. Once likely identifications are made, all less intense peaks are used to complete identification. Use of computer databases has simplified and speeded interpretation enormously, and the identification of several minerals in a mixture is now routinely realistic.

Electron microbeam techniques

Electron microprobe

The main use of an electron microprobe (see Reed 1993: 14, fig. 2.1) is the qualitative and quantitative chemical analysis of small volumes of solids (≤ 5 μm). A scanning electron microscope is often incorporated as part of the electron microprobe. The Periodic Table can be analyzed except for elements lighter than carbon. The minimum detectability is typically 100 ppm, although this is dependent on the sample. Maps of elemental concentrations can be obtained over a sample.

Advantages of the electron microprobe over other methods include the following. Sample preparation is relatively simple, requiring a polished surface on a block or glass section. Small volumes are needed, limited to 5 μm diameter and depth. The analysis is nondestructive. The sample can be viewed, ensuring that the analysis location is known. The disadvantages are that the technique cannot generally identify the oxidation state of the elements (exceptions are potentially Fe and S), groups such as –OH cannot be identified, and quantitative analysis is poor for elements lighter than carbon. A good polish is required which may be difficult for soft materials.

BASICS. Analysis is under a vacuum ($\leq 10^{-4}$ torr) to permit passage of the electron beam, and to prevent attenuation of the x-rays generated by lighter elements. A filament (e.g. tungsten wire) generates electrons which are drawn away by an anode plate to generate the electron beam. Two electromagnetic lenses (condenser and objective) focus the electron beam on to the sample surface. The beam electrons reaching the sample have a fixed energy defined by the accelerating potential.

Several processes occur when the electron beam hits the sample, most important of which include (see Reed 1993 [*Schematic diagram of electron microprobe*]):

i. Generation of diagnostic x-rays from the elements present in the sample
ii. Generation of a background radiation which is a continuum

iii. The ejection of secondary electrons from atomic orbitals by the electron beam (the basis of SEM)
iv. The reflection of beam electrons as backscattered electrons (also used in SEM)
v. Cathodoluminescence

The diagnostic x-rays are emitted from electrons around the atomic nucleus, provided the incident beam energy is sufficient (the critical excitation energy or 'binding' energy). The incident beam electron can 'hit' an orbital electron and be scattered (see Potts et al. 1995: 5, fig. 1.3: *Schematic representation of processes resulting from electron bombardment*). The orbital electron is also ejected.

The empty electron level is filled by an electron from an outer orbital shell, and the energy lost emitted as a photon. The photon may emit another electron from the same atom, termed auger electron emission (the basis of auger spectroscopy), or the photon may be emitted as an x-ray photon. The x-rays generated from the elements in the sample contain the following information: the wavelength (λ), which is dependent on the emitting element, and intensity, which is dependent on the concentration of elements in the sample.

If the electron is ejected from the K orbital, it is termed K radiation (Potts et al. 1995). If the replacing electron comes from the L shell, it emits K_α radiation, and if from the M orbital, it emits K_β radiation. An electron ejected from the L orbital generates L radiation, and if ejected from the M orbital it generates M radiation. A background radiation continuum is produced by deceleration of the incident beam electrons as they pass the atomic nuclei. The loss of energy generates the background radiation (also termed the *braking radiation* or *Brehmstrahlung*).

The generated x-rays hit a curved crystal in which the atomic planes are physically bent, and are reflected to a detector for amplification and recording. The angle of the crystal can be set at a specified angle (θ) to the incident x-rays. From Braggs Law (above), at a specific θ, only x-rays of a fixed wavelength will be detected. The intensity of the diagnostic peak, which is proportional to the concentration of the element in the sample, is subtracted from the background radiation continuum either side of the diagnostic peak.

This is the basis of wavelength dispersive spectrometry (WDS), in which detection and quantification is based by 'sitting' on a fixed wavelength. WDS is relatively time consuming, but is best suited to high quality quantitation and elemental mapping. A representative WDS analysis of brass is shown in a diagram in Reed (1993: 143; fig. 11.1), with the emission lines of Cu and Zn.

Quantitation acknowledges three factors which have to be considered in obtaining the best quantitative analyses: the ZAF correction. The Z factor (or generation factor) acknowledges that the incident beam not only interacts with the sample surface, but can interact to depths of approximately 5 μm. The depth to which the beam interacts depends on the atomic numbers (Z) of the elements in the sample and their atomic weights. Correction is needed for absorption (A) or generated x-rays will occur in the sample. The generated x-rays will cause fluorescence (F) by ionizing elements in the sample and generating further x-rays. The ZAF correction is now computerised.

The faster alternative to WDS is energy dispersive spectrometry (EDS). The detector registers the x-ray photon energy and its intensity, and the detector output is managed by a pulses height analyser. The data are presented as a plot of pulse height (corresponding to elemental concentrations in the sample) versus x-ray energy (diagnostic of the elements in the sample). Although quantitation is not of as high a calibre as WDS, data are often adequate to identify a material.

Scanning electron microscopy

In the electron microprobe, the incident electron beam is focused on a spot. The beam can be moved along a line to give a 'line analysis,' or rastered across the sample to give multiple line analyses, which is the basis of SEM. The advantage of SEM is that it gives topographic information.

Relatively low energy secondary electrons are lost from the surface sample during bombardment by the incident electron beam. The secondary electrons are directed to the detector by a positive grid, and then detected and amplified to give an image of the rastered surface. Back scattered electrons, derived from the incident beam, have higher energies than secondary electrons, and can provide higher contrast images than those derived from secondary electrons.

An x-ray detector (typically EDS) can provide elemental analyses in scanning electron microscopes.

PREPARATION. In both electron microprobe and SEM, the effects of the incident electron beam and the surrounding low pressure must be considered. The sample must be dry, or the low pressure will cause physical distortion of the sample during analysis. If the incident electron beam energy

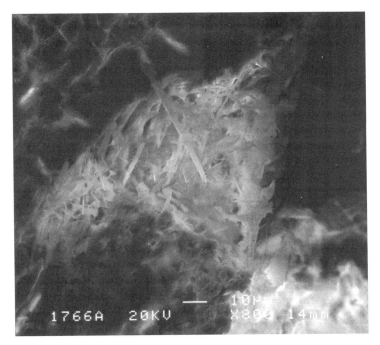

FIGURE 27. SEM image of natron crystals (based on morphology) in a desiccation crack in the bladder of the mummy of Asru, Manchester Museum. *Credit: Andrew Gize.*

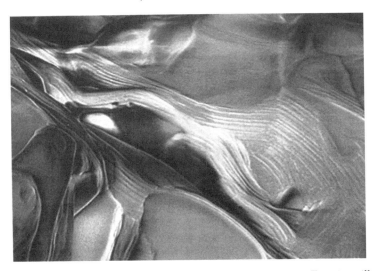

FIGURE 28. ESEM image of crystalline wax coating an ancient Egyptian pillow. Note the absence of any burning or charging of the wax by the electron beam. Field of view 90 μm. *Credit: Reproduced from Seath, J., Gize, A., David, A. R., Hall, K., Lythgoe, P., Speak, R., Caldwell, S. 2006. 'An atypical ancient Egyptian pillow from Sedment el-Gebel: evidence for migrant worker trading and technology'.* Journal of Archaeological Science 33: 548.

is too high, 'burn off' of lighter elements can occur (e.g. Na), or the sample itself can show signs of damage. A key requirement is that the electrons from the incident electron beam can flow from the sample to an electrical ground. If the concentration of electrons builds up in the sample through 'charging,' the incident electron beam will become unstable, resulting in poor analytical data and images.

A variety of sample holders are available in scanning electron microprobes and scanning electron microscopes. Samples can be in resin, on glass slides, or attached by an adhesive pad to an aluminium stub. In all cases, to prevent charging, the sample is either coated in gold (best) or carbon, prior to analysis.

To illustrate the advantages and disadvantages of SEM, Figure 27 shows an SEM image of presumed natron crystals along a desiccation crack in the bladder of the mummy Asru (Manchester Museum). The crystals can only be presumed to be natron on the basis of their morphology, as the elements in natron are too light to be easily detected and quantified. The conductive coating of the specimen, however, has ensured that these fragile crystals can be recorded.

Environmental scanning electron microscopy

SEM requires sample coating with a thin conductive film (e.g. Au, C) to conduct electrons away from the surface being impacted by the incident electron beam. In addition, the sample must be dry before coating. Although sample sizes are small, a hindrance in archaeological applications is that the coating can be permanent, and therefore analysis is not strictly destructive. Environmental scanning electron microscopy (ESEM) is a relatively new SEM design in which it not necessary to ensure that the sample is dry nor to coat it to prevent charging.

As in SEM, the electron beam needs to be generated and travel through low pressures. In an ESEM, a seal with small apertures (micrometre scale) is placed before the sample. The sample itself can then be exposed to a higher pressure atmosphere containing water vapour. The water vapour in the sample chamber excludes the need to desiccate samples.

The incident electron beam passes through the sample chamber and generates secondary electrons. The secondary ions impact vapour water molecules to produce additional secondary electrons, which in turn impact other water molecules to produce further secondary electrons. The generation of all these secondary electrons in a cascade amplifies the signal reaching the detector. The water molecules that have lost secondary electrons have a positive charge, which significantly reduces the effects of charging on the sample.

Currently, SEM with Au- or C-coated samples produces higher resolution images than ESEM. Nevertheless, ESEM is advantageous in that it requires no preparation, and imaging coupled with EDS elemental analysis is usually non-destructive.

Figure 28 shows crystalline wax coating a pillow, emphasising the non-destructive potential of ESEM. The wax crystals show no evidence of burning or partial melting under the beam, and charging is absent from the crystal edges.

CHAPTER 11

The facial reconstruction of ancient Egyptians

Caroline M. Wilkinson

Introduction

Facial reconstruction (otherwise known as facial approximation) is the process utilised to reproduce the facial appearance of an individual by relating the skeletal structure to the overlying soft tissue (Gerasimov 1971; Prag and Neave 1997; Taylor 2001; Wilkinson 2004). Facial reconstruction has been used to provoke recognition in forensic identification investigations worldwide, and is a powerful forensic tool that significantly enhances the chances of identification of the deceased.

The Manchester mummy team has been at the forefront of research into the facial depiction of ancient Egyptians since its conception in 1973 (David 1986; David and Tapp 1992). Initial forensic investigations of Egyptian mummies housed at The Manchester Museum involved Richard Neave, a medical artist from the University of Manchester (Neave 1979). In 1973, Neave reconstructed the faces of the Two Brothers, a pair of twelfth Dynasty (c. 1900 B.C.) Egyptians. This early work followed a rather simple, undeveloped method and Neave stated that 'whilst a great deal of attention was paid to the areas of muscle insertion and their probable effect upon the face, we put very little effort into developing the muscle groups themselves' (Prag and Neave 1997).

Neave used the tissue depth data produced by Kollman and Buchly (1898) from cadavers of White Europeans for these reconstructions and worked exclusively with skull casts and sculptors' clay and often built the neck structure onto the facial reconstructions to give the finished head a more balanced appearance. Guidelines set up by Krogman (Krogman and Iscan 1962) and Gerasimov (1971) were also used to interpret the facial features.

Although this early work was heavily based upon the work of Gerasimov (1971), Neave and his successors have developed and refined the facial reconstruction technique through research and experience and this method has been adopted by other practitioners across the world. The Manchester method attempts to interpret the skeletal detail of the skull to establish facial morphology, whilst using tissue thickness data as a guide to the soft tissue depth. Early work used tissue data from Black Americans (Rhine and Campbell 1980) or mixed-race Africans (Phillips and Smuts 1996), but more recent facial reconstructions have been able to use tissue depth data taken from a contemporary Egyptian population (El-Melhallawi and Soliman 2001).

Traditionally, the facial reconstructions of ancient Egyptians resulted from the invasive study of the mummified remains. Once the soft tissue had been removed, the skull could be analysed and a replica of the skull manufactured (Taylor and Angel 1998) on which to produce the facial reconstruction. Mould making is a complicated and time-consuming craft, and a great deal of specialised experience is necessary for skull replication. It is not recommended that inexperienced practitioners perform skull replication on human remains involved in forensic or archaeological investigations, as irreparable damage may occur that might preclude further forensic analysis or historical documentation.

With the development of clinical imaging, noninvasive assessment of mummified human remains has become possible. Cross-sectional data created by x-ray computed tomography (CT) scanning can be utilised to produce a three-dimensional digital model of the skull (Spoor et al. 2000) and replica skulls may be produced from digital data by using stereolithography (Hjalgrim et al. 1995) or another form of three-dimensional model manufacture (Seitz et al. 2005). There are varieties of software packages that render the surface cross-sectional CT data by extracting selected tissues and visualising the tissues as three-dimensional models. Surface rendering involves segmentation (isolation of the tissue by thresholding), interpolation between the slices to create a smooth surface and illumination of the surface. Digital three-dimensional models of the skull can also be imported into computer-based facial reconstruction systems.

The accuracy of facial reconstruction

To some extent, forensic identification investigations provide an opportunity to assess the accuracy of the facial reconstruction, when the individual is finally identified. Comparison of the identified individual with the reconstruction may be possible, although the results of such comparisons may be misleading because only successful cases may be used. Consequently, blind studies have been suggested to evaluate the accuracy of facial reconstruction, and several such studies have been produced by researchers from the Manchester mummy team to validate their methods.

Following his early work on the Two Brothers, Neave reconstructed the faces of four cadavers to establish the accuracy of facial reconstruction. Neave produced manual reconstructions and then correctly linked each to a photograph of the cadaver (Prag and Neave 1997).

Later in his career, Neave was provided with another opportunity to evaluate the technique when, as part of a challenge set up by the Dutch National Association for Oral and Maxillofacial Surgery, he was provided with a skull replica made from CT scans of a volunteer. The clay reconstruction was sufficiently similar to the individual for Neave to recognise him in a room full of people (Prag and Neave 1997).

Some years later, Wilkinson conducted a comprehensive accuracy study in which five female skulls were used (Wilkinson and Whittaker 2002). The faces were reconstructed by the manual method and evaluated by face pool identification, resemblance ratings and morphological assessment by image superimposition. Fifty volunteers correctly identified each reconstruction as the most frequently chosen face from a pool of ten faces, and there was an average identification rate of 34 per cent above chance (10 per cent). In addition the reconstructions were rated on average as a close resemblance to the identified individuals and image superimposition showed that facial proportions, nose shape and jaw line were the most accurate features whilst facial fatness and ear shape were the areas of most error. The authors concluded that it is possible to produce a better than approximate resemblance using this method.

Further research was conducted a few years later utilizing the computer-based facial reconstruction system developed by Wilkinson (2003, 2005). This blind study used the CT data of two live White North American subjects, and facial reconstructions were produced by two practitioners (Wilkinson et al. 2006). The reconstructions were evaluated by face pool identification and three-dimensional morphological superimposition. Seventy per cent of the volunteers correctly identified the reconstructions from the face pools (50 per cent above chance) and both reconstructions received identification rates at least 50 per cent greater than any other face in the pools. Even with differences at the cheeks caused by the position of the subject in the CT scanner, the shell-to-shell deviation maps suggested that 57.5 per cent of the facial reconstruction surfaces showed less than 2.5 mm error and 83 per cent showed less than 5 mm error. Both reconstructions showed upper lip and ear pattern errors.

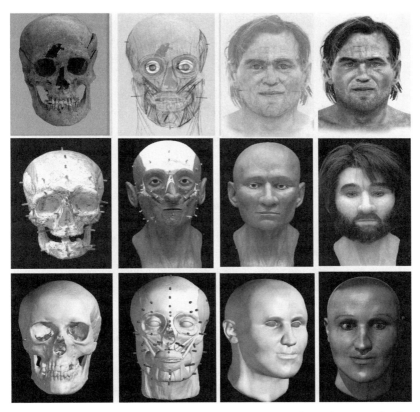

FIGURE 29. Facial reconstruction procedures. Top row: Manual two dimensional – the musculature and facial morphology are drawn over a photograph of the skull. Skin colour and texture are then added in Adobe Photoshop or with paint. Middle row: Manual three dimensional – the musculature and skin layer are modelled in clay onto a replica skull. The finished cast of the head can be painted and a wig, plastic eyes and facial hair added. Bottom row: Computerised three dimensional – the musculature is added from a database of premodelled muscles and distorted to fit the skull. A skin layer is then added in virtual clay, followed by colours and textures that are mapped onto the three-dimensional model. Facial reconstructions by Caroline Wilkinson, Dundee University. *Credits: Caroline Wilkinson, University of Manchester, and Image Foundry Ltd.*

The results of these studies suggest that this method of facial reconstruction will produce a better than approximate resemblance to the individual and therefore justifies the use of this method to recreate the faces of ancient Egyptians from mummified remains.

Facial reconstruction methods

Currently we can divide the facial reconstruction methods into two basic groups: two-dimensional and three-dimensional techniques. There are a variety of different methods within each group.

Two-dimensional facial reconstruction

MANUAL. Drawings and paintings of the face can be produced on overlays superimposed onto images of the skull or craniographs (see Figure 29). Frontal and profile views are often produced using this technique. There are a number of publications outlining the methodology (Krogman and Iscan 1986; Iscan and Helmer 1993; Taylor 2001).

Some practitioners prefer to draw the facial musculature onto an initial overlay before attempting the finished facial morphology (Needham et al. 2003), whereas others draw the finished face directly over the skull images (George 1993; Taylor 2001). A great deal of artistic ability and portraiture skills are necessary to produce a realistic facial likeness by using the two-dimensional manual method.

COMPUTERISED. A facial composite created from photographic or sketched features can be produced over an image of the skull by using computer software designed specifically for the reconstruction of facial appearance from skeletal remains. Facial outlines and features are chosen from a database dependent upon the skeletal structure, and the proportions of the skull determine the overall face shape and appearance.

A variety of software exists that create facial images similar to those of Efit, Identikit, or Profit composite systems. Usually, frontal view images only are produced (Evenhouse et al. 1992; Ubelaker and O'Donnell 1992; Miyasaka et al. 1995; Stratomeier et al. 2005).

Three-dimensional facial reconstruction

MANUAL. Facial sculptures are produced directly onto the skull or skull replica (see Figure 29). Some practitioners favour an anatomical approach (Gerasimov 1955; Prag and Neave 1997; Wilkinson 2004), modelling the facial musculature before applying a skin layer to depict the facial appearance, whereas others favour a morphometric approach, using mean tissue depth data to create a contour map of the facial surface into which the facial features are modelled (Gatliff and Snow 1979; Krogman and Iscan 1986; Iscan and Helmer 1993).

Current practitioners of the anatomical approach also use mean tissue depth data as guides, and most practitioners of the morphometric approach also apply some anatomical guidelines. There are a number of publications outlining these methodologies (Krogman and Iscan 1986; Iscan and Helmer 1993; Prag and Neave 1997; Clement and Ranson 1998; Taylor 2001; Wilkinson 2004).

COMPUTERISED. Over the last decade numerous systems have been developed to produce facial reconstruction using computer software, with the aim of increasing the levels of flexibility, efficiency, and speed. The first computer technique to be developed for forensic purposes was produced by Moss and his colleagues at University College London and was based upon a system used for cranial reconstructive surgery (Moss et al. 1987).

Currently computerised facial reconstruction systems can be divided into two groups – automated systems and modelling systems.

Automated systems are based on anthropometrical data and/or templates of skeletal and facial morphology. Tissue data from clinical images are included and facial templates (dependent upon the sex, age, and ethnic group of the skull) are 'morphed' to fit the skull. Additional manual intervention may also be necessary to apply external facial details. These systems create multiple variations for each skull, and impose a very specific set of facial characteristics onto the facial reconstruction, in that the resulting face will ultimately resemble the sample face (Michael and Chen 1996; Quatrehomme et al. 1997; Nelson and Michael 1998; Jones 2001).

Three-dimensional modelling systems have also been utilized to mimic the manual methods of facial reconstruction. Some modelling systems use three-dimensional animation software (Buhmann et al. 2003; Eliasova et al. 2003; Kahler et al. 2003; Kindermann 2003) to model the face onto the skull, whereas other systems utilise virtual sculpture systems with haptic feedback (Wilkinson 2003; Subke and Wittke 2005) (see Figure 29).

The systems with haptic feedback have the advantage of allowing the practitioner to feel the surface of the skull during analysis, which will provide some important skeletal details for facial reconstruction, such as determination of the malar tubercle or muscle attachment strength. Three-dimensional modelling systems may follow either the anatomical (Wilkinson 2003) or morphometric approaches (Subke and Wittke 2005).

The uses of facial reconstruction in Egyptological investigations

The facial reconstruction of ancient Egyptians has a long history and has been utilized for various purposes.

DEPICTION OF ANCIENT PEOPLE. Many archaeological investigations have concentrated upon the re-creation of the facial appearance solely as an exercise in depiction: namely, to show the public how these ancient people looked and to enable comparison with contemporary faces in Egypt and worldwide. Such examples include the facial reconstruction of Tutanhkamun (Gatliff 1980; Handwerk 2005), Nesperennub (Taylor 2004), and Janus (Tukker and Dassen 1999) (see Plate XVII).

DEPICTION FROM MUMMIFIED SOFT TISSUE. Often the assessment of mummified soft tissues will reveal details of facial morphology that cannot, as yet, be accurately determined from the skeleton alone (see Figure 30). Frequently, the ears will be preserved, with varying degrees of deterioration, and it may be possible to determine ear shape, size, protrusion and/or detail. Similarly, the nasal tip, vermillion line, hair line and facial wrinkle patterns may be visible.

Because shrinkage and distortion may affect the facial appearance, the skeletal detail should also be assessed where possible to establish feature morphology. Known effects of the mummification procedure should be taken into account when reconstructing mummified faces, because many facial features will be distorted by the bandages, the nose may be distorted by brain removal and the eyes may be sunken due to postmortem changes. For example, the large majority of Egyptian mummies appear to exhibit hooked noses in profile, yet this is typically a bandage distortion rather than the actual profile of the nose, and only experienced facial anthropologists will recognise this phenomenon.

THREE-DIMENSIONAL MODELS FROM TWO-DIMENSIONAL DATA. Where access to the original skull is not possible either directly or via three-dimensional clinical imaging, methods of three-dimensional model production from two-dimensional data (such as radiographs, photographs and craniometrics) may be utilised. Early researchers (Neave 1986) modelled the skull shape manually in clay, using outlines from radiographs as templates. Because only two templates could be utilised, there was a great deal of estimation involved in this method.

Computer systems may now be used to produce a three-dimensional model of the skull from radiographs and/or photographs. Multiple views are aligned using cranial points as registration marks (see Figure 31) and virtual sculpture (Wilkinson 2003) or mesh distortion of a template skull (Davy et al. 2005) reproduces the skull morphology. Extrapolation of surface morphology between the views is inevitable and the more views that are available, the more accurate the resulting three-dimensional model of the

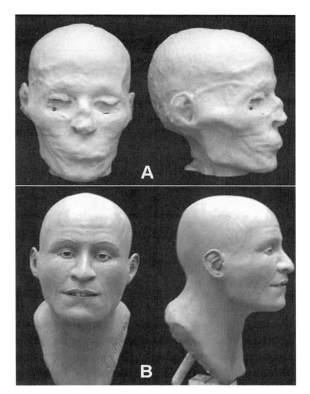

FIGURE 30. The preserved remains of an ancient Egyptian priest (A) and facial reconstruction (B). The replica of the mummified face was produced from CT scan data by using stereolithography, courtesy of The National Museums of Scotland and PDR, Cardiff. The facial reconstruction was produced by Caroline Wilkinson. *Credits: Caroline Wilkinson and University of Manchester.*

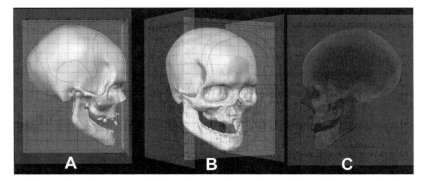

FIGURE 31. Production of a three-dimensional skull model from two-dimensional data. The skull was modelled utilising radiographs and scaled drawings as templates, whereas numerous craniometrics and photographs were used to provide the detail and enable accuracy. (A) Side view of skull model with scaled drawing as template. (B) Three-quarter view of skull model with all template images visible. (C) Side view of transparent skull model with radiographs as template. *Credits: Caroline Wilkinson and Chris Rynn, Dundee University.*

skull will be. As these methods include a certain degree of estimation and loss of detail on the surface of the bone, any resulting facial reconstruction would require photographic records of the skull and/or an appreciation of the decrease in accuracy of any resulting face.

This same procedure has also been applied to the reconstruction of mummified soft tissue (see Figure 32). One of the more interesting challenges was the depiction of Ramesses II. Ramesses II was an Egyptian pharaoh from the nineteenth Dynasty. He is believed to have taken the throne in his early twenties and to have ruled Egypt from 1304 B.C. to 1237 B.C. His unwrapped mummified remains are housed at the Egyptian Museum of Cairo and there are a small number of existing craniographs taken in 1976. Sadly, the craniographs are of poor quality and of limited views and it was impossible to recreate an accurate three-dimensional model of the skull of Ramesses II from this material.

The mummified soft tissues of the face of Ramesses II were visible and had been photographed from multiple angles and views. It was therefore possible to recreate the mummified face of Ramesses II by using virtual sculpture. The craniographs were used to establish the facial proportions and profile and the photographs were then utilised to model the feature detail and those areas not visible on the radiographs. The mummified face of Ramesses II was then 'dehydrated' to recreate his living appearance. Because Ramesses II was estimated to have been between 87 and 93 years of age when he died, he was given a rather emaciated facial appearance, consistent with an elderly statesman. Finally the three-dimensional computer model was given a coloured skin texture, eye colour and hair to realistically depict Ramesses II in his later years (see Figure 32).

Facial reconstruction has also been utilised in an attempt to investigate cultural, social, medical, genetic and environmental aspects of ancient Egyptian life.

COMPARISON WITH PORTRAITURE. The Egyptian mummy portraits (or Fayoum portraits) are well known to Egyptologists and all date from the first to second centuries A.D. Most were produced using the same encaustic technique and almost all the portraits are frontal, giving a haunting look, as if they are staring at the viewer.

These portraits have been analysed by Egyptologists to determine hairstyles, jewellery, fashion, and social status, but little was known about the accuracy of the portraits. Researchers questioned whether the portraits really portrayed the deceased or if they were stylized and whether they were produced during life or posthumously. It has been estimated that there are

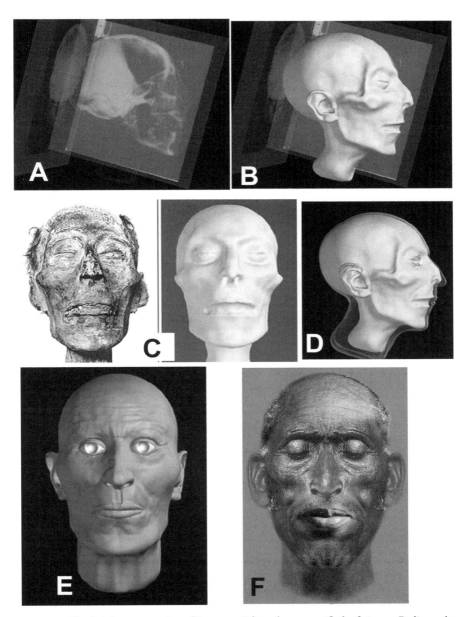

FIGURE 32. The facial reconstruction of Ramesses II from the mummified soft tissues. Radiographs showing the soft tissue outlines (A) were used as templates to create a three-dimensional model (B) of the mummified face, and the photographs (C) were used as reference for detail and accuracy. The soft tissues in life were produced by 'rehydrating' the mummified remains (D) to establish facial appearance prior to mummification (E). Skin tone and texture were estimated (F). Reconstruction by Caroline Wilkinson, Dundee University. *Credit: University of Manchester.*

FIGURE 33. Comparison of facial reconstructions of ancient Egyptians with portraits. Column 1: Facial reconstruction and portrait of fifty-year-old male. Reconstruction by Richard Neave. Courtesy of the British Museum. Column 2: Facial reconstruction and portrait of twenty- to twenty-five-year-old female. Reconstruction by Denise Smith. Courtesy of the British Museum. Column 3: Facial reconstruction and portrait of twenty-nine-to thirty year-old male. Reconstruction by Caroline Wilkinson. Courtesy of the Polish Centre for Archaeology, Cairo, Egypt. Column 4: Facial reconstruction and portrait of thirty-year-old male. Reconstruction by Caroline Wilkinson. Courtesy of the Glyptotek Museum. Column 5: Facial reconstruction and portrait of thirty- to thirty-five-year-old male. Reconstruction by Caroline Wilkinson. Courtesy of the Metropolitan Museum of Fine Arts, New York. *Credit for images of reconstructions: University of Manchester.*

more than a thousand mummy portraits, but fewer than a hundred are still bound into their mummies. Thus the number of candidates for a study of the realism of the portraits was relatively small.

Over the last ten years, facial anthropologists from the Manchester mummy team have studied five of these mummies with portraits (Wilkinson 2003; Brier and Wilkinson 2005). In all cases the reconstructions were produced blind and then compared to the attached portraits (see Figure 33). Three of the reconstructions were created using actual skulls and two reconstructions were created on skull replicas produced from the CT data.

FIGURE 33. *Continued*

Two examples were from the British Museum: a fifty-year-old male and a twenty- to twenty-five-year-old female; and another, a twenty-nine- to thirty-year-old male, was from the Polish Centre for Egyptology in Cairo. All three of these reconstructions showed high consistency with the facial features on the portraits, although the portrait of the young male was in poor condition and showed a fatter face than the reconstruction. These reconstructions were similar enough to the portraits to suggest that they were indeed painted during the lifetime of the individuals and were not idealised images (see Figure 33).

The other two cases produced differing results. The skull of a thirty-year-old male was provided by the Glyptotek Museum. The portrait and the reconstruction were very different and appeared to show individuals from different racial origins. The portrait revealed the face of an older man with a longer narrower face and longer nose. Superimposition of the skull and the portrait showed that the proportions of the face did not match those of the skull, and, therefore, it was suggested that the skull and the portrait may not be of the same individual (see Figure 33).

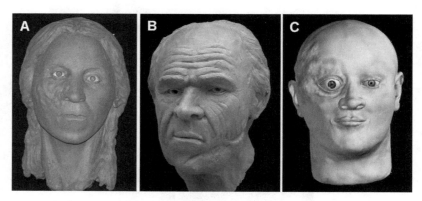

FIGURE 34. Depictions of disease and trauma in facial reconstruction work. (A) Iron Age woman with haemangioma, a fleshy growth to one side of the face. (B) Soldier from the Battle of Towton with healed wound to jaw. (C) Medieval woman with meningioma hyperostosis and related soft tissue changes. *Credit: Caroline Wilkinson.*

Finally, the skull of a thirty- to thirty-five-year-old male was provided by the Metropolitan Museum, New York. The portrait appeared to be of a younger man of a more Caucasian appearance, with a narrower nose, but there were many consistencies in facial proportions and face shape, with similar jaw lines and mouth shapes. Skull and portrait superimposition suggested similarity, except at the nose, where the nose of the portrait was narrower than the nasal aperture of the skull.

Because the facial proportions and other facial features were consistent between the skull, reconstruction and portrait, it was suggested that the artist may have 'stylised' the portrait of the individual, perhaps to fit more with the traditional Graeco-Roman fashion (see Figure 33). It is also possible that the CT data were not of high enough resolution to visualise the small endings to the bones at the nasal aperture, suggesting a misleading nasal width.

These five comparisons between facial reconstructions and portraits yielded somewhat different results, but provided insight into the accuracy and timing of the artwork. Future studies utilising other mummy and portrait combinations would shed further light on these enigmatic portraits.

DEPICTION OF DISEASE AND TRAUMA. Facial reconstruction can also be utilized to illustrate the effects and treatment of disease and trauma in ancient populations. Where wounds show signs of healing or where a pathological condition or long-standing disease has altered facial appearance, it may be necessary to demonstrate this as part of the reconstruction.

The first facial reconstruction case that involved facial trauma was Neave's work on Philip II, King of Macedon in c. 250 B.C. (Prag and Neave 1997).

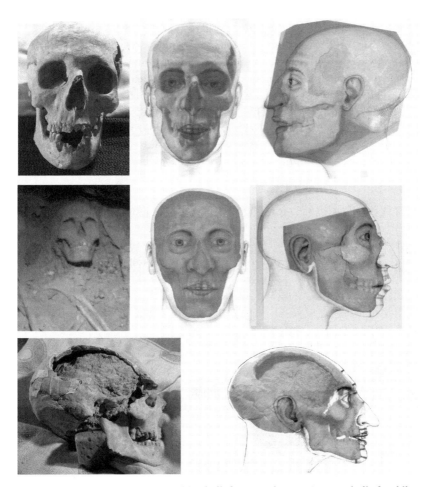

FIGURE 35. Facial reconstructions of the skulls from Tomb KV5. Top row: skull of middle-aged man in good condition and resulting two-dimensional facial reconstruction. Middle row: skull of middle-aged male partially excavated and resulting two-dimensional facial reconstruction. Bottom row: fragmented and partially reassembled skull of middle-aged male and resulting two-dimensional facial reconstruction. Reconstructions by Caroline Wilkinson and Caroline Needham. *Credit: University of Manchester.*

Wilkinson (Wilkinson and Neave 2003) reconstructed the face of a soldier from the Battle of Towton (c. 1461 A.D.), and the skull demonstrated a massive healed sword wound to the lower jaw. The reconstructed face exhibited the scar resulting from the treatment of this wound, and facial paralysis caused by the trauma (see Figure 34).

There have been a number of reconstructions depicting long-standing disease in ancient populations (see Figure 34). Neave produced a facial reconstruction of Robert the Bruce (Wilkinson 2004), exhibiting the effects of leprosy and also a number of healed wounds to the forehead. Where these conditions will have altered the facial appearance of the individuals significantly and for a long period of time prior to death, it is reasonable to include the visual symptoms as part of the reconstruction.

There has, however, been little attention to facial pathology with regards to the reconstructions of ancient Egyptians. Some reconstructions have shown dental abnormalities (see Figure 34), but there have been few examples of healed trauma or long-standing facial disease. Further research into this subject could be rewarding.

ASSESSMENT OF FAMILIAL LINKS. Facial reconstruction has been utilized to attempt to assess the genetic relationship between individuals. Certain facial features have a hereditary component, such as adherent ears and bifid noses. Consistency in feature morphology, proportions and characteristic features cannot, however, positively identify a genetic relationship, and may only be used to lend weight to such a theory.

Prag and Neave (1995) reconstructed the faces of seven individuals from an ancient Greek grave circle at Mycenae, with the aim of discovering whether, having recreated the faces, they might be able to judge whether these individuals were in any way related to each other. They found that those from the same graves showed family likenesses in facial proportions and nasal shape, and individuals from graves in different parts of the circle generally exhibited smaller lower facial proportions and differences in interorbital distance, nasal prominence and forehead shape.

Similarly, Wilkinson (Redknap 2002) reconstructed the faces of four of five individuals from a Viking period (c. 980–1000 A.D.) burial site in Llanbedrgoch, Wales, and discovered that the skulls all exhibited adherent ears and supraorbital notches, which are known hereditary characteristics. In addition, the nasal apertures of these skulls exhibited consistent features. The facial anthropology assessment suggested a possible familial relationship, even though this could not be positively confirmed.

The ancient Egyptian population has also been studied in this way. Wilkinson and Needham were involved with the Theban Mapping Project and the excavation of KV5, a tomb in the Valley of the Kings, thought to have housed the sons of Ramesses II. Weeks and his colleagues discovered the skulls of four individuals in KV5 (Weeks 2001) and a facial anthropology assessment was performed to ascertain whether these individuals could have been related to Ramesses II. Only three of the four skulls were available for

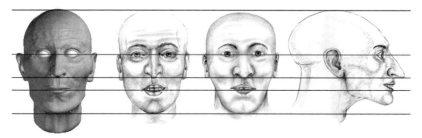

Ramesses II

FIGURE 36. Comparison of the facial reconstructions from Tomb KV5 and Ramesses II. The horizontal lines intersect the face of Ramesses II at the top of the head, outer canthus, base of the nose, mouth slit and base of the chin. Faces 2 and 3 show consistent proportions with those of Ramesses II. The horizontal proportions of face 3 are significantly different from all the other faces. *Credit: Caroline Wilkinson.*

assessment: one was intact and clean, one was still partially buried and one was fragmented.

Due to the condition of the skulls and limited access, only photographic evidence was possible and two-dimensional reconstructions were attempted. The fragmented skull could only be assessed in profile, as many pieces were missing and full reassembly was not possible; however, enough of the skull was intact to allow reassembly of the vertical proportions and the left profile. The remaining two skulls were reconstructed in frontal and profile views (see Figure 35) by two practitioners.

The facial reconstructions were then compared with the mummified face of Ramesses II and the facial reconstruction that had been produced from his mummified soft tissues (see Figure 32). All the faces had similar features, such as a long narrow face shape, long noses and prominent cheek bones, and two of the skulls had very similar vertical proportions to Ramesses II (see Figure 36). The face of Ramesses II exhibits long vertical distances between the nose and the mouth and the mouth and the chin. It could be said that this is one of the most striking features of Ramesses II. These vertical proportions were consistent in two of the faces from KV5; however, one of the skulls had very different vertical proportions to Ramesses II, exhibiting a very short nasolabial distance and chin (see Figure 36).

Wilkinson concluded that although two of the skulls were consistent with Ramesses II in facial proportions and morphology, one was not. Therefore, these results shed some doubt on this individual being directly related to Ramesses II.

The inclusion of facial reconstruction in the scientific investigation of ancient Egyptian mummies has a long history. In recent years, there have been many technological developments that have widened the possibilities and allowed the noninvasive study of mummified remains. With the rapidly developing computer technology and medical imaging availability, there is unlimited scope for future research.

PART 3

The treatment of disease in ancient Egypt

CHAPTER 12

The ancient Egyptian medical system

Rosalie David

Sources for the study of Egyptian medicine

The sources for the study of ancient Egyptian medicine include inscriptional, archaeological and palaeopathological evidence (Ghalioungui 1973). The most significant information regarding the Egyptian concept of the body system, and the medicinal and pharmaceutical treatments they used is preserved in twelve documents known as the Medical Papyri (see p. 186–193); also, funerary biographical texts inscribed on stone tablets (stelae) give the titles and brief career details of some doctors.

Those temples associated with medical training and healing procedures provide limited archaeological evidence; in one, the Temple of Kom Ombo, there is a Roman Period wall-relief, which may depict a set of surgical instruments. Until now, the only identified surgical instruments that have been discovered date to the Graeco-Roman Period; however, it is possible that earlier, but unidentified, examples of surgical appliances may exist in museum collections.

In Egyptian tombs, the wall-reliefs generally represented the tomb owner and his elite contemporaries as stylised figures with a youthful, healthy appearance. By portraying them in this way, and using magical rites to activate the life force in these figures, the Egyptians hoped to ensure that these individuals would spend the afterlife in a state of fitness. Because of this idealisation of the figures, the scenes do not provide an accurate record of the diseases and illnesses suffered by the elite, although signs and symptoms of ill health are sometimes depicted in the representations of servants and labourers.

Human remains (both naturally preserved and intentionally mummified bodies) are a very important resource for the study of disease, but so far, they have provided scant evidence regarding medical practices and treatments.

All the sources therefore provide limited information about the medical system, and sometimes, as with the principles of idealising the human figure in the tomb art, the 'evidence' can falsify the reality of everyday existence.

The role of magic in medical practice

The Egyptians believed that supernatural forces could be used to change the form of things and to influence events. The name for this force was *heka* (Pinch 1994: 9), which has been translated into English as 'magic;' the Egyptians personified this force as the goddess Heka.

According to Egyptian mythology, the universe was brought into existence through the divine creative word, and magic was the principle through which this spoken command was turned into reality. Although magic was considered to be more powerful than all the other forces of nature and had influence over all created forms, it was under the control of the creator god. Essentially, it provided the gods and the king with a potent weapon for their continuing struggle against chaos in the heavens and on earth.

Magic was integral to the Egyptian belief system and was widely used at all levels of society. It took many forms: state magic, performed in the temples, maintained the equilibrium of the universe; funerary magic ensured that the deceased attained the afterlife; everyone used spells and amulets to ward off evil; and magical rites, incantations, and spells played an important role in treating the sick.

The Egyptians adopted various approaches to treating and healing the sick. Modern studies classify these as 'rational' and 'irrational' or 'magical' methods, and although this distinction and categorisation would have been meaningless to the Egyptians, the source material does demonstrate that there were two medical routes, one based on magico-religious concepts and the other on scientific observation of the patient's condition.

Archaeological and literary evidence indicates that magic was an important aspect of religion for at least 4,500 years. The Medical Papyri (see below) clearly demonstrate that rational and irrational methods both played significant roles in treatment. Indeed, magic is as prominent in the earlier periods as in later times, and there is no evidence that medicinal procedures either 'progressed' from magical to rational methods or, conversely, declined from a scientific approach into superstitious practices.

A significant study at Manchester, the Pharmacy in Ancient Egypt Project, is currently assessing the therapeutic efficacy of ancient Egyptian medicaments (see Chapter 14); however, just a few examples can demonstrate the

Egyptians' flexible approach to treatment. Some pharmaceutical remedies, such as the use of honey, cream, and milk to treat throat and chest infections (e.g. Ebers Papyrus 190, 323), are clearly based on trial and error and observation of the patient.

Other remedies, however, rely exclusively on principles of magic. Some, for example, incorporate disagreeable substances such as urine and excrement to dispel 'evil spirits' from the patient, allowing 'good spirits' to attend him and assist his recovery (e.g. Ebers Papyrus 326; Edwin Smith Papyrus, Case 8). In another case, a 'transfer ritual' is used to treat migraine (Ebers Papyrus 250), and the spell sends the pain from the patient into the head of a fish. A magical incantation was also used to treat the common cold (Ebers Papyrus 763): 'Flow out fetid nose! flow out son of fetid nose! Flow out, you who break the bones, destroy the skull, and make ill the seven holes of the head!'

When magic was used to treat patients, either close at hand or at a distance, it usually consisted of three elements. The most important was the spell or incantation: it was thought that, once recited, the words of the spell followed a particular course, reaching and hopefully curing the patient. The spell was often accompanied by a ritual – acts and gestures performed on the patient or on a doll or wax image; this process might involve the use of water, wine, oil, perfumes and incense, and be accompanied by dances and music, to transform the patient's mental and physical state. Third, amulets (a type of jewellery worn since at least the fourth millennium B.C.) were frequently used in patient treatment: their symbolic shapes and materials were believed to have intrinsic powers that could provide magical protection for the owner.

The medical practitioners

Medicine, like every other aspect of life in ancient Egypt, came under the control of the gods. Various gods had different areas of responsibility: for example, the invention of healing prescriptions was attributed to Thoth, the god of writing; Isis, the devoted wife of Osiris whose body she reconstituted and restored after death, was the divine patroness of magicians; the gods Horus and Amun treated eye diseases, and the goddess Tauert was associated with childbirth and fertility.

Sekhmet, a destructive lioness-headed goddess who brought epidemics, received an important cult aimed at propitiating her anger. The Egyptians also worshipped a deified man as the founder of medical science: this was Imhotep, the vizier, architect and possibly physician of King Djoser of the third Dynasty, whom the Greeks later identified with their god of medicine, Aesculapius.

Some medical practitioners were closely associated with the temples. The Egyptian temple, never a place of congregational worship, was known as the 'House of the God.' The main function of the priesthood, which played a significant and influential role in society, was to perform temple rituals that fulfilled the needs of the resident deity whose spirit was believed to be present in the cult statue in the sanctuary.

During the Old and Middle Kingdoms, there was some overlap between priesthood and laity, as many held positions as priests on a part-time basis, combining it with a career as a lawyer, doctor, teacher, or scribe (Sauneron 1960). In the New Kingdom, this balance was changed when revised temple organisation resulted in many priestly offices becoming full-time, professional posts. Some priests continued to play a major role in medical practice, providing an important link between the temples and the external world.

Because the treatment of illness combined rational and magical methods, priest-doctors, doctors, and practitioners of magic were all involved in the healing processes. There is no reference to any rivalry among these practitioners, and the Ebers Papyrus (854a) indicates that they held parallel roles in treating the sick (Nunn 1996: 113).

One group of physicians, the 'Priests of Sekhmet' (von Kanel 1984), was attached to the temples. Many probably had specialist skills for treating specific illnesses, and these appear to have combined rational and magical methods; some also held titles associated with magic. They shared many practices with the *sunu*, another category of doctors sometimes connected to large communities such as the army, royal palaces and work sites; they also performed public hygiene duties in the cemeteries. Again, some of the *sunu* were attached to temples, whereas others were professional magicians.

There were apparently various groups to which professional magicians might belong. As well as the *sunu*, some held the title of *sau* (from the verb 'to protect'); these probably included midwives and women who practised community magic, particularly on behalf of pregnant women and children. Other magicians were priests of Heka (the goddess of magic) or Serqet (the scorpion goddess). By placating Serqet, the latter sought to acquire power against venomous reptiles and insects, and the Brooklyn Papyrus (Sauneron 1989) confirms that they used both magic and rational medicine to treat snakebites.

Although many magicians, who probably specialised in ritual magic and healing, appear to have been closely associated with the temples during pharaonic times, some may have functioned independently, perhaps even replacing the conventional doctor in some smaller communities. By the Roman Period, their association with state religion and the temples had largely ceased, and instead, they offered their services as independent, paid practitioners of secular magic.

The temple: a centre of healing and education

Priest-doctors may have made a significant contribution in temples that enjoyed a special reputation for healing, although it is not known if these centres provided medical treatments in addition to faith cures. At these temples, patients underwent ritual cleansing with sacred water, and therapeutic dream therapy, which involved 'incubation' or temple sleep, when the patients, in a trancelike state, encountered the gods and, according to some claims, were healed of their afflictions.

Until now, only two sites have revealed archaeological evidence that confirms the healing role of the temple, but inscriptions indicate that other sites had a similar use. In the enclosure of the Temple of Hathor at Denderah, archaeologists have identified a building (the 'sanatorium') where patients were accommodated in cells to undergo immersion and preparation for incubation (Daumas 1957). Here, they were either totally immersed or their limbs were bathed with holy water that was believed to possess curative properties.

Other evidence of temple treatment is provided by invalids who, seeking a cure, left graffiti at the temple of Deir el-Bahri (Milne 1914), on the walls of a chamber where Imhotep (a god of medicine) and Amenhotep, son of Hapu (a deified wise man) (Wildung 1977) were once worshipped. These inscriptions show that petitioners came from different, not necessarily wealthy, backgrounds and that some had travelled to Egypt from other countries to seek a cure.

The 'House of Life,' an important institution that was probably attached to many temples, may have played a significant part in the training and employment of priest-doctors and others associated with the medical system. Although its exact purpose is unclear, the prime role of the House of Life was probably to provide a centre where the rituals designed to protect the gods and the king could be prepared and developed; this would involve discussion of theology and the liturgy, the copying of earlier texts, and sometimes the composition of new, original works.

One interpretation of the House of Life (not however universally accepted [Gardiner 1938]) suggests that in some cases, in addition to being a scriptorium and temple library, this institution may have functioned as a centre of higher learning, where doctors received theoretical and practical training (Strouhal 1992).

The medical papyri

The ancient Egyptians developed a particular concept of the body system, which was based on observation of the sick and experience of mummification, but which reflected a lack of firsthand experience and knowledge of internal structures and functions that only extensive surgical intervention in living patients could have provided.

Perhaps directly influenced by their environment, with the great life force of the Nile and its network of irrigation channels, the Egyptians developed a unique concept of how the human body functioned, and this came to dominate their medical theory and practice. This concept was centred on the *metu*, a term used for a range of conduits (such as blood vessels), ducts, tendons, muscles, and possibly nerves, which spanned the body.

It was believed that these formed a network that was centred on the heart which, because it was supposed to be the seat of a person's thoughts and emotions, had a direct influence upon the *metu*. Sometimes the *metu* were envisaged as conduits for the blood, mucus, urine, semen, air, disease elements, and good or evil spirits that moved around the body, and therefore obstructions in the system could result in flooding or droughts in various parts of the body.

Discussion of this concept is preserved in the twelve surviving medical papyri, which also describe some of the pharmaceutical and surgical treatments that were used (Leitz 2000). A major study and translation (into German) of the most important medical papyri are included in the *Grundriss der Medizin der alten Agypter* (1954–73).

Inscribed on papyrus, many of these documents date from the Hyksos Period (c. 1570 B.C.) onwards, but were probably copies of earlier works. They appear to have originated from two sources. Some may have been compiled in the House of Life (these existed, for example, at Bubastis, Sais, Abydos, Edfu, and Amarna), where scribes copied and consulted books on medicine, magic, and theology. Generally, these papyri incorporate a wide range of information that may have been drawn from smaller collections of documents, which perhaps preserved both oral and written traditions.

Other papyri, however, may have been produced by individual physicians for their personal use. For example, the Hearst Papyrus, which was found in a house in an ancient provincial town, may have been a reference book for a local doctor.

The papyri seem to represent at least three types of documents. They probably include handbooks of instruction for doctor's regular use; outlines for medical lectures; and lecture notes and clinical notebooks that record the instruction received by medical students. Some may have served more than one purpose: for example, when a doctor became a practising physician, he may have retained his student notebook for reference.

The documents that were probably compiled in a temple context seem to present a more systematic, structured approach, but none of the papyri has any real unity of composition or subject matter. Each one deals with a variety of subjects, and some material occurs in more than one papyrus. In individual case studies, the proportion of treatment by 'rational' or 'nonrational' (magical) formulae differs considerably from one papyrus to another, and with the possible exception of the Edwin Smith Papyrus, none of the papyri describe firsthand accounts of clinical experience. In many instances, the prescriptions are given authority either by attributing authorship to a deity, king, high priest, or official or by using archaic grammar and vocabulary to indicate the antiquity of the text.

Most of the medical papyri identified to date were acquired by their modern owners in the nineteenth and early twentieth centuries. Because these papyri were generally obtained through private sales, little is known of their provenance; they may have originated from doctors' houses or tombs, temple libraries, or town archives. They must surely represent only a small fraction of the medical papyri that once existed but have subsequently been lost, destroyed, or remain unidentified in libraries or museum collections.

Brief descriptions of the Medical Papyri are given below. Three of them (Edwin Smith, Chester Beatty [V, VI, VII, VIII, XV], and Carlsberg [VIII]) are named after their modern owners; one (Hearst) was named after the woman who financed University of California expeditions to Egypt; four carry the name of the city where they are now housed (London [BM 10059], London(Leyden [BM 10072], Berlin, Brooklyn [snakebite papyrus]); others – Kahun, Ramesseum (III, IV, V), and Crocodilopolis – are called after the site of their discovery; and the Ebers Papyrus carries the name of its modern owner and editor.

The Kahun Gynaecological Papyrus

The Kahun Gynaecological Papyrus (Griffith 1898; Quirke 2002) is the earliest of the extant medical papyrus (c. 1825 B.C.); this document has a precise, well-documented archaeological provenance. It formed part of the archive of papyri discovered by Petrie in 1889 at the site of the pyramid workmen's town of Kahun, built to house the families of the craftsmen engaged in building the nearby pyramid of Senusret II at Lahun. The papyrus is now housed at University College London.

This is the earliest known document on gynaecology in the world. Parts of it are in a fragmentary state, but it provides prescriptions (mainly fumigations, pastes, and applications) for gynaecological conditions, contraception, pregnancy testing, sterility, and identifying the sex of unborn children. It does not, however, include any information about obstetrics.

Although exact parallels are not found in other papyri, there are similarities between Papyrus Kahun and the Berlin, Carlsberg, Ebers, London, and Ramesseum papyri.

The Ramesseum Papyri III, IV and V

The archaeologist Quibell discovered seventeen papyri, housed in a wooden box, which were part of a burial he excavated in 1896. This tomb (which probably dates to c. 1700 B.C.) was found under the brick magazines associated with the Ramesseum (the mortuary temple of Ramesses II) at Thebes. Although only three of the papyri (III, IV and V [Gardiner 1955; Barns 1956]) have medical content, the burial also contained a set of artefacts (now in The Manchester Museum), which may have had a magico-medical purpose. The burial goods possibly indicate that the unidentified tomb owner was a medical practitioner (Gardiner 1955).

The prescriptions, which deal with gynaecological, ophthalmic, and children's diseases, as well as remedies for relaxing stiffened limbs, are similar to examples in the Hearst and Ebers Papyri.

The Edwin Smith Papyrus

The Edwin Smith Papyrus (Breasted 1930) is the world's earliest known treatise on surgery. Edwin Smith purchased the document from a dealer at Luxor in 1862, and on his death in 1906, his daughter presented it to the New York Historical Society. Later, it was purchased by the Brooklyn Museum who donated it to the New York Academy of Medicine in 1948; it is currently housed in the New York Academy of Sciences. The provenance is unknown, but the document may have originated from a doctor's tomb at Thebes.

Breasted's translation and commentary emphasised the unique nature of this work. He demonstrated how it dealt with general surgery and surgery of the bones, providing the earliest extant evidence of the existence of objective, scientific medicine, based on observation of the patient's condition and a detailed knowledge of anatomy. In particular, he noted that the overall organisation of the document, with systematic discussion of each case, was unequalled in the other major papyri. It revealed a scientific mind at work, and demonstrated the existence of surgery as a specialisation. Most important, this provides the earliest extant evidence of the attribution of medical conditions to understandable physical causes rather than to demonic or magical causes.

Unlike most other medical papyri, this is an instruction manual rather than a collection of prescriptions. The forty-eight case studies demonstrate how the doctor examined the patient and reached a diagnosis. The facts of each case are observed, listed, and dealt with in a logical order; most deal with trauma and discuss injuries rather than disease processes. Each study includes a title, examination with list of symptoms, diagnosis, verdict (either recovery, probable recovery, or uncertain outcome), and suggested treatment.

More than any other source, this unique document clearly demonstrates the sophistication of medical knowledge in ancient Egypt. The injuries were studied in a way that marks significant progression in medical practice: for example, in each case, the symptoms were considered in groups (syndromes) rather than individually – a very important advance that is usually attributed to the Greeks. Also, in Breasted's opinion, this text demonstrates that the Egyptians already knew how to count the pulse, thousands of years before the Greeks recorded this practise. In addition, by noting how injury to the brain and skull affected the lower limbs, the author of this papyrus showed that the localisation of function within the brain was already understood.

The surviving copy of this text dates to c. 1570 B.C., but aspects of its grammar and vocabulary led Breasted to suggest that the original version possibly belonged to the Old Kingdom, and may have been compiled by Imhotep, the vizier accredited with founding medical science in Egypt. Others, however, dispute this early date.

The purpose and use of the papyrus also remain uncertain. Its damaged condition indicates that it had been frequently handled, and was perhaps a copy produced for, used by, and eventually buried with a local medical practitioner. Because it deals only with injuries suffered by male patients, it may have been an instruction manual to treat injuries sustained in warfare or at a building site.

The Ebers Papyrus

The Ebers Papyrus (Ebers 1875; Bryan 1930; Ebbell 1937) is currently housed in the University Library of Leipzig. Edwin Smith originally purchased the document in Luxor in 1862, and it was published as the 'Ebers Papyrus' by Georg Ebers who bought it in a sale in 1872. Its provenance is uncertain but it may have come from the tomb of a doctor at Thebes.

Until Breasted published the Edwin Smith Papyrus, the Ebers Papyrus was the most important resource for studying ancient Egyptian medicine and pathology. It is the longest of the medical papyri (110 pages), and dates to the ninth regnal year of Amenhotep I (c. 1538 B.C.), although one part claims to have been in use in the first Dynasty (c. 3000 B.C.). The Ebers Papyrus incorporates a variety of medical texts, apparently drawn from many sources, and arranged in a random order. Parallels for many examples in this document are found in the Hearst, Berlin, and London Papyri.

The Ebers Papyrus includes three very important paragraphs that present a treatise on the function of the heart and its vessels (*metu*). It also contains clinical cases in which symptoms and treatments relating to a range of illnesses and diseases are described. Some of these have not yet been satisfactorily translated and identified, but there are important sections on digestive disorders and intestinal worms; eye and skin diseases; fractures, burns, and bites; diseases of the ear, nose, and throat; stiff and painful limbs; gynaecological conditions; surgical treatments for tumours and abscesses; and the care of skin and hair.

The Hearst Papyrus

When the Hearst Egyptian Expedition was working near Deir el Ballas in 1901, a villager presented them with this papyrus (now housed at the University of California), which may have come from an ancient house at the site (Reisner 1905; Wreszinski 1912). It probably dates to the reign of Tuthmosis III (c. 1490 B.C.) and may have been used as a practical reference book by a local doctor.

The papyrus covers 18 pages and contains 260 case studies. It shares nearly one-third of the case studies with the Ebers Papyrus, and is clearly a compilation of material drawn from various sources. Although it is an inferior source, the Hearst Papyrus provides some information that is not present in the Ebers Papyrus.

Generally, it deals with conditions related to the teeth, bones, blood, bites, hair, the alimentary and urinary systems, and the *metu*. It also includes incantations and remedies to treat infectious diseases, most notably against major epidemics such as the unidentified 'Asiatic disease.'

The Carlsberg Papyrus VIII

Nothing is known of the origin or provenance of this papyrus (Iversen 1939), owned by the Carlsberg Foundation and now located in the University of Copenhagen. Although this document probably dates to the later New Kingdom (c. 1300 B.C.), it may derive from an earlier version (possibly c. 1900 B.C.). There is a parallel for its discussion of eye diseases in the Ebers Papyrus, and sections on conception, pregnancy, and identifying the sex of unborn children are very similar to parts of the Kahun and Berlin Papyri.

The London Medical Papyrus

This papyrus, BM 10059, which includes paragraphs on gynaecology, contains sixty-one prescriptions that represent a compilation of medical (twenty-five) and magical (thirty-six) treatments (Wreszinski 1912); some of these repeat sections of the Ebers Papyrus.

Now held in the British Museum, the papyrus was formerly owned by the Royal Institution of London, but details of its provenance are unknown. It has been assigned to the later New Kingdom (c. 1300 B.C.).

The Chester Beatty Papyri V, VI, VII, VIII and XV

These five papyri, BM 10685, BM 10686, BM 10687, BM 10688, and BM 10695, respectively, form part of an archive, which was started by a scribe in c. 1200 BC, and then added to and passed down through his family for over a century. The documents, finally buried in the family tomb chapel at Deir el-Medina (the village occupied by the royal necropolis workers of Thebes during the New Kingdom), were discovered by archaeologists in 1928 (Gardiner 1935).

Nineteen of the papyri (which include literary texts, spells, medical treatments, and rituals) were donated to the British Museum by the philanthropist Sir Alfred Chester Beatty. The papyri contain both rational and magical treatments: Papyrus VI discusses rectal diseases (some have parallels in the Ebers and Berlin Papyri), Papyrus VII contains spells for treating scorpion stings, and Papyrus V includes magical treatments for migraine.

The Berlin Papyrus

This papyrus, No. 3038, purchased in 1827 by Friedrich Wilhelm IV of Prussia for the Berlin Museum (where it is held today), was formerly owned by the archaeologist Passalacqua who acquired it at Sakkara (Wreszinski 1909). Although its exact provenance is unknown, studies of the language and writing style have enabled Egyptologists to assign it to the nineteenth Dynasty (c. 1200 B.C.). The text asserts the age and authenticity of an original document by claiming that it was discovered in an old chest containing antique writings. There are also several references to the author of the text.

Many sections of this significant papyrus repeat the Ebers Papyrus (particularly the discussion of the *metu*), and there are some parallels with the Kahun and Carlsberg Papyri. Subjects covered include breast diseases, contraception, fertility tests, and identification of the sex of unborn children.

The Brooklyn Papyri: 47,218.48 and 47,218.85

This papyrus, now in the Brooklyn Museum, has been cut into two parts (47,218.48 and 47,218.85). It provided a practical manual for the *kherep-*priests of Serqet (the snake goddess) to use when they treated their patients for snakebites (Sauneron 1989). Egyptologists have dated this document to c. 300 B.C., although the authors claim that the original was discovered during the Old Kingdom (c. 2200 B.C.).

This remarkable document includes, along with some magical treatments, many rational remedies that are based on observation of the patients' symptoms; it has provided convincing evidence that the *kherep-*priests (previously regarded as practising magicians) also used conventional treatments.

The London and Leiden Papyrus

This papyrus, written in Demotic in c. 250 A.D., contains sixty-one prescriptions of which only twenty-five are medical. Its content places it somewhere between the conventional medical papyri and those documents, such as the Turin 'Book of Magic' (c. 1160 B.C.), which prescribe entirely magical remedies. In addition to treatments to cure illness, the papyrus contains spells intended to kill or cause disease, and even prescribes mixtures to induce sleep (Griffith and Thompson 1904).

Because it was not recognised that the two parts of the papyrus (originally owned by Anastasi, the Swedish consul in Alexandria) were part of one document, they were sold to separate institutions: the Dutch government acquired one section (now in the Leiden collection) in 1828, and the other (BM 10072) entered the British Museum in 1857.

Papyrus Vindob

Despite its late date (c. 150 A.D.), this papyrus, D.6257, from Crocodilopolis (now in the Vienna collection) does not include any magical remedies but provides rational treatments for many conditions (Reymond 1976).

The contribution of human remains to the study of Egyptian medicine

In his account of the Edwin Smith Papyrus, Breasted (1930) states that preserved human remains from Egypt provided little evidence of any surgical or medical procedures that might have been attempted. He discussed some examples of wounds and injuries and cited some cases of medical intervention, including an Old Kingdom mandible with surgically bored holes to drain an abscess below the first molar, and two bodies in which splints, worn in life, had been left in place when the patients died.

Breasted concluded that palaeopathological evidence could contribute little to any reevaluation or interpretation of the contents of the Medical Papyri; however, over the past decades, considerable advances have been made in the study of preserved bodies from ancient Egypt. New techniques, many of them described in this book, have been used to diagnose disease and disease patterns. This evidence can now help Egyptologists and scientists to reassess the early translations of descriptions of disease, medical terms and words, and treatments that are listed in the Medical Papyri.

For example, in some cases, it is already possible to match physical conditions identified in the human remains with specific remedies and treatments in the papyri. One aim of a current study on ancient Egyptian pharmacy being conducted in Manchester may expand this possibility. The aim here is to identify scientifically any traces of therapeutic treatments that may remain in mummified tissue, and this may produce new knowledge that could inform future studies on the prescriptions in the Medical Papyri (see Chapter 14).

Ultimately, it is surely through interdisciplinary studies, using inscriptional evidence from the papyri, palaeopathological data from the bodies, and ethnographical studies of current traditional medicines, that researchers will be able to trace the practice of medicine and pharmacy in Egypt over the millennia.

CHAPTER 13

Intoxicants in ancient Egypt? opium, nymphaea, coca and tobacco

David J. Counsell

Introduction

Anthropologists recognise that all societies use intoxicants in aspects of their cultural lives (Lewin 1964; Rudgley 1993). Modern analysis of plants that early peoples believed to have intoxicating or healing properties has, in many cases, demonstrated the presence of pharmacologically active chemicals such as alkaloids and flavonoids that account for these effects.

In his work on drugs in ancient and primitive societies Emboden (1979), improving on previous work by Lewin (1964), classified intoxicants into the different groups summarised in Figure 37. Clearly, some well-known intoxicants do not fit easily into one category, opium, for example, being both narcotising and hallucinogenic, depending upon the circumstances of its use.

Although the use of animal- and mineral-derived drugs is well described in Egyptian medical practice (Nunn 1996), these do not tend to act as intoxicants, and thus, for this study, the subject materials of interest tend to be derived from plants.

Little is known about the use of intoxicants in ancient Egypt beyond the widespread consumption of beer, as part of the staple diet, and wine, by the elite. The cultural use of alcohol by the Egyptians is well documented and will not be considered here. This chapter will focus on a small number of intoxicants that may or may not have contributed to Egyptian society as a medicine, recreational drug or in sacred rituals.

Following the controversial TV documentary 'Mystery of the Cocaine Mummies,' first broadcast in 1994 (Schaffer Library 2005), I was invited to join the Manchester mummy team, to set up a project to look at cocaine and other intoxicants in Egyptian society.

For this research, we have concentrated principally on four drugs: opium, the 'blue lotus' (*Nymphaea caerulea*), cocaine and nicotine, and we have focused on analytical techniques such as gas chromatography-mass spectometry (GCMS) and liquid chromatography-mass spectrometry (LCMS). As reference for the reader, Chapter 10 includes a discussion of the techniques that have been used for this study, and this chapter presents the recent results obtained by the Manchester group. Together with a critical reappraisal of earlier work undertaken on this subject by other researchers, our results will be used to explore the history of these drugs in ancient Egypt.

Opium: its history in ancient Egypt and the Mediterranean

The origins of opium

Much of the evidence for opium around the ancient Mediterranean, including Egypt, is based upon artistic representations of the poppy capsule. Structurally, poppy capsules – the opium poppy (*Papaver somniferum*) included – have several clearly identifiable features, especially the 'torus' ring, a bulbous swelling on the stalk below the capsule, where the flower's petals were attached.

Opium, a resinous residue from dried sap, is obtained by incising the ripening capsule of the opium poppy, *Papaver somniferum*, and collecting the extruded sap as it dries. The resin has a variable composition depending upon many environmental factors but generally contains a number of physiologically active alkaloids, including the analgesics morphine and codeine and the vasodilator papaverine, all still used in medical practice.

The opium poppy has lost its ability to self-seed as the capsule does not split of its own accord, even when dried, thus requiring external assistance to split the poppy capsule and distribute the seeds. By definition therefore, opium poppies are a man-made cultivar, and not a natural plant. Its closest natural relation is *Papaver setigerum*, the only other poppy variety to produce opium alkaloids, and probably the precursor from which the opium poppy developed (De Cadole 1959).

Frequent finds of opium poppy seeds throughout Europe during the later Neolithic and early Bronze Age (Rudgley 1993), many associated with primitive open and closed systems for burning and smoking the drug (Kritikos and Papadaki 1967b), indicate an early use of opium in this area.

There seems little doubt that opium was used in Cyprus and Crete during the second millennium B.C. Finds of poppy remnants and primitive smoking devices attest to this (Kritikos and Papadaki 1967a, 1967b; Karageorghis

Category	Effects	Examples
Hallucinogens	Visual, auditory and other hallucinations.	LSD, magic mushrooms, henbane, cannabis.
Inebriants	Cause inebriation	alcohol, inhaled volatiles.
Hypnotics	Induce sleep	mandrake, opium.
Stimulants	Increase mental or physical stimulation	tea, coffee, betel, cocaine, tobacco.

FIGURE 37. *Summary of classification of intoxicants. Credit: David Counsell. Adapted from Emboden, W. 1979.* Narcotic Plants: Hallucinogens, Stimulants, Inebriants and Hypnotics, their Origins and Uses. *London: Studio Vista.*

1975). All these finds are, however, from religious contexts, suggesting that the use of opium was sacred rather than secular, and there is no indication of any medicinal application at this time. Artefacts and writings from these neighbouring societies in Cyprus and Crete have proved useful in investigating the use of intoxicants in Egypt.

The poppy in New Kingdom Egypt

Because the New Kingdom was contemporary with the Mediterranean Late Bronze Age, it might be expected that opium would be known to the Egyptians, although the sacred use of opium in Crete and Cyprus may have been a matter of secrecy.

Merrillees (1962, 1979) suggested that opium was imported into Egypt via trade with Cyprus at the height of the New Kingdom (c. 1500 B.C.) in the distinctive Cypriot Base II Ring Ware juglets known colloquially as *Bil-Bils*. His theory is based upon the design similarities of these small containers when compared with an opium poppy capsule. There is clear evidence of trade at that time: the *Bil-Bil* juglets, regardless of their contents, attest to that; but was opium really part of that trade?

Scenes in Egyptian tombs and temples show gardens and plants. The poppy is frequently depicted in New Kingdom art, including a scene in the tomb of Senedjem at Deir-el-Medina, Thebes. A necklace and matching earrings found in tomb KV56, Thebes, may also depict poppy capsules (Gabra 1937).

The names of many plants used as drugs have been identified in the Medical Papyri. The most important source, the Ebers Papyrus (Ebbell 1937) (see Chapter 12), refers to a large number of plant materials used in the manufacture of drugs. Unfortunately, these names are not always easy to translate. One important passage (782), known as *The Remedy for the Crying Child*, may refer to opium (Nunn 1996: 153). It includes the words '*shepnen* of *shepen*,' which have been translated (Erman and Grapow

1926–1931) as 'seeds' or 'petals' of 'poppy' (possibly the opium poppy). Neither the seeds nor the petals of the opium poppy contain any opium alkaloids and therefore would be unlikely to act as a sedative.

In summary, although Gabra (1937) and others have proposed that opium was cultivated as early as the New Kingdom, all the examples cited are now thought to be the red poppy (*Papaver rhoeas*) rather than opium poppy.

Bil-bil *juglets*

None of the above evidence supports the use of opium or the cultivation of the opium poppy in Egypt during the New Kingdom, but does Merrillees' theory provide a different perspective?

Opium could have arrived in Egypt during the New Kingdom from Cyprus, given the spread of its use to the central Mediterranean islands by that time. The shape of the *Bil-Bil* juglets is very reminiscent of an upturned poppy, and Merrillees suggests that some juglets are even decorated with striated markings similar to the parallel incisions used in modern day opium harvesting.

There are problems with this theory however. The contents of the juglets must have been liquid to pass through such a long narrow neck. Some juglets even have a pouring spout that clearly confirms the liquid nature of the contents. During the harvesting of opium, extruded sap is allowed to partially dry on the capsule before being scraped off with the resulting resin being packed into blocks after drying out further (White 1989).

For centuries, in European medicine, opium was administered by cutting a weighed amount from a solid block of material and then dissolving it in alcohol to make laudanum or as a constituent of Dover's powder (Scott 1969). Why then would the Cypriots come up with such an elaborate method of exportation when transporting the material in its solid form would be much less complicated? It is entirely possible that some as yet untested block of opium resin lies in a museum collection somewhere, awaiting identification.

Also, Cypriot Base II Ring Ware comes in forms other than *Bil-Bil* juglets; because these display the same type of markings as *Bil-Bil* juglets, it is evident that this decoration is not exclusive to *Bil-Bils*, and must surely indicate a decorative style rather than representing opium-harvesting scars. Nevertheless, despite these concerns, it seemed appropriate to investigate further Merrillees' theory by analysing the residues from these vessels for the presence of opium alkaloids.

Acquisition	Provenance	Egyptian	Sample	Opium	Palmitic
692	Gurob	XVII to XIX	Residues	Negative	Not tested
742	Il Lahun	XVII to XIX	Residues/Pottery	Negative	Not tested
743	Il Lahun	XVII to XIX	Residues/Pottery	Negative	Positive
744	Kahun	XXIV	Residues/Pottery	Negative	Not tested
2145	Gurob	XVII to XIX	Residues	Negative	Negative
2146	Gurob	XVII to XIX	Residues	Negative	Not tested
2147	Gurob	XVII to XIX	Residues/Pottery	Negative	Negative
2148	Gurob	XVII to XIX	Residues/Pottery	Negative	Not tested
2149	Gurob	XVII to XIX	Residues	Negative	Not tested
2978	Abydos	XVII	Residues	Negative	Not tested
6839	Abydos	XVII to XIX	Residues	Negative	Negative
6946A	Sedment	XIX	Residues	Negative	Positive
6946B	Sedment	XIX	Residues	Negative	Not tested

FIGURE 40. *Summary of provenance and forensic laboratory analysis on Manchester Cypriot Base II Ring Ware collection. Credit: David Counsell.*

Analytical work on opium in ancient Egypt

The first scientific attempt to identify opium from Egyptian artefacts was made by Muzio (1925) when residues from pottery removed from the tomb of the architect Kha at Deir el Medina were analysed. He 'confirmed' the presence of opium; however, in a review of this work, Bisset et al. (1994b) were unable to identify which jar had been analysed. Many of the jars, including the one thought to have been analysed, still appeared to have intact seals. None of the jars were of the *Bil-Bil* type, although Merrillees (1968) speculates that their design may have been inspired by Base II Ring-Ware.

Evans and Card (1986) first reported the detection of opium from a *Bil-Bil* jar by using thin-layer chromatography. Koschel (1996) subsequently reported the detection of opium using radioimmunoassay (RIA), thin-layer chromatography and GCMS on an unprovenanced pot in the Martin von Wagner Museum (University of Würzburg, Germany). Although they participated in this study, Bissett et al. (1996) were cautious in their interpretation of the result, indicating the need for the analysis of more juglets, particularly those with a firm provenance, to provide definitive proof.

In the Manchester project, the first step was to arrange for an analysis of the *Bil-Bil* juglets in The Manchester Museum collection. Samples from thirteen pots were analysed by the local forensic science laboratory at Exton Hall, Chorley, Lancashire. Residues were obtained from all of the complete pots, and broken pots were scraped on the inside surface to remove any dried-on residues. In some cases the pottery surface itself was removed with a surgical bur, thus increasing the chance of detection of opium even if that pot had been reused.

The treatment of each juglet and its provenance are summarised in Figure 40. At the laboratory, the samples were extracted with methanol and tested using high- pressure liquid chromatography (HPLC), GCMS and then derivatised to increase the detection of morphine, using further GCMS analysis. The results were disappointing because no evidence of opium alkaloids was detected in any of the samples. Five pots were then subjected to more extensive GCMS analysis, and in two of these, palmitic acid was found.

The maximum morphine yield in modern opium is approximately 10 per cent. Thus, given that the actual samples weighed between 0.25 and 0.5 g, a maximum content of 25–50 mg per sample might be expected. Speculating that the likely content would be much lower than this, given the age and inevitable degradation of any residual alkaloids over time, possibly to a residual factor of 0.1 per cent of the original, it would be expected that the remaining morphine content would be between 25 and 50 µg, well within the 2–5 µg per sample reference sensitivity assured by the laboratory.

Despite this, it was decided that further, more sensitive and in-depth analysis was required, and subsequent analytical work was performed at Hall Laboratories in Manchester. Reevaluation of a number of pots from the collection, using GCMS capable of a sensitivity of 0.2–0.5 µg, equivalent to 0.2–0.5 parts per million in a 1 ml resuspension, detected no opium alkaloids.

In the 1990s, Nunn and Evans took samples from *Bil-Bil* pots in The Manchester Museum collection. Subsequent analysis of this material involved the use of HPLC with ultraviolet detection and RIA (techniques that paralleled our own work). They informed us that morphine had been detected in two of three pots (Manchester No. 744 and Manchester No. 6946A), confirmed by both techniques. Review of our own results on these pots using GCMS could not confirm the presence of morphine or other opium alkaloids.

To address these conflicting results, Evans brought the extracts they had obtained from the 'positive' pots to Hall Laboratories, where they were tested further, using a system linking LCMS against a known sample of opium. Although morphine, codeine and noscapine were all easily detected from the opium sample, it again proved impossible to demonstrate the presence of these alkaloids in the pot extracts. Thus, it had to be accepted that the

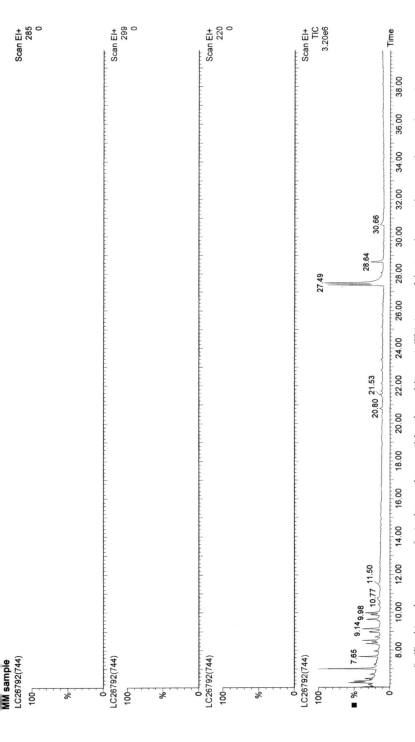

FIGURE 38. *Total ion chromatogram for juglet number 744 (Manchester Museum)*. This is one of the jugs that tested positive for morphine when using RIA and HPLC. Above are selected ion chromatograms for molecular weights 220 (noscapine), 299 (codeine) and 285 (morphine), which are the major alkaloids in opium. The lack of any peaks confirms that this sample is devoid of these compounds. If any of the compounds seen in the total ion chromatogram (TIC) have certain key functionalities present, for example, primary binding sites such as hydroxyl and amino groups on an aromatic framework, it could explain the positive result obtained with RIA. This will be explored in further work. *Credit: David Counsell.*

previous positive results were unreliable and that LCMS, being both highly sensitive and highly specific, now provided the definitive answer.

Later evidence for opium in ancient Egypt

In later times, information regarding plant use in Egypt is found in Classical writers, the most important source being Dioscoridus Pedanius of Anazarbus (first century A.D.) whose *Materia Medica* remained a significant pharmacological thesis until the fifteenth century A.D. (Gunther 1934). This makes it clear that opium was known in Egypt and the Roman World in the first century A.D. His description suggests that there had been a lively debate over the previous four centuries regarding the safety of the drug in medical use.

A wall scene in an intact tomb at Saqqara which belonged to Psamtek (Psammeticus), Royal Physician to Amasis (c. 500 B.C.), depicts a basket of seeded bread under a sheaf of what appear to be poppies, a 'torus' being clearly identifiable. This association of a physician, poppies and seeded bread raises the possibility of the medical use of opium at this time.

Cypriot base II ring ware juglets: an alternative explanation

Detailed chromatographic-mass spectrometric analysis of the contents of these jars has revealed no firm evidence of their use. The chromatograms appear to fit two profiles, which either suggest two different uses for the juglets or their reuse after the initial contents have been drained. A distinguishing feature between these two groups is the presence of nonanal ($C_9H_{18}O$).

Two samples from the Manchester collection suggest a further possibility: the pots comprised a pair of holders whose contents were mixed when the time came to use them. Manchester No. 2149 is actually a double vase, comprising two juglets fused together during manufacture, and Manchester No. 6946 A and B were found tied together by a piece of ancient string. Figure 39 shows that these two pots seem to be different in their contents, with pot B containing nonanal in contrast to pot A.

Nonanal is known to be a breakdown product of civetone ($C_{17}H_{30}O$). Civetone, derived from the anal glands, modified sweat glands, of the palm civet or civet cat is still used in perfume as a fixative, although its use is declining in favour of modern synthetic fixatives. Sebacic acid (C10 dicarboxylic acid), derived from sweat glands, is also present in small traces in some of the samples containing nonanal, lending further support to this possibility.

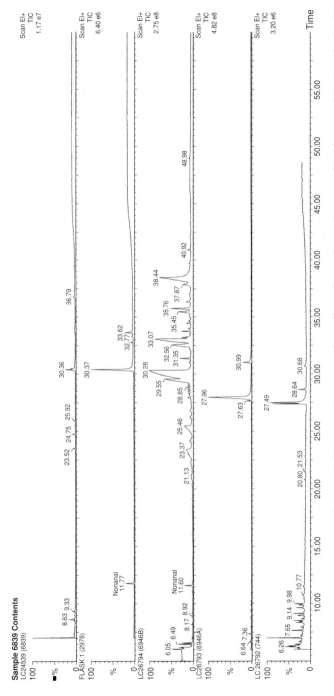

FIGURE 39. *Total ion chromatograms for four Bil-Bil juglets.* The main peaks in all samples are fatty acids, principally palmitic acid (C16). Juglet 6946B shows an extended series of fatty acids not seen in the other samples from C16 through to C22. Note the presence of nonanal in two of the juglets and the different profiles in 6946A and 6946B. *Credit: David Counsell.*

There is no known evidence for civet species in ancient Egypt or Cyprus, as their natural habitats are sub- Mediterranean Africa and Southeast Asia, but the possibility of a trade route for civetone or a civetone-based perfume from Southeast Asia via Cyprus cannot be discounted.

The Egyptian lotus: narcotic or perfume?

The lotus is one of the most potent symbols of ancient Egypt, expressing the unity of the 'Two Lands,' a tradition referring back to the unification of the Egyptian nation in c. 3100 B.C. It was also the emblem of Nefertum, the god of fragrance, and was associated with creation myths, rebirth and solar imagery. Although the lotus, and particularly the blue lotus, were of great religious importance to the Egyptians, this does not preclude their use in a secular context.

Emboden (1979, 1981) suggested the possibility that ancient Egyptians and the Maya used water lilies as intoxicants. Subsequently, Harer (1985) suggested that the Egyptians used the blue lotus (*Nymphaea caerulea*) and white lotus (*Nymphaea lotus*) as intoxicants in a recreational context. He proposed that the flowers of these plants were immersed in wine to extract active alkaloids into a fortified, that is, more intoxicating, drink. Although not all Egyptologists accept this idea, Harer presents considerable circumstantial evidence to support his hypothesis. The theory warrants further investigation, and here, we reassess the evidence presented by Harer in the light of our own investigations into the alkaloid content of these plants.

Our investigations formed the subject of a Channel 4 (UK) television documentary, as part of the series 'Private Lives of the Pharaohs' (Tyldesley 2000). Unfortunately, this documentary presented an oversensational interpretation of our results, implying that we had discovered that the blue lotus was the ancient Egyptian equivalent of Viagra®. The following discussion therefore provides the first opportunity to set the record straight.

Botany and phytochemistry of Nymphaea spp.

Three species of water lily are known from ancient Egypt. The white lotus (*Nymphaea lotus*) and the blue lotus (*Nymphaea caerulea*) are widely depicted in Egyptian art and decoration throughout the historical period. Identification and phytochemical interpretations are complicated by the introduction (probably c. 500 B.C.) of a third, nonnative species, the pink lotus (*Nelumbo nucifera*), also known as the Persian lotus (Harer 1985).

	Nymphea caerulea	*Nymphea lotus*	*Nelumbo nucifera*
Flower Colour	Blue	White	Pink
Flower Size	3-6 ins	5-10 ins	5-10 ins
Leaves	12-16 ins, wavy.	12-20 ins, serrate.	12-36 ins, sinuate.
Blooming	Night - noon	Dawn - noon	?

FIGURE 41. *Summary of botanical features of ancient Egyptian 'lotuses.' Credit: David Counsell. Adapted from Bailey, H. L. and Bailey, E. Z. 1976.* Hortus Third: A concise dictionary of plants cultivated in the United States and Canada. *New York: Macmillan.*

Also, confusion persists regarding the nomenclature of these plants (Harer 1985). In modern botany, the term 'lotus' refers to the genus *Nelumbo* and not to the *Nymphaea* spp., which should more correctly be called blue and white 'water lilies.' Thus, it would seem that the term 'lotus,' when found in a context pertaining to Egyptology, is used incorrectly. The characteristics of the blue and white water lilies are summarised in Figure 41.

According to Harer, *Nymphaea* spp. contain a number of alkaloids, namely, nymphaeine, nuciferine, nupharidine and α-nupharidine, that exist in both the flower and the rhizome of the plant. This has proven difficult to confirm even using Harer's references. In contrast to *Nymphaea* spp., the alkaloid profile of *Nelumbo* spp. is well described and includes nuciferine, nupharidine and α-nupharidine (Wróbel, 1977). It appears that the only alkaloid exclusive to the *Nymphaea* genus is nymphaeine, an 18-carbon structure, about which very little is known. This is in contrast to the 15-carbon alkaloids from *Nelumbo* spp., which are well understood and include apomorphine derivatives (Dr Duke).

Apomorphine itself is a toxic substance used extensively in the past as an emetic and more recently as a sexual stimulant (Dula et al. 2001; Montorsi et al. 2003), giving *Nelumbo nucifera* a far better claim to be an intoxicant, with possibly aphrodisiac properties, than the two *Nymphaea* varieties.

The evidence for ingestion of water lily

Several writers, including Dioscorides and Herodotus (c. 450 B.C.) (*The Histories*, Book 2, para. 92), have recorded that the ancient Egyptians ingested various parts of the lily plant, but unfortunately they do not describe the resultant effects. Neither do these accounts confirm which plant was being consumed, although it is possible that they both refer to *Nelumbo*.

It is generally agreed that, in the Medical Papyri (see Chapter 12), the ancient Egyptian word for *Nymphaea* spp. is *seshen*, although it is unclear whether they made any distinction between the white and blue lotus, or indeed with the pink lotus after its introduction in the Persian Period. It is evident, however, that any mention of *seshen* before this time refer to *Nymphaea* spp.

The medical texts contain a number of early references to *seshen*. In many examples, the plant appears to have been consumed as a constituent of a remedy (Manniche 1989), although any untoward effects are not recorded.

The case for lotus-spiced wine

Immersion of lotus flowers in wine would almost certainly facilitate the extraction of any alkaloids present in the flower because they are generally readily soluble in alcohol compared to water. Even if the plant contains alkaloids, this does not necessarily imply that these compounds are present throughout all parts of the plant, and they may or may not be present in the flower. As yet, the pharmacological effects, psychotropic or otherwise, of the alkaloids named by Harer are not well understood but, in support of his theory, there is evidence of an association between blue lotus and wine in ancient Egypt.

The Medical Papyri (see Chapter 12) contain two references to the immersion of *seshen* in alcohol. Ebers 209 and 479 describe *seshen* 'spending the night' in alcoholic mixtures. It cannot, however, be concluded that the Egyptians knew the importance of this in terms of extracting potentially active agents. They used many other vehicles such as water, milk and honey in drug production. The use of alcohol as a vehicle is not restricted to lotus-containing remedies and similarly, not all lotus-containing remedies utilise alcohol as a vehicle.

The uninhibited woman depicted in the Turin Erotic Papyrus (No. 55001) is consistently depicted with a lotus above her head, suggesting that she may have been intoxicated by its use or that it was being used as an aphrodisiac (Schumann et al. 2001).

Other archaeological evidence cited by Harer includes tomb reliefs depicting the lotus in banqueting scenes, implying that it was used as a recreational intoxicant, and artifacts associated with the immersion and consumption of lotus-enhanced wine.

Analysis of the Egyptian water lilies

Although blue water lilies are fairly common, most are modern varieties cultivated to bloom all day or for longer periods. True *Nymphaea caerulea*

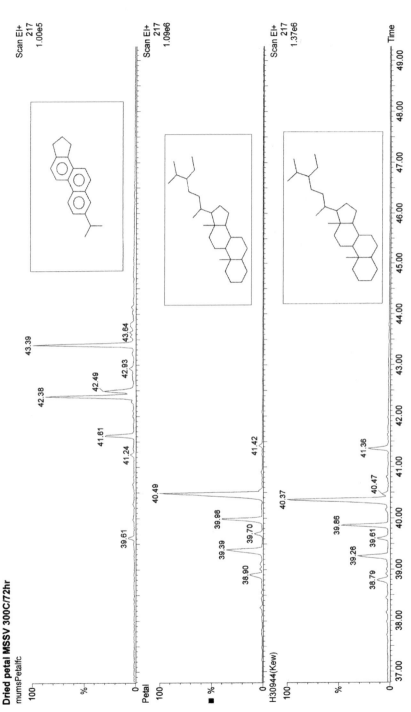

FIGURE 42. *Phytosterol profile of ancient sample (from Royal Botanical Gardens, Kew) and modern petal of* Nymphaea caerulea *compared with a petal of* Impatiens walleriana *(Busy Lizzie). Note the preservation of the profile of the two samples of* Nymphaea caerulea *and the difference in comparison with a different species. The structure of the major phytosterol component for each sample is shown alongside. Credit: David Counsell.*

is now a rare plant, seldom found in the wild and only occasionally in botanical collections. For our research, blue lotus flowers were generously provided by Stapeley Water Gardens in Staffordshire, UK.

Extraction of these flowers was performed using three techniques, each performed on fresh blooms. Head space analysis allowed evaluation of the plant's scent for intoxicating possibilities. A freon-based supercritical extraction technique was used to extract the essential oils of the flowers, and finally a methanol solvent extraction was performed. The extracts were subjected to analysis by GCMS and LCMS.

Later, the Royal Botanic Gardens at Kew, Richmond (UK), provided a small sample for the project: this was a *Nymphaea caerulea* petal, previously identified by Dr Nigel Hepper (1990), which had been taken from funerary garlands from Hawara (first century A.D.). This small petal sample and an equivalent modern sample from the Stapeley flowers were subjected to micro-scale sealed vessel pyrolysis GCMS, and the results obtained from the ancient and modern plant were then compared.

Generally, the results were disappointing, as no alkaloids were identified in any of the analyses performed on the blue lotus; however, in agreement with other published material (Fossen et al. 1999), high levels of bioflavonoid were found. Comparison with an extract of *Ginkgo biloba* showed the level of these compounds was higher in the fresh blue lotus flowers. Bioflavonoids are known to have beneficial effects, being oxygen free radical scavengers and vasodilators that enhance tissue blood flow, so it is likely that like ginkgo, ginseng and other herbal remedies rich in bioflavonoids, blue lotus has health promoting properties.

The micro-scale sealed vessel studies on the blue lotus demonstrated preservation of the phytosterol profile of the two samples, despite the time gap of some 2,000 years. These compounds are found predominately in the cell walls of the plant, and their demonstrable stability over time opens up the possibility that this method might be useful in identifying ancient plant remains, if consistent species differences in these profiles can be demonstrated and catalogued.

The general conclusion, however, is that consumption of blue lotus flowers, either by eating or as a wine-based infusion, would not give any additional intoxicating effect.

Water lilies as aphrodisiacs

Two clear mechanisms exist in which drugs can be used to enhance sexual performance. Best known is the mechanism of sildenafil (Viagra®)

and similar drugs, which produce a specific vasodilator effect to help produce and sustain the male erection. Research has suggested a benefit may be derived from the use of *Ginkgo biloba* in male impotence although this research is limited and it is unclear whether the effect is due to the bioflavonoid or ginkgolide content (Sikora et al. 1989).

Certainly, bioflavonoids produce vasodilation but this is a non-specific effect that is not proven to influence the male erection; therefore, no aphrodisiac properties can be ascribed to plants that contain them. It is tempting to interpret the blue lotus as an aphrodisiac on the grounds of its appearance in scenes in the Turin Erotic Papyrus, but this association cannot be supported by any scientific evidence. Many substances used today are believed to have aphrodisiac properties although they contain no active ingredients, so perhaps the same pertained to the blue lotus in ancient Egypt.

The Persian lotus, *Nelumbo nucifera*, is more interesting. Differing from Viagra® in action, certain compounds are now known to act centrally to increase libido (the desire for sex), rather than enhancing the ability to perform. In this regard, small doses of apomorphine have been demonstrated to be effective (Dula et al. 2001; Montorsi et al. 2003), although in large doses, it is a profound emetic that causes prolonged and uncontrolled vomiting. This presents the possibility that the Persian lotus might act in this way, although there is no evidence that the ancient Egyptians used it in this manner.

Cocaine and nicotine

The report of the discovery of cocaine and nicotine in Egyptian mummies (Balabanova et al. 1992; Parsche et al. 1993) raised the possibility of transatlantic trade in the second millennium B.C. Although nicotine is not exclusive to the tobacco plant, as it is found in a number of plants from the eastern Atlantic landmass, Balabanova considered that the levels discovered in the mummies were too high to have been derived from a dietary source. This implied, by default, that they were the result of chewing or smoking tobacco.

On the other hand, cocaine is only found in the 'New World' and could only be obtained from the South American coca plant (*Erythroxylum coca*). There is no clear evidence in the Egyptian archaeological record of any regular transatlantic trade at this time, although critics might claim that is because no one has looked properly. If trade did exist, it seems hardly likely that it was limited to these two plants, and other evidence of cultural exchange between the two areas would be expected, in terms of artefacts and even written records. If it is assumed from this basic analysis that Balabanova's results are incorrect, then an explanation is required as to how these results have come about.

Overview of hair analysis for cocaine and other drugs

The detection of the cocaine metabolite benzoylecgonine (BZE) was first reported in 1981 (Arnold and Püschel 1981), using RIA. There was difficulty with quantification in early studies due to confusion between specificity of antibodies for cocaine and BZE and loss of drug during the digestion processes.

Standard techniques for drug analysis use hair samples of about 100 mg that are first washed in methanol to remove surface materials such as cosmetics and oils. Extraction is by acid or alkali digestion or using organic solvents, followed by analysis using RIA or GCMS with quantification against known concentrations. Alkali digestion is the most efficient method but cannot be used for cocaine as it completely degrades the drug. Methanol is the preferred solvent for cocaine extraction. RIA is popular for screening, due to the high sensitivity of commercial kits working in nano- or picogramme per milligramme concentrations. GCMS is then used for confirmation and quantification (Henderson et al. 1995).

The collective experience of modern drug analysis is based on contemporary samples from known or anticipated drug users, with predictable contamination and a proven track record in these circumstances. Given the potential for contamination in archaeological samples, and bearing in mind our earlier experience with opium (described above), it is questionable if the rigour of standard techniques is adequate when applied to the more complex situation seen in Egyptian mummies.

Sampling from Egyptian mummies: the problems

Sampling from ancient human remains, particularly Egyptian mummies, is fraught with problems seldom encountered in the modern sphere of drug analysis. Mummified materials (complete mummies and various body parts) are held in museum collections around the world. Much of this material is unprovenanced, and some may even have a relatively modern date, as there was a thriving trade in fake mummies during the nineteenth century. It is quite likely therefore that positive results for cocaine and nicotine could be obtained from these post-Colombian individuals.

	Parsche (1993)	Cartmell (1991 and 2001)
Cocaine in Hair Egypt	0.024 – 0.2 ng/mg	nil
Cocaine in Hair Peru	0.22 – 13.9 ng/mg	0.02 – 15.8 ng/mg
Nicotine in Hair Egypt	0.14 – 0.9 ng/mg	0.7 – 2.2 ng/mg
Nicotine in Hair Peru	0.028 – 1.4 ng/mg	Not measured.

FIGURE 43. *Comparison of hair analysis for cocaine and nicotine in Egypt and South America.* Data given in papers corrected to nanogrammes/milligrammes of sample. *Credit: David Counsell.*

Contamination of samples can occur from many sources (Cartmell and Weems 2001). Plant material and gums and resins were applied internally and externally in the process of mummification, and the hair of Egyptian mummies is often densely matted by these ancient unguents. Further contamination of the mummy could occur from spillage or leaching of other grave goods at the time of burial or during the subsequent millennia when vermin, insects, bacteria and moulds could enter the body or the wrappings.

After excavation, exposure to environmental factors or poor storage could lead to further contamination (see Chapter 16). Smoking has only recently been banned in our museums, and it is likely that many esteemed archaeologists of the past were users of tobacco. Photographic evidence supports this; for example, H. A. Harris can be seen smoking a cigarette while examining an Egyptian mummy in 1930 at University College London (Dawson 1938).

In time, the extensive organic compounds from the mummy itself and from the mummification and other contaminating processes will undergo a process known as diagenesis. Compounds that are present become degraded as the result of oxidation, fermentation and other processes, including cross reactivity between compounds. This in turn produces new materials and compounds that were not necessarily present on the mummy at the start, causing problems with interpretation, and increasing the chances of a false positive result with RIA and HPLC.

Cocaine and nicotine in ancient populations

Not surprisingly, cocaine has been detected in Peruvian mummies (Cartmell et al. 1991; Balabanova et al. 1992). In 1992, Balabanova's team also published their first identification of drugs in Egyptian mummies, followed in 1993 by a further paper (Parsche et al.1993) reporting the detection of

nicotine, cocaine and hashish in a variety of tissues from ancient populations from Peru and Egypt, with nicotine, but not cocaine or hashish,
detected in bone from ancient Sudan and members of the ancient 'Bell'
culture from Germany. More recently, Cartmell and Weems (2001) have
reported the detection of nicotine, but not cocaine, in Egyptian mummies
from the Dakhleh Oasis. The reported levels for hair samples in the Parsche
and Cartmell papers adjusted to microgrammes per milligram of material
are summarised in Figure 43.

NICOTINE. Cartmell and Weems (2001) suggest a cut-off point of 2 ng/mg
to distinguish between regular tobacco smokers and those exposed passively
to smoke or ingesting nicotine in the diet, with levels greater than 20 ng/mg
being reported in previous studies on South American mummies. This is
consistent with the range reported by Parsche et al. (1993) in modern addicts.
It seems clear therefore that the nicotine found in Egyptian mummies is
from a dietary source. The ubiquitous presence of nicotine in all the populations tested, all at dietary levels, supports the validity of these results.

Duke's *Phytochemical and Ethnobotanical Database* lists twenty-three
nicotine-containing plants in addition to tobacco (*Nicotiana tabacum*). Of
these, two – *Withania somnifera* and *Apium graveolens* – were known to the
Egyptians (Manniche 1993), and the latter, celery, was the more likely to
be used as a food. In 1994, as a result of the 'Cocaine Mummies' television
documentary, seven samples (six of tissue and one of hair), taken from
mummies in The Manchester Museum collection, were sent for analysis
at the Medical Toxicology Laboratory at Guy's and St Thomas' Hospital in
London, UK. Three of these samples tested positive for nicotine and none
for cocaine. Concentration levels were not reported.

All the nicotine-positive samples were taken from disarticulated heads of
unknown provenance. Further investigation and closer inspection demonstrated that two, No. 7700/ES8(10p) and No. 7700/ES6(4p), originated from
the collection of G. Elliot Smith, former professor of anatomy in Cairo and
Manchester. Neither head showed any evidence of intentional mummification. It seems likely, from the evidence of the Dawson (1938) picture,
that environmental contamination could be a factor in these results. The
antiquity of the third head, No. 7700/1981.575(3p), could be confirmed by
the signs of resin use on the hair and residual traces of gilding on the face,
attributing it to the Ptolemaic Period (c. 300 B.C.).

COCAINE. The level of cocaine found in Peruvian hair is reassuringly consistent in the two studies shown, with significantly lower levels detected in

the Egyptians. Assuming that the identification of cocaine is correct, this difference might be explained either by a lower level of exposure during life or greater deterioration of the cocaine present in the hair, over the additional centuries since death, in the Egyptian sample.

In addition to the seven aforementioned samples, hair, bone and tissue samples have been tested from a variety of mummies in the Manchester and Leicester collections. These include four mummies from Manchester: Asru (No. 1777, Thebes, c. 700 B.C.), Nekht-Ankh (No. 21470, Rifeh, c. 1900 B.C.), No. 1770 (Ptolemaic Period, c. 300 B.C.) and No. 1766 (Fayoum, c. 100–200 A.D.) and four mummies from Leicester. To date, none have tested positive for cocaine, using methanol solvent extractions of tissue samples, tested using GCMS to a sensitivity of 0.1 μg/mg of material.

If the theory of transatlantic trade were correct, surely the results obtained by either Cartmell or Manchester would corroborate the discovery of cocaine in at least one of the Egyptian mummies that have been tested by these teams. This lack of results suggests that either Balabanova and her associates are misinterpreting their results or that the sample of mummies tested by them have been mysteriously exposed to cocaine.

The levels of cocaine recorded for South American mummies in these studies compare favourably with reported levels in modern coca chewers in the range of 1.0–28.9 ng/mg (Henderson et al. 1992) and 1.4 and 50.6 ng/mg (Möller et al. 1992). By comparison, the levels in the Egyptian mummies are very low – close to the 0.1 ng/mg limit of detection reported by many investigators at the time of the study (Henderson et al. 1992, 1995) and consistently lower than the 0.3 ng/mg suggested by Cartmell et al (1993) as a cut-off point 'to differentiate a "negative" and a "positive" result consistent with previous hair studies.' (The paper actually states 3 ng/mg, which would contradict the interpretation of the results given by the authors. We therefore suspect that a decimal point error has been made, as a cut-off value of 0.3 ng/mg would be consistent with the results shown and the interpretation given.) According to this interpretation, the results for cocaine reported by Parsche and Balabanova are negative.

Critique of Dr Balabanova's work on drug analysis in mummies

It is clear from the general literature on hair analysis for drugs that Balabanova was one of the pioneers of hair analysis, being the first to report the determination of cocaine in human hair by using GCMS, thus demonstrating that the primary analyte in hair is cocaine itself, rather than the metabolite BZE as previously thought (Henderson et al. 1995; Balabanova and Homoki 1987). She obviously has expertise in this area in the context of modern forensic analysis.

Her papers reporting the discovery of cocaine in hair from Egyptian mummies are lacking in detail with regard to the methodology used. It can only be speculated that the method used was similar to that reported in her original work, but this does not provide important detail, particularly relating to the GCMS analysis, in terms of retention times in the chromatography phase, use of control samples and whether identification was based on detection of a molecular ion or the full mass-spectrometric profile.

Parsche reports using samples weighing 1 g, which is acceptable for tissue samples but represents a significant amount of hair (the norm being 100 mg) to remove from a mummy. Without proven experimental rigour, it is difficult to accept Balabanova's findings, particularly as the concentrations are so low in the presence of heavy contamination when such small quantities of a drug can be difficult to detect against the background contamination, even when modern computer programmes are used to facilitate interpretation.

Our own experience with the analysis of Base II Ring Ware, considering the conflicting results obtained, has highlighted the potential problems encountered when conclusions are based on the application of modern tests to ancient materials. Analytical methods that have proven accurate and reliable in modern uncontaminated samples must be used and interpreted with caution when applied to ancient samples, particularly mummified material, which frequently contains many unidentified materials.

Even hair samples from a typical Egyptian mummy are often contaminated by the gums and resins used to coat the hair or glue it to the skull, as compounds from the decaying embalming materials inevitably penetrate the hair shaft as they do the rest of the body. For example, work in progress has demonstrated the penetration of camphor and naphthalene, as markers of embalming material, even into the marrow of intact longbones.

Cocaine: an alternative explanation

If Balabanova's results are indeed correct (and without reevaluation of her extracts or retesting of the original mummies she worked on, this is difficult to accept), then other possible explanations must be considered. The evidence for transatlantic trade, as presented by the *Cocaine Mummies* documentary, is unconvincing. A much simpler explanation is that the Munich mummies could have been inadvertently contaminated, either in the laboratory or at some earlier point in their history.

Historically, the coca leaf has been a gift of nature, fuelling the extraordinary high-altitude achievements of the Inca Empire. It is only as a result of its identification and extraction into the pure form by Gaedcke in the 1850s and Niemann's later improvement of the earlier technique, that cocaine became available in its powdered and highly concentrated form. In the late nineteenth and early twentieth centuries, cocaine, devoid of its modern social stigma, was widely used by members of the upper social classes across Europe and America, eventually finding its way into popular 'pick me up' products such as 'Coca Cola' and 'Forced March.'

According to the *Cocaine Mummies* documentary and notes from the Munich Museum where Balabanova's team obtained their samples, the mummies were once in the private ownership of the King of Bavaria. The habits of the king are unknown, but given the fashions of the time, it is not implausible that the mummies were contaminated with cocaine whilst in his possession or subsequently.

Conclusions

In summary, Merrillees' proposal that opium was imported into Egypt from Cyprus during the New Kingdom cannot be confirmed. Reevaluation of Cypriot Base II Ring Ware seems unlikely to implicate *Bil-Bil* juglets, which more probably contained a perfume product, possibly civetone based. As for the blue lotus, scientific evidence does not support the use of *Nymphaea caerulea* as a narcotic or aphrodisiac, although it may have health benefits due to its high bioflavonoid content.

Nicotine has been found in Egyptian mummies in small quantities consistent with a trace dietary source, possibly derived from celery, but not at the levels expected from tobacco use.

The levels of cocaine reported in South American mummies are consistent with the habit of coca leaf chewing. The levels reported in Egyptian mummies are very low, below the level agreed upon for a positive result by some laboratories and at the limit of detection by the technical standards for GCMS in the early 1990s. The results are therefore unreliable. The possibility of modern contamination cannot be ruled out, but either way, it seems highly unlikely that the ancient Egyptians were exposed to cocaine during their lifetimes.

CHAPTER 14

Pharmacy in ancient Egypt

Jacqueline M. Campbell

Introduction

Pharmacy is the practice of sourcing, preparing and dispensing pharmaceutical preparations to treat ailments. The use of medicinal plants as remedies, from ancient to current times, precedes any formal medical record knowledge being transmitted from generation to generation. This is manifested in traditional medicine today, in which treatments are characteristic of a local community.

This century has witnessed a revived interest in natural drug resources and the reestablishment of sustainable species to satisfy demand (Demerdash 2001). Herbal remedies are now regulated (*British Herbal Pharmacopoeia*), whereas scientific interest focuses on pharmacognosy and pharmacology (Evans 2002).

The classical history of pharmacy

History attributes medicine to Hippocrates, c. 460 B.C., and drugs to the mythical Chiron. Asclepiades (100 B.C.) communicated Hippocratic medicine to Rome whilst Dioscorides (c. 50 A.D.) compiled the first pharmacopoeia of 500 drugs (Gunther 1934). His contemporary, Pliny, wrote of medicinal plants, whereas Celsus recorded the *materia medica* of the Roman world. In c. 150 A.D., Galen developed pharmacy, thereby influencing medicine for 1,500 years (Brock 1952; Sarton 1954; Nutton 2001). In the fifth century A.D., Oribasius translated Galenic texts into Syriac, which remained medical doctrine for 200 years. When Islam united Near Eastern countries under one religion in the seventh century A.D., Galen's teachings were embraced (Elgood 1951) and continued to influence Arabic medicine until the eleventh century.

Avicenna combined Galenic tradition with Persian medicine, which had its origins in the Code of Hammurabi, c. 1950 B.C. (Sigerist 1987:386). Avicenna's *Canon on Medicine* (Gruner 1930) was brought to Salerno, and subsequently transmitted to Moslem Spain whence the twelfth century Jewish exodus carried his teaching to France and England. Translated into Latin by Gerard of Cremona, the work influenced medicine until the sixteenth century when the advent of the printing popularised medicinal herbals (Gerard 1597; Culpeper 1653), the precursors of modern pharmacopoeia.

Elizabethan trade introduced plants and spices to Britain, and many were incorporated into *materia medica*. The Society of Apothecaries (1617) established their physic garden in Chelsea, which survives today. Indeed, Galenic protocol influenced orthodox medicine until the eighteenth century, and botanical preparations remain known as 'Galenicals.'

The origin of pharmacy is readily traced to ancient Greece, but the medical records of the ancient Egyptians are very much earlier. The Medical Papyri (see Chapter 12) not only describe symptoms, but also cite approximately 2,000 remedies, many in sufficient detail to permit reproducibility.

Ancient Egyptian records

Ancient Egyptian physicians were meticulous in their medical recordings, but difficulties remain in translating drug sources which have no parallel attestation elsewhere (Quirke 1998). Comprehensive studies on ancient Egyptian botany have emerged (Loret 1892; Täckholme 1941–1974; Germer 1985; Hepper 1990; Manniche 1999) and much is known of agriculture (Bowman and Rogan 1999), food supplies (Darby et al. 1977), and materials and food technology (Nicholson and Shaw 2003). Consequently, knowledge of Egyptian flora is increasing but identification in the Egyptian texts remains uncertain.

Translational uncertainties

Loret (1892) translated *m3tt* as celery, Dawson (1933) proposing mandrake, herbs considerably different in pharmacological application. Dawson (1926) translated *snj-t3* as fenugreek, yet Ebbell (1937: 30) determined it to be colocynth. Manniche (1999: 122) proposes that *b3k* is moringer oil, whereas Ebbell (1937: 33) and Jonckheere (1947: 32) suggest Balanites. To Ebbell (1937: 32), *s'm* remains unknown and Manniche (1999: 80) proposes absinthe. *The Grundriss* (1954–1973) and Ghalioungui (1987) offer different translations, whereas Charpentier (1981) reviewed many in the context of botanical evidence. The diverse *materia medica* of ancient Egypt, however, is comprehensively recorded (Estes 1993: 139–157; Ebeid 1999: 249–271; Nunn 2000: 136–162).

The translator not only considers the literal translation, but also assigns a plant that fits the criteria of both language and medicinal application, consistent with the literary and artistic evidence (Dawson 1926). Philology is unlikely to resolve the uncertainties, although there is greater consensus on trees, cereals and foodstuffs, because these words were used daily, but less agreement on shrubs and herbs. The identities of fifty-five plants and minerals are disputed, and 145 ingredients remain unidentified.

Forensic pharmacy provides the potential for validation, enabling translation to be considered from contemporary pharmacological application. Common names are used throughout the texts to describe minerals and plants; for the latter, these names can represent numerous species, so this type of definitive identification is very important. Awareness of the prevalence of individual plants at various historical periods, indicating their availability, is another significant factor.

Forensic evaluation

The undigested remains of the cereal-based diet in ancient Egypt provide essential forensic evidence. The last meal eaten, including medication, may be identified by analysing stomach contents in mummified remains (Ogell 2005). Additionally, the nutrition and diet of a population may be determined by studying faecal remains (Aufderheide 2003). Humans have always taken supplementary food to improve health, and hence it is difficult to distinguish between food and drug. Hair analysis (Cartmel et al. 2005; Watson 2005) affords longer term evidence of food and toxins while indicating famine, disease and stress.

Archaeologists have determined the flora available in ancient Egypt (de Vartavan and Asensi Amorós 1997) but provenance is uncertain in nineteenth century museum collections (Germer 1998: 84; Quirke 1998). Moreover, tomb finds do not necessarily indicate the burial cache. Seeds, carried on the feet of excavators, or burrowing animals can contaminate archaeological sites, as can animal dung residues. Surface finds are neither representative nor reliable. Unless present in the abundance of a granary or bouquet, the only reliable plant evidence is in a sealed container, as in the Tutankhamun collection (Newberry 1927: 189–196) or the Tomb of Kha (Egyptian Museum, Turin).

Plants significant to a later era can be placed in or near an earlier tomb in tribute or when human remains were relocated or rewrapped. Furthermore, tomb offerings may represent the best of what was available and not necessarily what was abundant. Consequently, plant evidence should not be considered in isolation. Authenticity of a burial may be determined by evaluating the phytogeography (Boulos 1999–2005), supported by evidence of cultivation or importation.

Seeds and twigs are sufficiently robust to survive transportation, but flowers are usually too delicate. Ancient Egyptians were prolific collectors, preserving many items of daily use for the next life, which provide not only archaeobotanical evidence but patterns of progression in the pharaonic period and beyond. Techniques now used to recover archaeobotanical specimens (Murray 2003: 509) are more sophisticated than those of the nineteenth century because they represent the general populace as opposed to individual tomb finds.

Identification of plants presents greater difficulties (Germer 1985, 1998). It is possible to classify family and genus, but not the species which may be medicinally unique. For example, poppies from the same family and genus have species with markedly different properties, one a decorative flower (*Papaver rhoeas*), the other a potent narcotic (*Papaver somniferous* [see Chapter 13]). The climate that preserved human remains equally preserved plants, and morphological examination, the least destructive process, enables identification of some species by observing shape, size, stem, leaf, fruit or seed.

Fruits and seeds are the most abundant and most extensively identified, but when dehydrated, the evidence can confuse the observer. Although dehydration and carbonisation cause shrinkage, physical cellular characteristics, unique to each species, can be identified microscopically (Gale and Cutler 2000). Provenance can also assist in identification, as can natural habitat. Fruits are noticeably smaller and often shrivelled; seeds are robust and change shape the least, but their characteristic morphology is less defining.

A control specimen, often required, is available in various herbaria (the Royal Botanic Gardens Kew [RBGK] and the Vivi Tackholme Herbarium, the University of Cairo). Living specimens can be sourced at RBGK and the Chelsea Physic Garden, London. Texts of Egyptian flora are invaluable aids (Täckholme 1941–1969; Boulos 1999–2005).

Palynology permits reconstruction of past flora, from observation of pollen grains preserved on artefacts, soil, sand and human remains. The resistant outer coats of the pollen grain, each with a uniquely patterned surface, afford qualitative and quantitative estimates of species that occurred thousands of years previously. A typical pollen grain is 30 μm in diameter; it is visible under the light microscope and reveals even more detail under scanning electron microscopy (Ayyad and Moore 1995).

Archaeobotany indicates when plants were harvested. Constant availability requires storage and this is confirmed archaeologically (Caton Thompson and Gardner 1934; Fahmy 2003: 20). Archaeobotanical remains, however, do not necessarily indicate function. The purpose of inclusion may be agricultural, nutritional, medical, decorative, symbolic or ritual. Climate and environment influence active principles within plants and, subsequently, in their evolution.

Mass spectrometry (Chapter 10) provides the chemical fingerprint of the plant, which may be compared with contemporary samples. Gas chromatography/mass spectrometry isolates the individual components, typically essential oils, alkaloids and glycosides that are significant pharmaceutically. Only molecular investigation will afford comparison of species. The DNA data bank at RBGK is a vital resource to this infant area of interest. The biodiversity present in pharaonic times may have subsequently diminished, and thus species once prolific (Balanites and juniper) may be scarce today.

Pharmacy, one of the few ancient Egyptian technologies which provides the recipe for formulation, is disadvantaged because there is no known ancient pharmaceutical preparation. The raw materials, however, are described and many are identified. Furthermore, Egyptian remedies may be evaluated for pharmaceutical merit against modern protocols. These include drug source (habitat, origin, harvesting and storage), pharmacognosy (active principles, extraction and phytochemistry), formulation, preparation, administration, dosing regime, clinical properties and therapeutic value. Applied with archaeobotany, these can be used to authenticate species in ancient Egyptian remedies, and to propose plants as candidates for previously untranslated words in the Egyptian texts (Campbell 2007).

Pharmacy practise in ancient Egypt

The Kahun (Griffiths 1898; Quirke 2002), Edwin Smith (Breasted 1930), Ebers (Ebbell 1937; Ghalioungui 1987) and the Chester Beatty (Jonckheere 1947) Papyri, containing a thousand prescriptions, representing 50 per cent of all known remedies, are pivotal in pharmaceutical history (see Chapter 12). Initial assessment, supplemented by the observations of Dawson

(1926–1935), Jonckheere (1944, 1955), *The Grundriss* (1954–73), Manniche (1999), and Nunn (2000), indicate 107 drug sources of plant origin (utilising the leaf, fruit, seed, resin, bark and root), twenty-eight minerals and twenty-four animal ingredients. It is instinctive to assume the *materia medica* of ancient Egypt parallels contemporary application, but uncertainties in identification of substances used and the diseases they treated necessitate pharmacological evaluation.

Formulation of remedies

Ingredients in ancient Egyptian remedies indicate the character of the finished preparation. Oils used 4,000 years ago remain oils today; similarly, honey has changed little, and the description 'powder' dictates the character, behaviour and nature of a formulation. Raw materials are relatively unchanged: frankincense and terebinth trees are still cut to permit the flow of resin, ricinus seed is pressed for castor oil, aloe leaves are tapped, fruits are picked, and seeds are harvested and stored. Ancient Egyptian formulations can therefore be directly compared with standard formulations cited in *The British Pharmaceutical Codex* (1973), at a time when much was still formulated within the dispensary.

The ancient Egyptians used creams, draughts, enemata, extracts, eye lotions, drops, ointments, infusions, inhalations and insufflations. Juices and linctuses soothed coughs, while liniments, lotions and mixtures soothed skin and muscles. They used mouthwashes, ointments and pastes, pessaries, poultices, powders, solutions, suppositories and tablets (Campbell and David 2005; Campbell 2006).

Formulations include the active ingredient, ancillary drugs to alleviate the side effects of the principal drug, flavourings to disguise a bitter or unpleasant taste, and a vehicle to carry the ingredients in even distribution and permit measurement of a suitable volume. Nonconforming preparations include excrement or wholesome, nutritious foodstuffs.

Raw materials

Drugs from plant sources would have been harvested from their agricultural industry or the wild. Cereals, barley, emmer and flax, which dominated in antiquity, were sown in November when the Nile waters receded (Murray 2003: 506–536); from these, alcohol, fibre, oils, demulcents and emollients were sourced. Dates, carob pods, figs and pomegranate were harvested, yielding stabilisers, laxatives, antiseptics, astringents and anthelminthics.

The acacia flowered from October, followed by the pod, which is useful in medicine. In January, gum is scraped from acacia main stems and stored as hard chips to be used as stabilisers and demulcents, which are useful in respiratory and skin problems. In January, beans and peas would be sown. In April, sycamore figs, vegetables and cereals were harvested, and melons, cucumbers and colocynth would ripen, each with potent pharmaceutical constituents. Flax was harvested whilst young, to produce fine cloth (Vogelsang-Eastwood 2003: 269–274), and the seed heads, the source of pharmaceutically active linseed oil, were removed in May.

Cumin and dill seed, yielding essential oils, were harvested in June, as well as garlic, so that its bulb could be readily stored for six months. July brought a second harvest of sycamore figs. By August, the abundant water lily flower was harvested and dried, and its centre was ground and made into bread (Herodotus 2:92) (see Chapter 13); it was also used pharmaceutically. Grapes were gathered in August and, although less commonly available than beer, wine was used as an extraction medium, or for its acidic and antiseptic properties, when soured.

Onions, plums and juniper berries were gathered, each with its own medicinal use. Herodotus (2:94) describes the Egyptian marsh dwellers, pressing castor seeds for oil, and the medicinal uses of castor oil is recorded in the Ebers Papyrus (Ebell 1937: 59). In October, the agricultural cycle would recommence when olives, Ziziphus fruit, and a third crop of sycamore fig were collected; these were pharmaceutically useful as laxatives, diuretics and astringents. Frankincense, cedar and coriander were obtained through trade with the Near East, Nubia, Libya and the southern Mediterranean. Animal sources originated from husbandry or hunting, and inorganic sources were the products of mining, smelting, building or jewellery industries. Drug availability probably parallelled food availability and was subject to the same threats.

Medicinal plants available at the onset of the New Kingdom – typically the dom palm, garlic and safflower – although not knowingly cited in any papyri, can possibly be identified with some of the untranslated drug names. If evidence for the onset of botanical appearance occurs later, this does not conclusively exclude the plant's medicinal use, but the likelihood is reduced, although its introduction through trade must always be considered.

Preparation of remedies

Method of preparation influences the availability of the drug and hence its ultimate efficacy. Ancient Egyptian preparations show remarkable consistency, embracing techniques familiar to contemporary manufacturing pharmacy: boiling; warming; dry heating; vaporising; straining; cold or warm infusion; extraction in water, alcohol or fat; pressing; triturating; powders; sieving and moulding.

Instructions are often explicit, reproducible and supplemented by directions for use. Each details the drug sources to be used, with the most potent ingredient being cited first, the lesser next, and the vehicle cited last. Drug extraction demonstrates an awareness of selective solubility. Acacia and other gums are extracted in water or fat, colocynth is extracted in alcohol, and hyoscyamus is correctly extracted in nonaqueous solution. Some preparations use a two-stage extraction, the first being water or alcohol and the second, acid, from sour milk or wine. Grinding increases the surface area of the drug to the medium in which it is extracted, and the Egyptian remedies demonstrate manufacturing control, from coarse to a fine powder. They were cognisant of storage and shelf life, remedies being prepared daily but usually no more than four days ahead, unless prepared in alcohol, fat, sugar or dried.

Measurement

Measurement affords reproducibility and may indicate value, potency, and the vehicle in which the medication is mixed, as well as any secondary drugs or flavourings. It greatly influences efficacy, and is significant to the formulation of remedies.

The papyri cite capacity, based on a standard volume, the units following a binary halving of the previous subdivision:

$$\tfrac{1}{2}, \tfrac{1}{4}, \tfrac{1}{8}, \tfrac{1}{16}, \tfrac{1}{32} \text{ and } \tfrac{1}{64}, \text{ the whole equalling } \tfrac{63}{64}.$$

This dyadic system of notation was based on the Horus Eye fractions (Nunn 2000: 142–143). Believed to equate to the standard unit of measure, one *heqat* estimated to be 4.5–4.8 L (Robins and Shute 1998). The smallest and medicinally used unit, the *ro*, had a value of $\tfrac{1}{320}$th *heqat*, c. 15 ml. Pommerenering (2003, 2004, 2005) proposes that the Horus Eye fractions were a quadruple *heqat*, corresponding to the *dja*, first used in the New Kingdom. This impacted on the efficacy of some remedies, quadrupling the *ro*. Ebbell (1937) adopts the numerical notation throughout whereas Jonckheere (1947) used the fractional representation subsequently detailed in *The Grundriss* (1973: 5).

When measurements are not detailed, the pattern previously established affords nomination of the quantity. The smallest quantity measured is 0.5 *ro*, the largest 160 *ro*. Characteristic of the varying drug levels in any plant, this means that no two recipes would have had the same efficacy, even if equal quantities were used. Indeed, this was the motivation for the development of synthetic substitutes that revolutionised the twentieth century A.D. Measurements are detailed in 230 remedies; 450 can be estimated by precedent, leaving 320 in doubt. Those without measurement are generally used topically, where quantities are not critical. When quantities are omitted from a suppository or enema, volumes were presumably small to accommodate the rectal capacity.

Prescription format

The format of remedies consistently commences 'a treatment for' or, if in successive order, the term 'another' is used. Instructions accompany remedies: 'swallow with beer;' 'take for four, eight or sixteen days;' 'introduce into anus, nostril, ear, nose or vagina;' 'take in one day;' 'take at night;' 'bandage in place;' and 'place on wound.' Prescriptions were detailed for the ailment, with the dose, quantity and frequency usually specified. There is no evidence that drugs were considered in relation to the risk involved but they knew when not to treat 'a case with which I will contend.' They amended remedies for neonates, children and adults.

Ebers Papyrus 273 stipulates an amendment for an infant, 'to put right the urine of a child,' with instructions to the woman to take the remedy and issue to the infant. This technique of maternal administration is used to wean the infants of drug addicts off methadone. Palliative care (Edwin Smith Papyrus 29) was practised, maintaining wound treatment, rest and nutrition. A number of their prescriptions would satisfy geriatric care today, including remedies for the cardia, rheumatism, frequent micturition and constipation. There is no evidence of the holistic approach characteristic of homeopathy and traditional medicine (WHO 1991).

Administration of remedies

Nunn (2000: 143) describes the administration of drugs from a medical aspect. Pharmaceutically, to be effective, the drug must arrive at the site of action, having survived the route of administration, with hazards including gastric acid, rectal motility or vomiting reflex. Absinth, acacia, aloe, ammi, Balanites oil, barley, beer, bayberry, bryony, carob, castor oil, celery, cumin, coriander, colocynth, dill, dates, figs, grapes, honey, henbane, lettuce, milk, myrtle, oils, wheat and wine were all taken orally in extracts, mixtures, solutions, infusions, pills, draughts or linctuses. Demulcent or palatable ingredients were incorporated in most remedies to counter bitter or unpleasant tastes. Rarely (crocodile dung: Ebers Papyrus 334) was any toxin prescribed orally.

Topical applications include rubefacient pine resin and turpentine or liniments based on alcohol and resins. Emollients included animal fat or plant oils expressed from ricinus, Balanite or moringer fruit. Insufflations to treat wounds included copper, malachite or limestone. Others were ointments, creams and honey. Poultices of high specific heat were used to relieve pain or bring infection to a focus, utilising, clay, dung, barley or wheat. Seldom used today, they were popular until the twentieth century, and deployed similar materials. Pharmaceutically, all topical ingredients were conveyed in a medium affording even distribution of the medicament to maintain it in intimate contact with the skin.

Rectal administrations include enemata based on drugs dispersed in a liquid base of oil, milk or water. Others were demulcent ointments of vegetable oils or animal fats incorporating mildly antiseptic honey or antibacterial resins. Suppositories were administered to deliver a drug, demulcent or stimulate defecation, containing finely powdered medicament incorporated into a fat or mucilage basis, which melted or rehydrated with body fluids at body temperature.

Inhalation utilises the vapour of pine resins or bitumen, heated on hot stones and inhaled through a hollow reed or resin inserted directly into the nostril. Inhalations remain for respiratory problems, although inhalers are used now rather than hot vapours, which were common only fifty years ago.

Fumigation with mercury, although no longer applied, was used in the late nineteenth century to treat syphilis, and frankincense was utilised as a powerful antiseptic. In the Kahun Papyrus (c. 1900 B.C.), frankincense was cited as a fumigant for the womb.

Vaginal drugs were administered in ancient Egypt as ointments, douches, pessaries or fumigants, bringing the drug in close contact with the mucous membrane.

Aural, nasal and ophthalmic preparations are now invariably ointments or solutions, with ophthalmic preparations being sterile and isotonic. Ancient Egyptians had no concept of sterility but their remedies were site specific, consisting of antibacterial agents such as copper, malachite and resins, and additionally, biocides of antimony and lead, mixed in any vehicle that would afford application.

Ancient Egyptian dressings

Ghalioungui (1983: 6–8) cites the term *wt* to describe the medical dresser, a term also used in embalming (Nunn 2000: 133–134). Dressings are an essential adjunct to medical care, affording comfort, protection and physical support, and ensuring medicaments have close contact with the wound and thereby increasing efficacy. Vogelsang-Eastwood (2003: 294) reports wax-impregnated bandages to keep the dressing in place. The type of wound and stage of healing determines the dressing. Lint, a soft linen product, was used to apply grease and honey. Bandages were applied in strips (*sehed*), to act as a suture and close the wound. Splints were used for (Edwin Smith Papyrus 35) a 'fracture of the clavicle' to hold the arm firmly in place once the bone had been reset. Stiffened rolls of linen were used to protect injured tissues for a split ear (Edwin Smith Papyrus 27) or a broken nose. Rolls of linen served as tampons (Edwin Smith Papyrus 11–15) to absorb body fluids, and form soft templates for damaged tissue.

Secondarily, dressings must maintain the wound in a moist condition, and keep it free from infection, toxins and fibre. Lint or seed wool were soaked in medicaments and applied to the anus. As the wound heals or deteriorates, differing dressing types are appropriate (British National Formulary [BNF] 2001: 689–696), and this staging is exhibited in the Edwin Smith Papyrus 11. They also reported when not to dress wounds to allow any infection to drain (Edwin Smith Papyrus 47). The need to change dressings daily was recognised for ulcerated or infected wounds (Edwin Smith Papyrus 46). Construction of ancient bandages is remarkably consistent with contemporary dressings (Campbell et al. 2005).

Therapeutic effect of drugs in ancient Egypt

The medicinal chemistry and pharmacology of many plants is well documented (Martindale 1958–1977; Nunn 2000: 215; Evans 2000). Efficacy depends on the correct drug and dosage regime, appropriately formulated and administered for the medical indication. Today, calculations are based on the dynamics of drug absorption, distribution, and elimination from the body (Wilkinson 2001: 3–31). A direct relationship exists between the blood concentration of a drug and its pharmacological action. This may be the required therapeutic, subtherapeutic or a toxic effect.

Patients respond differently, a dose which is subtherapeutic to one being efficacious to another. Following administration, drugs follow a recognised fate. A lag phase precedes the minimum effective concentration (MEC) for the drug, the intensity of effect increasing as absorption continues. This peaks at a specific time, after which elimination dominates, resulting in a decreased effect.

Once the drug level falls below the MEC, a second dose is normally administered, its lag phase overlapping the declining phase of the previous dose. Dose frequency is designed to maintain drug concentration between the MEC and toxic concentration – the 'therapeutic window.' The ancient Egyptian dosing regimes, probably based on empirical observation that a single dose rarely works (save for laxatives), satisfies this pharmacokinetic pattern. Using knowledge of pharmacognosy, pharmacokinetics, formulation, preparation and drug administration, ancient Egyptian remedies may be pharmaceutically assessed against early twentieth century A.D. pharmacy protocols (Campbell 2006).

Efficacy must be evaluated against a medical indication: *Ricinus communis*, the castor oil plant, has a physiological action as a laxative, but acts physically as an emollient or demulcent. Acacia gum is a physical skin emollient, and physiologically a respiratory demulcent. Pharmacy today utilises food substances, but this does not preclude its primary nutrient role nor diminish its pharmaceutical function. Fig (*Ficus caricus*), a nutritious fruit, has bulk laxative properties; Balanite nut, a high calorific famine food, has antidiabetic and anthelminthic properties, its oil being a lubricant.

The efficacy of drugs used in ancient Egypt

GASTROINTESTINAL DRUGS. Laxatives promote defecation. They are irritant, bulk forming or lubricant. The irritants, castor oil and colocynth, stimulating fluid secretion and gut motility, were used in ancient Egypt in therapeutic amounts. Luminally active bulk formers such as whole grain, figs and fruits, increase the volume of the gastrointestinal tract and are without therapeutic limit. Oils lubricate the intestine and facilitate the passage of stools. Without therapeutic limit, these were utilised by the ancient Egyptians, but rarely taken in more than one dose. No archaeobotanical evidence exists to support the use of senna or aloes.

Antacids increase the stomach pH. Calcium carbonate (limestone) was used at unknown therapeutic levels; however, excess would produce metabolic alkalosis. Digestants, based upon hydrochloric acid and bile salts, were not available, although they used sour milk, yielding butyric acid, a digestant. Barley water, milk and honey were used as stomach demulcents, properties utilised today, each physical in action and without therapeutic limit.

Hyoscyamus muticus controls diarrhoea by reducing intestinal motility and is efficacious in small doses, although no measurement is cited in any Ebers Papyrus remedy. Gypsum, similar to kaolin, was cited for diarrhoea. It is hydroscopic and acts physically, binding excess gut water which causes the diarrhoea. It also adsorbs enterotoxins (Jafri and Pasricha 2001: 1038).

CARDIOVASCULAR DRUGS. Some plant glycosides demonstrate powerful cardioactivity, and aloe and mustard contain subtherapeutic amounts (Ebers Papyrus 191–200). *Ammi*, a cardioactive vasodilator at 2.5 mg, was prescribed at therapeutic levels (Ebers Papyrus 215).

Diuretics increase the rate of urine flow by reducing superfluous extracellular fluid. Before synthetic diuretics, plant substances were used for this. Glucose, sucrose and mannitol, present in fruits, carob and honey, promote diuresis, and the ancient Egyptians utilised them to treat the heart. Owing to its hypertensive effect, acacia is contraindicated as a diuretic but is cited in Ebers Papyrus 200 for the 'cardia.'

CENTRAL NERVOUS SYSTEM. The ancient Egyptians had access to hemp (*Cannabis sativa*) but there is no evidence of its sedative properties. Ghalioungui (1987: 19) proposed š3š3 as the sedative valerian but no ancient Egyptian remedy is consistent with this property, nor is there any archaeobotanical evidence of valerian.

Hyoscine, extracted from *Hyoscyamus muticus*, controls muscle motility by depressing motor function. Its extraction and use in Ebers Papyrus 66 is compatible with its pharmacological properties. Rubefacients and biocides, each without central nervous system activity, were used in the Ebers Papyrus for epilepsy (Case 210), and for paralysis (Cases 758–760).

ANALGESICS AND ANTIPYRETICS. Pain is often synonymous with fever in the papyri. Salt and alum without analgesic value are antipyretic. Celery, frankincense, cinnamon, coriander, juniper and benzoin, vogue in contemporary aromatherapy, have little analgesic value. Ebers Papyrus 766 and 294 cite Willow but demonstrate no awareness of the analgesic properties of salicin, a precursor to salicylic acid. Hemp incorporated in a suppository to refresh the anus (Chester Beatty Papyrus 24) is without therapeutic benefit but is physically supportive. There is no Egyptian archaeobotanical evidence of the opium poppy before the Roman Period (see Chapter 13).

MUSCULOSKELETAL DISORDERS. Many disorders result from strain, and the remedy is immobilisation and heat until the bone or muscle heals. The ancient Egyptians used vasodilating rubefacients, which increased blood circulation and imparted comfort and warmth. Turpentine and mustard, long utilised in this capacity, were used in ancient Egypt together with Juniper, pine resins and frankincense, enhanced by warming poultices and bandages. Tolerance of the irritant determines the therapeutic limit. As today, the ancient Egyptians used rubefacients to control rheumatism, and also the recognised antirheumatics, celery and saffron (Ebers Papyrus 655, 296) (Evans 2000).

GENITOURINARY SYSTEM. Drugs to influence labour, menstruation, vaginal infections or contraception were used in ancient Egypt, although diagnosis is vague (Nunn 2000: 196–197). Prior to the advent of hormonally based drugs, treatment differed little from the formulations described in the papyri, which utilised fumigation, demulcents and topical applications. Crocodile dung used as a contraceptive (Kahun Papyrus 21) putatively possesses spermicidal properties, but would be an effective barrier contraceptive. Juniper oil, a uterine stimulant (Ebers Papyrus 805), would induce labour and is contraindicated today in pregnancy. Reference to hordenine, an alkaloid from sprouting barley that has adrenergic properties, occurs in Kahun Papyrus 17, in connection with a woman's bleeding.

Urinary drugs influence urine retention, incontinence, pain and infection. Demulcents, such as wheat, barley, honey and acacia mucilage, create an alkaline environment hostile to bacterial growth, while relieving burning and pain associated with parasitic or bacterial infection. Their action is physical and effective. Natron and northern salt influence electrolyte balance. Balanite oil, an anthelminthic, was only used sporadically, suggesting that the physicians did not recognise its true therapeutic value. Diagnosis may not always be possible (Nunn 2000: 161 and 91–92), but nevertheless, remedies affording symptomatic relief may be therapeutically evaluated.

ANTIBACTERIALS, ANTIBIOTICS AND INFESTATION. Anthelminthics rid the gastrointestinal tract of worms. Those cited in the papyri remained in pharmaceutical practice until fifty years ago. Pelletierine, from pomegranate, depresses intestinal smooth muscle, while simultaneously paralysing the tapeworm, which is then removed by purgatives. Antimony, a biocide, has long been used in the treatment of fluke parasites. Laxatives dominated their treatment and current protocols advocate their use.

Martindale (1958) cites phenols, alcohols, acids, halogens, oxidising agents, metals, their salts and dyes as antiseptics, germicides and fungicides. Phenols denature the protein of bacterial cells. As a phenol, the ancient

Egyptians used bitumen, available from the neighbouring Near East; their alcohol was provided by beer or fermented wine; and their acid came from soured wine. Copper bases, safflower and indigo dyes were commonplace and used in painting and textiles. Oil excludes air, preventing bacterial growth. Heavy metals are astringent, and in particular, copper salts, with their germicidal and fungicidal properties, were frequently used in ancient Egyptian medicine.

Honey was widely used bacteriocidally, inhibiting bacterial growth and extracting water from wounds by osmosis, thereby providing a dry environment that was hostile to bacteria. Today, Mesitran, a new hydroactive range of dressings, delivers the therapeutic benefits of honey for all stages of wound healing (Medlock Medical 2005: 10–11). Zinc and aluminium, cited in the papyri, are locally applied primary astringents, possessing germicidal properties, that damage the surface protein of the bacterial cell.

RESPIRATORY SYSTEM. Expectorants promote removal of lung secretion, and antimony was used to loosen a dry cough. Bitumen was poured on hot stones and inhaled as a stimulant expectorant (Ebers Papyrus 326). Turpentine had similar application forty years ago. The ancient Egyptians used acacia and carob as demulcents to soothe irritated membranes, but there is no evidence that they utilised anodyne expectorants. Asthma (Ebers Papyrus 327–336) was treated inappropriately although *Ammi*, a respiratory vasodilator, was prescribed for a cough (Ebers Papyrus 319 and 323).

OPHTHALMIC. Nowadays, eye infections are treated with antibiotics and antivirals, whereas fifty years ago, mercury and antimony were used. Although they were effective biocides, absorbed through the conjunctival capillaries, they were renotoxic. The Egyptians used lead (galena), malachite, copper and possibly antimony to treat eye infection, as well as some outlandish preparations that contained pathogens and irritants.

EAR, NOSE AND OROPHARYNX. Antibiotics are currently used to alleviate ear infections although ribbon gauze soaked in astringent aluminium acetate was formerly prescribed. The therapeutic equivalent in Egypt was malachite, oil and honey on seed wool (Ebers Papyrus 766). Wax, which causes pain and deafness, requires removal if it is impacted, and today, olive oil is prescribed to soften the wax. In the Ebers Papyrus (764 and 765), the equally efficacious goose fat and Balanites oil were utilised.

Today, sodium chloride drops relieve nasal congestion by liquefying the mucous secretions, and the Ebers Papyrus (761) prescribes the equally

therapeutic date wine. The ancient equivalent of contemporary deconges-
tants was the fragrant gum placed in the nostril (Ebers Papyrus 763).

Pain from ulceration of the mouth is relieved by mouthwashes, antiseptics
and antifungals. The papyri similarly cite demulcent acacia, carob, milk and
grease to soothe, and yellow ochre, cumin, copper and manna as antiseptics;
all these formulations are prescribed for a number of days. Thymol, from
thyme, is used today, but has no archaeobotanical representation until the
Roman Period. The local anaesthetic properties of celery seed is cited (Ebers
Papyrus 701), although its duration is short term.

SKIN. Demulcents, comprising gums, mucilage, aloe and starches, which
coat the surface and protect the underlying irritated tissue, were applied as
lotions. Vegetable oils, animal fats and waxes protect, soothe and hydrate
the skin, and as emollients, they are commonly used to treat eczema;
the Egyptians also used them for these purposes. Today, these treatments
are based on wax, liquid paraffin, lanolin, cod liver oil and urea, whereas
the ancient Egyptians used castor oil, Balanites oil and urine of an ass or of
women who had recently borne a male child.

These contemporary remedies incorporate antimicrobials, but the Egyptian ones included, as antiseptics, salt, frankincense, ochre, alabaster, styrax
and myrrh, as well as antimicrobial honey, each of which demonstrates
pharmaceutical merit. Jaundice, viewed as a skin complaint, was treated
by laxatives, which had no effect on liver function, but improved pallor by
removing bile.

Scalp dermatitis (dandruff) responds to antimicrobials in oil. The papyri
cite ladanum (Ebers Papyrus 357), a mild antiseptic oil, although there is no
archaeobotanical evidence of the shrub. Baldness was treated ineffectively,
with oils, fats, copper and hedgehog quills (Ebers Papyrus 776).

Burns (Ebers Papyrus 484–509) were treated with soothing demulcents,
protective antiseptics and biocides, which were all effective, but the astringents they used – turpentine, copper and frankincense – would be painful,
although this was ameliorated to some extent by oils, animal fats and honey.
The pathogenic sheep dung recommended in Ebers Papyrus 483 would
have been deleterious.

Trauma and wound management

The Edwin Smith Papyrus (1–48) and Ebers Papyrus (510–588) used honey,
grease and lint, after debriding and suturing. Infected wounds were treated

with biocides such as malachite, copper, zinc and antimony, each of which
has an infinite therapeutic window.

Conclusions

Although the ancient Egyptian pharmacopoeia was unsophisticated, there
is compelling evidence of recognisable formulation, preparation, administration, dosing regime and efficacy. Principal, secondary drug, vehicle and
flavouring are recognisable in 70 per cent of remedies, with only 30 per cent
of remedies characterised by polypharmacy.

The first scientific estimate of pharmaceutical merit demonstrates
that 64 per cent of remedies have therapeutic value, equally divided
between physiological and physical action. Of these 3 per cent are toxic,
1.5 per cent subtherapeutic and 20 per cent undetermined, the remainder
having no known therapeutic activity. If the *ro* is 60 ml, there is evidence
that colocynth, in some recipes, was occasionally prescribed at a toxic dose.
The placebo effect cannot be overlooked (Nunn 2000: 97 and 137–138).

There is consensus on the translation of 45 per cent of drug sources,
supported by archaeobotany and pharmacognosy. Plants of uncertain identification can be verified by applying these techniques, which supports the
translation of *dȝrt* as carob, *snj-tȝ* as colocynth, *pšd* as hyoscyamus, *šȝw* as
coriander, *mȝtt* as celery, *bȝk* as Balanite and *s'm* as artemisia; however, this
does not support *innk* as thyme, *inst* as aniseed, *šȝšȝ* as valerian or *ims.t*
as dill, although there is significant archaeobotanical evidence of dill in
predynastic times (Fahmy 2003).

A single reference confirms that Balanites, an anthelminthic, was used to
treat schistosomiasis (Ebers Papyrus 265), and there is artistic and archaeobotanical evidence that mandrake, a potent soporific, existed, although it is
not apparently cited in the texts. The medicinal worth of other plants used in
ancient Egypt is now recognised: for example, saffron, *safflower* and celery
are antirheumatic and juniper is abortifacient.

There is compelling information to indicate that the food which sustained
their good health in times of plenty was also used selectively in potent
amounts to cure them in sickness. Preliminary research (Campbell 2006)
has demonstrated that prescriptions originated in distinct areas of Egypt or
abroad, closely reflecting the phytogeography of the species.

Finally, the role of the ancient Egyptian pharmacist should be considered. Prescriptions begin 'thou shalt prepare for him,' indicating the existence of the pharmacist, although this role was synonymous with that of the
physician. The Ebers Papyrus (Ebbell 1937: 75) describes an ointment to be

made by Chui the venerable, the high priest of Heliopolis. This man did not have the title of pharmacist, but he was probably the first to be named as a preparer of drugs.

The pharmaceutical foundations established in early dynastic Egypt were adopted by the developing Greek and Persian civilisations, particularly from 650 B.C. onwards, and their subsequent political stability, military domination and communication skills provided the historical context and continuity in which pharmacy could flourish and develop. Consequently, the Greeks were recognised as the fathers of pharmacy, but credit for this most certainly belongs to the ancient Egyptians who practised a credible form of pharmacy and pharmacotherapy a thousand years previously.

PART 4

Resources for studying mummies

CHAPTER 15

The International Ancient Egyptian Mummy Tissue Bank

Rosalie David

Introduction

The late twentieth century saw various initiatives to address issues surrounding the ethics and treatment of the dead in museum and other collections (e.g. in papers produced by the World Archaeological Congress [1989] and the Museum Ethnographers Group [1994]). By the early twenty-first century, these matters warranted even greater attention, and in May 2001, Britain established a Working Group on Human Remains, with the remit 'to examine the current status of human remains within the collections of publicly-funded Museums and Galleries in the United Kingdom, and consider the desirability and possible form of legislative change in this area' (DCMS Report 2005:5).

This Working Group produced a report (DCMS 2003), and there was subsequent consultation on this document (DCMS 2004). Together, these formed the basis for the DCMS Report (2005), which sets out nonstatutory guidance for museums in England, Wales, and Northern Ireland, who own permanent collections of human remains, and other organisations where human remains form part of their teaching, research, or display functions.

The DCMS Report (2005) provides information relating to a legal and ethical framework for the treatment of human remains; the curation, care and use of remains; and a framework for handling claims, where appropriate, for the repatriation of human remains to indigenous communities.

This report recognises the contribution to the modern world that research, teaching and, where appropriate, display of human remains can make, but also acknowledges that, because of their 'personal, cultural, symbolic, spiritual or religious significance to individuals and, or, groups' (DCMS 2005:7), human remains have a unique status in museum and other collections, and therefore require special attention.

There is acknowledgment that access to human remains for practical study is an essential component of higher education courses that have a medical or osteological element, with the insistence, however, that students should be made aware of their ethical and legal obligations when working on these remains (DCMS 2005: 20).

The report also provides guidelines on sampling human remains for scientific analysis (DCMS 2005: 21); it recognises the importance of access to this material for some research projects, even though the work may ultimately involve destruction of the sample. It explicitly recommends that only appropriately qualified staff and students should undertake the sampling, that it should be performed to the highest standards, and that only the smallest samples required for the investigation should be removed.

The guidelines also state that the holding institution should ensure that there are good scientific justifications for taking the samples, that the samples will form part of a carefully planned research programme that can be expected to produce useful results, and that sampling should only be performed after researchers have considered and confirmed that the research question cannot be answered by nondestructive methods. If appropriate (e.g. if the effectiveness of the chosen research technique needs to be proven), the report recommends that a pilot study should be conducted on a small number of samples before permission is sought for a full project. If any samples are not destroyed during analysis, they should be returned to the collection.

Aspects of any research programmes involving sampling should be fully documented by the holding institution. These records should include: the application and justification for the project, details of sampling (sample location and size and sampling process), and, ultimately, a full account of the results of the analysis. This ensures that such information will be accessible to future researchers.

This guidance also states that institutions holding ancient human remains for research purposes should ensure that there is public access to information about these collections and the associated research programmes. Presented within a research framework, this should identify the nature of the material and the current state of knowledge in the related research areas, any potential areas of research to which the holdings might contribute, and a strategy to indicate priorities and methods of research.

Many of the above issues had already been addressed by the Manchester Mummy Research Project when, in 1994, the International Ancient Egyptian Mummy Tissue Bank was established at the University of Manchester, initially to provide a resource for the team's work.

Establishing the International Ancient Egyptian Mummy Tissue Bank

The tissue bank was set up to ensure that a sufficient quantity of tissue samples from Egyptian mummified remains were available for the Ancient Schistosomiasis Project (see Chapters 1, 8, and 9). The Manchester team's studies since 1973 had made the members aware that as well as contributing to knowledge about health, disease, medical conditions, diet, and occupations in ancient Egypt, Egyptian mummies are a repository of evidence about other areas, including mummification practices, funerary beliefs and customs, chronology and radiocarbon dating techniques, and familial relationships.

The foundation of the bank was also timely because, by the mid-1990s, researchers had access to increasingly sophisticated techniques that could be applied to small tissue samples. These included histology, pathology, DNA techniques, immunology, chemical analysis, pharmacology, virology, spectrometry, and radiocarbon dating methods. Therefore, from the beginning, the tissue bank had the potential to provide a resource for a wide range of studies undertaken both by the Manchester team and other researchers (Lambert-Zazulak 2000).

There were several factors that had to be addressed when the tissue bank was established: the methods of study that could be applied to the tissues; knowledge that might be gleaned from this research; and various archaeological, practical, and ethical issues related to collecting, storing, and studying mummy tissue samples. For example, the Manchester group was fully aware that in addition to its primary role as a research resource, the tissue bank would address some of the conservation and display concerns associated with requests for access to mummies for scientific investigation (see Chapter 16).

The removal of full-body mummies or even mummified parts from permanent museum displays for repeated access and sampling can cause disruption and will involve additional handling of the human remains. In contrast, the establishment of the tissue bank contributes to conservation of the remains because it reduces the need to handle the mummy. Researchers can make good use of a single occasion to examine, radiograph, and collect small tissue samples from the mummy. Using endoscopic techniques (see Chapter 4), scientists can obtain samples from inside the bodily cavities, with minimal destruction to the mummy, and these samples can then be kept in the tissue bank where they are readily available for future studies.

The concept of tissue banking originated many years ago to support medical research, and it has continued to contribute to studies that advance disease diagnosis and treatment. For example, some banks store tissues for transplant surgery, whereas others hold blood and blood products. There has also been a historical tradition to create institutional resources in museums, and in some university departments, research institutes, and learned societies, where many types of artefacts are held and made available for research. In some cases, these have included 'libraries' of samples taken from ancient and modern material, which include, for example, animal tissues, groups of insects and plants, stone artefacts, and textiles. In many cases, the holding institutions also compile and store information about these collections. Researchers who work in these institutions or elsewhere can gain access to this material and associated documentation, which provides them with the opportunity to add new knowledge to the subject area. Some of these collections also present excellent opportunities for interdisciplinary research.

Although tissue banking had already been introduced elsewhere for samples obtained from South American mummies, the establishment of the Ancient Egyptian Mummy Tissue Bank at Manchester was the first formal project, on an international scale, to seek material from Egyptian mummies held in collections outside Egypt. This initiative posed the challenge of trying to combine the concept of tissue banking with the creation of an institutional resource of samples, with its associated documentation.

The formation and development of the tissue bank

Initially funded by a research grant (1996–1999) from The Leverhulme Trust (UK), the tissue bank project set out to obtain samples from a maximum number of individual mummies held in collections outside Egypt (Lambert-Zazulak et al. 2003). There was no true precedent for the creation of this tissue bank. For example, in medical tissue banks, the collection, storage, distribution, and study arrangements for each bank are dictated by the uses for which the samples are intended, and each type of bank has its own scientific and ethical criteria, which represent the bank's specific mission. These criteria have little direct relevance to the Ancient Egyptian Tissue Bank, and so, new criteria had to be established.

The first step was to identify and locate the whereabouts of Egyptian mummies and mummified parts in collections around the world (excluding Egypt). A starting point was provided by the International Egyptian Mummy Database (Pettitt and Fildes 1984). This was established in Manchester in 1984, in response to an urgent request made at the international symposium, *Science in Egyptology*, held at Manchester in 1984, that information about

Egyptian mummies held in collections throughout the world should be collected, collated, and computerised as soon as possible (Pettitt and Fildes 1986). This database was now used as a primary resource for identifying potential collaborating institutions.

Searches were also made through directories and other listings of museums, universities, research institutes, medical schools, learned societies, libraries, stately homes, and schools. As well as the expected locations, mummies were also successfully traced to some unusual sources, including castles, monasteries, a morticians' college, a school cupboard, and a lido.

This stage of the work provided a fascinating insight into the reasons why people had collected mummies (which were as varied as their collectors) and the routes by which the mummies had reached their present locations. Generally, the mummy collections reflect the interests and resources of the collectors, and, in some cases, the fashions that prevailed at the time.

In past centuries, some travellers and others with a dilettante interest in Egyptology purchased mummies on the open market from dealers who, residing in Egypt or elsewhere, supplied an ever-growing demand for antiquities and curiosities. For example, the tissue bank includes samples taken from a mummy now displayed in a stately home, which was brought back by a relative of the current owner from her honeymoon in Egypt (Rowley-Conwy et al. 1998). There is also tissue from a mummy purchased by a leading member of the Leeds Philosophical and Literary Society (England) in order that the Society's members could undertake a detailed philological and scientific investigation of the mummy and its coffins in 1825 (Osburn 1828).

Mummies from excavations funded by museums, learned societies, and private art collectors are the most likely to have an archaeological provenance ('find-spot') and are therefore particularly important for epidemiological and other studies that require this information. Other mummies were acquired because of the study interests of their collectors, which included medicine, pathology, the history of medicine, anthropology, ethnology, ancient history, art, archaeology, Bible studies, and pharmacology. There were also more unusual areas, such as phrenology, eugenics, and even the history of circuses and showmanship.

In recent years, an unusual opportunity for interdisciplinary research and university outreach studies was provided when a partial mummy was discovered in a cupboard at a school in England. The mummy had been donated to the school by its former owner, a pathologist whose daughter had attended the school; many years earlier, he and his colleagues had unwrapped and performed a partial autopsy on the mummy. When the remains were first found, teachers and pupils from the school brought them to the KNH Centre for Biomedical Egyptology at the University of Manchester.

Here, samples were removed for the tissue bank, and the mummy provided the basis for various scientific projects undertaken by students pursuing the Master of Science Degree in Biomedical Egyptology. The mummy, which has now been returned to the school where it is housed in appropriate conditions, and all the new information derived from the studies undertaken at Manchester, are providing a unique and fascinating resource for the school's ongoing science, history, and art projects.

In the past, Egyptian mummified remains have been put to some unexpected uses: for centuries, *mumia* was acclaimed as a medicinal and pharmaceutical ingredient (see Chapter 16; Dawson 1926–1927), and 'mummy brown,' made from pulverised mummy tissue, was popular as an artists' pigment (Woodcock 1996). For the tissue bank, it was thought likely that the main sources of samples (which include mainly tissue but also some bone and hair) would be full-body mummies, mummified parts, the visceral contents of Canopic jars, and samples of *mumia*.

To identify the presence and location of these potential sources, the Manchester researchers approached more than 8,000 possible owners and holders of this material. An excellent response brought confirmation of material in many countries, including Australia, Brazil, Chile, Canada, Iceland, India, Germany, Italy, Portugal, South Africa, and the United States of America, as well as collections in institutions throughout Britain. The types of collection varied considerably, ranging from a single body part, such as a mummified finger, to human remains representing hundreds of individuals that were excavated in Nubia as part of a rescue operation associated with the construction of modern dams on the Nile.

Collecting the samples

The methods and extent of sampling, and the subsequent research that can be undertaken on the samples, will be largely dictated by the physical state and degree of preservation of each source of mummified material. Factors that have most impact in this respect are the natural environmental conditions in Egypt; the provenance of the mummy; the method and quality of the mummification process; activities of tomb robbers in antiquity; methods of acquiring, transporting, and storing the body in its more recent history; and the techniques used by previous scientific investigators and conservators (see Chapter 16).

Acquisition of samples for the tissue bank involves several stages. Once the mummified remains have been identified and located, permission to undertake tissue sampling is sought from the owner/holder of the material. If this is granted, then deposits are requested of approximately 1 to 2 g of dried soft tissue (which can include skin, brain, muscle, or viscera) from each mummy or mummified part. Also, the bank will receive samples of hair, bone, and teeth.

These samples can either be collected by the owner/holder (in which case, the bank administrators will provide advice and detailed instructions), or, if requested and it is feasible, an experienced member of the Manchester Mummy Project will undertake this procedure.

During this process, the researchers should ensure that the mummies are treated ethically and handled with respect at all times, and tissue should only be collected from sites where this would not be detrimental to the overall physical condition of the mummy. Recommended routes for sampling include any area of the body that has already been opened up through damage or previous investigation, the severed area of a separate limb or head, or the use of endoscopy to gain access to internal areas of the body (see Chapter 4).

At the University of Manchester, the tissue bank samples are held in a metal fireproof cabinet that provides a physically secure store, and this is housed in a dedicated area that provides the correct environmental conditions for fragile organic material.

When a sample enters the bank, it is allocated a unique identification code that remains with it throughout its subsequent history. The sample is always left intact, because preserving its integrity in this way ensures that it can be used for as many studies as possible; also, a single sample will often include various tissue types and the macroscopic appearance of an intact sample can help a researcher to identify and decide which area of the sample may be most suitable for any proposed research.

The tissue bank documentation system

As well as collecting tissue samples, a major function of the tissue bank is to provide central record keeping and to store information relating to the samples, so that this will be available for future research.

A 'Material Transfer Agreement' is sent to each depositor of tissue or other samples. This states that the sample(s) is transferred to the bank for a renewable period of ten years, and that it can be loaned on approved application for use in well-planned, documented, and achievable research projects. Under the terms of this agreement, reports will be issued to each depositor on any research conducted on their samples.

Researchers who borrow samples from the tissue bank are asked to sign a 'Researcher's Agreement,' which allows them to retain the material for one year, in the first instance. The agreement requires that they report their results to the tissue bank administrators, and that, in any publications, they record the reference code of the sample(s) and acknowledge its depositor.

Other documentation kept by the bank includes a central listing of the location of all mummies and mummified parts that are identified through the bank's searches and studies, whether or not these institutions contribute samples to the bank. Sometimes, for example, biopsy sampling cannot be performed on the human remains, either because of existing general agreements regarding ethical issues over human remains, or because the remains are physically inaccessible due to thick or tight wrappings.

Nevertheless, the existence of the remains can still be recorded, and it may be possible to photograph or radiograph them, thus providing valuable information for the tissue bank records. The tissue bank documentation, continually updated, is believed to represent the largest centralised record of ancient Egyptian human remains held in collections outside Egypt.

The role of the tissue bank in supporting research

As the tissue bank has now been in existence for some eleven years, it is possible to assess the role it can play in supporting research projects, and providing material for postgraduate and postdoctoral studies. In addition to the major programmes undertaken by the Manchester Mummy Project on disease studies and pharmacy in ancient Egypt (see Chapters 1, 8, 9, 13, and 14), the bank provides material for various studies undertaken by other researchers based elsewhere.

One of its new and most significant functions is to provide material for research undertaken by postgraduate students as part of their Master of Science and Doctor of Philosophy courses in the recently established KNH Centre for Biomedical Egyptology at Manchester (see Chapter 17).

Stating that 'Research into human remains and their context are an important source of direct evidence about the past,' the DCMS Report (2005: 8) specifies several specific areas of study, and it is evident that many of the research projects undertaken by students in Manchester are making important contributions to these fields. For example, in the category defined as 'human evolution and adaptation, and genetic relationships' (DCMS 2005: 8), student research has explored the retrieval of parasite, nuclear, and mitochondrial DNA (see Chapter 9), and the genetic relationships between individual mummies or family groups.

In two other specified areas, 'disease and causes of death' and 'history of disease and of medicine' (DCMS 2005: 8), there have been disease studies on sickle cell anaemia, parasitic infestations including schistosomiasis, tuberculosis, parvoviral infections, malaria, thoracic bacteria, and therapeutic treatments. New knowledge about 'burial practices, beliefs and attitudes' (DCMS 2005: 8) has been contributed by forensic studies on the materials used in mummification such as resin and natron, analyses of the preservation state of mummified tissue (see Chapter 6), and a scientific investigation of the mummification process itself.

In relation to 'diet, growth and activity patterns' (DCMS 2005: 8), studies have been undertaken on the drug content in modern and ancient hair, and ancient Egyptian hair and its treatment with henna have been the subject of analysis. Other projects have addressed conservation issues, such as bone decomposition or the identification of fungi in human remains.

Techniques used in these projects include histology, histochemistry, DNA identification, immunology, mass spectrometry, and micro-scale sealed-vessel pyrolysis coupled with gas chromatography/mass spectroscopy. Samples from the tissue bank have also been used for studies on problems that can occur when radiocarbon dating techniques are applied to Egyptian material.

In addition to the tissue bank, museums preserve a wealth of other evidence from ancient Egypt. The Manchester students have had access to ancient plant remains and tissue from mummified animals, and this has facilitated some very interesting projects. These include a molecular analysis of ancient cereal crops (see Chapter 9), a mass spectrometric analysis of ancient Egyptian plant remains (see Chapter 10), a histological examination of tissue from an ancient Egyptian cat (see Chapter 6), and a comparative study of DNA extracted from modern domestic and ancient Egyptian cats (see Chapter 9).

The future of the tissue bank

The tissue bank is in the process of moving from The Manchester Museum to the KNH Centre for Biomedical Egyptology, where it can now fulfil its role more appropriately. It is important that the bank continues to grow and develop so that it can provide a valuable resource for palaeoepidemiological, biomedical, and scientific studies in Egyptology. The recent introduction of Biomedical Egyptology as a university subdiscipline at Manchester (see

Chapter 17) will also help to shape the direction this development may take in the future.

The bank, which currently holds some 1,400 samples, has plans to expand in several ways. A key issue will be the acquisition of more tissue samples with a specific provenance to facilitate epidemiological research. Also, it is hoped that the bank can extend its remit to include more samples of bone, hair, and resin, and the establishment of a complementary palaeopharmacognosy bank is also planned.

It is envisaged that this will preserve fragile plant samples, and also include digital records of plant specimens known to have been used in ancient Egyptian medicine (see Chapter 14). Future studies on plant development and ancient therapeutic treatments will be able to access this data. The tissue bank and the palaeopharmacognosy bank will provide a unique, joint resource for studies in palaeopathology, palaeoepidemiology, genetic research, mummification techniques, archaeobotany, and pharmacognosy.

Another major step, already in progress, is the computerisation of all the records and documentation associated with the tissue bank and the International Egyptian Mummy Database, which will improve the administrators' facility to handle, retrieve, and manage information. This development will be accompanied by the introduction of a system to establish a specific, appropriate schedule of analytical study for each full or part sample, so that the maximum amount of information can be retrieved from examining each fragment (see Chapter 17).

Workers in this field of research are always aware that mummy tissue is a valuable and irreplaceable scientific resource. Continuing efforts to build up the International Ancient Egyptian Mummy Tissue Bank will hopefully ensure that, in the twenty-first century, this unique collection can effectively support and enhance the research of scientists and Egyptologists.

CHAPTER 16

Conservation treatment for mummies

Antony E. David

Introduction

Conservation issues relating to Egyptian mummies are discussed in detail in David and David (1995) and David (1986: 87–89); a survey of the subject is provided in Aufderheide (2003: 502–514).

Some human remains have survived in skeletal form whereas others consist of the skeleton and soft tissues. The latter occur in many areas of the world (Aufderheide 2003) and are often described as 'mummies,' although, originally, the word 'mummy' was used exclusively for the preserved bodies of the ancient Egyptians. The term mummy is reputedly derived from the word *mumia*, meaning 'bitumen' or 'pitch.' The word *mumia* was apparently first applied to a black, bituminous substance that coagulated with the water that brought it down from mountain tops (particularly the 'Mummy Mountain' in Persia).

For centuries, it was claimed that this *mumia* had medicinal properties, and it was an increasingly popular ingredient in medieval and later prescriptions. When demand outstripped supply, another source of *mumia* was sought, and the preserved bodies of the ancient Egyptians, which often had a blackened, bituminous appearance, came to be credited with the same properties as *mumia*. Consequently, tissue from these bodies began to be used as a medicinal ingredient, and they became known as 'mummies.'

In various countries around the world, some mummies (defined as bodies consisting of the skeleton and soft tissues) are preserved unintentionally, as the result of the natural circumstances of the burial site or place of death. Here, the most important factors (which can occur singly or in combination) are environmental conditions: dryness of the sand in which the body is interred, heat and coldness of the climate, and an airtight burial location.

In some instances, a conscious decision was reached to take the process further. This process resulted in intentional natural mummification, which involved the deliberate enhancement of these natural circumstances by means of, for example, heat drying or smoking the body, or ensuring that air was excluded from the burial (David and David 1995). Finally, some early societies introduced 'true' or 'intentional' mummification, which involved the use of sophisticated procedures and chemical or other agents to preserve the body.

Archaeological evidence indicates that religious and social factors probably acted as the impetus to develop intentional mummification, and the procedure was undoubtedly the result of experimentation conducted over many years. In Egypt, both natural, unintentional mummification and intentional mummification occurred in tandem to meet the perceived needs of different social classes (see Chapter 2).

Deterioration of mummies

The various factors involved in the deterioration of mummies can occur singly or in combination, but the deterioration will be due to environmental conditions (Meier 1997; Carter and Walker 1999); physical damage which can be the result of inept handling, or attack by rodents, insects, or microbiological agents (bacteria and fungi); or damage caused by previous conservation attempts.

General deterioration in mummies is discussed more fully in David and David (1995: 77–80) and Aufderheide (2003: 502–505), and an extensive literature considers the various causative agents involved in this process. These causes include the environmental factors that have an impact on the condition of a mummy, such as light and temperature levels (Paine 1992), and relative humidity; and various studies that deal with the occurrence and destructive effects of insects found in mummies, such as Curry (1979), Strong (1981), Stefan (1982), Parsche and Seifert (1992), Pinniger (1994), Rae (1996), and Pinniger and Harmon (1999). Also, the role of microbiological agents in the destruction of mummified remains has been quite extensively recorded (see Chapter 6; Hino et al. 1982; Arene et al. 1992; Subert et al. 1993; Horne 1995; Daniels 1996; Ridgway et al. 1996; English et al. 2002).

In most cases, deterioration and damage can either be avoided or rectified to some extent, but in some mummies, it is not possible to arrest or remedy these processes. Any damage or deterioration usually occurred in antiquity – during the mummification or burial processes and the subsequent period in the burial context; however, in some cases, the problems have arisen after the mummy was excavated, as the result of inadequacies in transportation, handling, or storage.

Conservation treatments for Egyptian mummies

The environmental conditions in which the mummy was found, the type of mummification procedure it represents, and the extent and type of damage and deterioration it has suffered will inevitably dictate the conservation methods that have to be devised and adopted in each case. Sometimes, measures to rectify a problematic storage environment, which has caused the deterioration, will suffice, but for other mummies, it is necessary to adopt more interventionist techniques which affect the whole body, or to take measures regarding the physical repair and support of the mummy. In many instances, a combination of these procedures will be required.

A number of studies describe the various conservation treatments applied to a range of preserved bodies from many areas of the world. Various projects have involved Egyptian mummies (e.g. Melville 1995; Maekawa and Valentin 1996; Fulcheri 1997; David 1998; Johnson and Wills 1988). Studies have also been performed on other 'dry mummies' discovered, for example, in the Canary Islands (Herraez and Morales 1992) and South America, and on 'wet mummies' such as bog bodies (Glob 1969; Delaney and O'Floinn 1995; Daniels 1996; Fischer 1998), and frozen bodies (Johansson 1989; Boguchi 1996; Reinhard 1998; Ceruti 2003), of which the 'Iceman' is a particularly famous example (Gaber 2003; Vigl 2003; Spindler 1994; Bruttini 2005). This chapter, however, will concentrate on the methods available for the intentional and natural mummies found in Egypt, which are essentially 'dry mummies.'

Complete intentional mummies from Egypt usually incorporate body wrappings and funerary artefacts, in addition to the preserved human remains. These include bandages and funerary artefacts, such as face and chest covers, amulets, and sometimes, painted panel portraits (see Chapter 11), which are made from a variety of materials ranging from textiles, cartonnage, wood, and faience through to metals. These associated materials have to be taken into account when conservation treatments are selected (Leveque 1987; Laurin 1988). The treatments indicated in this chapter will focus on the mummified body itself, where some of the basic choices are dictated by the overall condition of the mummy – whether, for example, the body retains its bandages and casing or if the mummy has been unwrapped at some point in its history.

Environmental control

Mummified remains are most effectively kept in an environment with a relative humidity of 35–50 per cent and a constant temperature of 10–15°C. When mummies are stored as part of reserve collections in museums, this control can be achieved by providing storage areas which meet these optimum conditions (Horie 1988), or when exhibited on public galleries, they can be housed in specially designed display cases that will provide the appropriate environmental control (Pope 1992).

INERT GAS ENVIRONMENT. This method was devised by Professor Silvo Curto for the Egyptian mummies in the University of Turin collection. Inert gas is used within the display case, with a constant regeneration of the gas to achieve a positive leak as a fail-safe measure if the airtightness of the case fails. This method, however, is only appropriate if no existing deterioration can be detected in the mummy, and disadvantages of this system include the cost of preparing the gallery and the cases, installing the equipment, and providing a means of monitoring the system indefinitely.

Another approach was developed at the Getty Conservation Institute in California, USA, in particular response to the criticism of a technique – the use of high-energy gamma rays – that had been utilised earlier (see below) to disinfect the mummy of Ramesses II (Balout 1985; Bucaille 1987). This innovative display and storage system, designed to preserve mummified objects by statically controlling the levels of oxygen and relative humidity, has been used since 1989 in the gallery in the Egyptian Museum, Cairo, where the royal mummies are now exhibited. The aim of the system is to prevent deterioration resulting from the constant or repeated fluctuation of humidity levels, and 'biological attack by insects and microorganisms, thermally and photolytically induced oxidation, and degradation by gaseous and particulate air pollutants' (Maekawa et al. 1992: 213).

This method uses a hermetically sealed, nitrogen-filled case that 'maintains its pressure equilibrium with surrounding atmosphere by compensating with inflation or deflation of a bellows. The case contains sensors for oxygen and humidity, humidity buffer, oxygen scavenger and pollution sorbent' (Maekawa 1992: 213). The main principle is that all oxygen will be excluded from the case, but despite precautionary measures, it is recognised that some air will leak into the case, but to prolong its maintenance-free life from eleven to twenty years, an oxygen scavenger (Ageless™) can be introduced into the case.

CLEAN-AIR-CYCLE ENVIRONMENT. A method devised by H. Howarth and A. E. David (David and David 1995: 81–82) was originally incorporated into a gallery display at Blackburn Museum, Lancashire (UK). The mummy is placed in an ordinary museum case, and the existing air outside the case is cleaned through filters and humidified to the correct level (not exceeding 50 per cent relative humidity). Environmental sensors inside the case can be used to monitor the relative humidity and temperature there; this information can be made available through a radio connection which, in the Blackburn Museum example, was incorporated into a monitor supplied by Exeter Environmental Systems.

The cleaned and filtered air is then constantly pumped through a sulfur dioxide filter and sucked through a plenum unit mounted on the case containing the mummy. Within the case, the mummy is supported on a construction made of stainless-steel tubing across which polyester has been stretched, which allows the preconditioned internal environment to circulate freely around the mummy.

A constant circulation of air is achieved inside the case, because the case allows a positive leakage of treated air back into the gallery where it is cleaned, re-humidified to the correct level, and then sucked back into the case. This system prevents insect attack and fungal growth.

Treatments to counteract fungal, bacterial, and insect attack

Environmental control is effective as a preventative and maintenance measure; however, if the mummy is already in a state of deterioration, then direct intervention using methods such as gas fumigation or wet treatments with fungicides, bactericides, and insecticides is also required to arrest the damage.

GAS FUMIGATION. Chemical sterilization must be toxic and volatile so that it can eliminate the cause of the deterioration in the mummy and effectively sterilize it. This can be achieved by means of gas fumigation, and two methods are available. In the first, the mummy, appropriately supported, is placed inside a fumigation chamber from which the air is then evacuated by using vacuum pressure. A fumigant is then introduced, effected under vacuum so that it will achieve optimum penetration of the mummy.

In the second method, the fumigant is introduced into a tightly sealed polythene bag that contains the mummy. This is not the preferred option, however, as penetration of the fumigant is less effective because the process is not assisted by vacuum, and the method can be dangerous if certain fumigants are used.

In general, the choice of fumigants is a key factor in this procedure. They must be effective and must comply with all precautions of the European/ British Health and Safety Regulations. The fumigants vary in their ability to penetrate the mummy; this, and whether or not the mummy is wrapped, will determine the length of time that is required for each treatment.

In any case, this process cannot permanently eliminate the causative agents of deterioration, and therefore the treatment should be repeated at three yearly intervals. The search for safe, more effective fumigants is an ongoing process for conservators, but there is also an increased emphasis on preventative pest control measures within museums (Pinniger and Harmon 1999), so that the need for actively intrusive methods of treatment will be reduced.

WET STERILIZATION. If a fumigation chamber is not available, then an alternative, if the mummy is totally or partially unwrapped, is to apply the fungicide or insecticide solutions directly to the mummified tissue. First, the conservator can use dry brushes, with the assistance of a controlled suction vacuum cleaner, to remove fungal spores and salt recrystalliza-tion. The operator should be protected from inhaling dust or spores. If required, an internal inspection of the mummy can then be performed using an industrial endoscope, so that severe infestations can be identified and receive concentrated treatment (for further discussion of endoscopy, see Chapter 4).

The next step is to apply the solution, either with a soft brush or using very low pressure sprays. This ensures that there is equal distribution inside and outside the cavities and on the body surface. Again, the operator should observe all the necessary safety precautions, such as using a mask and pro-tective gloves and conducting the procedure in a fume cupboard. It was reported (David and David 1995: 83) that good results had been achieved using pentachlorophenol (sodium salt) in pure alcohol (see Plates XVIII and XIX); however, because of its toxicity, pentachlorophenol, although effective in preventing further microbiological infestations in mummies, is no longer considered an appropriate method of treatment, and, follow-ing new European/British Health and Safety Regulations, an alternative fungicide is used.

CONTROLLED DRYING. This method is most successfully used for unwrapped bodies, although follow-up treatment, using a chemical application (see p. 251–252) is required. The procedure works by removing water from the mummy so that the destructive microorganisms that infect the body are deprived of an essential element for their survival and growth.

To reduce the water content of the mummy, the body is placed in a controlled environment where the relative humidity in the atmosphere is slowly and gradually reduced. This can be achieved either by using dehumidifiers to remove moisture from a controlled volume of air or by means of hygroscopic agents (e.g. silica gel), but these need to be monitored and checked regularly to ensure their continued effectiveness.

ULTRAVIOLET IRRADIATION, THE USE OF X-RAYS, GAMMA RAYS AND ELECTRON BEAM RADIATION. For many years, various methods that can destroy microorganisms or bring about physical and chemical changes in their cells have been used as conservation measures for the treatment of wood, paper, and plaster-covered walls (Belyakova 1960; Van der Molen and Garty 1980) and to arrest deterioration in human remains (Johansson 1989). This was perhaps most famously exemplified by the now criticised treatment of the mummy of Ramesses II (Balout and Roubet 1985; Bucaille 1987).

Physical repair, handling, and support of mummies

Any modern treatment of physical damage in mummies should be conducted in such a way that in the future there is no chance that it will be mistaken for an ancient repair. The aesthetics of the mummy should be a key consideration: its original appearance should be retained as far as possible and, if practicable, any original materials should be incorporated in the repair. It is also important that any modern repair should be easily reversible.

Care should always be taken when handling mummies or moving them from one location to another. Methods of support for mummies, when they are in storage collections or displayed on public locations, are also a major consideration for conservators and curators (Gabrielli 2005). For example, to ensure that minimum stress is placed on sensitive areas such as knee joints, it is important that mummies are stored or displayed horizontally and not in the vertical position.

At The Manchester Museum, various methods were developed to provide support for the mummies both on the gallery and in the reserve stores, and to facilitate the handling and moving process when, for example, the mummies were taken to other areas of the university for scientific examination. These provisions included a foam bed for each mummy, moulded to its individual shape; in the stores, the mummies, supported on these beds, were then placed on specially constructed 'mortuary-type' trolleys (Horie 1988).

The impact of conservation treatments on future scientific investigations

It is acknowledged that mummification techniques undertaken in the past can significantly affect the quality of the samples obtained today for scientific research (see Chapter 7). There is also a growing recognition that, although conservation measures are essential to preserve the mummy as an important source of evidence, some treatments may damage or destroy information that scientific analysis might otherwise recover (David 1998; Aufderheide 2003: 514). This is particularly important, for example, in relation to DNA identification.

This is an urgent conflict that should be addressed so that resolutions can be sought before further evidence is irretrievably lost. Although some studies have already been undertaken (Brooks et al.1996; Paterakis 1996), and these issues have been discussed at the First (Tenerife, Canary Islands, 1992), Second (Cartagena, Colombia, 1995), Third (Arica, Chile, 1998), Fourth (Nuuk, Greenland, 2001), Fifth (Turin, Italy, 2004) and Sixth (Lanzarote, Canary Islands, 2007) World Congresses on Mummy Studies, generally this is an area that has not received due attention. Hopefully, future research will address some of these issues.

PART 5

The future of biomedical and scientific studies in Egyptology

CHAPTER 17

Biomedical Egyptology: some future possibilities and contributions

Rosalie David

Introduction

It is hoped that the research outlined in this book has demonstrated how the subdiscipline of Biomedical Egyptology, based on the analytical investigation of mummies and associated material, has added a new dimension to the study of ancient Egypt. Effectively, each mummy can be regarded as a 'museum of disease,' preserving unbiased evidence about its owner's lifestyle, diet, illnesses, and sometimes, the cause of death. There may be additional information about medical or pharmaceutical treatment, mummification techniques, religious practices, and familial connections. Increasingly, the use of sophisticated analytical techniques enables us to extract this information and, provided that investigators interpret their data correctly, this type of research can provide evidence that cannot be gained from archaeology, art history, or ancient literature.

This information can add fascinating insights into other aspects of Egyptian society. For example, the author is currently researching dietary links between the incidence of atherosclerosis identified in mummies belonging to priests and temple chantresses, and the access these groups had to the food offered daily in the temple rituals and then divided up amongst the clergy. Although most of the population ate a mainly vegetarian diet, the gods' food included large quantities of meat supplied from the animals specially slaughtered in the temple precinct. Ultimately, it may be possible to demonstrate that these dietary variations had a direct impact on the disease patterns observed in different social groups.

Sometimes, biomedical and scientific analyses will challenge or overthrow theories that archaeologists, historians, and other scientists have proposed. In our own work, for example, pharmacological studies are questioning previous suggestions about the use of narcotics in ancient Egypt

(Chapter 13), and research on pharmacy is seeking to demonstrate the efficacy, if any, of their medicaments (Chapter 14).

Biomedical Egyptology is based on a multidisciplinary approach, often combining not only a range of analytical techniques but also providing a bridge between the sciences and humanities. In fact, it is the interdisciplinary nature of the subject that presents workers with both their greatest opportunities and their greatest challenges. Most modern educational systems provide a narrow perspective, dividing 'arts' from 'sciences' at an early stage, and most researchers pursuing projects in biomedical and scientific Egyptology will have received their basic training either in an area of science or in Egyptology/archaeology in which the main focus is usually on history, art history, language studies, or archaeological techniques.

To make progress in biomedical Egyptology, it is essential that workers drawn from both backgrounds learn to 'speak each other's language.' Egyptologists need to understand the application, potential, and limitations of the scientific techniques that are available and be able to present specific and well-considered questions. Conversely, some knowledge of Egyptian civilisation will make scientists aware of any issues relating to the historical context of the material on which they are working, and this in turn will inform their assessment and interpretation of the analytical results.

The Manchester Mummy Project has been notable for its interdisciplinary approach. This has been possible because of the project's continuity and, particularly, the long-established working relationships of the team members who, although drawn from different backgrounds in science or Egyptology, understand each other's perspective. Throughout the past thirty years, there have been some inevitable changes in the group's membership, and some new techniques have been introduced while others are no longer used; nevertheless, it has always been possible for the project to adopt a fully integrated approach to its research.

This was first established during the early stages of the project (Chapter 1), when the team developed the 'Manchester Method,' a protocol designed for the examination of mummies. This method sets out a sequence for investigating a mummy, moving from a general overview (radiology), to sampling techniques (endoscopy), and then to specific studies (e.g. palaeohistology, immunology, and DNA identification) performed on material removed from the mummy.

The KNH Centre for Biomedical Egyptology

In order that future workers are aware of the huge potential of 'mummy studies,' it is essential that appropriate opportunities should exist to train those who wish to pursue a career in this field. In his excellent survey of scientific studies on mummies, Aufderheide (2003: xiii) stated that this was still an 'orphan discipline,' and, in the United States of America, for example, there were 'no committed academic training programs, standing university faculty positions, students, dedicated funding sources or journals.' The situation in Europe was little better.

The KNH Centre for Biomedical Egyptology, recently established at the University of Manchester, now provides a unique facility devoted specifically to biomedical and scientific studies in Egyptology. The centre, which carries the initials of its patroness, was opened by His Royal Highness The Earl of Wessex in 2003 and is located in the Faculty of Life Sciences.

The KNH Centre, recently designated as one of the University's 'centres of excellence,' has developed rapidly. Directed by the KNH Professor of Biomedical Egyptology, the centre has two lecturers (one also holding a Fellowship in The Manchester Museum), a Teaching Fellow, and a postdoctoral research group. With its new laboratories and access to the extensive facilities of a leading science faculty, the centre provides a base for the continuing work of the Manchester Mummy Research Project, as well as a new location for the International Ancient Egyptian Mummy Tissue Bank. One of the centre's main purposes is to provide training in biomedical and scientific studies in Egyptology. At the undergraduate level, the centre currently offers a very popular final year option on 'ancient Egyptian mummies,' for students pursuing a Bachelor of Science degree in Biological Sciences, but currently, postgraduate studies are the centre's main training focus.

At present, there are twelve students in the Doctor of Philosophy programme, and since 1995, Manchester has run a unique Master of Science degree course in Biomedical and Forensic Studies in Egyptology, which is now a mainstay of the centre's work. The main aim of this course is to demonstrate how a range of scientific techniques can be applied to ancient Egyptian mummified remains and associated material.

The students (who come from various countries) pursue units in both Egyptology and scientific and analytical techniques, which are taught by members of the Manchester Mummy Project; each student also produces a research dissertation which presents them with the opportunity to undertake original research on ancient material (examples are given in Chapters 6 and 9). This course, which is available to students with either a science or an Egyptology/archaeology background, provides specific training to ensure that students can relate to and work in either aspect of the subject.

The opportunities that Manchester can offer for study in this field include not only excellent science facilities, but also the extensive resources of the tissue bank and the university's major Egyptology collection, held in The

Manchester Museum. Also, a formal Agreement between the Faculty of Life Sciences at Manchester and the National Research Centre, one of Egypt's leading scientific establishments, has opened up new opportunities for bioanthropologists at both institutions to cooperate in research and training programmes. Staff and students from both centres have participated in joint training workshops held in Cairo in 2004 and 2005, and there are plans for exchange programmes and conferences on ancient pharmacy and medicine. In general, this international association of two groups of scientists holds out considerable prospects for the development of new avenues of research and training in this field.

Some future possibilities

Egypt provides the palaeopathologist with a unique set of circumstances. Not only have natural and intentional mummification processes preserved evidence of disease in the skeletal and tissue remains of every social class in an ancient society but, for the most part, the modern inhabitants of Egypt can trace their direct descent from that ancient population. This provides a rare opportunity for scientists to undertake epidemiological studies over a time span of some 7,000 years, comparing data from contemporary health studies performed in Egypt, with evidence derived from studies on the mummies. An important future goal will be to trace the evolution and development of specific diseases within this Egyptian context – evidence which could eventually make a major contribution to a universal history of disease.

The success of such epidemiological research can only be guaranteed if sufficient quantities of provenanced samples are available, and if there continues to be development of the immunological, genetic, and other techniques that can be applied to mummified remains. It is important to recognise, however, that even with the emergence of these techniques, palaeohistology should remain a key investigative tool in the study of any sample.

Palaeohistological examination should always be undertaken as the first step to identify the true nature of any sample taken from a mummy (e.g. is it tissue, resin, or plant remains?) and to confirm which other analyses are required. This procedure ensures that time and expense are not wasted in pursuing techniques that may not be suitable for a particular sample. Indeed, to extract maximum information with minimal destruction, a specific analytical plan should be prepared for every sample.

Future researchers will need to ensure that collections of mummified remains – the basic resource for biomedical and scientific studies – are preserved and developed. This will involve the expansion of the tissue bank, and close cooperation amongst scientists, Egyptologists, and conservators, so that there can be an urgent dialogue about the possible effects that some conservation treatments may have on future scientific studies, and how these problems can be addressed.

With the new training opportunities that are now being established, and the career possibilities that should result from this, we can perhaps hope that, in the twenty-first century, Biomedical Egyptology will start to fulfil its true potential.

References

Aceves-Avila, F. J., Medina, F., Fraga, A. 2001. 'The antiquity of rheumatoid arthritis: A reappraisal,' *Journal of Rheumatology* 28(4): 751–757.

Adams, J. E. 2003. 'Dual energy x-ray absorptiometry,' in S. Grampp (ed.), *Radiology of Osteoporosis*. Berlin, Heidelberg: Springer, pp. 87–100.

Al-Sherbiny, M., Osman, A. M., Hancock, K., Deelder, A. M., Tsang, C. W. 1999. 'The application of immunodiagnostic assays: Detection of antibodies and circulating antigens in human schistosomiasis and correlation with clinical findings,' *American Journal of Tropical Medicine and Hygiene* 60: 960–966.

Appenzeller, O., Stevens, J. M., Kruszynski, R., Walker, S. 2001. 'Neurology in ancient faces,' *Journal of Neurology, Neurosurgery and Psychiatry* 70(4): 524–529.

Araujo, R., Reinhard, K., Ferreira, L. F. 2000. 'The role of mummy studies in paleoparasitology,' *Chungara, Revista de Anthropologica Chilena* 32: 111–117.

Arene, E., Chavez, R., Rivas, V., Padilla, A., Holguin, E., Rivera, H., Otazo, R. 1992. 'Preservation of Mummies: a study of destructive biological mechanisms of mummy tissues,' in A. C. Aufderheide (ed.), *Proceedings of the I World Congress on Mummy Studies*, Vol. 1. Tenerife: Museo Arqueologico y Etnografico de Tenerife, pp. 241–246.

Ariazza, B. T. 2005. 'Arseniasis as an environmental hypothetical explanation for the origin of the oldest artificial mummification practice in the world,' *Chungara, Revista de Anthropologica Chilena* 37(2): 255–260.

Armitage, P. L., Clutton-Brock, J. 1981. 'A radiological and histological investigation into the mummification of cats from ancient Egypt,' *Journal of Archaeological Science* 8: 185–196.

Arnold, W., Püschel, K. 1981. 'Experimental studies on hair as an indicator of past or present drug use,' *Journal of the Forensic Science Society* 21: 83.

Ashby, R. 2001. *An investigation of Harris lines in Egyptian mummies.* Unpublished MSc thesis, University of Manchester, Manchester (UK).

Aufderheide, A. C., Rodriguez-Martin, C. 1998. *The Cambridge Encyclopedia of Human Paleopathology.* Cambridge: Cambridge University Press.

Aufderheide, A. C. 2003. *The Scientific Study of Mummies.* Cambridge: Cambridge University Press.

Aufderheide A. C., Salo, W., Madden, M., Streitz, J., Buikstra, J., Guhl, F., Arriaza, B., Renier, C., Wittmers, L. E., Fornaciari, G., Allison, M. 2004. 'A 9,000-year record of Chagas' disease,' *Proceedings of the National Academy of Science of the United States of America* 101(7): 2034–2039.

Aufderheide, A. C., Salo W., Madden, M., Streitz, J., de la Cruz, K. D., Buikstra, J., Arriaza, B., Wittiners, L. E. 2005. 'Aspects of ingestion transmission of Chagas disease identified in mummies and their coprolites,' *Chungara, Revista de Antropologia Chilena* 37(1): 85–90.

Ayyad, S. K., Moore, P. D. 1995. 'Identification of Fossil Water Lily Pollen Grains in the Sediments of Egypt,' *Electronic Journal of Biotechnology* 35, No 2: 119–132.

Balabanova, S., Homoki, J. 1987. 'Determination of cocaine in human hair by gas chromatography/mass spectrometry,' *Zeitschrift fur Rechtsmedizin* 98: 235–240.

Balabanova, S., Parsche, F., Pirsig, W. 1992. 'First identification of drugs in Egyptian mummies,' *Naturwissenschaften* 8: 358.

Balout, L., Roubet, C. 1985. *La Momie de Ramsès II (1976–1977). Contribution Scientifique a l'Egyptologie*. Ed. Recherche sur les Civilisations. Paris: Musee National d'Histoire Naturelle, Musee de l'Homme.

Banwell, C. N. 1983. *Fundamentals of Molecular Spectroscopy*. 3rd ed. London: McGraw-Hill.

Barakat, A. O., Mostafa, A., Quian, Y., Kim, M., Kennicutt, M. C. 2005. 'Organic geochemistry indicated Gebel El Zeit, Gulf of Suez, is a source of bitumen used in some Egyptian mummies,' *Geoarcheology-an International Journal* 20(3): 211–228.

Barns, J. W. B. 1956. *Five Ramesseum Papyri*. Oxford: Oxford University Press.

Begg, P. R. 1954. 'Stone Age man's dentition,' *American Journal of Orthodontics* 40: 373–383.

Begg, P. R., Kesling, P. C. 1977. 'Correct occlusion, the basis for orthodontics,' in P. R. Begg, *Orthodontics, Theory and Technique*. Philadelphia: W. B. Saunders Co., pp. 7–40.

Belyakova, L. A. 1960. 'Gamma irradiation as a means of disinfection of books against spores of mould fungi,' *Microbiology (Moscow)* 29: 762–765.

Bennike, P., Fredebo, L. 1986. 'Dental treatment in the Stone Age,' *Bulletin of the History of Dentistry* 34 no. 2: 81–87.

Bibby, P. M. G. 2005. *A genetic analysis of mummy 7717*. Unpublished MSc thesis, University of Manchester. Manchester (UK).

Biemann, K. 1962. *Mass Spectrometry, Organic Chemical Applications*. NewYork: McGraw-Hill.

Binladen, J., Wiuf, C., Gilbert, M. T., Bunce, M., Barnett, R., Larson, G., Greenwood, A. D., Haile, J., Ho, S. Y., Hansen, A. J., Willerslev, E. 2006. 'Assessing the fidelity of ancient DNA sequences amplified from nuclear genes,' *Genetics* 172: 733–744.

Bissett, N. G. (ed.). 1994. *Max Wichtl; Herbal Drugs and Phytopharmaceuticals*. Medpharm Scientific Publications. London: CRC Press.

Bissett, N. G., Bruhn, J. G., Curto, S., Holmstedt, B., Nyman, U., Zenk, M. H. 1994. 'Was opium known in 18th dynasty ancient Egypt? An examination of materials from the tomb of the chief royal architect Kha,' *Journal of Ethnopharmacology* 41: 99–114.

Bissett, N. G., Bruhn, J. G., Curto, S., Holmstedt, B., Nyman, U., Zenk, M. H. 1996a. 'Was opium known in 18th dynasty ancient Egypt? An examination of materials from the tomb of the chief royal architect Kha,' *Ägypte und Levante* 6: 199–201.

Bissett, N. G., Bruhn, J. G., Zenk, M. H. 1996b. 'The presence of opium in a 3,500 year-old Cypriot base-ring juglet,' *Ägypte und Levante* 6: 203–204.

Blair, D., van Herwerden, L., Hirai, H., Taguchi, T., Habe, S., Hirata, M., Lai, K., Upatham, S., Agatsuma, T. 1997. 'Relationships between *Schistosoma malayensis* other Asian schistosomes deduced from DNA sequences,' *Molecular Biochemistry Parasitology* 85 (2): 259–263.

Blancou, J. 2001. 'History of trichinellosis surveillance,' *Parasite* 8: S16–S19.

Blau, S., Yagodin, V. (2005). 'Osteoarchaeological evidence for leprosy from western Central Asia,' *American Journal of Physical Anthropology* 126(2): 150–158.

Blom, D. E., Buikstra, J. E., Keng, L., Tomczak, P. D., Shoreman, E., Stevens-Tuttle, D. 2005. 'Anemia and childhood mortality: Latitudinal patterning along the coast of pre-Columbian Peru,'. *American Journal of Physical Anthropology* 127(2): 152–169.

Bogucki, P. 1996. 'Pazyryk and the Ukok Princess' in P. G. Bahn (ed.), *Tombs, Graves and Mummies*. London: Weidenfeld and Nicholson, pp. 146–151.

Boldsen, J. L. 2001. 'Epidemiological approach to the paleopathological diagnosis of leprosy,' *American Journal of Physical Anthropology* 115(4): 380–387.

Boni, T., Ruhli, F. J., Chhem, R. K. 2004. 'History of palaeoradiology: early published literature, 1896–1921,' *Journal of the Canadian Association of Radiology* 55(4): 211–217.

Boom, R., Sol, C. J. A., Salimans, M. M. M., Jansen, C. L., Wertheim-van dillen, P. M. E., Van der Noordaa, J. 'Rapid and simple method for purification of nucleic acids,' *Journal Clinical Microbiology* 28 (3): 495–503.

Boulos, L. 1999–2005, *Flora of Egypt*. Volumes I-IV. Cairo: Al Hadara Publishing.

Bowles, J., Blair, D., McManus, D. P. 1995. 'A Molecular phylogeny of the human schistosomes,' *Molecular Phylogenetics and Evolution* 4: 103–109.

Bowman, A. K., Rogan, E. 1999. *Agriculture in Egypt from Pharaonic to Modern Times*. Proceedings of the British Academy 96. Oxford: Oxford University Press.

Boyd, W. C., Boyd, L. G. 1934. 'An attempt to determine the blood groups of mummies,' *Proceedings of the Society for Experimental Biology* 31: 671.

Bratcher, H. 2006. *Paleopathology of malaria: An analysis of ancient liver tissue from the Dakhleh Oasis Tombs for the presence of Plasmodium infection*. Unpublished MSc thesis, University of Manchester. Manchester (UK).

Braunstein, E. M., White, S. J., Russell, W., Harris, J. E. 1988. 'Palaeoradiological evaluation of the Egyptian royal mummies,' *Skeletal Radiology* 17: 348–352.

Breasted, J. H. 1930. *The Edwin Smith Surgical Papyrus*, 2 vols. Chicago: University of Chicago Press.

Brewer, D. J., Redford, D. B., Redford, S. 1994. *Fruits, Domestic Plants and Animals. The Egyptian Origins*. Warminster, England: Aris and Phillips Ltd., pp. 47–64.

Brickley, M., Ives, R. 2006. 'Skeletal manifestations of infantile scurvy,' *American Journal of Physical Anthropology* 129 (2): 163–172.

Brier, B. 1996. *Egyptian Mummies*. London: Michael Mara Books.

Brier, B., Wilkinson, C. M. 2005. 'A preliminary study on the accuracy of mummy portraits,' *Zeitschrift für Agyptische Sprache* 132: 107–112.

British Herbal Pharmacopoeia. 2003. Bournemouth: British Herbal Medicine Association.

British National Formulary. 2001. London: British Medical Association and Royal Pharmaceutical Society of Great Britain.

British Pharmaceutical Codex. 1973, 2004. London: The Pharmaceutical Press.

Brock. A. J. 1952. *Galen on the Natural Faculties*. London: Heinemann, Ltd. Loeb Series.

Brooks, M., Lister, A., Eastop, D., Bennett, T. 1996. 'Artifact or information? Articulating the conflicts in conserving archaeological textiles,' in R. Ashok and P. Smith (eds.), *Archaeological Conservation and Its Consequences*. London: International Institute for Conservation of Historic and Artistic Works, pp. 16–21.

Brown, K. W. 2001. 'Workers' health and colonial mercury mining at Huancavelica, Peru,' *The Americas* 51(4): 467–496.

Brown, T. A., Allaby, R. G., Brown, K. A., O'Donoghue, K., Sallares, R. 1994. 'DNA in wheat seeds from European archaeological sites,' *Experientia* 50: 571–575.

Bruttini, R., Samadelli, M. 2005 'The effects of energy sources on the Iceman's low temperature storage conditions in the South Tyrol Museum of Archaeology' in E. Rabino Massa (ed.), *Proceedings V World Congress on Mummy Studies*. *Journal of Biological Research*, 80, N.1. Turin: Universita di Torino, pp. 308–312.

Bryan, C. P. 1930. *The Papyrus Ebers*. London: Geoffrey Bles.

Bucaille, M. 1987. *Les Momies des Pharaons et la Medicine*. Paris: Librairie Seguier.

Budavari, S., O'Neil, M. J., Smith, A., Heckelman, P. E. (eds.), *The Merck Index*.11th ed. Rahway, NJ: Merck & Co.

Budzikiewicz, H., Djerassi, C., Williams, D. H. 1967. *Mass Spectrometry of Organic Compounds*. San Francisco: Holden-Day.

Buffington, R., and Wilson, M. K. 1991. *Detectors for Gas Chromatography – A Practical Primer*. Avondale: Hewlett-Packard.

Buhmann, D., Bellman, D., Kahler, K., Haber, J., Seidel, H. P., Wilske, J. 2003. 'Computer-aided soft tissue reconstruction on the skeletonised skull,' *Proceedings of the 1st International Conference on Reconstruction of Soft Facial Parts (RSFP)*. Potsdam, Germany, pp. 37–39

Bull, I. D., Simpson, I. A., Dockrill, S. J., Evershed, R. P. 1999. 'Organic geochemical evidence for the origin of ancient anthropogenic soil deposits at Tofts Ness, Sanday, Orkney,' *Organic Geochemistry* 30: 535–556.

Bull, I. D., van Bergen, P., Nott, C. J., Poulton, P. R., Evershed, R. P. 2000. 'Organic geochemical studies of soils from the Rothamsted classical experiments – V. The fate of lipids in different long-term experiments,' *Organic Geochemistry* 31: 389–408.

Bullard, F. 2001. A brief introduction to Bayesian statistics. NCTM 2001 lecture notes, The North Carolina School of Science and Mathematics. Available online at: http://courses.ncssm.edu/math/TALK/PDFS/BullardNCTM2001.pdf

Burger, J., Hummel, S., Herrmann, B., Henke, W. 1999. 'DNA preservation: a microsatellite DNA study on ancient skeletal remains,' *Electrophoresis* 20: 1722–1723.

Burlingame, A. L., Schnoes, H. K. 1969. 'Mass spectrometry in organic geochemistry,' in G. Eglinton and M. T. J. Murphy (eds.), *Organic Geochemistry*. Berlin, Heidelberg: Springer-Verlag, pp. 89–160.

Byers, S. N., Roberts, C. A. 2003. "Bayers' theorem in paleopathological diagnosis,' *American Journal of Physical Anthropology* 121(1): 1–9.

Bzdega, J. 2006. *A comparative study of modern and ancient barley DNA using established methods and commercial kits.* Unpublished MSc thesis, University of Manchester. Manchester (UK).

Campbell, J. M., David, A. R., Campbell, J. R. 2005. 'An insight into the practise of pharmacy in ancient Egypt,' *Pharmaceutical Historian* 35, No. 4, December 2005: 62–68.

Campbell, J. M., David, A. R. 2005. 'Some aspects of the practise of pharmacy in Ancient Egypt 1850 BC to 1300 BC,' in E. Rabino Massa (ed.), *Proceedings V World Congress on Mummy Studies, Journal of Biological Research* 53, No.1. Turin: Universita di Torino, pp. 331–334.

Campbell, J. M. 2006. *The application of archaeobotany and pharmacognosy, to assess the pharmaceutical merit of remedies within the Kahun, Edwin Smith, Ebers and Chester Beatty Medical Papyri, to establish an ancient Egyptian pharmacopoeia.* University of Manchester: Unpublished MSc Thesis.

Candela, P. B. 1936. 'Blood group reactions in ancient human skeletons,' *American Journal of Physical Anthropology* 21: 429–432.

Cano, R. J., Pioner, H. N., Pieniazek, N. J., Acra, A., Poiner Jr., G. O. 1993. 'Amplification and sequencing of DNA from a 120–135 million year old weevil,' *Nature* 363: 536–538.

Cano, R. J., Tiefenbrunner, F., Ubaldi, M., Del Cueto C., Luciani, S., Cox, T., Orkand, P., Kunzel, K. H., Rollo, F. 2000. 'Sequence analysis of bacterial DNA in the colon and stomach of the Tyrolean Iceman,' *American Journal of Physical Anthropology* 112: 297–309.

Capasso, L. L. 2005. 'Antiquity of cancer,' *International Journal of Cancer* 113(1): 2–13.

Carter, D. J., Walker, A. K. 1999. 'Collection environment,' in D. J. Carter and A. K. Walker (eds.), *Care and Conservation of Natural History Collections*. Oxford: Butterworth and Heinemann, pp. 139–151.

Cartmell, L., Aufderheide, A., Caprara, J., Klein, J., Koren, G. 2005. 'What were they drinking? A preliminary study of alcohol metabolites in Andean mummy hair,' in E. Rabino Massa (ed.), *Proceedings V World Congress on Mummy Studies, Journal of Biological Research* 53, No.1. Turin: Universita di Torino, pp. 114–116.

Cartmell, L. W., Aufderheide, A. C., Springfield, A., Weems, C., Arriza, B. 1991. 'The frequency and antiquity of prehistoric coca leaf chewing practices in Northern Chile: radioimmunoassay of a cocaine metabolite in human mummy hair,' *Latin American Antiquity* 2(3): 260–268.

Cartmell, L. W., Weems, C. 2001. 'Overview of hair analysis: a report of hair analysis from Dakhleh Oasis, Egypt,' in *Chungara, Revista de Antropologia Chilena* 33(2): 289–292.

Cartmell, L. W., Aufderheide, A. C., Witmers, E., Weems, C. 2003. 'The predictive value of cocaine hair/visceral ratios in Andean mummies – a pilot study,' in N. Lynnerup, C. Andreasen, and J. Berglund (eds.), *Mummies in the*

New Millenium, Proceedings of the 4th World Congress on Mummy Studies. Copenhagen: Greenland National Museum and Archives and Danish Polar Centre, pp. 79–81.

Caton-Thompson, G., Gardner, E. W. 1934. *The Desert Fayum.* Royal Anthropological Institute of Great Britain. London: John Fellows.

Cattaino, G., Vicario, L. 1999. 'Myotonic dystrophy in Ancient Egypt,' *European Neurology* 41(2): 59–63.

Cecil, R. L., Loeb, R. F. 1960. 'Bacterial diseases,' in *A Textbook of Medicine.* Phildelphia and London: W. B. Saunders Co., pp. 194–201.

Celsus. C. *De Medicina.* Books I–VIII (Volumes 1–4). Transl. by W. G. Spencer, 1971. Loeb Series. London: William Heinemann Ltd.

Ceruti, M. C. 2003. 'First steps in the recovery and preservation of the frozen Inca mummies from volcano Llullaillaco (Northwestern Argentina)' in N. Lynnerup, C. Andreasen, and J. Berglund (eds.), *Mummies in a New Millennium, Proceedings of the 4th World Congress on Mummy Studies. Nuuk, Greenland, September 4th to 10th, 2001.* Copenhagen: Greenland National Museum and Archives and Danish Polar Centre, pp. 182–186.

Charpentier, G. 1981. *Recueil de Matériaux Épigraphiques relatifs à la Botanique de L'Égypte Antique.* Paris: Trismegiste.

Charron, D. (ed.) 1997. *Genetic Diversity of HLA: Functional and Medical Implications.* Paris: EDK.

Cheever, A. W. 1969. 'Quantitative comparison of intensity of *Schistosoma mansoni* infections in man and experimental animals,' *Transactions of Royal Society of Tropical Medicine and Hygiene* 63: 781–795.

Chhem, R. K. and Ruhli, F. J. 2004. 'Palaeoradiology: current status and future challenges,' *Journal of the Canadian Association of Radiology* 55(4): 198–199.

Chhem, R. K., Schmit, P., Faure, C. 2004. 'Did Ramesses II really have ankylosing spondylitis? A reappraisal,' *Journal of the Canadian Association of Radiology* 55(4): 211–217.

Cipollaro, M., Di Bernardo, G., Galanom G., Galderisi, U., Guarino, F. 1998. 'Ancient DNA in human bone remains from Pompeii archaeological site,' *Biochemical and Biophysical Research Communication* 247: 901–904.

Ciranni, R., Giusti, L., Fornaciari G. 2000. 'Prostatic hyperplasia in the mummy of an Italian Renaissance prince,' *Prostate* 45(4): 320–322.

Ciranni, R., Caramella, D., Nenci, R., Fornaciari, G. 2005. 'The embalming, the scientific method and the paleopathology: the case of Gaetano Arrighi (1836),' *Medicina nei Secoli* 17(1): 251–262.

Ciranni, R., and Fornaciari, G. 2006. 'The aortic coarctation and the Etruscan man: morphohistologic diagnosis of an ancient cardiovascular disease,' *Virchows Archives* 449(4): 476–478.

Clement, J. G., Ranson, D. L. 1998. *Craniofacial Identification in Forensic Medicine.* Sydney: Arnold Publishers.

Cockburn, A., Cockburn, E. (eds.) 1980. *Mummies, Disease and Ancient Cultures.* Cambridge: Cambridge University Press.

Cockburn, A., Cockburn, E., Reyman, T. A. 1998. *Mummies, Disease and Ancient Cultures.* 2nd ed., revd. Cambridge: Cambridge University Press.

Colombini, M. P., Modugno, F., Silvano, F., Onor, M. 2000. 'Characterization of the balm of an Egyptian mummy from the 7th century BC,' *Studies in Conservation* 45(1): 19–29.

Connan, J., Nissenbaum, A. 2004. 'The organic geochemistry of the Hasbeya asphalt (Lebanon): comparison with asphalts from the Dead Sea area and Iraq'. *Organic Geochemistry* 35: 775–789.

Contis, G., David, A. R. 1996. 'The epidemiology of Bilharzia in ancient Egypt: 5000 years of schistosomiasis,' *Parasitology Today* 12 no.7: 253–255.

Cotte, M., Walter P., Tsoucaris, G., Dumas, P. 2005. 'Studying skin of an Egyptian mummy by infrared microscopy,' *Vibrational Spectroscopy* 38(1–2): 159–167.

Crubezy, E., Goulet, J., Bruzek, J., Jelinek, J., Rouge D., Ludes, B. 2002. 'Epidemiology of osteoarthritis and enthesopathies in a European population dating back 7700 years,' *Joint Bone Spine* 69 (6): 580–588.

Culpeper, N. 1826. *Culpeper's Complete Herbal and English Physician*. Manchester: J. Gleave and Sons.

Currie, K. 2002. *Ancient Egyptian skin: a comparative histological investigation*. Unpublished MSc Dissertation. Manchester: University of Manchester.

Curry, A. 1979. 'The insects associated with the Manchester mummies,' in A. R. David (ed.), *The Manchester Museum Mummy Project*. Manchester: Manchester Museum, pp. 113–118.

Curry, T. S., Dowdey, J. E., Murry, R. C. 1990. *Christensen's Physics of Radiology*. 4th ed. Philadelphia: Williams and Wilkins.

Czermack, J. 1852. 'Beschreibung und mikroskopische Untersuchung zweier ägyptischer Mumien,' *Sonderberichte Akademie Wissenschaft Wein* 9: 427–469.

Danforth, M. E. 1999. 'Nutrition and politics in prehistory,' *Annual Review of Athropology* 28: 1–2.

Daniel, T. M. 2000.'The origins and precolonial epidemiology of tuberculosis in the Americas: can we figure them out?' *International Journal of Tuberculosis and Lung Disease* 4(5): 395–400.

Daniels, V. (1996), 'Selection of a conservation process for Lindow Man,' in K. Spindler, H. Wilfing, E. Rastbichler-Zissernig, D. zur Nedden, and H. Nothdurfter (eds.), *Human Mummies: A Global Survey of their Status and the Techniques of Conservation*. New York: Springer-Verlag, pp. 3–8.

Darby, W. J., Ghalioungui, P., Grivetti, L. 1977. *Food: The Gift of Osiris*. London: Academic Press.

Daumas, F. 1957. 'Le sanatorium de Dendara,' *Bulletin de l'Institut Français d'Archéologie Orientale* 56: 35–58.

David, A. E. 1986. 'Conservation of mummified Egyptian remains,' in A. R. David (ed.), *Science in Egyptology. Proceedings of the 'Science in Egyptology' Symposia*, Manchester: Manchester University Press, pp. 87–89.

David, R. (ed.) 1978. *Mysteries of the Mummies*. London: Book Club Associates.

David, A. R. (ed.) 1979. *The Manchester Museum Mummy Project: Multidisciplinary Research on Ancient Egyptian Mummified Remains*. Manchester: Manchester Museum.

David, R., Tapp, E. (eds.) 1984. *Evidence Embalmed. Modern Medicine and the Mummies of Ancient Egypt*. Manchester: Manchester University Press.

David, A. R. (ed.) 1986. *Science in Egyptology. Proceedings of the 'Science in Egyptology' Symposia*, Manchester: Manchester University Press.

David, A. R., Tapp, E. (eds.) 1992. *The Mummy's Tale. The Scientific and Medical Investigation of Natsef-Amun, Priest in the Temple of Karnak*. London: Michael O'Mara Books Limited.

David, A. R., David, A. E. 1995. 'Preservation of human mummified specimens,' in C. Collins (ed.), *The Care and Conservation of Palaeontological Material*. Oxford: Butterworth-Heinemann, pp. 73–88.

David, A. R. 1997. 'Disease in Egyptian mummies: the contribution of new technologies,' *The Lancet* 349: 1760–1763.

David, A. R. 1998. 'Benefits and disadvantages of some conservation treatments for Egyptian mummies.' Paper read at the 3rd World Congress on Mummy Studies held at Arica, Chile, May 14–18.

David, R., Archbold, R. 2000. *Conversations with Mummies*. London: HarperCollins.

Davies, W. V., Friedman, R. 1998. *Egypt*. London: British Museum Press.

Davy, S. L., Schofield, D., Evison, M. P. 2005. 'Creating a three-dimensional skull model from two-dimensional images: problems and practicalities in computerised facial reconstruction.' *Proceedings of the 2nd International Conference on Reconstruction of Soft Facial Parts (RSFP), Remagen, Germany.*

Dawson, D. P., Giles, S., Ponsford, M. W. (eds.). 2002. *Horemkenesi, May He Live Forever! The Bristol Mummy Project.*Bristol: Bristol Museums and Art Gallery.

Dawson, W. R. 1926. 'The plant called "Hairs of the earth",' *Journal of Egyptian Archaeology* 12: 240–241.

Dawson, W. R. 1926–1927. 'Mummy as a drug,' *Proceedings of the Royal Society of Medicine* 20 (1–2): 87–94.

Dawson, W. 1929. *Magician and Leech*. London: Methuen.

Dawson, W. R. 1932, 1933, 1934, 1935. 'Studies in the Egyptian medical texts,' *Journal of Egyptian Archaeology* 18: 150–154; 19: 133–137; 20: 41–46, 185–188; 21: 37–38.

Dawson, W. R. (ed.). 1938. *Sir Grafton Elliot Smith: A Biographical Record by his Colleagues*. London: Jonathan Cape, opposite p. 178.

Dawson, W. R., Gray, P. H. K. 1968. *Catalogue of Egyptian Antiquities in the British Museum*, vol. 1. *Mummies and Human Remains*. London: Trustees of the British Museum.

De Cadolle, A. 1959. *Origin of Cultivated Plants*. New York: Hafner Publishing Co.

Deelder, A. M., Miller, R. L., De Jonge, N., Krijger, F. W. 1990. 'Detection of schistosome antigens in mummies,' *Lancet* 335 (8691): 724–725.

Delaney, M., O'Floinn, R. 1995. 'A bog body from Meenybradden Bog, County Donegal, Ireland,' in R. C. Turner and R. G. Scaife (eds.), *Bog Bodies*. London: British Museum Press, pp. 123–132.

Demerdash, M. 2001. 'The medicinal plants of Egypt,' in P. K. Saxena (ed.), *Development of Plant Based Medicines: Conservation, Efficacy and Safety*. Amsterdam: Kluwer Academic Press, pp. 69–93.

Demirjian, A., Goldstein, H., Tanner, J. M. 1973. 'A new system of dental assessment,' *Human Biology* 45(2): 211–227.

Dendy, P. P., Heaton, B. 1999. *Physics of Diagnostic Radiology*. 2nd ed. London: Institute of Physics (IOP) Publishing.

Denton, J. 1998. 'Silicone gel Breast implants,' *The Report of the Independent Review Group*©.

Department for Culture, Media and Sport (DCMS). 2003. '*The Report of the Working Group on Human Remains.*' London: Department for Culture, Media and Sport.

Department for Culture, Media and Sport (DCMS). 2004. '*Care of Historic Human Remains. A Consultation Report of the Working Group on Human Remains.*' London: Department for Culture, Media and Sport.

Department for Culture, Media and Sport (DCMS). 2005. '*Guidance for the Care of Human Remains in Museums.*' London: Department for Culture, Media and Sport.

Despommier, D. D., Gwadz, R. W., Hotez, P. J. 1995. *Parasitic Diseases*. 3rd ed. New York: Springer-Verlag.

Dhanjal K. S., Bhardwaj, M. K., Liversidge, H. M. 2006. 'Reproducibility of radiographic stage assessment of third molars,' *Forensic Science International* 159 S1:S74–77. Epub 2006 Mar 10.

Dioscorides. 'Materia Medica IV, 64,' in M. Wellman (ed.), *Pedanii Dioscuridis Anazarbei De Materia mediica*. 3 vols. Berlin: 1906–1914; reprint 1958, vol. 2.

Dittmar, K., Teegen, W. R. 2003.'The presence of *Fasciola hepatica* (liver fluke) in humans and cattle from a 4,500 year old archaeological site in the Saale-Unstrut Valley, Germany,' *Memorias do Instituto Oswaldo Cruz* 98 (Suppl. 1): 141–143.

Donoghue, H. D., Spigelman, M., Zias, J., Gemaey-Child, A. M., Minnikin, D. E. 1998. 'Mycobacterium tuberculosis complex DNA in calcified pleura from remains 1400 years old,' *Letters in Applied Microbiology* 27: 265–269.

Dowling, J. 2002. 'Faculty profile: planted in stone, William Stein, associate professor of Biological Sciences,' *Binghamton Alumni Journal* 11, No. 2, online edition: http://alumni.binghamton.edu/AJ/2003/winter/profile01.htm

Dr Duke's Phytochemical and Ethnobotanical Databases. http://www.ars-grin.gov/duke/

Drancourt, M., Aboudharam, G., Signoli, M., Dutour, O., Raoult, D. 1998. 'Detection of 400-year-old *Yersinia pestis* DNA in human dental pulp: An approach to the diagnosis of ancient septicemia,' *Proceedings of the National Academy of Sciences of America* 95(21): 12637–12640.

Drancourt, M., Raoult, D. 2002. 'Molecular insights into the history of plague,' *Microbes and Infection* 4(1): 105–109.

Dula, E., Bukofzer, S., Perdok, R., George, M. 2001. 'Double-blind, crossover comparison of 3 mg apomorphine SL with placebo and with 4 mg apomorphine SL in male erectile dysfunction,' *European Urology* 39: 558–564.

Ebbell, B. 1937. *The Papyrus Ebers*. London: Oxford University Press.

Ebeid, N. I. 1999. *Egyptian Medicine in the Days of the Pharaohs*. Cairo: General Egyptian Book Organisation Press.

Ebers, G. M. 1875. *Papyrus Ebers*. 2 vols. Leipzig: Englemann.

Elgood, C. L. 1951. *Medical History of Persia and the Eastern Caliphate*. London: Cambridge University Press.

Eliasova, H., Dvorak, D., Prochazka, I. O. 2003. 'Facial three-dimensional reconstruction,' *Proceedings of the 1st International Conference on Reconstruction of
Soft Facial Parts (RSFP), Potsdam, Germany*, pp. 45–48.

Elles, R., Turnbull, L., Ivinson, A., Dyer, P., Harris, R., David, A. R. 1993. 'A
beginning to the routine analysis of DNA from ancient Egyptian mummies,' in
N. Kanawati (ed.), *The Tombs of El-Hagarsa*. Sydney: Australian Centre for
Egyptology, vol. 2, pp. 40–50.

El-Mehallawi, I. H., Soliman, E. M. 2001. 'Ultrasonic assessment of facial soft
tissue thicknesses in adult Egyptians,' *Forensic Science International* 117: 99–107.

Emboden, W. 1979. *Narcotic Plants: Hallucinogens, Stimulants, Inebriants and
Hypnotics, Their Origins and Uses*. London: Studio Vista.

Emboden, W. 1981. 'Transcultural use of narcotic water lilies in ancient Egyptian
and Maya drug ritual,' *Journal of Ethnopharmacology* 3: 39–83.

English, M., Madelin, M., Campbell, R. 2002. 'Report on the mycological
examination of the bandages,' in D. P. Dawson, S. Giles and M. W. Ponsford
(eds.), *Horemkenesi. May He Live Forever. The Bristol Mummy Project*. Bristol:
Bristol Museums and Art Gallery, pp. 177–178.

Estes, J. 1993. *The Medical Skills of Ancient Egypt*. Science History Publications.
U.S.A., pp. 139–157.

Evans, W. C. 2002. *Trease and Evans Pharmacognosy*. London: W. B. Saunders.

Evenhouse, R. M., Rasmussen, M., Sadler, L. 1992. 'Computer-aided forensic
facial reconstruction,' *Journal of Biological Chemistry* 19: 22–28.

Evison, M. P., Fieller, N. R. J., Smillie, D. M. 1998. 'Ancient HLA: a preliminary
survey,' *Ancient Biomolecules* 3: 1–28.

Exner, S., Bogusch, G., Sokiranski, R. 2004. 'Cribra orbitalia visualized in
computed tomography,' *Annals of Anatomy-Anatomisher Anzeiger* 186(2):
169–172.

Fahmy, A. 2003. 'A fragrant mixture: Botanicals from the basket in B333,' *Nekhen
News* 15, (Fall).

Farooq, N. 1973. 'Historical development,' in N. Ansari (ed.), *Epidemiology and
Control of Schistosomiasis (Bilharziasis)*. Basel: S. Karger, pp. 1–16.

Farr, R. F., Allisy-Roberts, P. J. 1997. *Physics for Medical Imaging*. Philadelphia: W.
B. Saunders.

Finch, J. L. 2005. *Prosthesis or restoration? A detailed study of the left forearm of the
Durham mummy, DURON 1999.32.1*. Unpublished MSc Thesis, University of
Manchester, Manchester (UK).

Fischer, C. 1998. 'Bog bodies of Denmark and northwestern Europe,' in A.
Cockburn, E. Cockburn, and T. A. Reyman, *Mummies, Disease and Ancient
Cultures*. 2nd ed. Cambridge: Cambridge University Press, pp. 237–262.

Flaherty, T., Haigh, T. J., 1984. 'Blood groups in ancient Egypt,' in A. R. David and
E. Tapp (eds.), *Evidence Embalmed*. Manchester: Manchester University Press,
pp. 96–103.

Flaherty, T., Haigh, T. J. 1986. 'Blood groups in mummies,' in A. R. David (ed.),
Science in Egyptology. Manchester: Manchester University Press, pp. 379–
382.

Fornaciari, G., Marchetti, A. 1986. 'Intact smallpox virus particles in an Italian
mummy of sixteenth century,' *Lancet* 339: 128–129.

Fornaciari, G., Castagna, M., Tognetti, A., Tornaboni, D., Bruno, J. 1989. 'Syphilis in a Renaissance Italian mummy,' *Lancet*, September 9, 2(8663): 614.

Fornacairi, G., Castagna, M., Viacava, P., Tognetti, A., Bevilacqua, G., Segura, E. L. 1992. 'Chagas' disease in a Peruvian Inca mummy,' *Lancet* 339: 128–129.

Fornaciari, G. 1999. 'Renaissance mummies in Italy,' *Medicina nei Secoli* 11(1): 85–105.

Fornaciari, G., Ciranni, R., Ventura, L. 2001. 'Paleoandrology and prostatic hyperplasia in Italian mummies (XV-XIX century),' *Medicina nei Secoli* 13(2): 269–284.

Fornaciari, G., Zawaglia, K., Giusti, L., Vultaggio, C., Ciranni R. 2003. 'Human papilloma virus in a 16th century mummy,' *Lancet* 362 (9390): 1160.

Fossen, T., Larsen, A., Kiremirec, B. T., Andersen, O. M. 1999. 'Flavenoids from blue flowers of *Nymphea caerulea*,' *Phytochemistry* 51(8): 1113–1137.

Fricker, E. J., Spigelman, M., Freicker, C. R. 1997. 'The detection of Escherichia coli DNA in the ancient remains of Lindow Man using the polymerase chain reaction,' *Letters in Applied Microbiology* May 24 (5): 351–4.

Fulcheri, E. 1997. 'Esame istologico random nel controllo periodico della stato di conservacione dei resti umani mummificati' [Random histological sections as part of a periodic control of the state of conservation of human mummified remains], in M. Girotti (ed.), *Nuove Tecnologie nella Tutela e nal Recupero delle Raccolte Naturalistiche, Museali e Scientifiche*. Turin: University of Turin, pp. 81–89.

Fulcheri, E., Baracchini, P., Rabino Massa, E. 1992. Immunocytochemistry in histopaleopathology,' in A. C. Aufderheide (ed.), *Proceedings of First World Congress of Mummy Studies, Tenerife* Vol. 2: 559. Abstract.

Furniss, B. S., Hannaford, A. J., Smith, P. W. G., Tatchell, A. R. (eds.). 1989. *Vogel's Textbook of Practical Organic Chemistry*. 5th ed. Harlow: Longman Scientific & Technical.

Gaber, O., Kunzel, K. H., Poisel, S. 2003. 'The Ice Man, preservation and endoscopy,' in N. Lynnerup, C. Andreasen, and J. Berglund (eds.), *Mummies in a New Millennium, Proceedings of the 4th World Congress on Mummy Studies. Nuuk, Greenland, September 4th to 10th, 2001*. Copenhagen: Greenland National Museum and Archives and Danish Polar Centre, pp. 146–149.

Gabra, S. 1956. 'Papaver species and opium through the ages,' *Bulletin de l'Institut d'Égypte* 37: 39–56.

Gabrielli, N. 2005. 'Some suggestions for approaching the study and conservation of ancient human biological remains. A synthesis of the conservation work in the body of Blessed Margherita of Savoia,' in E. Rabino Massa (ed.), *Proceedings of V World Congress on Mummies. Journal of Biological Research* 80, N.1. Turin: Universita di Torino, pp. 279–283.

Gale, R., Cutler, D. 2000. *Plants in Archaeology*. Otley, England: The Royal Botanic Gardens, Kew.

Gardiner, A. 1961. *Egypt of the Pharaohs*. Oxford: Oxford University Press, pp. 19–40.

Gardiner, A. H. 1935. *Hieratic Papyri in the British Museum*. London: British Museum.

Gardiner, A. H. 1938. 'The House of Life,' *Journal of Egyptian Archaeology* 24: 157–179.

Gardiner, A. H. 1955. *The Ramesseum Papyri*. Oxford: Oxford University Press.

Gatliff, B. P., Snow, C. C. 1979. 'From skull to visage,' *Journal of Biocommunication* 6 2: 27–30.

Gatliff, B. P. 2001. 'Facial Reconstruction of Tut Ankh Amun (1980),' in K. T. Taylor (ed.), *Forensic Art and Illustration*. Boca Raton: CRC Press, pp. 466–467.

Geer, R. (transl.). 1954. *Diodorus of Sicily*, 12 vols. London: Loeb Classical Library.

George, R. M. 1993. 'Anatomical and artistic guidelines for forensic facial reconstruction,' in M. Y. Iscan and R. P. Helmer (eds.), *Forensic Analysis of the Skull*. New York: Wiley Liss Inc., pp. 215–227.

Gerasimov, M. M. 1971. *The Face Finder*. New York: Lippincott.

Germer, R. 1985. *Flora des pharaonischen Ägypten*. Mainz am Rhein: Philipp von Zabern.

Germer, R. 1998. 'The plant remains found by Petrie at Lahun and some remarks on the problems of identifying Egyptian plant names,' in S. Quirke (ed.), *Lahun Studies*. New Malden, Surrey, UK: SIA Publishing.

Gerrad, J. 1633. *The Herbal or General History of Plants*. Facsimile, 1975. New York: Dover Publications.

Gerszten, P. C. and Martinez, A. J. 1995. 'The neuropathology of South American mummies,' *Neurosurgery* 36: 756–761.

Ghalioungui, P. 1973. *Magic and Medicine in Ancient Egypt*. 2nd ed. Amsterdam: B. M. Israel.

Ghalioungui, P. 1987a. *The Ebers Papyrus*. Cairo: Academy of Scientific Research and Technology.

Ghalioungui, P. 1987b. *Translation of the Ebers Papyrus*. By kind permission of W. Benson Harer, San Bernardino, CA.

Giger, W., Blumer, M. 1974. 'Polycyclic aromatic hydrocarbons in the environment: Isolation and characterization by chromatography, visible, ultraviolet, and mass spectrometry,' *Analytical Chemistry* 46: 1663–1667.

Gill, R. (ed.). 1997. *Modern Analytical Geochemistry*. Harlow: Pearson Education Limited.

Gize, A. P. 1984. *The organic geochemistry of three Mississippi Valley-type deposits*. Unpublished Ph.D. thesis, University Park, The Pennsylvania State University.

Glob, P. V. 1969. *The Bog People*. London: Faber & Faber.

Goldenberg, E. M., Giannassi, D. E., Clegg, M. T., Smiley, C. J., Durbin, M., Henderson, D., Zurawski, G. 1990. 'Chloroplast DNA sequence from a Miocene Magnolia species,' *Nature* 344: 656–658.

Goncalves, M. L. C., Araujo, A., Ferreira, L. F. 2003. 'Human intestinal parasites in the past: new findings and a review,' *Memorias do Instituto Oswaldo Cruz* 98 (Suppl. 1): 103–118.

Grant, M. 2000. *Galen on Food and Diet*. London: Routledge.

Granville, A. B. 1825. 'An essay on Egyptian mummies; with observations on the art of embalming among ancient Egyptians,' *Philosophical Transactions of the Royal Society of London* 1: 269–316.

Gray, P. H. K. 1966. 'Radiological aspects of the mummies of ancient Egyptians in the Rijksmuseum van Oudheden, Leiden.' Reprinted from *Oudheidkundige mededelingennuit het Rijksmuseum van Oudheden, Leiden*, p. 47.

Gray, P. H. K. 1967a. 'Calcinosis intervertebralis, with special reference to similar changes found in human mummies of ancient Egypt,' in D. Brothwell, A. T. Sandison (eds.), *Diseases in Antiquity*. Springfield: Charles C Thomas, pp. 22–30.

Gray, P. H. K. 1967b. 'Embalmers' restorations,' *Journal of Egyptian Archaeology* 52: 138.

Gray, P. H. K., Slow, D. 1968. *Egyptian Mummies in the City of Liverpool Museums*. Liverpool: Liverpool Corporation.

Gray, P. H. K. 1971. 'Artificial eyes in mummies,' *Journal of Egyptian Archaeology* 57: 125–126.

Gray, P. H. K. 1973. 'The radiography of Mummies of Ancient Egyptians,' *Journal of Human Evolution* 2: 51–53.

Greulich, W. W., Pyle, S. I. 1971. *Radiographic Atlas of Skeletal Development of Hand and Wrist*. Stanford: Stanford University Press.

Griffith, F.Ll. 1898. *Hieratic Papyri from Kahun and Gurob*. London: Bernard Quaritch.

Griffith, F.Ll., Thompson, H. 1904. *The Demotic Magical Papyrus of London and Leiden*. London: H. Grevel & Co.

Grilletto, R. 1973. 'Caries and dental attrition in the early Egyptians as seen in the Turin Collections,' in D. R. Brothwell and B. A. Chiarelli (eds.), *Population Biology of the Ancient Egyptians*. London and New York: Academic Press, pp. 325–331.

Grundriss der Medizin der alten Agypter. 1954–1973. 9 vols. Berlin: Akademie-Verlag. *Grundriss der Medizin der Alten Agypter*. 1954. Vol. 1. Grapow, H. *Anatomie und Physilogie*; 1955. Vol. 2. Grapow, H. *Von den medizinischen Texten*; 1956. Vol. 3. Grapow, H. *Kranker, Krankheiten und Arzt*; 1958. Vol. 4. Von Deines, H., Grapow, H., Westendorf, W., Part 1. *Ubersetzung der medizinischen Texte*. Part 2. *Erläuterungen*; 1958. Vol. 5. Grapow, H. *Die medizinischen Texte in Hieroglyphischer Umschreibung Autographiert*; 1959. Vol. 6. Von Deines, H., Grapow, H. *Wörterbuch der ägyptischen Drogennamen*; 1961, Vol. 7. Von Deines, H., Westendorf, W. *Wörterbuch der mediziniscen Texte*; 1962. Vol. 8. Westendorf, W. *Grammatique de medizinshen Texte*; 1973. Vol. 9. Von Deines, H., Grapow, H., Westendorf, W., *Ergänzungen, Drogenquanten, Sachgruppen, Nachträge, Bibliographe, Beneralregister*. Berlin: Akademie-Verlag

Gruner, O. C. 1930. *A Treatise on the Canon of Medicine of Avicenna*. London: Luzac & Co.

Grushka, E. (ed.) 1974. *Bonded Stationary Phases in Gas Chromatography*. Ann Arbor: Ann Arbor Science Publishers.

Guhl, F. 1997. '*Trypanosoma cruzi* DNA in human mummies,' *Lancet* 349: 1370.

Guhl, F., Jaramillo, C., Vallejo, G. A., Yockteng, R., Cárdenas-Arroyo, F., Fornaciari, G., Arriaza, B., Aufderheide, A. C. 1999. 'Isolation of *Trypanosoma cruzi* DNA in 4,000-year-old mummified human tissue from Northern Chile,' *American Journal of Physical Anthropology* 108: 401–407.

Gunther, R. 1934. *The Greek Herbal of Dioscorides*. Oxford: Oxford University Press.

Haas, C. J., Zink, A., Palfi, G., Szeimies, U., Nerlich, A. G. 2000. 'Detection of leprosy in ancient human skeletal remains by molecular identification of *Mycobacterium leprae*,' *American Journal of Clinical Pathology* 114 (3): 428–436.

Hagelberg, E. 1994. 'Mitochondrial DNA from ancient bones,' in B. Herrmann and S. Hummel (eds.), *Ancient DNA*. New York: Springer-Verlag, pp. 195–204.

Hall, P. A., Watson, A. F. R., Garner, G. V., Hall, K., Smith, S., Waterman, D., Horsfield, B. 1999. 'An investigation of micro-scale sealed vessel thermal extraction-gas chromatography-mass spectrometry MSSV-GC-MS and micro-scale sealed vessel pyrolysis-gas chromatography-mass spectrometry applied to a standard reference material of an urban dust organics' in *The Science of the Total Environment*, pp. 235, 269–276.

Halperin, E. C. 2004. 'Paleo-oncology: the role of ancient remains in the study of cancer,' *Perspectives in Biology and Medicine* 47(1): 1–14.

Handt, O., Hoss, M., Krings, M., Pääbo, S. 1994. 'Ancient DNA: methodological challenges,' *Experientia* 50: 524–529.

Handt, O., Krings, M., Ward, R. H., Pääbo, S. 1996. 'The retrieval of ancient human DNA sequences,' *American Journal of Human Genetics* 59: 368–376.

Handwerk, B. 2005. 'King Tut's new face: behind the forensic reconstruction,' *National Geographic Magazine* May 11.

Harer, W. B. 1985. 'Pharmacological and biological properties of the Egyptian lotus,' *Journal of the American Research Center in Egypt* 22: 49–54.

Harper, A. L. 2003. *A molecular analysis of ancient cereal crops*. Unpublished MSc thesis, University of Manchester. Manchester (UK).

Harris, H. A. 1933. 'Rickets,' in Oxford Medical Publications, *Bone Growth in Health and Disease*. London: Oxford University Press, p. 87.

Harris, J. E., Iskander, Z., Farid, S. 1975. 'Restorative dentistry in ancient Egypt: an archaeological fact,' *Journal of the Michigan Dental Association* 57(12): 401–404.

Harris, J. E., Storey, A. T., Ponitz, P. V. 1980. 'Dental disease in the royal mummies,' in J. E. Harris and E. F. Wente (eds.), *An X-Ray Atlas of the Royal Mummies*. Chicago: University of Chicago Press, pp. 328–346.

Harris, J. E., Wente, E. S. (eds.) 1980. *An Atlas of the Royal Mummies*. Chicago and London: University of Chicago Press.

Harrison, R. G., Connolly, R. C. 1969. 'Kinship of Smenkhkare and Tutankhamen affirmed by serological micro method,' *Nature* 224: 325–326.

Harwood-Nash, D. C. F. 1979. 'Computed tomography of ancient Egyptian mummies,' *Journal of Computer Assisted Tomography* 3: 768–773.

Hauswirth, W. W., Dickel, C. D., Rowold, D. J., Hauswirth, M. A. 1994. 'Inter and Intrapopulation studies of ancient humans,' *Experientia* 50: 585–592.

Hawthorne, F. C. (ed.).1988. 'Spectroscopic methods in mineralogy and geology,' in P. H. Ribble (series ed.), *Reviews in Mineralogy. Mineralogical Society of America* 18. Michigan: BookCrafters, Inc.

Hayes, R. G., and Schurr, M. R. 2002. 'Electron spin resonance studies to explore the thermal history of archaeological objects,' in K. A. Jakes (ed.), *Archaeological Chemistry, Materials, and Meaning*. American Chemical Society Symposium Series 831. Washington DC: American Chemical Society, pp. 151–167.

Hayes, W. C. 1964. 'Neolithic and Chalcolithic communities in Northern Egypt,' in K. C. Seele (ed.), *Most Ancient Egypt*. Chicago: University of Chicago Press, pp. 91–146.

Haynes, S., Searle, J. B., Bretman, A., Dobney, K. M. 2002. 'Bone preservation and ancient DNA: the application of screening methods for predicting DNA survival,' *Journal of Archaeological Science* 29: 585.

Henderson, G. L., Harkey, M. R., Zhou, C., Jones, R. T. 1992. 'Cocaine and metabolite concentrations in the hair of South American coca chewers,' *Journal of Analytical Toxicology* 16(3): 199–201.

Henderson, G. L., Harkey, M. R., Jones, R. T. 1995. 'Analysis of hair for cocaine,' in E. J. Cone, M. J. Welch, and M. B. Grigson (eds.), *Hair Testing for Drugs of Abuse: International Research on Standards and Technology*. Bethesda, MD: NIH Publication No. 95–3727, pp. 91–120.

Hepper, F. N. 1990. *Pharaoh's Flowers: The Botanical Treasures of Tutankhamun*. London: Her Majesty's Stationery Office.

Herodotus. *The Histories*. Book II, para 92. Transl. by A. de Selincourt. 1961. Penguin Classics. Harmondsworth: Penguin Books, pp. 134–135.

Herraez, I., Morales, M. G. 1992. 'Conservation y embalaje de restos antropologicos momificados del Museo Arqueologico de Tenerife,' in A. C. Aufderheide, *Proceedings of the I World Congress on Mummy Studies*, Vol. 2. Tenerife: Museo Arqueologico y Etnografico de Tenerife, p. 879.

Heryet, A. R., Gatter, K. C. 1992. 'Immunocytochemistry for light microscopy,' in C. S. Herrington, J. O. McGee (eds.), *Diagnostic Molecular Pathology*, Vol. 1. Oxford: IRL Press, pp. 7–46.

Higuchi, R., Bowman, B., Freiberger, M., Ryder, O. A., Wilson, A. C. 1984. 'DNA sequences from quagga, an extinct member of the horse family,' *Nature* 312: 282–284.

Hino, H., Ammitzboli, T., Moller, R., Asboe-Hansen, G. 1982. 'The ultrastructure of bacterial spores in the skin of an Egyptian mummy'. *Acta Pathologica et Microbiologica Scandinavica, Section B, Microbiology (Denmark)* 90(1): 21–24.

Hinton, R. J. 1982. 'Differences in interproximal and occlusal wear among prehistoric Tennessee Indians,' *American Journal of Physical Anthropology* 57: 103–115.

Hippocrates Vol. 4. Jones, W. H. S. 1931. *Affections; Diseases I; Diseases II*. Loeb Classical Collection. London: Harvard University Press.

Hjalgrim, H., Lynnerup, N., Liversage, M., Rosenklint, A. 1995. 'Stereolithography: potential applications in anthropological studies,' *American Journal of Physical Anthropology* 97: 329–333.

Hockett, B., Haws, J. A. 2005. 'Nutritional ecology and the human demography of Neandertal extinction,' *Quarternary International* 137: 21–34.

Hoering, T. C. 1981. 'Monomethyl, acyclic hydrocarbons in petroleum and rock extracts' in *Carnegie Institution of Washington Year Book* 80, pp. 389–394.

Hoffman, H., Hudgins, P. A. 2002. 'Head and skull base features of nine Egyptian mummies: evaluation with high resolution CT and reformation techniques,' *American Journal of Roentgenology* 178: 1367–1376.

Hoffman, H., Torres, W. E., Ernst, R. D. 2002. 'Palaeoradiology: advanced CT in the nine Egyptian mummies,' *Radiographics* 22: 377–385.

Hofreiter, M., Serre, D., Poiner, H. N., Kuch, M., Pääbo, S. 2001. 'Ancient DNA,' *Nature Reviews Genetics* 2: 353.

Holland, T. 1937. 'X-rays in 1896,' *Journal of Liverpool Medico-Chirurgical Society* 45: 61.

Hopfgartner, G., Veuthey, J.-L., Gulacar, P. O., Buchs, A. 1990. 'Extraction of biomarkers from sediments with supercritical carbon dioxide: A comparative study with solvent extraction and thermodesorption methods,' *Organic Geochemistry* 15: 397–402.

Horie, C. V. 1988. 'Storage improvements to Manchester's mummies,' in S. C. Watkins and C. E. Brown (eds.), *Conservation of Ancient Egyptian Materials*. London: United Kingdom Institute for Conservation, Archaeology Section, pp. 95–100.

Horne, P. 1995. 'Aspergillosis and dracunculiasis in mummies from the tomb of Parennefer,' *Palaeopathology Newsletter* 92: 10–12.

Horton, W. A., Dwyer, C., Goering, R., Dean, D. C. 1983. 'Immunohistochemistry of types I and II collagen in uncalcified skeletal tissues,' *Journal of Histochemistry and Cytochemistry* 31(3): 417–425.

Hoss, M., Pääbo, S. 1993. 'DNA extraction from Pleistocene bones by a silica based purification method,' *Nucleic Acids Research* 21(16): 3913–3914.

Hoss, M., Jaruga, P., Zastawny, T. H., Dizdaroglu, M., Pääbo, S. 1996. 'DNA damage and DNA sequence retrieval from ancient tissues,' *Nucleic Acids Research* 24: 1304–1307.

Hounsfield, G. N. 1973. 'Computerized transverse axial scanning (tomography). 1. Description of system,' *British Journal of Radiology* 46(552): 1016–1022.

Hounsfield, G. N. 1976. 'Historical notes on computerized axial tomography,' *Journal of the Canadian Association of Radiology* 27(3): 135–142.

Hounsfield, G. N. 1980. 'Nobel Lecture 8 December 1979. Computed medical imaging,' *Journal of Radiology* 61(6–7): 459–468.

Hukuda, S., Inoue, K., Ushiyama, T., Sarruhashi, Y., Iwasaki, A., Huang, J., Mayeda, A., Nakai, M., Li, F. X., Yang, Z. Q. 2000. 'Spinal degenerative lesions and spinal ligamentous ossifications in ancient Chinese populations of the Yellow River Civilization,' *International Journal of Osteoarcheology* 10: 108–124.

Hummell, S., Herrmann, B. (eds.). 1994. *Ancient DNA*. New York: Springer-Verlag, pp. 205–210.

Hunt, A. S. 1911. *Catalogue of the Greek and Latin Papyri in the John Rylands Library Manchester*. Vol. 1. Literary Texts. Manchester: Manchester University Press.

Iscan, M. Y., Helmer, R. P. 1993. *Forensic Analysis of the Skull*. New York: Wiley-Liss Publishers.

Isherwood, I., Jarvis, H., Fawcett, R. A. 1979. 'Radiology of the Manchester mummies,' in A. R. David (ed.), *The Manchester Museum Mummy Project*. Manchester: Manchester University Press, pp. 25–64.

Iversen, E. 1939. *Papyrus Carlsberg, no. VIII*. Copenhagen: Munksgaard.

Jafri, S., Pasricha, P. J. 2001. Agents used for diarrhoea, constipation and inflammatory bowel disease,' in J. G. Hardman et al. *Goodman & Gilman's: The Pharmacological Basis of Therapeutics*. 10th ed. New York: McGraw-Hill.

Jastrow, M. 1913. 'The medicine of the Babylonians and Assyrians,' *Proceedings of the Royal Society of Medicine*, 2(October 10th): 110–145.

Jeziorska, M., Lambert-Zazulak, P., Appenzeller, P., David, R., Guillien, E. E. 2005a. 'Natural preservation of tissues not so bad after all,' *Journal of Biological Research* 80(1): 221–224.

Jeziorska, M., Wade, R., Wakler, M. G., Appenzeller, O. 2005b. 'Egyptian versus natural mummification: tracking the differences in loss of tissue antigenicity,' *Journal of Biological Research* 80(1): 229–232.

Johansson, A. 1989. 'Final preservation of mummies by gamma radiation,' in J. P. H. Hansen and H. C. Gulos (eds.), *The Mummies from Qilakitsoq – Eskimos in the 15th Century*. Man and Society series, Vol. 12. Copenhagen: Meddelelser om Gronland, pp. 134–136.

Johnson, C., Wills, B. 1988. 'The conservation of two pre-dynastic Egyptian bodies,' in S. C. Watkins and C. E. Brown (eds.), *Conservation of Ancient Egyptian Materials*. London: United Kingdom Institute for Conservation, Archaeology Section, pp. 79–84.

Johnson, P. H., Olson, C. B., Goodman, M. 1985. 'Isolation and characterisation of deoxyribonucleic acid from tissue of the woolly mammoth, *Mammuthus primgenius*,' *Comparative Biochemistry and Physiology* 81B: 1045–1051.

Jonckheere, F. 1944. *Une Maladie Égyptienne. L'hématurie Parasitaire*. Brussels: Fondation Égyptologique Reine Elisabeth.

Jonckheere, F. 1947. *Le Papyrus Médical Chester Beatty*. Brussels: Fondation Égyptologique Reine Elisabeth.

Jonckheere, F. 1955. *Le Preparateur de Remedies dans Organisation de la Pharmacie Égyptienne*. Institut für orientforshung. Berlin: Deutsche Akademie Wissenschaften 29, pp. 160–161.

Jones, J. 2002. 'Towards mummification: new evidence for early developments,' *Egyptian Archaeology. The Bulletin of the Egypt Exploration Society* 21: 5–7.

Jones, M. W. 2001. 'Facial Reconstruction using volumetric data.' *Presented at: Vision, Modeling and Visualisation Conference, Stuttgart, Germany.*

Jordan, P., Webbe, G., Sturrock, R. F. (eds.). 1993. *Human Schistosomiasis*. Oxford: CAB International.

Junker, H. 1929–55. *Giza Grabungen auf dem Friedhof des Alten Reiches bei den Pyramiden von Giza*, 12 vols. Vienna: Akademie der Wissenschaften in Wien Denkschriften.

Kaestle, F. A., Horsburgh, K. A. 2002. 'Ancient DNA in anthropology: methods, applications and ethics,' *Yearbook of Physical Anthropology* 45: 92–130.

Kahler, K., Haber, J., Seidel, H. P. 2003. 'Reanimating the dead: reconstruction of expressive faces from skull data,' in *ACM/SIGGRAPH Computer Graphics Proceedings* 22 3: 554–567.

Kalender, W. A. 2000. *Computed Tomography – Fundamentals, System Technology, Image Quality, Applications*. Munich: Publicis MCD Werbeagentur, GmbH.

Kalender, W. A. 2006. 'X-ray computed tomography,' *Physics in Medicine and Biology* 51(13): R29–43.

Karageorghis, V. 1976. 'A twelfth century BC opium pipe from Kition,' *Antiquity* 50: 125–129.

Karlsen, F. A. 2006. *A comparative study of histological embedding media as used for ancient decalcified and undecalcified bone*. Unpublished MSc Dissertation. Manchester: University of Manchester.

Kaup, Y., Schmid, M., Middleton, A., Weser, U. 2003. 'Borate in mummification salts and bones from pharaonic Egypt,' *Journal of Inorganic Biochemistry* 94(3): 214–220.

Kindermann, K. 2003. 'Innovative approaches to facial reconstruction using digital technology,' *Proceedings of the 1st International Conference on Reconstruction of Soft Facial Parts (RSFP), Potsdam, Germany*, pp. 127–132.

Koenig, W. 1896. *14 photographien von Roentgen-Strahlen*. Leipzig: Verlag von Johann Ambrosius Barth.

Koller, J., Baumer U., Kaup, Y., Schmid, M., Weser, U. 2003. 'Analysis of a pharaonic embalming tar,' *Nature* 425: 784.

Koller, J., Baumer, U., Kaup, Y., Weser, U. 2005. 'Herodotus' and Pliny's embalming materials identified on ancient Egyptian mummies,' *Archaeometry* 47: 609–628.

Kollman J., Buchly, W. 1898. 'Die persistenz der rassen und die reconstruction der physiognomie prähistorischer schädel,' *Archiv für anthropologie* 25: 329–359.

Krebs, O., Hummel, S., Wischmann, H., Herrmann, B. 2000. 'Purifying ancDNA extracts by high performance liquid chromatography (HPLC),' *Abstract in Proceedings of the 5th International Ancient DNA Conference, Manchester*.

Krikorian, A. D. 1975. 'Were the opium poppy and opium known in the ancient Near East?,' *Journal of the History of Biology* 8(1): 95–114.

Kritikos, P., Papadaki, S. 1967. 'The history of the poppy and of opium and their expansion in antiquity in the eastern Mediterranean area,' (parts 1 and 2). *Bulletin on Narcotics* 19(3): 17–38; 19(4): 5–10.

Koschel, K. 1996. 'Opium alkaloids in a Cypriot base ring I vessel (Bil Bil) of the Middle Bronze Age from Egypt,' *Ägypte und Levante* 6: 159–166.

Krogman, W. M., Iscan, M. Y. 1962. *The Human Skeleton in Forensic Medicine*. 1st ed. Springfield, Ilinois: Charles C Thomas.

Krogman, W. M., Iscan, M. Y. 1986. *The Human Skeleton in Forensic Medicine*. 2nd ed. Springfield, Illinois: Charles C Thomas.

Krypczyk, A., Tapp, E. 1986. 'Immunocytochemistry and electron microscopy of Egyptian mummies,' in A. R. David (ed.), *Science in Egyptology*. Manchester: Manchester University Press, pp. 361–365.

Kupper, L., Heise, H. M., Bechara, F. G., Stucker, M. 2001. 'Micro-domain analysis of skin samples from moor-mummified corpses by evanescent wave infrared spectroscopy using silver halide fibres,' *Journal of Molecular Structure* 565: 497–504.

Lagier, R. 2006. 'Bone eburnation in rheumatic diseases: a guiding trace in today's radiological diagnosis in palaeopathology,' *Clinical Rheumatology* 25: 127–131.

Lambert, J. B., Wu, Y., Santiago-Blay, J. A. 2002. 'Modern and ancient resins from Africa and the Americas,' in K. A. Jakes (ed.), *Archaeological Chemistry, Materials, Methods, and Meaning*. American Chemical Society Symposium Series 831. Washington DC: American Chemical Society, pp. 64–83.

Lambert-Zazulak, P. I. 2000. 'The International Ancient Egyptian Mummy Tissue Bank at the Manchester Museum,' *Antiquity* 74: 44–48.

Lambert-Zazulak, P. I., Rutherford, P., David, A. R. 2003. 'The International Ancient Egyptian Mummy Tissue Bank at the Manchester Museum as a resource for the palaeoepidemiological study of schistosomiasis' in P. Mitchell (ed.), *World Archaeology* 35, No. 2, *Archaeology of Epidemic and Infectious Diseases*. Oxford: Routledge, pp. 223–240.

Lampert, C. D., Glover, I. C., Heron, C. P., Stern, B., Shoocongdej, R., Thompson, G. B. 2002. 'Characterization and radiocarbon dating of archaeological resins from Southeast Asia,' in K. A. Jakes (ed.), *Archaeological Chemistry, Materials, Methods, and Meaning*. American Chemical Society Symposium Series 831. Washington DC: American Chemical Society, pp. 84–109.

Laurin, G. 1988. 'Conservation of an Egyptian mummy from Swindon,' in S. C. Watkins and C. E. Brown (eds.), *Conservation of Ancient Egyptian Materials*. London: United Kingdom Institute for Conservation, Archaeology Section, pp. 85–94.

Lee, M. L., Novotny, M. V., Bartle, K. D. 1981. *Analytical Chemistry of Polycyclic Aromatic Compounds*. London: Academic Press.

Leek, F. F. 1967a. 'The practice of dentistry in ancient Egypt,' *Journal of Egyptian Archaeology* 53: 51–58.

Leek, F. F. 1967b. 'Reputed early Egyptian dental operation, an appraisal,' in D. Brothwell and A. T. Sandison (eds.), *Diseases in Antiquity*. Springfield, Illinois: Charles C Thomas, pp. 702–705.

Leek, F. F. 1969. 'The problem of brain removal during embalming by the ancient Egyptians,' *Journal of Egyptian Archaeology* 55: 112–116.

Leek, F. F. 1973. 'Bite, attrition and associated oral conditions as seen in ancient Egyptian skulls,' in D. R. Brothwell and B. A. Chiarelli (eds.), *Population Biology of the Ancient Egyptians*. London and New York: Academic Press, pp. 290–295.

Leek, F. F. 1979. 'The dental history of the Manchester mummies,' in A. R. David (ed.), *The Manchester Museum Mummy Project*. Manchester: Manchester Museum, pp. 65–77.

Leek, F. F. 1984. 'Dental problems during the Old Kingdom,' in A. R. David and E. Tapp (eds.), *Evidence Embalmed*. Manchester: Manchester University Press, pp. 104–133.

Leek, F. F. 1986. 'Dental health and disease in ancient Egypt with reference to the Manchester mummies,' in A. R. David (ed.), *Science in Egyptology*. Manchester: Manchester University Press, pp. 35–48.

Leitz, C. 2000. *Magical and Medical Papyri of the New Kingdom*. London: British Museum Press.

Leveque, M. A. 1987. 'An approach to the conservation of Egyptian mummies: the mummy of Lady Nesmutaatneru.' *Recent Advances in Conservation and the Analysis of Artifacts*. London: Summer Schools Press for University of London Institute of Archaeology, pp. 239–242.

Lewin, L. 1964. *Phantastica: Narcotic and Stimulating Drugs, Their Use and Abuse*. London: Routledge and Kegan Paul.

Lewin, P. K. and Harwood-Nash, D. C. 1977. 'X-ray computed axial tomography of an ancient Egyptian brain,' *RCS Medical Science: Anatomy, Human Biology, Biomedical Technology, Nervous System* 5: 78.

Li, H. C., Fujiyoshi, T., Lou, H., Yashiki, S., Sonoda, S., Carier, L., Nunez, L., Munoz, I., Horai, S., Tajima, K. 1999. 'The presence of ancient human

T-celllymphotropic virus type 1 provirus DNA in an Andean mummy,' *Nature Medicine* (12): 1428–1432.

Lindahl, T. 1993. 'Instability and decay of the primary structure of DNA,' *Nature* 362: 709–715.

Liversidge, H. M., Chaillet, N., Mornstad, H., Nystrom, M., Rowling, K., Taylor, J., Willems, G. 2006. 'Timing of Demirjian's tooth formation stages,' *Annals of Human Biology* 33(4): 454–470.

Loreille, O., Orlando, L., Patou-Mathis, M., Philippe, M., Taberlet, P., Hanni, C. 2001. 'Ancient DNA analysis reveals divergence of the cave bear, *Ursus specaeus* and brown bear, *Ursus arctos*, lineages,' *Current Biology* 11: 200–203.

Loret, V. 1892. *La flore Pharaonique. Les Documents Hiéroglyphiques et les Spécimens Découverts dans les Tombeaux*. 2nd ed. Paris: Ernest Leroux.

Lucas, A. 1962. *Ancient Egyptian Materials and Industries*. 4th ed., rev. J. R. Harris. London: Edward Arnold.

Maekawa, S., Preusser, F., Lambert, F. 1992. 'An hermetically sealed display and storage case for mummified objects in inert atmospheres,' in A. C. Aufderheide (ed.), *Proceedings of the I World Congress of Mummy Studies*, Vol.1. Tenerife: Museo Arqueologico y Etnografico de Tenerife, pp. 213–220.

Maekawa, S., Valentin, N. 1996. 'Development of a prototype storage and display case for the royal mummies of the Egyptian Museum in Cairo,' in K. Spindler, H. Wilfing, E. Rastbichler-Zissernig, D. zur Nedden, and H. Nothdurfter (eds.), *Human Mummies*. New York: Springer-Verlag, pp. 47–56.

Manialawi, M., Meligy, R., Bucaille, M. 1978. 'Endoscopic examination of Egyptian mummies'. *Endoscopy* (Stuttgart) 10: 191–194.

Manley, B., Eremin, K., Shortland, A., Wilkinson, C. 2002. 'The facial reconstruction of an ancient Egyptian queen,' *Journal of Audiovisual Medicine* 25(4): 155–159.

Manniche, L. 1993. *An Ancient Egyptian Herbal*. London: British Museum Press.

Marchand, A., and Conard, J. 1980. 'Electron paramagnetic resonance in kerogen studies,' in B. Durand (ed.), *Kerogen*. Paris: Editions Technip, pp. 243–270.

Mark, S. 2002. 'Alexander the Great, seafaring, and the spread of leprosy,' *Journal of History of Medicine and Allied Sciences* 57(3): 285–311.

Mariotti, V., Dutour, O., Belcastro, M. G., Facchini, F., Brasili, P. 2005. 'Probable early presence of leprosy in Europe in a Celtic skeleton of the 4th–3rd century BC (Casalecchio di Reno, Bologna, Italy),' *International Journal of Osteoarcheology* 15(5): 311–325.

Marmion, J. 2003. *An investigation into the evidence of malaria in ancient mummified tissue*. Unpublished MSc thesis, University of Manchester. Manchester (UK).

Marota, I., Rolla, F. 2002. 'Molecular paleontology,' *Cellular and Molecular Life Sciences* 59: 97–111.

Martindale. 1958, 1977, 2004. *The Extra Pharmacopoeia*. London: The Pharmaceutical Press.

Maurer, J., Mohring, T., Rullkotter, J., Nissenbaum, A. 2002. 'Plant lipids and fossil hydrocarbons in embalming material of Roman Period mummies from the Dakhleh Oasis, Western Desert, Egypt,' *Journal of Archeological Science* 29(7): 751–762.

McLafferty, F. W. (ed.) 1963. *Mass Spectrometry of Organic Ions*. New York: Academic Press.

McLafferty, F. W. and Turecek, R. 1993. *Interpretation of Mass Spectra*. 4th ed. Mill Valley: University Science Books.

Medlock Medical. 2005. *A Natural Alternative in Wound Healing*. Community Pharmacy, October. Sidcup, Kent, UK: United Business Media.

Meier, D. (1997). 'Conserving mummies: A problem for museums,' *South American Explorer* 50: 15.

Melville, B. 1995. 'Examination and conservation considerations of an unwrapped mummy in the National Museums of Scotland,' in C. E. Brown, F. Macalister, and M. M. Wright (eds.), *Conservation in Ancient Egyptian Collections*. London: Archetype Publications, pp. 77–84.

Mekota, A. M., Vermehren, M. 2005. 'Determination of optimal rehydration, fixation and staining methods for histological and immunohistochemical analysis of mummified soft tissues,' *Biotechnic and Histochemistry* 80(1): 7–13.

Merrillees, R. 1962. 'Opium trade in the Bronze Age Levant,' *Antiquity* 36: 287–292.

Merrillees, R. 1968. 'The Cypriot Bronze Age pottery found in Egypt,' *Studies in Mediterranean Archaeology*, Vol. 18.

Merrillees, R. 1979. 'Opium again in antiquity,' *Levant* 11: 167–171.

Merriwether, D. A., Rothhammer, F., Ferrell, R. E. 1994. 'Genetic variation in the New World: ancient teeth, bone and tissue as sources of DNA,' *Experientia* 50: 592–601.

Michael, S. D., Chen, M. 1996. 'The 3-D reconstruction of facial features using volume distortion,' *Proceedings of 14th Annual Conference of Eurographics UK*, pp. 297–305.

Midant-Reynes, B. 1992. *The Prehistory of Egypt*. Oxford: Blackwell Publishers, pp. 1–12.

Miller, E., Ragsdale, B. D., Ortner, D. J. 1996. 'Accuracy in dry bone diagnosis: a comment on paleopathological methods,' *International Journal of Osteoarcheology* 6(3): 221–229.

Miller, R., Callas, D. D., Kahn, S. E., Rixxhiuti, V., Aple, F. S. 2000. 'Evidence of myocardial infarction in mummified human tissue,' *Journal of the American Medical Association* 284(7): 831–832.

Miller, R. L., Armelagos, G. J., Ikram, S., De Jonge, N., Krijer, F. W., Deelder, A. M. 1992. Palaeoepidemiology of *Schistosoma* infection in mummies,' *British Medical Journal* 304: 555–556.

Miller, R. L., De Jonge, N., Krijger, F. W., Deelder, A. M. 1993. 'Predynastic schistosomiasis,' in W. V. Davies and R. Walker (eds.), *Biological Anthropology and the Study of Ancient Egypt*. London: British Museum Press, pp. 55–60.

Millet, N. B., Hart, G. D., Reyman, T. A., Zimmerman, M. R., Lewin, P. K. 1980. 'ROM1: mummification for the common people,' in A. Cockburn and E. Cockburn (eds.), *Mummies, Disease and Ancient Cultures*. Cambridge: Cambridge University Press, pp. 71–84.

Milne, J. G. 1914. 'The sanatorium of Deir el-Bahri,' *Journal of Egyptian Archaeology* 1: 96–98.

Mitchell, P. D. 2003. 'Pre-Columbian treponemal disease from 14th century AD Safed, Israel, and implications for the medieval eastern Mediterranean,' *American Journal of Physical Anthropology* 121(2): 117–124.

Miyasaka, S., Yoshino, M., Imaizumi, K., Seta, S. 1995. 'The computer-aided facial reconstruction system,' *Forensic Science International* 74: 155–165.

Möller, M. R., Fey, P., Rimbach, S. 1992. 'Identification of cocaine and its metabolites, benzoylecgonine and ecgonine methyl ester, in hair from Bolivian coca chewers by gas chromatography/mass spectrometry,' *Journal of Analytical Toxicology* 16(5): 291–296.

Molnar, S. 1972. 'Human tooth wear, tooth function and cultural variability,' *American Journal of Physical Anthropology* 34: 175–190.

Montiel, R., Garcia, C., Canadas, M. P., Isidro, A., Guijo, J. M., Malgosa, A. 2003. 'DNA sequences of Mycobacterium leprae recovered from ancient bones,' *FEMS Microbiology Letters*, September 26(2): 413–414.

Montorsi, F., Perani, D., Anchesi, D. 2003. 'Apomorphine-induced brain modulation during sexual stimulation: a new look at central phenomena related to erectile dysfunction,' *International Journal of Impotence Research* 15: 203–209.

Moodie, R. L. 1926. 'Studies in palaeopathology, XIII: the element of the Haversian system in normal and pathological structures among fossil vertebrates,' *Biologia Generalis* 2: 63–95.

Moodie, R. L. 1931. *Roentgenological Studies of Egyptian and Peruvian Mummies.* Chicago: Field Museum of Natural History.

Moss, J. P., Linney, A. D., Grindrod, S. R., Arridge, S. R., Clifton, J. S. 1987. '3-dimensional visualisation of the face and skull using computerised tomography and laser scanning techniques,' *European Journal of Orthodontics* 9: 247–253.

Mughal, M. Z., Ward, K., Adams, J. 2005. 'Assessment of Bone status in children by densitometric and quantitative ultrasound techniques,' in H. Carty, F. Brunelle, D. A. Stringer, and S. C. Kao (eds.), *Imaging in Children.* 2nd ed. Oxford: Elsevier Ltd; vol. 1, pp. 477–486.

Mullis, K. B., Faloona, F. A. 1987. 'Specific synthesis of DNA in vitro via a polymerase-catalysed chain reaction,' *Methods in Enzymology* 155: 335–350.

Murphy, M. T. J. 1969. 'Analytical methods,' in G. Eglinton and M. T. J. Murphy (eds.), *Organic Geochemistry.* Berlin: Springer-Verlag, pp. 74–88.

Murray, M. A. 1910. *The Tomb of Two Brothers.* Manchester: Sherratt and Hughes.

Murray, M. A. 2003. 'Cereal production and processing,' in P. T. Nicholson and I. Shaw (eds.), *Ancient Egyptian Materials and Technology.* Cambridge: Cambridge University Press.

Museum Ethnographers Group. 1994. 'Professional guidelines concerning the storage, display, interpretation and return of human remains in ethnographical collections in United Kingdom museums'. *Journal of Museum Ethnography* 6.

Muzio, I. 1925. 'Su di un olio medicato della tomba di Cha,' *Atti della Società Liguistica di Scienze e Lettere* 4: 249–253. (English translation, see Bissettet al. 1994, appendix).

Natusch, D. F. S., and Thorpe, T. M. 1973. 'Element selective detectors in gas chromatography,' *Analytical Chemistry* 45: U84A–1194A.

Naville, E., Hall, H. R. 1907–13. *The Eleventh Dynasty Temple of Deir el-Bahari,* 2 vols. London: Egypt Exploration Fund, 3 vols.

Neave, R. 1979. 'Reconstruction of the heads of three ancient Egyptian mummies,' *Journal of Audiovisual Medicine* 2(4): 156–164.

Needham, C., Wilkinson, C. M., Knusel, C. J. 2003. 'Reconstructing visual manifestations of disease and trauma from archaeological human remains,' in L. R. Collett (ed.), *Graphic Archaeology: The Journal of the Association of Archaeological Illustrators and Surveyors 2003*. Exeter: Short Run Press, pp. 15–20.

Nelson, L. A., Michael, S. D. 1998. 'The application of volume deformation to 3-D facial reconstruction; a comparison with previous techniques,' *Forensic Science International* 94: 167–181.

Nerlich, A. G., Parsche, F., Kirsch, T., Wiest, I., von der Mark, K. 1993. 'Immunohistochemical detection of intestinal collagens in bones and cartilage tissue remnants in an infant Peruvian mummy,' *American Journal of Physical Anthropology* 91(3): 269–285.

Nerlich, A. G., Rohrbach, H., Zink, A. 2002. 'Paleopathology of ancient Egyptian mummies and skeletons. Investigations on the occurrence and frequency of specific diseases during various time periods in the necropolis of Thebes-West,' *Pathologie* 23(5): 279–385.

Neva, F. A., Brown, H. W. 1994. *Basic Clinical Parasitology*. 6th ed. Connecticut: Appleton and Lange.

Newberry, P. E. 1927. 'Report on the floral wreaths found in the coffin of Tutankamen,' in H. Carter (ed.), *The Tomb of Tutankamen*. London: Cassell and Company Ltd.

Nicholson, P. T., Shaw, I. (eds.) 2000. *Ancient Egyptian Materials and Technology*. Cambridge: Cambridge University Press.

Notman, D. N. H., Tashjian, J., Aufderheide, A. C., Cass, O. W., Shane, O. C., Berquist, T. H., Gray, J. E., Gedgaudas, E. 1986. 'Modern imaging and endoscopic techniques in Egyptian mummies,' *American Journal of Roentgenology* 146: 93–96.

Nunn, J. F. 2000. *Ancient Egyptian Medicine*. London: British Museum Press.

Nutton, V. 2001.'The rise of medicine,' in R. Porter (ed.), *Cambridge Illustrated History of Medicine*. Cambridge: Cambridge University Press.

Oeggl, K., Fofler, W., Schmidl, A. 2005.'New Aspects about the Diet of the Neolithic Tyrolean Iceman Ötzi,' in E. Rabino Massa (ed.), *Proceedings V World Congress on Mummy Studies, Journal of Biological Research* 53, No. 1. Turin: Universita di Torino, pp. 344–347.

Osburn, W. 1828. *An Account of an Egyptian mummy presented to the Museum of the Leeds Philosophical and Literary Society by the Late John Blayds, Esq*. Leeds: Leeds Philosophical and Literary Society.

Owen, L. M. 2001. *A radiographic investigation of the ancient Egyptian animal mummies from the Manchester Museum*. Unpublished MSc Thesis, University of Manchester, UK.

Pääbo, S. 1985. 'Molecular cloning of ancient Egyptian mummy DNA,' *Nature* (314)6012: 644–645.

Pääbo, S. 1986. 'DNA is preserved in ancient Egyptian mummies,' in A. R. David (ed.), *Science in Egyptology, Proceedings of the 'Science in Egyptology' Symposia*. Manchester: Manchester University Press.

Pääbo, S. 1989. 'Ancient DNA: Extraction, characterization, molecular cloning, and enzymatic amplification,' *Proceedings of the National Academy of Sciences of the USA* 86: 1939–1943.

Pääbo, S., Irwin, D. M., Wilson, A. C. 1990. 'DNA damage promotes jumping between templates during enzymatic amplification,' *Journal of Biological Chemistry* 265(8): 4718–4721.

Pääbo, S., Wilson, A. C. 1991. 'Miocene DNA sequence – a dream come true?' *Molecular Evolution* 1(1): 45–46.

Pääbo, S. 1994. *Amplifying Ancient DNA, In: A Guide to Methods and Applications.* San Diego, CA: Academic Press Inc., pp. 159–166.

Pääbo, S., Pioner, H., Serre, D., Jaenicke-Despres, V., Hebler, J., Rohland, N., Kuch, M., Krause, J., Vigilant, L., Hofreiter, M. 2004. 'Genetic analysis from ancient DNA,' *Annual Review of Genetics* 38: 645–679.

Pain, S. 2001. 'Parasites in paradise,' *New Scientist* 172(2320): 34–37.

Paine, C. 1992. *Standards in the Museum Care of Biological Collections.* Series: Standards in the Museum Care of Collections. No. 2. London: Museums and Galleries Commission

Parker, J. L. 2003.*The analysis of DNA extracted from modern domestic and ancient Egyptian cat samples.* Unpublished MSc thesis, University of Manchester. Manchester (UK).

Parr, R. L., Carlyle, S. W., O'Rourke, D. H. 1996. 'Ancient DNA analysis of Fremont Amerindians of the Great Salt Lake Wetlands,' *American Journal of Physical Anthropology* 99(4): 507–518.

Parsche, F., Seifert, P. 1992. 'A contribution to the problem of beetles attack in Egyptian mummies,' in A. C. Aufderheide (ed.), *Proceedings of the I World Congress on Mummies,* Vol. 2. Tenerife: Museo Arqueologico y Etnografico de Tenerife, p. 877.

Parsche, F., Balabanova, S., Pirsig, W. 1993. 'Drugs in ancient populations,' *The Lancet* 341: 503.

Paterakis, A. B. 1996. 'Conservation: preservation versus analysis?,' in A. Roy and P. Smith (eds.), *Archaeological Conservation and its Consequences.* London: International Institute for Conservation of Historic and Artistic Works, pp. 143–148.

Peters, K. E., Moldowan, J. M. 1993. *The Biomarker Guide.* New Jersey: Prentice-Hall, Inc.

Petersen, S., Nielsen, O. F., Christensen, D. H., Edwards, H. G. M., Farwell, D. W., David, R., Lambert, P., Gniadecka, M., Wulf, H. C. 2003. 'Near-infrared Fourier transform Raman spectroscopy of skin samples from the 'Tomb of the Two Brothers,' Khnum-Nakht and Nekht-Ankh, XIIth Dynasty Egyptian mummies (ca. 2000 BC),' *Journal of Raman Spectroscopy* 34(5): 375–379.

Petrie, W. M. F. 1892. *Meydum.* London: Nutt.

Petrie, W. M. F. 1898. *Deshasheh.* Fifteen memoirs of the Egyptian Exploration Fund. London: The Egyptian Exploration Fund.

Petrie, W. M. F. 1901. *Royal Tombs,* 2 vols. London: Egypt Exploration Fund.

Pettigrew, T. J. 1834. *A History of Egyptian Mummies.* London: Longman.

Pettitt, C. W., Fildes, G. 1984. 'Organising the information: the International Mummy Database' in A. R. David and E. Tapp (eds.), *Evidence Embalmed.* Manchester: Manchester University Press, pp. 150–157.

Pettitt, C. W., Fildes, G. 1986. 'The International Egyptian Mummy Database,' in A. R. David (ed.), *Science in Egyptology. Proceedings of the 'Science in Egyptology' symposia*. Manchester: Manchester University Press, pp. 175–181.

Phillips, V. M., Smuts, N. A. 1996. 'Facial reconstruction; utilisation of computerised tomography to measure facial tissue thickness in a mixed population,' *Forensic Science International* 83: 51–59.

Phornphutkui, C., Introne, W. J., Perry, M. B., Bernardini, I., Murphey, M. D., Fitzpatrick, D. L., Anderson, P. D., Huizing, M., Anikster, Y., Gerber, L. H., Gahl, W.A, 2003. 'Natural history of alkaptonuria,' *New England Journal of Medicine* 347(26): 2111–2121.

Pierce, A. E. 1979. *Silylation of Organic Compounds*. Rockford: Pierce Chemical.

Pinch, G. 1994. *Magic in Ancient Egypt*. London: British Museum Press.

Pinniger, D. B. 1994. *Insect Pests in Museums*. London: Archetype Publications.

Pinniger, D. B., Harmon, J. D. 1999. 'Pest management, prevention and control,' in D. Carter and A. K. Walker (eds.), *Care and Conservation of Natural History Collections*. Oxford: Butterworth/Heinemann, pp. 153–176.

Pliny. *Natural History*. Jones, W. H. S. 1999, 2001. Vol. 7, Books 24–27; Vol. 8, Books 28–32; Vol. 9, Books 33–35. Loeb Series. London: Harvard University Press.

Poinar, H. N., Hoss, M., Bada, J. L., Pääbo, S. 1996. 'Amino acid racemization and the preservation of ancient DNA,' *Science* 272: 864–866.

Poinar, H. N., Kuch, M., McDonald, G., Martin, P., Pääbo, S. 2003. 'Nuclear gene sequences from late Pleistocene sloth coprolite,' *Current Biology* 12: 1150–1152.

Pollard, A. M., Heron, C. 1996. *Archaeological Chemistry*. Cambridge: The Royal Society of Chemistry Paperbacks.

Pommerenering, T. 2003a. 'Altägyptische Rezepturen metrologisch neu interpreiert,' *Berichte zur Wissenshaftsgescchichte* 26: 1–16.

Pommerenering, T. 2003b. 'Neus zu de Hohlmassen und zum Medizinalmasssytstem,' *Aegyptica Helvetica* 17: 201–219.

Pommerenering,T. 2005. '"Altagyptische HohlmaBe metrologisch neu interpretiert" and relevance to historical pharmaceutical knowledge,' in H. von Hartwig Altenmuller and N. Kloth (eds.), *Studien zur Altagyptischen Kultur Beihfte*.

Pope, F. 1992. 'After the autopsy: the continuing conservation, research and interpretation of an Egyptian Mummy, Nakht (ROM 1)' in A. C. Aufderheide (ed.), *Proceedings of the I World Congress on Mummy Studies*, Vol. 1. Tenerife: Museo Arqueologico y Etnografico de Tenerife, pp. 231–235.

Potts, P. J., Bowles, J. F. W., Reed, S. J. B., Cave, M. R. 1995. *Microprobe Techniques in the Earth Sciences*. The Mineralogical Society Series 6. London: Chapman and Hall.

Prag, A. J. N., Neave, R. A. H. 1995. 'Seven Faces from Grave Circle B at Mycenae,' *British School of Athens* 90: 107–134.

Prag, J., Neave, R. A. H. 1997. *Making Faces*. London: British Museum Press.

Preston, W. L. 2002. 'Portents of plague from California's prehistoric period,' *Ethnohistory* 49(1): 69–121.

Quatrehomme, G., Cotin, S., Subsol, G., Delingette, H., Garidel, Y., Grevin, G., Fidrich, M., Bailet, P., Ollier, A. 1997. 'A fully three-dimensional method for facial reconstruction based on deformable models,' *Journal of Forensic Science* 42: 649–652.

Quibell, J. E. 1923. *Saqqara, 1912–1914*. Cairo: Service des Antiquites de l'Égypte.

Quirke, S. (ed.). 1998. *Lahun Studies*. New Malden, Surrey, UK: SIA Publishing.

Quirke, S. 2002a. *Manuscript for Health of Mother and Child. The Kahun Medical Papyrus or Gynaecological Papyrus*. London: University College (unpublished transcript).

Quirke, S. 2002b. A caution on reading the ancient Egyptian writings on good health. www.digitalegypt.ucl.ac.uk

Rae, A. 1996. 'Dry human and animal bones: their treatment at the British Museum,' in K. Spindler, H. Wilfing, E. Rastbichler-Zissernig, D. zur Nedden, and H. Nothdurfter (eds.), *Human Mummies: a Global Survey of their Status and the Techniques of Conservation*. New York: Springer-Verleg, pp. 3–8.

Raven, M. J., Taconis, W. K. 2005. *Egyptian Mummies. Radiological Atlas of the Collections in the National Museum of Antiquities at Leiden*. Turnhout, Belgium: Brepols.

Redknap, M. 2002. *Recreations – Visualising our Past*. Cardiff: National Museums & Galleries of Wales Press.

Reed, S. J. B. 1993. *Electron Microprobe Analysis*. 2nd ed. Cambridge: Cambridge University Press.

Reed, S. J. B. 1996. *Electron Microprobe Analysis and Scanning Electron Microscopy in Geology*. 1st ed. Cambridge: Cambridge University Press.

Reinhard, J. 1998. 'New Inca Mummies,' *National Geographic* 194(91): 128–135.

Reisner, G. A. 1905. *The Hearst Medical Papyrus*. Leipzig: Hinrichs.

Reisner, G. A. 1913. 'A family of builders of the sixth Dynasty, about 2600 BC,' *Bulletin of the Museum of Fine Arts, Boston*, vol. 11, no. 66: 53–66.

Reisner, G. A. 1928. 'The empty sarcophagus of the mother of Cheops,' *Bulletin of the Museum of Fine Arts Bulletin, Boston*, vol. 26, no. 157: 76–88.

Resnick, D., Niwayama G. 1976. 'Radiographic and pathologic features of spinal involvement in diffuse idiopathic skeletal hyperostosis (DISH),' *Radiology* 119: 559–568.

Reymond, E. A. E. 1976. *A Medical Book from Crocodilopolis*. Vienna: Verlag Bruder Hollinek.

Rhine, J. S., Campbell, H. R. 1980. 'Thickness of facial tissues in American Blacks,' *Journal of Forensic Science* 25(4): 847–858.

Ridgway, G. L., Powell, M., Mirza, N.1986. 'The microbiological monitoring of Lindow Man,' in I. M. Stead, H. B. Bourke and D. Brothwell (eds.), *Lindow Man: The Body in the Bog*. Ithaca, NY: Cornell University Press, p. 21.

Roberts, C. A., Buikstra, J. E. 2003. *The Bioarcheology of Tuberculosis: A Global View of the Reemerging Disease*. Gainesville: University Press of Florida.

Robins, G., Shute, C. 1998 *The Rhind Mathematical Papyrus*. London: British Museum Press.

Rothschild, B. M., Hershkovitz, I., Dutour, O. 1998. 'Clues potentially distinguishing lytic lesions of multiple myeloma from those of metastatic carcinoma,' *American Journal of Physical Anthropology* 105(2): 241–250.

Rothschild, B. M., Tanke, D. H., Helbling, M., Martin, L. D. 2003a.
'Epidemiologic study of tumors in dinosaurs,' *Naturwissenschaften* 90(11): 495–500.

Rothschild, B. M., Rothschild C. 2003b. 'Thermodynamic resolution of periosteal reaction and taphonomic change,' *Reumatismo* 55(3): 195–201.

Rothschild, B. M. 2005. 'History of syphilis,' *Clinical Infectious Diseases* 40: 1454–1463.

Rouxhet, P. G. Robin, P. L., Nicaise, G. 1980. 'Characterization of kerogens and of their evolution by infrared spectroscopy,' in B. Durand (ed.), *Kerogen*. Paris: Editions Technip, pp. 163–190.

Rowley-Conwy, P., Rowley-Conwy, J., Rowley-Conwy, D. 1998. 'A honeymoon in Egypt and the Sudan: Charlotte Rowley, 1835–1836,' in P. Starkey and J. Starkey (eds.), *Travellers in Egypt*. London: I. B. Tauris, pp. 108–120.

Ruffer, M. A. 1909. 'Note on the histology of Egyptian mummies,' *British Medical Journal* 1: 1005–1006.

Ruffer, M. A. 1910. 'Notes on the presence of *Bilharzia haematobium* in Egyptian mummies of the XXth Dynasty,' *British Medical Journal* 1: 16.

Ruffer, M. A. 1921a. 'Histological studies of Egyptian mummies,' in R. L. Moodie (ed.), *Studies in the Palaeopathology of Egypt*. Chicago: University of Chicago Press.

Ruffer, M. A. 1921b. 'On arterial lesions found in Egyptian mummies,' in R. L. Moodie (ed.), *Studies in the Palaeopathology of Egypt*. Chicago: University of Chicago Press, pp. 20–31.

Ruhli, F. J., Hodler, J., Boni, T. 2002. 'Technical note: CT-guided biopsy: a new diagnostic method for paleopathological research,' *American Journal of Physical Anthropology* 117(3): 272–275.

Ruhli, F. J., Chhem, R. K., Boni, T. 2004.'Diagnostice paleoradiology of mummified tissue: interpretation and pitfalls,' *Canadian Association of Radiology* 55(4): 218–227.

Rutherford, P. 1997. *The diagnosis of schistosomiasis by means of immunocytochemistry upon appropriately prepared modern and ancient mummified tissues*. Unpublished MSc thesis, University of Manchester. Manchester (UK).

Rutherford, P. 1999. 'Immunocytochemistry and the diagnosis of schistosomiaisis; ancient and modern,' *Parasitology Today* 15, No. 9: 390–391.

Rutherford, P. 2000. 'The diagnosis of schistosomiasis in modern and ancient tissues by means of immunocytochemistry,' *Chungara, Revista de antropologia Chilena* 32, No. 1: 127–131.

Rutherford, P. 2002. *Schistosomiasis: The dynamics of diagnosing a parasitic disease in ancient Egyptian tissue*. Unpublished Ph.D. thesis, University of Manchester. Manchester (UK).

Rutherford, P. 2005. 'Schistosomiasis in modern and ancient tissues,' in E. Rabino Massa (ed.), *Proceedings V World Congress on Mummy Studies, Journal of Biological Research* 80, N. 1. Turin: Universita di Torino, pp. 80–83.

Saffirio, L. 1972. 'Food and dietary habits in ancient Egypt,' *Journal of Human Evolution* 1: 297–305.

Sallares, R., Gomzi, S., Richards, A., Anderung, C. 2000. 'Evidence from ancient DNA for malaria in antiquity,' *Abstract in Proceedings of the 5th International Ancient DNA Conference, Manchester.*

Salleh, A. 2005. 'Prehistoric poo yields DNA clue,' *News in Science.* ABC online.

Sambrook, J., Fritch, E. F., Maniatis, T. 1989. *Molecular Cloning: A Laboratory Manual.* 2nd ed. Cold Spring Harbor, NY: Cold Spring Harbor Laboratory Press.

Sandison, A. T. 1955. 'The histological examination of mummified material,' *Stain Technology* 30(6): 277–283.

Sandison, A. T. 1962. 'Degenerative vascular disease in the Egyptian mummy,' *Medical History* 6: 77–81.

Sarton, G. 1954. *Galen of Pergamon.* Lawrence: University of Kansas.

Sauneron, S. 1960. *The Priests of Ancient Egypt.* New York: Grove Press.

Sauneron, S. 1989. *Un Traité Égyptien d'Ophiologie.* Cairo: L'Institut Français d'Archéologie Orientale.

Schaffer Library of Drug Policy. 2005. Transcript of the video: *Mystery of the Cocaine Mummies.* http://www.druglibrary.org/schaffer/Misc/mummies.htm

Schneider, G. M. 1978. 'Physicochemical principles of extraction with supercritical gases'. *Angewandte Chemie.* International edition, 17, pp. 716–727.

Schreiber-Goshe, S. 2005. *Adaptation of a modern breast cancer genetic screening test to ancient Egyptian mummified remains.* Unpublished MSc thesis, University of Manchester. Manchester (UK).

Schultz, M. 2001. 'Paleohistopathology of bone. A new approach to the study of ancient diseases,' in *Yearbook of Physical Anthropology 44.* New York: Wiley-Liss, Inc., pp. 106–147.

Schulze-Hagen, K., Steinheimer, F., Kinzelbach, R., Gasser, C. 2002. 'Avian taxidermy in Europe from the Middle Ages to the Renaissance,' *Journal für Ornithologie* 144(4): 459–478.

Schwager, G. P. 1969. 'The frequency of the appearance of transverse lines in the tibia in relation to childhood illness,' *American Journal of Physical Anthropology* 31: 17–22.

Schumann Antelme, R., Rossini, S. 2001. *Sacred Sexuality in Ancient Egypt: The Erotic Secrets of the Forbidden Papyrus.* Rochester: Inner Traditions International.

Seath, J., Giże, A. P., David, A. R., Hall, K., Lythgoe, P., Speak, R., Caldwell, S. 2006. 'An atypical Ancient Egyptian pillow from Sedment el-Gebel: evidence for migrant worker trading and technology,' *Journal of Archaeological Science* 33: 546–550.

Seitz, H., Tille, C., Rieder, W., Irsen, S. H., Bermes, G. 2005. 'Rapid prototyping models for facial reconstruction.' *Presented at 2nd International Conference on Reconstruction of Soft Facial Parts (RSFP), Remagen, Germany.*

de Selincourt, A. (transl.) 1961. *Herodotus. The Histories,* 9 vols. Book 2. Harmondsworth, England: Penguin Books.

Shafer, W. G., Hine, M. K., Levy, B. M. 1958. *Oral Pathology.* Philadelphia: W. B. Saunders Co., pp. 206–230.

Shaw, I., Nicholson, P. 1995. *British Museum Dictionary of Ancient Egypt.* London: British Museum Press.

Shin, D. H., Youn, M., Chang, B. S. 2003. 'Histological analysis on the medieval mummy in Korea,' *Forensic Science International* 137: 172–182.

Sigersist, H. E. 1987. *A History of Medicine*. Vol. 1. Primitive and Archaic Medicine. Facsimile of 1951. HarperCollins ed. Oxford: Oxford University Press.

Sikora, R.1989. 'Ginkgo biloba extract in the treatment of erectile dysfunction,' *Journal of Urology* 141: 188A.

Silverstein, R. M., Bassler, G. C., Morill, T. C. 1974. *Spectrometric Identification of Organic Compounds*. 3rd ed. New York: Wiley.

Simmonds, P. 2001. 'The origin and evolution of hepatitis viruses in humans,' *Journal of General Virology* 82(4): 693–712.

Simoneit, B. R.T and Giże, A. P. 2000. 'Analytical techniques for organic matter characterization in ore deposits,' in T. H. Giordano, R. Kettler, and S. A. Wood (eds.), *Ore Genesis and Exploration; the Roles of Organic Matter*. Reviews in Economic Geology 9: 27–61 Colorado: Society of Economic Geologists.

Smith, C. I., Chamberlain, A. T., Riley, M. S., Cooper, A., Stringer, C. B., Collins, M. J. 2001. 'Neanderthal DNA: not just old but old and cold?,' *Nature* 10, 771–772.

Smith, G. E., Wood-Jones, F. 1910. 'Report of the human remains,' in G. A. Reisner (ed.), *The Archaeological Survey of Nubia. Report for 1907–1908*. Cairo: National Printing Department, vol. 2, pp. 7–367.

Smith, G. E. 1912. *The Royal Mummies. Catalogue Général des Antiquités Égyptiennes de la Musée du Caire, Nos. 61051–61100*. Cairo: Service des Antiquités de l'Égypte.

Smith, G. E., Dawson, W. R. 1924. *Egyptian Mummies*. London: Allen and Unwin (repr. 1991. London: Kegan Paul International).

Smith, J. H., Torky, H., Mansour, N., Cheever, A. W. 1974. 'Studies on egg excretion and tissue egg burden in urinary schistosomiasis,' *American Journal of Tropical Medicine and Hygiene* 23: 163–168.

Smith, M. B., March, J. 2000. *March's Advanced Organic Chemistry. Reactions, Mechanisms, and Structure*. 5th ed. New York: Wiley-Interscience.

Smith, N. J. D. 1986. 'Dental pathology in an ancient Egyptian population,' in A. R. David (ed.), *Science in Egyptology*. Manchester: Manchester University Press, pp. 43–49.

Smyth, K. 2005. *Analysis of mitochondrial DNA from mummies Nekht-Ankh and Khnum-Nakht*. Unpublished MSc thesis, University of Manchester. Manchester (UK).

Soames, J. V., Southam, J. C. 1998. *Oral Pathology*. 3rd ed. Oxford: Oxford University Press.

Spindler, K. 1994. *The Man in the Ice. The Preserved Body of a Neolithic Man Reveals the Secrets of the Stone Age*. London: Weidenfeld and Nicholson.

Spoor, F., Jeffery, N., Zonneveld, F. 2000. 'Imaging skeletal growth and evolution,' in P. O'Higgins and M. Cohn (eds.), *Development, Growth and Evolution: Implications for the Study of the Hominid Skeleton*. London: Academic Press.

Stefan, J.-R. 1982. 'L'entomofaune de la momie de Ramsès II'. *Annales de la Société Éntomologique de France* 18: 531–537.

Stevens, J. M. 1975. 'Gynaecology from ancient Egypt: the Papyrus Kahun,' *The Medical Journal of Australia* 2: 949–952.

Stone, A. C., Milner, G.R, Pääbo, S., Stoneking, M. 1996. 'Sex determination of ancient human skeletons using DNA,' *American Journal of Physical Anthropology* 99: 231–238.

Stratomeier, H., Spee, J., Wittwer-Backofen, U., Bakker R. 2005. 'Methods of forensic facial reconstruction'. *Presented at the 2nd International Conference on Reconstruction of Soft Facial Parts (RSFP), Remagen, Germany.*

Strong, L. 1981. 'Dermestids – an embalmer's dilemma,' *Antenna* 5(1): 136–139.

Strouhal, E. 1986. 'Embalming excerebration in the Middle Kingdom,' in A. R. David (ed.), *Science in Egyptology*. Manchester: Manchester University Press, pp. 141–154.

Strouhal, E. 1992. *Life in Ancient Egypt*. Norman: University of Oklahoma.

Subert, F., Dvorak, V., Spalek, E., Navratilova, D., Vachala, B., Kucera, A. 1993. *Problems of Contemporary Mummy Conservation*. Prague: Charles University.

Subke J., Wittke M. 2005. 'CAD enhanced soft-tissue reconstruction in forensics with phantom- three-dimensional touch – an electronic modelling tool with haptic feedback.' *Presented at the 2nd International Conference on Reconstruction of Soft Facial Parts (RSFP), Remagen, Germany.*

Täckholm, V. 1941, 1950, 1954, 1969. *Flora of Egypt*. Vols. 1–4. Fouad University. Bulletin of the Faculty of Science, Vol. 17. Cairo: Cairo University Press.

Tanner, J. M., Whitehouse, R. H., Marshall W. A., Healy, M. J. R., Goldstein, H. 1975. *Assessment of Skeletal Maturation and Prediction of Adult Height (TW2 Method)*. London: Academic Press.

Tapp, E. 1979. 'Diseases in the Manchester mummies,' in A. R. David (ed.), *The Manchester Museum Mummy Project*. Manchester: Manchester University Press, pp. 95–102.

Tapp, E., Curry, A., Anfield, C. 1979. 'Electron Microscopy of the Manchester mummies,' in A. R. David (ed.), *The Manchester Museum Mummy Project*. Manchester: Manchester University Press, pp. 103–111.

Tapp, E. 1984. 'Disease in the Manchester mummies: the pathologist's role,' in A. R. David and E. Tapp (eds.), *Evidence Embalmed: Modern Medicine and the Mummies of Ancient Egypt*. Manchester: Manchester University Press, pp. 78–95.

Tapp, E., Stanworth, P., Wildsmith, K. 1984. 'The endoscope in mummy research,' in R. David and E. Tapp (eds.), *Evidence Embalmed*. Manchester: Manchester University Press, pp. 65–77.

Tapp, E., Wildsmith, K. 1986. 'Endoscopy of Egyptian mummies,' in A. R. David (ed.), *Science in Egyptology. Proceedings of the 'Science in Egyptology' Symposia*. Manchester: Manchester University Press, pp. 351–354.

Tapp, E., Wildsmith, K. 1992. 'The autopsy and endoscopy of the Leeds Mummy,' in A. R. David and E. Tapp (eds.), *The Mummy's Tale: the Scientific and Medical Investigation of Natsef-Amun, Priest in the Temple of Karnak*. London: Michael O'Mara Books, Ltd., pp. 132–153.

Taylor, J. H. 2004. *Mummy: The Inside Story*. London: British Museum Press.

Taylor, K. 2001. *Forensic Art and Illustration*. Boca Raton: CRC Press.

Taylor, R. G., Angel, C. 1998. 'Facial reconstruction and approximation,' in: J. G. Clement, and D. L. Ranson, *Craniofacial Identification in Forensic Medicine.* Sydney: Arnold Publishers, Chapter 14, pp. 178–181.

Terra, M. A. B. L., Bello, A. R., Bastos, O. M., Amendoeira, M. R. R., Coelho, J. M. C. D., Ferreira, L. F., Araujo, A. 2004. 'Detection of Toxoplasma gondii DNA by polymerase chain reaction in experimentally desiccated tissue,' *Memorias do Instituto Oswaldo Cruz* 99(2): 185–188.

Thompson, R. C. 1923. *The Assyrian Medical Texts.* Milford: Oxford University Press.

Thompson, R. C. 1924. *The Assyrian Herbal.* London: Luzak & Co.

Tukker, W., Dassen, H. 1999. 'Mummie – scannen door de eeuwen heen,' *Triakel,* 17 Dec: 14–17.

Turner, P. J., Holtom, D. B. 1981. 'The use of a fabric softener in the reconstitution of mummified tissue prior to paraffin wax sectioning for light microscopical examination,' *Stain Technology* 56: 35–38.

Tuross, N. 1994. 'The biochemistry of ancient DNA in bone,' *Experientia* 50: 530–535.

Tyldesley, J. 2000. *The Private Lives of the Pharaohs.* London: Channel 4 Books, Macmillan Publishers Ltd.

Ubelaker, D. H., O'Donnell, G. 1992. 'Computer assisted facial reproduction,' *Journal of Forensic Science* 37: 155–162.

Van der Molen, J. R., Garty, J., 1980. 'Growth control of algae and cyanobacteria on historical monuments by a mobile uv unit (muvu),' *Studies in Conservation* 25: 71–77.

Vartavan de, C. T., Amoros, V. 1997. *Codex of Ancient Egyptian Plant Remains.* London: Triad Exploration Ltd.

Vigl, E. E., Conci, P., Samadelli, M., Fichtel, G. 2003. 'The Iceman Mummy in the Archaeology Museum of South Tyrol: development of a new method of conservation,' in N. Lynnerup, C. Andreasen and J. Berglund (eds.), *Mummies in a New Millennium, Proceedings of the 4th World Congress on Mummy Studies. Nuuk, Greenland, September 4th to 10th, 2001.* Copenhagen: Greenland National Museum and Archives and Danish Polar Centre, pp. 82–85.

Vogelsang-Eastwood, G., 2003 'Textiles,' in P. T. Nicholson and I. Shaw (eds.), *op cit.* Cambridge: Cambridge University Press, pp. 268–298.

Von Hunnius, T. E., Roberts, C. A., Boylston, A., Saunders, S. R. 2006. 'Histological identification of syphilis in pre-Columbian England,' *American Journal of Physical Anthropology* 129(4): 559–566.

Von Kanel, F. 1984. *Les Prêtres-ouab de Sekhmet et les Conjurateurs de Serket.* Paris: Presses Universitaires de France.

Walgren, J. E., Caple, R., Aufderheide, A. C. 1986. 'Contributions of nuclear magnetic resonance to the question of alkaptonuria (onchronosis) in an Egyptian mummy,' in A. R. David (ed.), *Science in Egyptology.* Manchester: Manchester University Press, pp. 321–327.

Wampler, T. P. 1999. 'Introduction to pyrolysis–capillary gas chromatography,' *Journal of Chromatography* A, 842: 207–220.

Wapler, U., Crubezy, E., Schultz, M. 2004. 'Is cribra orbitalia synonymous with anemia? Analysis and interpretation of cranial pathology in Sudan,' *American Journal of Physical Anthropology* 123(4): 333–339.

Weast, R. C. (ed.). 1976. *The Chemical Rubber Company Handbook of Chemistry and Physics*. 57th ed. Cleveland: CRC Press Inc.

Weeks, K. R. 1980. 'Ancient Egyptian dentistry,' in J. E. Harris and E. F. Wente (eds.), *An X-Ray Atlas of the Royal Mummies*. Chicago: University of Chicago Press, pp. 99–121.

Weeks, K. R. (ed.). 2001. *KV5: A Preliminary Report on the Excavation of the Tomb of the Sons of Ramesses II in the Valley of the Kings*. 1st ed. Cairo: American University in Cairo Press.

Weinberger, B. W. 1947. 'The dental art in ancient Egypt,' *Journal of the American Dental Association* 34: 170–184.

Weinberger, B. W. 1948. *History of Dentistry*. St. Louis: C. V. Mosby Co., pp. 22–25.

Wells, C., Maxwell, B. M. 1962. 'Alkaptonuria in an Egyptian mummy,' *British Journal of Radiology* 35: 679–682.

Wells, C. 1964. *Bones, Bodies and Disease*. London: Thames and Hudson.

Weser, U., Kaup, Y. 2002. 'Borate, an effective mummification agent in pharaonic Egypt,' *Zeitschrift für Naturforschung Section B – A Journal of Chemical Sciences* 57(7): 819–822.

White, P. T. 1985. 'The poppy – for good and evil,' *National Geographic* 167, No 2: 143–189.

Wick, G., Kalischrug, G., Maurer, H., Mayeri, C., Muller, P. U. 1980. 'Really old palaeoimmunology: immunohistochemical analysis of extracellular matrix proteins in historic and prehistoric material,' *Experimental Gerontology* 30: 1565–1579.

Wildung, D. 1977. *Imhotep und Amenhotep*. Munich: Deutscher Kunstverlag.

Wilkinson, C. M., Whittaker, D. K. 2002. 'Juvenile forensic facial reconstruction – a detailed accuracy study,' *Proceedings of the 10th Meeting of the International Association of Craniofacial Identification, Bari, Italy*, pp. 98–110.

Wilkinson, C. M. 2003a. 'The facial reconstruction of the Marina El-Alamein Mummy,' *Polish Archaeology in the Mediterranean* XIV: 66–71.

Wilkinson, C. M. 2003b. 'Virtual sculpture as a method of computerized facial reconstruction'. *Proceedings of the 1st International Conference on Reconstruction of Soft Facial Parts, Potsdam, Germany*, pp. 59–63.

Wilkinson, C. M., Neave, R. A. H. 2003. 'The reconstruction of faces showing healed wounds,' *Journal of Archaeological Science* 30: 1343–1348.

Wilkinson, C. M., Motwani, M., Chiang, E. 2003. 'The relationship between the soft tissues and the skeletal detail of the mouth,' *Journal of Forensic Science* 48(4): 1–5.

Wilkinson, C. M. 2004. *Forensic Facial Reconstruction*. Cambridge: Cambridge University Press.

Wilkinson, C. M. 2005. 'Computerised facial reconstruction: a review of current systems,' *Journal of Forensic Science, Medicine & Pathology* 1, 3: 173–177.

Wilkinson, C. M., Rynn, C., Peters, H., Taister, M., Kau C. H., Richmond, S. 2006. 'A blind accuracy assessment of computer-modelled forensic facial reconstruction using computed tomography data from live subjects,' *Journal of Forensic Science, Medicine & Pathology* 2: 179–187.

Wilkinson, G. R. 2001. 'Pharmacokinetics: the dynamics of drug absorption, distribution, and elimination,' in J. G. Hardman et al. *Goodman & Gilman's: The Pharmacological Basis of Therapeutics*. 10th ed. New York: McGraw-Hill.

Williams, L. 2006. *An investigation to determine the optimum decalcification agent for ancient tissue*. Unpublished MSc Dissertation. Manchester: University of Manchester.

Wilson, A. S., Richards M. P., Janaway, R. C., Pollard, M. A. 2004. 'High resolution diet and seasonality information from archaeological hair.' *Paper presented at The V World Congress on Mummy Studies at Turin, Italy, 2nd to 5th September, 2004.*

Wilson, M. R., Polanskey, D., Butler, J., Dizinno, J. A., Replogle, J., Budowle, B. 1995. 'Extraction, PCR amplification and sequencing of mitochondrial DNA from human hair shafts,' *Biotechniques* 18: 662–669.

Winlock, H. E. 1921. 'Egyptian expedition 1920–1921,' *Bulletin of the Metropolitan Museum of Art, New York*, vol. 16, no.11: 37–52. New York: Rees, Omre, Brown, Green and Longman.

Woodcock, S. 1996. 'Body colour: the misuse of mummy.' *The Conservator* 20: 87–94.

Woodward, S. R., King, M. J., Chiu, M. N., Kuchar, M. J., Griggs, C. W. 1994 *Amplification of Ancient Nuclear DNA from Teeth and Soft Tissues, PCR Methods and Applications*. Cold Spring Harbor, NY: Cold Spring Harbor Laboratory Press, pp. 244–247.

World Archaeological Congress. 1989. *The Vermillion Accord. Archaeological Ethics and the Treatment of the Dead, A Statement of Principles Agreed by Archaeologists and Indigenous Peoples at the World Archaeological Congress.*

World Health Organisation. 1991. *Traditional Medicine and Modern Health Care.* World Health Organisation, Switzerland, Doc. No. A44/10: 22 March 1991.

Wreszinski, W. 1909. *Der Grosse Medizinische Papyrus des Berliner Museums.* Leipzig: Hinrichs.

Wreszinski, W. 1912. *Der Londoner Medizinische Papyrus (British Museum No. 1005) und der Papyrus Hearst in Transkription, Übersetzung, und Kommentar.* Leipzig: Hinrichs.

Wróbel, J. T. 1977. 'Nuphar alkaloids,' in *The Alkaloids*, vol. XVI. Manske: RHF ed. London: Academic Press.

Zias, J., Numeroff, K. 1987. 'Operative dentistry in the second century BCE,' *Journal of the American Dental Association* 114: 665–666.

Zink, A., Rohrbach, H., Scheimies, U., Hagedorn, H. G., Haas, C. J., Weyss, C., Bachmeier, B., Nerlich, A. G. 1999. 'Malignant tumors in ancient Egyptian population,' *Anticancer Research* 19(5B): 4273–4277.

Zink, A., Nerlich, A. G., 2003. 'Molecular analysis of the pharaohs: feasibility of molecular studies in ancient Egyptian material,' *American Journal of Physical Anthropology* 121: 109.

Website references

www.1 http://www.ox.ac.uk/blueprint/2004-2005/1301/15.shtml

Index